DESERT

Japanese American Kids Behind Barbed Wire

DIARY

May 18, 1943.

We have a large box filled with nails. Every day we bring more and more nails for Uncle Sam. Yesterday a big bomber flew over Topaz. Our paper folders tear so easily that we have decided to pay 5¢ each for some material to make new folders. Edwin brought us a baby horned toad. It is now living with our five lizards. Kimiko's mother was burned very badly by hot water. Yesterday little Drayton Nuttall found Don's money. Don was surely happy to have it returned.

OUR
DAILY DIARY

DESERT

Japanese American Kids Behind Barbed Wire

DIARY

Michael O. Tunnell

ini Charlesbridge

For Mayzie, Henry, Evelyne, and Jack

Published by Charlesbridge
9 Galen Street
Watertown, MA 02472
(617) 926-0329 • www.charlesbridge.com

Library of Congress Cataloging-in-Publication Data
Names: Tunnell, Michael O., author.
Title: Desert diary: Japanese American kids behind barbed wire / Michael O. Tunnell.
Description: Watertown, MA : Charlesbridge, [2020] | Includes bibliographical references and index. | Summary: "In March 1943, twenty-seven children began third grade in a strange new environment: the Topaz Relocation Center in Utah. Together with their teacher, Miss Yamauchi, these uprooted young Americans began keeping a classroom diary, with a different child illustrating each day's entry. Their full-color diary entries paint a vivid picture of daily life in a so-called 'internment camp': schoolwork, sports, pets, holidays, health—and the mixed feelings of citizens who were loyal but distrusted."—Provided by publisher.
Identifiers: LCCN 2019014251 (print) | LCCN 2019018675 (ebook) | ISBN 9781580897891 (reinforced for library use) | ISBN 9781632896131 (ebook) | ISBN 9781632896148 (ebook pdf)
Subjects: LCSH: Central Utah Relocation Center—Juvenile literature. | Japanese Americans—Evacuation and relocation, 1942–1945—Juvenile literature. | World War, 1939–1945—Japanese Americans—Personal narratives—Juvenile literature. | Japanese American children—Diaries—Juvenile literature. | World War, 1939–1945—Children—United States—Juvenile literature. | Japanese American children—Diaries.
Classification: LCC D769.8.A6 T863 2020 (print) | LCC D769.8.A6 (ebook) | DDC 940.53/177924509253—dc23
LC record available at https://lccn.loc.gov/2019014251
LC ebook record available at https://lccn.loc.gov/2019018675

Printed in China
(hc) 10 9 8 7 6 5 4 3 2 1

Display type set in Colby Compressed by Jason Vandenberg
Text type set in Minion Pro by Adobe Systems Incorporated
Printed by 1010 Printing International Limited in Huizhou, Guangdong, China
Production supervision by Brian G. Walker
Designed by Diane M. Earley

Page i: Third graders at Mountain View School in Topaz Camp kept a classroom diary from March 8 through August 12, 1943. In it they recorded their observations of daily life in a wartime prison camp.

Pages ii–iii: The cover of the classroom diary is pictured on this book's title page, along with the shoelace that held it together. The desert terrain of the former site of Topaz Camp appears in the background.

CONTENTS

Japanese American children at Raphael Weill Elementary School in San Francisco recite the Pledge of Allegiance.

PROLOGUE

"I Pledge Allegiance"

IN 1943 EIGHT-YEAR-OLD MAE YANAGI stood and recited the Pledge of Allegiance with her classmates. Then, like any other third grader, she began a day of math, reading, and spelling. Mae's teacher, Miss Yamauchi, always included time for the children to discuss what was happening in school and at home. Afterward she would summarize their words on a piece of art paper—a new page to be added to the class's daily diary. Mae most likely couldn't wait for her turn to decorate the day's diary page with pencil and crayon drawings.

Lots of classrooms keep diaries—but this diary was different. It told the story of a strange and isolated school with children from uprooted families.

As a third grader, Mae might not have fully realized that her school day was anything but normal. Still, she must have understood that "liberty and justice for all" did not apply to her, her classmates, her teacher, or her parents. A year earlier she had attended school in the San Francisco Bay

Area. Her classroom was filled with children of many backgrounds, including white children and kids of Japanese American descent. Now nearly every face was Japanese, like her own. And when Mae looked out the window, instead of the green of Northern California, she saw a parched landscape framed by Utah mountains. Instead of regular houses, she saw row after row of what looked like army barracks. Beyond the barracks stood guard towers with searchlights and soldiers carrying rifles—and a barbed-wire fence.

Mae Yanagi, US citizen, was a prisoner.

Mae, her classmates, and their families lived in these army-like barracks when they were held captive in the Utah desert. The government photographer avoided showing the guard towers.

"I pledge allegiance to the Flag of the United States of America and to the Republic for which it stands, one nation, indivisible, with liberty and justice for all."

—The Pledge of Allegiance as it read in 1942, when it was officially recognized by the US Congress

Mae Yanagi poses for the famous photographer Dorothea Lange on her Evacuation Day, May 8, 1942, when she and her family were forced to leave their home in California. To help maintain their dignity, families dressed in their best clothes, in stark contrast to the ID tags dangling from their necks. Photograph colorized by Benjamin Thomas, Colours of Yesterday.

Chapter 1

Unwanted

MAE YANAGI WAS SEVEN YEARS OLD in December 1941, when her life was tipped head over heels. Almost overnight, she and her family found themselves torn from their home in Hayward, California. And they weren't the only ones forced to leave—anyone with a Japanese face had to go.

By the end of 1942, everyone of Japanese ancestry, or Nikkei (*neek-kay*), had disappeared from the coastal regions of California, Oregon, and Washington. Most Nikkei from the San Francisco Bay Area ended up in hastily constructed "internment camps"—prison camps enclosed by barbed wire—in the mountain deserts of Utah. Other Americans of Japanese descent were transported away from the West Coast to similar camps in other interior states. But how could this happen in America, the land of the free?

Most first-generation Japanese immigrants, or Issei (*ees-say*), were on the West Coast, where they faced fierce bigotry. National laws denied them American citizenship. Some states prohibited them from owning land and banned all Nikkei from intermarriage with white Americans.

"Japanese are not bona fide citizens. They are not the stuff of which American citizens can be made."

—San Francisco mayor James Duval Phelan, 1900

Despite the prejudice, many Japanese immigrants managed comfortable lifestyles through hard work. Although jobs with white employers were scarce, many Issei started successful businesses. Others turned substandard plots of rented ground into prosperous fruit and vegetable farms. Some even purchased land by placing it in the names of their children, the Nisei (*nee-say*), who were born in the United States and therefore American citizens.

Often Nikkei worked hard to become "Americanized," while preserving many of their Japanese cultural traditions. Yoshiko Uchida's family lived in a three-bedroom bungalow in Berkeley, California. Her family owned a Buick and subscribed to *National Geographic*. As a grade-schooler, Yoshiko roller-skated and played cops and robbers, just like any other American kid. At the same time her family ate Japanese dishes and kept alive Japanese traditions, such as Hinamatsuri (*hee-nah-mah-tsoo-ree*), or Doll Festival, a day celebrating girls. Later, in high school, Yoshiko wore stylish clothing and listened to popular music. But the doors to white society were still closed to her and other Nisei teenagers. White employers wouldn't hire Nisei college graduates. And many white beauty salons wouldn't even cut Yoshiko's hair. But all in all, she remembered her life in California as pleasant and happy.

Then, on December 7, 1941, everything changed. Early that morning, Japanese aircraft launched a surprise attack on the US naval base at Pearl Harbor, in Hawaii. Bombs poured down on the unsuspecting base, destroying much of the United States' Pacific Fleet and killing more than two thousand people. Though World War II was already raging in other parts of the world, Japan's attack brought America into the conflict.

Suddenly all Nikkei, even those who were American citizens, came under suspicion. Despite a complete lack of evidence, newspapers printed rumors of Nikkei collusion with Japan. One story claimed that "Japs" (the name used for the enemy) in Hawaii had cut arrows in their crops to guide enemy aircraft to the target. Another reported that "Japs" in California planned to sabotage airports, power plants, and other military

The battleship USS Arizona *sinking during the Japanese air attack on Pearl Harbor.*

targets. Not a single case of such traitorous behavior was ever confirmed, but restaurants and stores suddenly refused to serve those of Japanese descent. Tombstones in Japanese cemeteries were smashed. Homes were vandalized. Farmers were terrorized. Mae and Yoshiko found themselves barred from movie theaters, roller rinks, and public parks.

Strident voices of fear and prejudice soon drowned out voices of reason. "I am for immediate removal of every Japanese on the West Coast to a point deep in the interior," wrote well-known newspaper columnist Henry McLemore. "Let 'em be pinched, hurt, hungry, and dead against it. . . . Personally, I hate the Japanese. And that goes for all of them." The US Congress strongly supported removing all people of Japanese ancestry from the West Coast, where (it was incorrectly rumored) spies might cooperate with the Japanese military likely lurking in submarines offshore.

In the end, President Franklin Roosevelt signed Executive Order 9066, which authorized the army to oust Nikkei from the West Coast and created the War Relocation Authority (WRA) to manage their

A barber in Seattle proudly displays a hate-filled sign after the forced removal of Nikkei from the West Coast. The offensive term Japs *refers to people of Japanese descent.*

Satsuo and Kinuye Yanagi and their seven children in one of their
Meekland Nursery greenhouses. Mae is at the front of the group, in the center.

removal and confinement. It didn't matter that most of them were American citizens. It didn't matter that they posed no military threat. The WRA would round up Mae, Yoshiko, and all other people of Japanese ancestry and forcibly move them away from their homes.

Though Mae and her parents knew they would be compelled to leave, it was still a shock to receive removal orders. Yoshiko's Evacuation Day, or E-day, was May 1, 1942. The family was given only ten days to pack up. "How can we clear out our house in only ten days?" her mother asked. "We've lived here for fifteen years!" For Mae's family, the upcoming E-day meant shutting down their nursery business. What would they do with the greenhouses, delivery truck, and other equipment? For most Nikkei in this situation, the only answer was to sell, but with only a few days to unload their property, they were at a disadvantage. Families sold pianos for $25 or less. A twenty-six-room hotel sold for $500! The Oda family parted with a $1,200 tractor, three cars, three trucks, all their crops, and thirty acres of farmland for only $1,300. Mae Yanagi even had to leave behind her new bicycle, a gift for her seventh birthday.

At first the army carted Bay Area Nikkei to a temporary holding site, the Tanforan Assembly Center, in San Bruno, California. Detainees could bring only what they could carry. They received ID tags for themselves

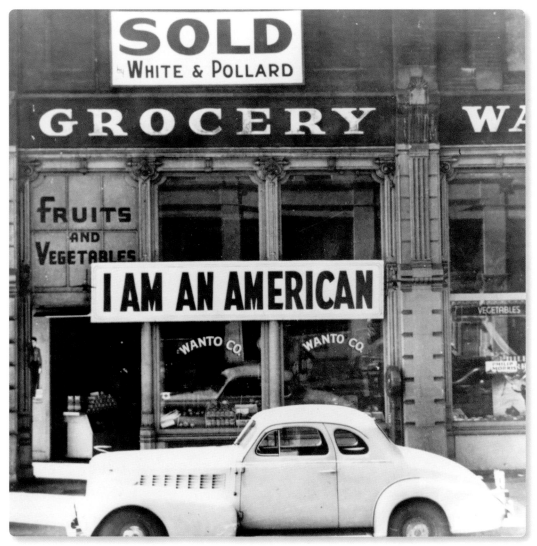

Torasaburo and Kuni Masuda had little choice but to sell their grocery store, but they made it clear to everyone passing by that they were loyal Americans.

Wooden planks bridged the open ditches in front of the horse-stall "apartments" at the Tanforan Assembly Center.

and their baggage. Each person was assigned a number, as was each family. The Yanagis were family 21578, and Mae was 21578G. The Uchidas were 13453; Yoshiko, 13453C. On their E-day, Mae and Yoshiko were loaded on buses and driven to Tanforan. Mae wouldn't see the Bay Area again for three years, and she would never return to her home in Hayward.

Tanforan was a horse-racing track that the army hastily converted into a temporary detention center. Mae's family was assigned to a horse stall, where they lived for four and a half months while their permanent "home" in Utah was being built. Though linoleum had been laid over the rough floorboards, the place reeked of horse manure, and it was furnished only with army cots. Yoshiko found herself in a similar stall, a rude replacement for her family's sunny bungalow with its indoor plumbing and modern kitchen. After a brief time in Tanforan, a young child was heard to say, "Mommy, let's go back to America."

Nikkei bound for Utah rode in stuffy, swaying train cars that caused waves of sickness. Ken Fujii remembers his train being dubbed "the diarrhea train."

After the train ride, the prisoners rode buses out to the desert, where they were greeted by the grim sight of guard towers looming over their new home.

Chapter 2

A Square Mile of Desert

WHEN MAE YANAGI, Yoshiko Uchida, and the rest of the nearly eight thousand inhabitants of Tanforan finally left for Utah, the two-day train trip was like a tiny taste of freedom. After nearly five months of captivity, Yoshiko drank in the sights outside the train car window: "Houses, gardens, stores, cars, traffic lights, dogs, white children riding bicycles. All these ordinary things seemed so strange and wonderful to us."

The train pulled into the station at Delta, Utah, the small town nearest to the WRA's Central Utah Relocation Center, or Topaz Internment Camp. Yoshiko and the other passengers then boarded buses for the fifteen-mile trip out into the desert. As her bus neared Topaz, Yoshiko's heart must have dropped at the grim sight of the unfinished barbed-wire fence and guard towers surrounding a square mile of desert terrain. A drum and bugle corps of camp Boy Scouts greeted the new arrivals, but a spirited welcome couldn't make up for the barrenness of their new home.

This was a bone-dry world of searing heat and biting cold—of scorpions and rattlesnakes. Mae's classmate Raymond Akashi described his sharpest Topaz memory as "pound[ing] the heel of [his] boot" on scorpions. The ground was so parched that little grew except for the drab, tough-as-nails greasewood bush. Temperatures skyrocketed as high as 106°F in the summer and plummeted as low as 30° below zero in the winter. A fifty-degree swing during a single day was not surprising.

Internees, the term the government used for the prisoners, soon discovered that the wind blew most of the time, making things hotter or colder—and drier and dirtier. Mae's earliest memory of Topaz was of "the fine alkali dust that blew in . . . and covered everything." If the wind picked up enough speed, the outcome could be dangerous: a dust storm.

A Boy Scout drum and bugle corps welcoming later arrivals to Topaz.

This diary drawing shows a dust devil (whirlwind), a bleached cow skull, dry brush, and a jackrabbit, as well as a seagull in the sky. The children were surprised to see the familiar coastal birds, which came from Great Salt Lake, a hundred miles to the north.

There were times when storms lasted for days, with winds so fierce the flying sand made legs bleed.

One of Yoshiko's first encounters with a dust storm turned into a near-death experience. She was walking across camp when "the wind suddenly gathered ominous strength" and "swirling masses of sand" filled the air. A dust cloud "eclipsed barracks only ten feet away." Yoshiko dove into a laundry building for cover, though the monstrous storm threatened to shake the flimsy structure to pieces. During a brief lull in the winds, she made a break for home but was caught again and nearly choked to death. "Fear gave me strength to fight," she later wrote.

"Yesterday there was a fierce whirl-wind near Block 2. A boy on a bicycle was whirled around and around."

—*Our Daily Diary*, May 13, 1943

When the rain did come, it transformed the dust and sand into sludge. Streets turned into quagmires. Some of the detainees made their traditional wooden clogs, called geta (*gay-tah*), a foot high because of

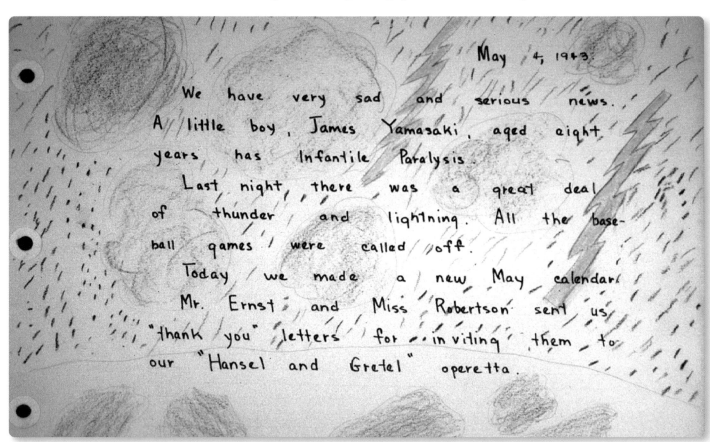

May 4, 1943

We have very sad and serious news. A little boy, James Yamasaki, aged eight years has Infantile Paralysis.

Last night, there was a great deal of thunder and lightning. All the baseball games were called off.

Today we made a new May calendar. Mr. Ernst and Miss Robertson sent us "thank you" letters for inviting them to our "Hansel and Gretel" operetta.

Though it didn't rain often at Topaz Camp, the thunderstorms could be spectacular, as rendered by the class artist of the day.

mud puddles, but geta didn't work to traverse the deeper muck in the middle of the streets. Sato Hashizume remembers that "until they put the planks down so we could walk we were losing our shoes and getting stuck and screaming for help." Third graders like Mae would have sunk up to their knees!

The camp was named for nearby Topaz Mountain, which was named in turn for the semiprecious gemstone found there. The masthead of the first edition of the camp newspaper, the *Topaz Times*, included a drawing of a fac-

A man fighting with bog-like mud in the street.

eted topaz stone and the slogan "Jewel of the Desert." For the rest of their imprisonment, the detainees sarcastically referred to the camp as a jewel.

Despite the bleak conditions, the Nikkei could occasionally recognize the beauty of the surrounding landscape. "As time passed, we became familiar with the desert," remembers Edwin Narahara, another of Mae's classmates. "To this day, I still appreciate [it]." In their diary drawings, Miss Yamauchi's students often depicted striking mountain and desert scenery, including the crystal clarity of the starry heavens. The entry for July 26 reports Raymond's excitement at spotting a shooting star, while the drawing shows a brilliant streak flashing across the dark and star-laced mountain sky.

Resident firefighters pose beside their fire truck. They were kept busy because the tinderbox-like barracks were always catching on fire.

Chapter 3

Barracks, Mess Halls, and Latrines

MAE YANAGI LIVED IN A FIRETRAP. Her family, like all the other Topaz detainees, had been moved into a wooden barrack covered with flammable tar paper and heated with coal-burning iron stoves that belched sparks. It was a formula for disaster. A top-notch fire department was a camp necessity.

Mae's firetrap home was an icebox as well. Cold weather came early in 1942, and her barrack lacked a stove at first. Mae's family waited weeks for crews to install a stove and interior drywall. Even then, the barrack remained uninsulated. As Roger Walker, a worker in the camp, later reported, "The sheeting had cracks at least a quarter of an inch between each board. . . . No insulation whatsoever. . . . It is really difficult to see how they survived." To help keep out the cold, Edwin Narahara collected milkweed pods, which his family stuffed into gaps in the walls and floor.

Eight thousand people were packed into that square mile of desert. Mae found herself crowded into one of thirty-four "neighborhoods," called blocks. Each block was made up of twelve barracks, plus a mess hall, a recreation hall, a laundry, and a public bathroom. Toilets lacked seats at first, and stalls for showers and toilets had no doors. Many older Nikkei, particularly women, found showering in public humiliating.

"Running to the restroom in the middle of the night was a frightening experience. I imagine[d] the 'Boogey Man' lurking in the shadows of the barracks."

—Roy Takeuchi, Mae's classmate

Each barrack was divided into six apartments. Yoshiko Uchida's address was 7-2-C, for Block 7, Barrack 2, Apartment C. Mae's family was so large that it had two apartments: 9-11-C and 9-11-D. Because the blocks were identical, people would get lost. On March 16, Mae's class diary reports that a new student "was absent this afternoon because he could not find his way to school." Later "signs were put up showing the names of the streets of Topaz"—Sage Street, Greasewood Way, Agate Avenue, and other streets named for local plants and minerals.

Yoshiko's apartment was twenty feet long and twenty feet wide, a bit larger than some because it housed a family of four. It came with a pot-bellied stove, army cots with straw-filled cotton bags for mattresses (later exchanged for cotton-stuffed mattresses), and a light bulb hanging by a wire from the ceiling. For other furnishings, the Uchidas had to scavenge building materials and make their own. Detainees were able to rig up hot plates to heat water and warm food, but the appliances were an added fire hazard. Mae's friend Jane Kawaguchi set her barrack on fire when

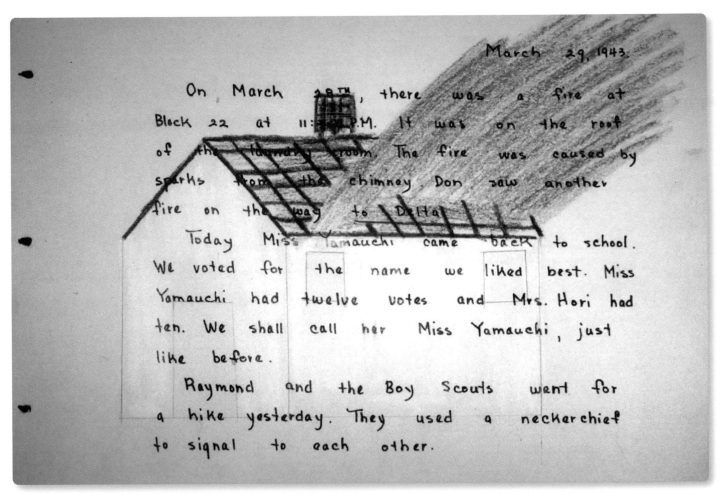

Fires were commonplace in Topaz. The diary reports many conflagrations, including the one pictured here and a July 4 barrack fire caused when "some careless children threw sparklers on the roof."

heating oil to fry some rice. "While waiting for the oil to get hot, some friends came by and asked if I wanted to go to the playground," she recalls. "So I ran off without turning off the hot plate. Needless to say, I got the worst spanking and scolding of my life!"

White teachers and administrators lived in barracks, too, but theirs were different. When Yoshiko Uchida visited a couple who were teachers, she discovered that "they lived in half a barrack . . . with linoleum and carpeting on the floor, a houseful of comfortable furniture, a fully equipped kitchen." Included was a private bathroom. After visiting her white friends, Yoshiko was "filled with envy, longing, and resentment." Such inequality surfaces in the classroom diary, too: in March the children noted that "Lynn will get a new refrigerator today." Lynn Johnson was the son of white camp employees who decided not to send him into Delta for school. No one else in the class had a refrigerator.

For detainees, running water was available only in the laundries, latrines, and mess halls. But the quality of the water was the same for everyone. It came from three wells and was heavily laced with salty alkaline. Margaret Hamachi, another of Mae's friends, remembers that the water was "dirty" and that her mother kept a pot on the stove to boil it

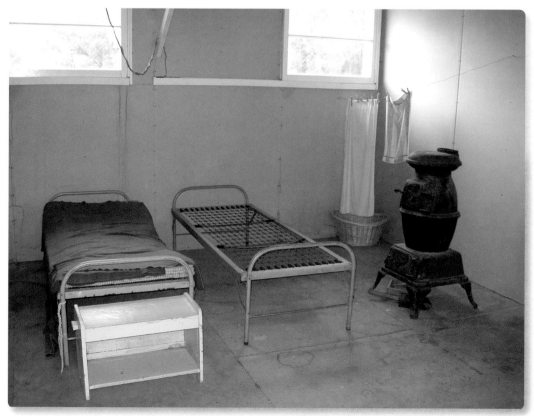

A restored barrack at the Topaz Museum. When the Nikkei first arrived, interior walls and floors lacked coverings, unlike in this photo. Wind and dust blew through gaps in the boards. Some windows had no glass.

before use. But at least there was water—mostly. Blocks often lost their supply when the flimsy pipes corroded in the alkaline soil and sprang leaks. The pipes would run dry without warning, sometimes catching people in the middle of showers, covered with soap. "When the water was running [again]," Yoshiko Uchida recalled, "a neighbor would bang on our door and shout." Then family members would rush to the laundry with pans or buckets to bring back an emergency supply. After a year the entire water system was unearthed and replaced, remedying most of the

Detainees work on the Topaz electrical system. The towers in the background stored the camp's water. Although the alkaline-laced water wasn't pleasant to drink, Miné Okubo reported that it was good for washing clothes.

Camp administrators allowed detainees to collect limited amounts of scrap lumber to build household furnishings. There was never enough to go around, so pilfering lumber from camp building projects was common. In at least one instance, a guard used his gun to threaten teenagers scavenging wood.

problems. But washing laundry with a wooden washboard was still exhausting work—and a rude shock for those detainees who had once owned washing machines.

Though Topaz Camp didn't look like the California towns Mae and Yoshiko knew, it had the same basic services: a post office, a Western Union telegraph office, a telephone switchboard for routing calls (for administrative use only), a motor pool for maintaining camp work vehicles, a police department, a hospital, and a fire department. Workers were needed, so most adult Nikkei had jobs. Most earned only $16 per month, while white employees earned $150 to $200.

The government had frozen the bank accounts of the Nikkei, so they were restricted to their small camp salaries. But the meager money bought Mae tickets for in-camp movies, the occasional ice-cream bar, or perhaps a hairbrush from the Topaz dry-goods store. Her parents could also order items from the Montgomery Ward or Sears, Roebuck catalogs.

As time passed and more materials became available, some detainees created Japanese gardens in an effort to beautify their drab surroundings. This simple garden features a shrine.

Nikkei held every sort of job in Topaz, from electrician to block manager to farmer. Mae's father worked as a glazier, installing windows and replacing glass, while her mother became a custodian, cleaning the camp photography studio. Yoshiko Uchida and Miné Okubo, both in their early twenties, also had jobs. Miné worked at the *Topaz Times*. Yoshiko became a second-grade teacher. Later in life Yoshiko became a well-known author, as did Miné, who was also an illustrator. Both wrote books about Japanese American incarceration.

Yoshiko, Miné, Mae, and the rest of the detainees ate their meals in mess halls. Back in California, they had eaten family meals around their own dining-room tables. Now iron bells clanged in each block, calling them

Yoshiko Uchida (left) with her family (her mother, Iku; her father, Dwight; and her sister, Keiko) on June 15, 1943.

*Detainees ate their meals in crowded mess halls
with picnic-style tables and unfinished interior walls and ceilings.*

to be fed with 250 others. Main dishes were served at a counter, side dishes were placed on the tables, and Nikkei "waiters" brought around tea.

At first many were unhappy with the camp food. Mrs. Yanagi had prepared Japanese foods at home in California, so Mae and her siblings found the strange fare unpalatable. Her brother particularly despised the curried mutton stew. Some of Mae's classmates vividly recall their "unfavorites." Roy Takeuchi hated "liver, liver, liver (ugg)!!!" For Betty Sugiyama, it was kidney. Raymond Akashi and Grace Hayashi couldn't stand the

SPECIAL TOPAZ TIMES *News Daily* **SPECIAL**

Vol. I No. 46 TOPAZ, UTAH Thursday, December 24, 1942

MISSING RESIDENT FOUND ALIVE

HORSEMEN FIND FUKAGAI 10 MI. FROM MT. TOPAZ

Three-day search for Kozo Fukagai was ended yesterday when a group of horsemen discovered his prostrate figure on the desert sand about 10 miles west of Mt. Topaz. Alive and conscious, though greatly exhausted by hunger, thirst and exposure, the 32-year old nisei immediately inquired about his parents, according to Katsumi D. Wakamatsu, 26-2-C, who was first to locate him.

After some nourishment was given to him, some of the horsemen galloped ahead to the searching party's base camp to Mt. Topaz and obtained a cattle truck to transport him into the City. He arrived at the Hospital at about 4 PM, a little more than an hour after he was found.

The clue to his whereabouts came when footprints were found along a dry river wash yesterday afternoon. Wakamatsu, Hakaru Oda and George Fukui from the Agricultural Division's cattle ranch accompanied by 6 Caucasian cowboys from neighboring ranches quickly trailed the tracks. Wakamatsu, who was about 50 yards apart from the others, finally perceived a lone figure clothed in brown slacks and government winter mackinaw and cap at about 3:30 PM.

After the discovery was confirmed, the Internal Security Division recalled all of the 85 members of the searching groups dispatched from the City yesterday.

Now under the care of Dr. Mas Harada, Fukagai was met at his bedside by his parents, Mr. and Mrs. Kazo Fukagai of 31-2-D, and Rev. I. Kyogoku.

"The safe return of their son is probably Mr. and Mrs. Fukagai's finest Christmas gift, and the City rejoices with them in these good tidings," Project Director Charles F. Ernst commented.

Formerly of San Francisco, Kozo Fukagai is a graduate of the High School of Commerce and was a student of Heald's Business College. At Topaz he was working with the individual survey group.

CANDIDATES NAMED FOR ELECTION

Candidates to run in the general election for councilmen on Dec. 29 were chosen last Tuesday evening at nomination assemblies held in all of the City's 9 districts. At the polls next week residents of each district are expected to elect a number of representatives equal to the number of occupied blocks within the district.

Following residents were nominated on Dec. 22: (Dist. 1) Paul Fujii, Frank Fukuda, Kaoru Kimura; (Dist. 2) Hachiro Yuasa, Koji Marata, Yoshio Taira, James Yamamoto, Masao Miho, Takashi Takahashi, Ray Kaneko; (Dist. 3) Henry Takahashi, Shigeru Kosakura, Masanki Sakakihara, Dr. Carl Hirota, Harry Tawa, T. Yatabe, Saburo Matsumoto, Lincoln Tokunaga, Kiyosuke Nomura; (Dist. 5) Mas Yamada, Clarke Harada, Saiki Muneno, George Ochikubo, Kenji Fujii, Don Onumo; (Dist. 6) Hiro Katayama, John Iwatsu, Eiichi Sato, Shiro Shibata, George Hoshide, Hi Korematsu, Victor Abe, Shigeo Isaki; (Dist. 7) Paul Sugawara, George Hagiwara, James Nishimura, Tsune Baba, Taro Katayama, Hiro Bando, Masato Maruyama, Yoshifume Sakauye, Vernon Ichisaka; (Dist. 8) Takatoshi Yamamoto, George Shigezumi and Shigetoshi Shigeo.

News Briefs

CLINIC: Effective immediately, the clinic will be open only for emergencies during regular clinic hours. There will be no special clinic until next week. The clinic will be closed all day Dec. 25th.

SOLDIERS: The Christmas committee extends a personal invitation to all nisei soldiers to attend all the functions being planned for the Christmas holidays.

CO-OP: The barber shop in Block 41 opened Tuesday. A beauty shop will be open soon, it was announced by the Cooperative Enterprise.

MEMORIAL SERVICE: Memorial for the late Kikui Mizuhara will be held this Saturday, 7:30 PM at the Buddhist Church, Rec 28.

Library

HOLIDAY HOURS: The Public Library will close at 5 PM today (Thursday), all day Christmas; open from 2 to 5 PM only on Saturday and Sunday.

SOMETHING NEW: A newly constructed charge counter takes the place of the former table, as part of the furnishing program. Christmas decorations have been made by staff members under the direction of Margaret Tsuda and Esther Tani of the catalog dept.

RENTAL: Beginning Jan. 1st, books in the rental collection will circulate for 5 days for 5¢ - 2¢ per day over due. Books may be renewed if not on reserve.

VISITOR: J.P. McEvoy, roving editor of Reader's Digest and writer, was a recent visitor to the Library. "The Library looks professional; it is more than an attempt." he commented.

WEATHER REPORT	
Max. (Tues. night)	45° F.
Min. (Wed. morn)	29° F.

The Topaz Times, *written and published by detainees, was duplicated on a mimeograph machine and ran articles on camp-related news (elections, library hours, sporting events, and holiday plans), as well as some national news.*

powdered eggs, and Frankie Kawasaki thought the rice tasted bitter. "I couldn't understand how anyone could spoil rice," he says.

To offset mess-hall fare, many people cooked on their stoves and hot plates. Frankie remembers his family baking bread on the pot-bellied stove and churning their own butter. Edwin Narahara discovered a fondness for peanut butter and jam on saltine crackers, which he bought at the camp store. He snacks on them to this day. When camp administration finally allowed detainees to build a tofu

A worker in the camp's tofu factory. Tofu, or soybean curd, is a popular part of the Japanese diet.

plant in February 1943, people were jubilant. At last Mae and her friends could eat a traditional Japanese food!

As there were many mouths to feed, the Topaz construction plan included farms and ranches beyond the barbed wire. Detainees managed and worked on hog and turkey farms, a cattle ranch, and farms growing crops such as alfalfa. Once the farms began producing, the meals in the mess halls improved.

At one point the Utah state legislature sent a delegation to Topaz to check on reports that the prisoners were being coddled, but the legislators "pronounced themselves satisfied with what they saw." To this day, there are old-timers who believe the "internees" ate better than most Americans. To this day, Mae will tell you that just wasn't so.

Miss Yamauchi's third-grade class.
Mae Yanagi is in the front row, second from the right.

This diary page lists the names of students in the class on March 8, 1943, the date of the first diary entry.

This diary is kept by the members of the High Third Grade. Their names are:

Don Adams	Frankie Kawasaki	Shizuko Nishitani
Raymond Akashi	Jane Kawaguchi	Makoto Oda
David Crowton	George Kitagawa	Betty Sugiyama
Grace Hayashi	Jackie Kitajima	Robert Suzuki
Margaret Hamachi	Kiku Kitow	Kei Takemoto
June Inouye	Harry Mayeda	Roy Takeuchi
Lynn Johnson	Ben Morita	Kimiko Tsutsui
Richard Kaneko	Johnny Moritomo	Bobby Hirano
Robert Kerr	Edwin Narahara	Mae Yanagi

Chapter 4

School Days

A MONTH AFTER ARRIVING AT TOPAZ, Mae started school. Two elementary schools, a junior high school, and a high school opened their doors on October 20. Mae's classroom was bare and cold: no tables, chairs, stoves, books, or teaching supplies. The children had to sit on the floor.

The unfinished barrack offered little protection from dust storms, freezing temperatures, and snow. When Yoshiko Uchida reported to teach second grade, she found her classroom "as cold as the inside of a refrigerator." It even had a hole in the roof! No sooner had Mae started school than it ended. Early snowstorms forced the schools to shut down in November, and they didn't reopen until well into December, when the rooms had drywall walls and stoves.

When the classrooms were finally warm enough, Mae returned to Mountain View School, which occupied half of Block 8. Mae's older brothers, Takehiko and Takeshi, attended Topaz High School in Block 32. Tak and Keshi had a harder time adjusting to camp school than Mae did because they better understood the injustice of so-called "relocation," which included an inferior education. They and many other Nisei high-schoolers were headed for college. They knew Topaz High, with its lack of supplies, equipment, and well-trained teachers, was crippling their academic progress. In fact most of the Topaz High class of 1943 reported that they felt they could no longer be successful in college. "I really don't think I learned anything [at Topaz High]," said Robert Utsumi. "I just felt I didn't get a high school education."

Mae and her third-grade classmates tended to be happier. They weren't worried about college. And they were so much younger that parents and teachers could sometimes shelter them from the worst realities of imprisonment. As a result some children, like Edwin Narahara, grew up remembering Topaz as a prolonged campout. It was a similar experience for Betty Sugiyama. "When we made our journey to Topaz, I thought we were going on vacation," she remembers. "Riding on the Pullman train was new and fun to me."

Graduating seniors from Topaz High receive their diplomas.

Three children help clean up their classroom. Younger children tended to be more content than high-school students, who realized their education was suffering in Topaz.

The diary kept by Miss Yamauchi's class seems to reflect this effort to make captivity bearable for the younger children. Elementary school in Topaz appears to have been a happy, safe, and busy place. Some of Mae's classmates, including Grace Hayashi and June Inouye, remember feelings of comfort at being surrounded by so many Japanese American faces—and having a Japanese American teacher for the first time!

Because the children had missed so much school in the fall, school extended through the summer of 1943. The seventy-two pages of *Our Daily Diary* start on March 8 and end on August 12. By spring Topaz had settled into its routine, allowing the diary to reveal the normal, day-to-day events of grade-school life in a prison camp. Of course, life could never be truly normal, as though these kids were back home in the Bay

Area. But both teachers and children made the best of what might have easily become an intolerable situation. Their resilient attitude is reflected in their class diary.

Naturally schoolwork takes front and center in the diary. On May 10 the children noted that they made new spelling books and started learning their multiplication tables—like any other third-grade class. More unusual was the strong focus on nature. Miss Yamauchi's class took

The children of Topaz adjusted to their strange new surroundings, settling into the comforting daily routine of school. This photograph was taken at a point when the classrooms finally had tables, chairs, and chalkboards.

advantage of being trapped in a mountain desert by studying their surroundings in science and social studies. Many of their art projects, field trips, and writing assignments also centered on the natural world. This meant the classroom was often populated by wild things. The children wrote that Edwin brought in a prairie dog (how he managed to catch it remains untold) and that Margaret and Mae brought in fish for the classroom zoo. Kiku Kitow added a horned toad in May.

"Our ants have started to dig their tunnels. Margaret brought some sugar for our ants because ants are so fond of sweet things."

—*Our Daily Diary*, March 26, 1943

In social studies the class learned about early Native American cultures from the area. The third graders watched a film about Pueblo people and how they lived in their environment. Later they made their own

Miss Yamauchi's students built an enclosure for their lizards, which were part of an ever-growing classroom zoo made up of small desert creatures.

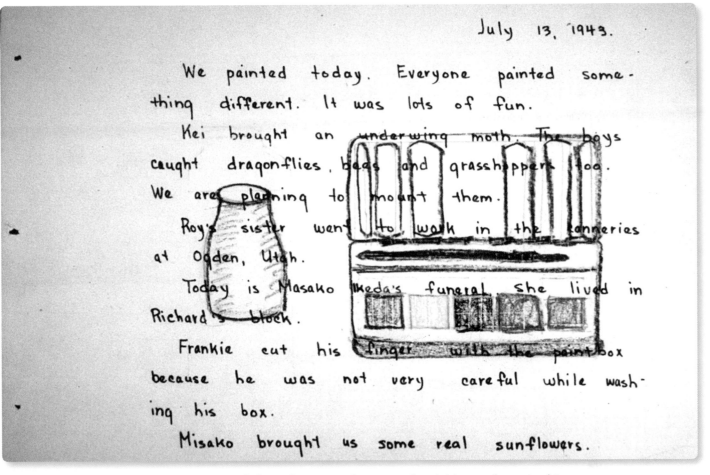

July 13, 1943.

We painted today. Everyone painted something different. It was lots of fun.

Kei brought an underwing moth. The boys caught dragonflies, bees and grasshoppers too. We are planning to mount them.

Roy's sister went to work in the canneries at Ogden, Utah.

Today is Masako Ikeda's funeral. She lived in Richard's block.

Frankie cut his finger with the paintbox because he was not very careful while washing his box.

Misako brought us some real sunflowers.

Miss Yamauchi's class recorded a wide variety of events and activities, as shown in this diary entry. The illustration features a set of watercolor paints.

books and a frieze, or banner, about human shelter. As they reported on May 25, "many pupils in our class were flat on their stomachs working very hard on our frieze."

Art projects like the frieze brightened up the classroom. In the spring Mae and her classmates decorated the room with handcrafted flowers. They also painted with watercolors, sculpted clay, and made their own monthly calendars.

Drywall carving was a more unusual art project. There must have been plenty of drywall scraps left over after the interior walls of the barracks were completed. First the children sponged the scraps with water to loosen the paper coating until it could be peeled away. Each student then drew an outline on the surface and scraped away the chalk-like material to create a three-dimensional picture. The children were pleased enough with their work that they gifted the camp director, Charles Ernst, three of their carvings.

Spring was also the season of school performances in the elementary grades. Miss Yamauchi's class performed an operetta, "Hansel and Gretel." After weeks of listening to music, building sets, and rehearsing, the class presented their operetta on April 30 at Recreation Hall Number 8.

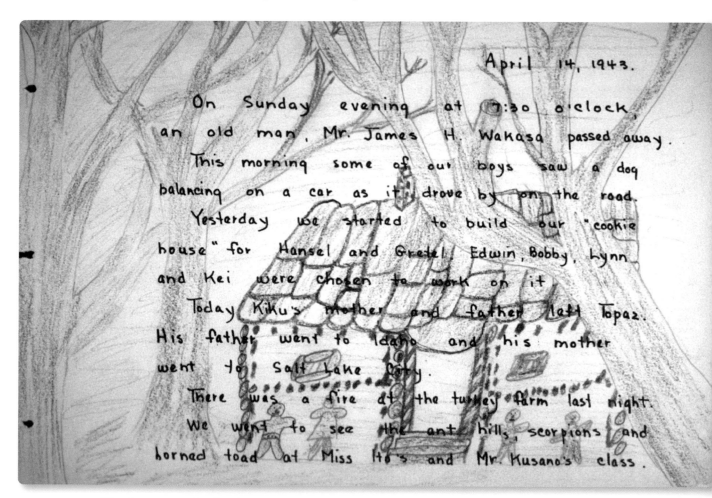

April 14, 1943.

On Sunday evening at 7:30 o'clock, an old man, Mr. James H. Wakasa passed away. This morning some of our boys saw a dog balancing on a car as it drove by on the road.

Yesterday we started to build our "cookie house" for Hansel and Gretel. Edwin, Bobby, Lynn and Kei were chosen to work on it.

Today Kiku's mother and father left Topaz. His father went to Idaho and his mother went to Salt Lake City.

There was a fire at the turkey farm last night. We went to see the ant hills, scorpions and horned toad at Miss Ito's and Mr. Kusano's class.

The diary artist for this day rendered a scene from the class play, "Hansel and Gretel."
The class was just beginning work on the "cookie house" scenery for the play.

Roy Takeuchi was Hansel, and what he best remembers is crawling into the "cardboard box we'd fashioned into an oven." There were some tense moments the night of the performance because Gretel had a mosquito bite on her eye that almost kept her off the stage! But she bravely pushed on, and the production was a great success. Soon after, the class traveled across camp to Desert View School's rendition of "Hansel and Gretel." With great humility, the children determined that "they were just as good as we were."

Whether the school day included measuring the children's height and weight, peering through Harry Mayeda's telescope, or voting in class elections (Edwin was elected class president on April 1), it seems clear that Miss Yamauchi's classroom activities gave a great deal of purpose to these third graders' life in camp. The children preferred going to school over staying home because it seemed more like their old lives back in California. Yoshiko Uchida once braved a dust storm to get to her second-grade classroom, not expecting her students to be there. When she arrived, she found some of them waiting in the dust-filled room. As she later wrote, "I was touched . . . to see their eagerness to learn despite the desolation of their surroundings, the meager tools for learning, and, in this case, the physical dangers they encountered just to reach school."

March 11, 1943.

Yesterday we started to join the American Junior Red Cross.

Please remember to put 10% of your pay into war bonds and stamps. We should not kill spiders because Uncle Sam needs them for the war.

Lynn will get a new refrigerator today.

Blocks 3, 16, 22, 23 had no running water this morning because the water pipe broke at the high school grounds. The people in these blocks went to other places to wash their faces and brush their teeth.

May 18, 1943.

We have a large box filled with nails. Every day we bring more and more nails for Uncle Sam.

Yesterday a big bomber flew over Topaz.

Our paper folders tear so easily that we have decided to pay 8¢ each for some material to make new folders.

Edwin brought us a baby horned toad. It is now living with our five lizards.

Kimiko's mother was burned very badly by hot water.

Yesterday little Drayton Nuttall found Don's money. Don was surely happy to have it returned.

World War II was always on the minds of detainees, including children. These patriotic diary pages urge the class to contribute to the war effort.

Chapter 5

The War

WORLD WAR II LOOMED over the lives of every Japanese American person, including children. Despite what the government had done to them, the detainees in Topaz worked hard to support the fight against Japan, Germany, and Italy. *Our Daily Diary* reports that class members joined the American Junior Red Cross, which sent supplies and other aid to American soldiers. The diary reads, "Please remember to put 10% of your pay into war bonds and stamps"—a plea to help fund the war. The page also admonishes everyone "not to kill spiders because Uncle Sam needs them for the war." Spiderwebs (especially those of the black widow) are some of the thinnest yet strongest materials known, and they do not stretch or fray. The children knew that American bombers used webs for the crosshairs of their sighting scopes.

Miss Yamauchi's class showed their patriotism in other ways, too. The diary page for May 18 is decorated with two waving American flags surrounded by a border of bent nails. "We have a large box filled with nails," the children say. "Every day we bring more and more nails for

Uncle Sam." Americans were recycling anything and everything that could be turned into tanks, planes, guns, or other vital wartime supplies. The iron in old nails fit the bill, but relinquishing nails was a serious sacrifice for detainees, who needed them to make furniture. The third graders also collected "rubber, money, spiders, paper, and lots of other things to help Uncle Sam." Used rubber was recycled into tires, and rags and old clothes were turned into parachutes and uniforms. The girls in Mae's class also knitted small squares. "After we finish many many pieces, we shall put them all together and make a blanket for the American Red Cross," they write.

In the spring, Miné Okubo later recalled, "practically everyone set up a victory garden." Americans from coast to coast planted victory

Children and adults planted victory gardens in the alkaline soil of Topaz.

A bus carries volunteers from Topaz to Fort Douglas, near Salt Lake City, Utah, to be inducted into the army.

gardens. The idea was to feed American families, thus freeing up other sources of food for the soldiers. In Topaz watering the vegetables was difficult because there was no running water near the garden plots. Detainees had to form bucket brigades from the laundry, lining up and passing buckets of water from person to person.

Before long the Topaz community was saying goodbye to young men who volunteered to go to war. Immediately after Pearl Harbor, Japanese Americans had been barred from joining US military forces. However, young men of Japanese descent in Hawaii wanted to prove their loyalty. Their determination impressed Lieutenant General Delos Emmons, and he pushed hard for permission to form the 100th Battalion, an all-Nisei unit shipped off to Italy to fight the Germans. Still, the Nisei boys on the mainland were not considered fit to serve. In February 1943 President Roosevelt finally decided that they should have the right to volunteer for a new all Japanese American army unit called the 442nd Regimental Combat Team. Many young women also decided to serve by joining the

Women's Auxiliary Army Corps, which challenged the traditional Japanese belief that females should not be involved in the military. They went through rigorous basic training and then served as typists, clerks, drivers, nurses, and interpreters.

"This afternoon the second group of the Japanese American Combat Team left Topaz to join Uncle Sam's Army. Edwin's uncle is a volunteer too."

—*Our Daily Diary*, May 21, 1943

While many Nisei were eager to volunteer, others were unhappy with the idea of a segregated unit. Why weren't there German American combat teams or Italian American units? As a matter of fact, why hadn't German and Italian "enemy aliens" been thrown in prison camps, too? They were also unhappy about having to pass a loyalty questionnaire. One of

Like the women in this photo, several hundred young women in Topaz volunteered for the Women's Auxiliary Army Corps. Their male counterparts didn't want to appear less patriotic, so the number of male army volunteers increased as well.

The Topaz service flag displayed a star for each detainee serving in the military.

the questions asked the Nisei boys to swear allegiance to the United States and disavow allegiance to the Japanese emperor. To these native-born American citizens, the assumption that they might be loyal to Japan's emperor was insulting, and many would not volunteer to fight for the government that had imprisoned them. But in January 1944, young Nisei men suddenly had no choice. Uncle Sam decided to draft them into service. Mae and the other children of Topaz watched as their brothers, uncles, and fathers left a barbed-wire compound to fight for freedom in a faraway land.

On the battlefront in Italy, the 100th Battalion was merged with the new 442nd Regimental Combat Team. This elite unit continued to be as formidable as the 100th had been on its own. Their motto was "Go for Broke" and that's exactly what they did, in part to prove their loyalty. As a result, the 442nd had one of the highest casualty rates of any regiment in the war. In the end the young men received 18,143 medals and citations, making the regiment "the most decorated unit of its size and length of service in the history of the United States."

Japanese American soldiers were also deployed against Japan in the Pacific, mostly as interpreters and scouts. The army was shocked to discover that the Nisei were so Americanized that only about 10 percent knew the Japanese language well. The army trained thousands of Nisei, both men and women, at the Military Intelligence Service Language School.

On furlough before being shipped to the battlefront in Europe, two Nisei soldiers visit their families inside Topaz Camp, likely in the presence of an armed guard.

Soldiers of the 442nd Regimental Combat Team at Camp Shelby, in Mississippi. Their fighting spirit is exemplified by their rescue of the "Lost Battalion," which was surrounded by Germans. US attempts to rescue the battalion were unsuccessful until the 442nd was given the task. In a rain of Nazi gunfire, the Nisei soldiers charged up a hill, firing their weapons and tossing grenades. The 442nd rescued the 211 remaining soldiers but suffered huge losses: approximately 150 dead and 1,800 wounded.

The Japanese military often sent uncoded messages, assuming their language was indecipherable to Americans. The young Nisei interpreters became the army's secret weapon. In April 1943 they translated a radio transmission giving the whereabouts of Admiral Isoroku Yamamoto. American fighter planes intercepted and shot down the admiral's aircraft, killing the architect of the Pearl Harbor attack.

Many interpreters did more than translate and decode messages. Kenny Yasui fought alongside other US troops, as did many of the soldier linguists. Once Kenny pretended to be a Japanese colonel and captured sixteen enemy soldiers by commanding them to drop their weapons and march to his orders. Roy Matsumoto got close enough to a group of Japanese soldiers to overhear their assault plan, enabling the Americans to

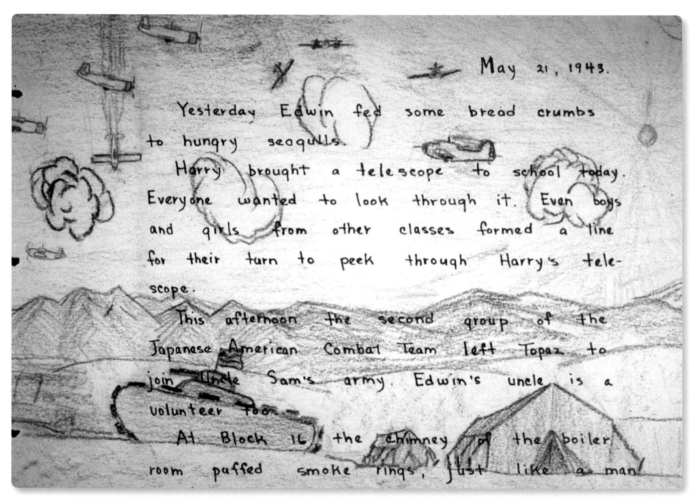

May 21, 1943.

Yesterday Edwin fed some bread crumbs to hungry seagulls.

Harry brought a telescope to school today. Everyone wanted to look through it. Even boys and girls from other classes formed a line for their turn to peek through Harry's telescope.

This afternoon the second group of the Japanese American Combat Team left Topaz to join Uncle Sam's army. Edwin's uncle is a volunteer too.

At Block 16 the chimney of the boiler room puffed smoke rings, just like a man

This entry reports the departure of Topaz's members of the 442nd Regimental Combat Team. Toward the end of the war, the 442nd liberated Dachau, the horrific Nazi concentration camp, and found the inmates near death. Thinking Germany's Japanese allies were there to finish them off, a prisoner cried out, "Why don't you just shoot us and get it over with?" A Nisei soldier dropped to his knees. "We are liberators," he said, weeping. "We are American Japanese."

Grieving mothers in Topaz Camp hold the flags that would have draped the coffins of their fallen soldier sons had their bodies been shipped home.

annihilate the first wave of attackers. Major General Charles Willoughby, chief of intelligence in the Pacific, believed the work of the Nisei linguists "shortened the Pacific war by two years."

Meanwhile, back in Topaz no news was good news for many families. They feared receiving the Western Union telegram with the fateful words "I regret to inform you . . ." The Gold Star banner hanging in a window meant a son or daughter would not be coming home from the war. Their bodies were typically buried in that faraway soil, which made parting all the more difficult. All American families who lost sons or daughters, brothers or sisters, to the war suffered this tragedy. But a Gold Star banner hanging in the dusty window of a tar-papered barrack, within a barbed-wire enclosure, must have been especially heartrending.

Sixth-grade boys in Manzanar Camp (Owens Valley, California) use a rock as home plate. Similar softball and baseball games took place in Topaz.

Chapter 6

Take Me Out to the Ball Game

BEING IMPRISONED AND HELPLESS while war raged across the planet was reason enough for Topaz detainees to feel anxious. Some suffered from depression. Finding ways to escape the gloom was imperative in the struggle to survive, and so sports, games, and other recreational activities became lifesavers.

In their classroom diary, the third graders report that their class squared off against Miss Kushida's class in baseball. Though the diary doesn't report who won, the contest was one of many, many games of baseball played in Topaz Camp by young and old alike. On May 26 the "Military Police beat the Administration by the score of 11–5," and, in Block 30, "the little boys played baseball against the old men" and won 21–10! The detainees built a dozen baseball diamonds around the camp. Instead of green grass, the fields were patches of desert dirt cleared of greasewood bushes and rocks, then leveled and drenched with water to pack and harden the surfaces. Equipment was often donated by friends back home or purchased by the detainees themselves.

May 19, 1943.

Today Miss Kushida's class and our class played baseball.

Kei received a new sweater and two books from his grandmother.

Last night Don and Robert helped the people of their block. They stacked fire wood until 10:30 P.M. They are very tired today.

Today Miss Yamauchi told us a story about snakes.

A man at Block 23 was running and he suddenly fell forward in a faint.

Betty's sister was lost but she was found wandering around in another block. Each block is so much alike that it is easy

The third graders reported about several baseball games in their diary. Later many detainees said that the sport had been a real blessing to their sanity.

The other major team sports were basketball and football. At least eight blocks had basketball courts. Block football leagues played games on the high-school field. Youngsters played, too, pulling together sandlot football games and pickup basketball games. Other sports included Ping-Pong, volleyball, and judo. Whatever the sport, competitions drew large and enthusiastic crowds of spectators—fans needing distraction from what could be a dispiriting and tedious existence.

Sixth-grade girls in Manzanar Camp playing volleyball on an outdoor court.

Judo students practicing throws in Rohwer Camp, in Arkansas.

Boys playing a pickup game of basketball in Tanforan.

A Nikkei golfer putting a ball across a sand "green." The Topaz course was a short one, as players had to stay in view of the guard towers.

Though difficult to imagine, Topaz even had a tennis club and a nine-hole golf course with dirt fairways and sand "greens." The golf course was outside the fence but in view of the guard towers. The cost of maintaining and operating the golf course and tennis courts came from small fees and membership dues.

Cards—as well as checkers, chess, and other board games—were also popular. Players would visit recreation halls to compete in fierce tournaments—or to just pick up a game. The older generation particularly enjoyed go (*goh*) and shōgi (*shoh-gee*), Japanese games resembling chess. Children often learned to play, too, sometimes even beating their elders.

Like kids everywhere, the children of Topaz made their own fun. Frankie Kawasaki remembers marble matches in the dirt, and Johnny Moritomo played war in the recreation hall with blow darts made from Sears catalog pages. Roy Takeuchi loved games of jintori (*jeen-toh-ree*) (Capture the Flag) on summer evenings, best "when the sun set and it was easier to flank the opposing team." And during the first Topaz spring, as reported by Miss Yamauchi's class, kite flying became all the rage. Both adults and children enjoyed taking advantage of the ever-present Topaz wind—although the homemade kites sometimes tumbled and tangled in the barbed wire.

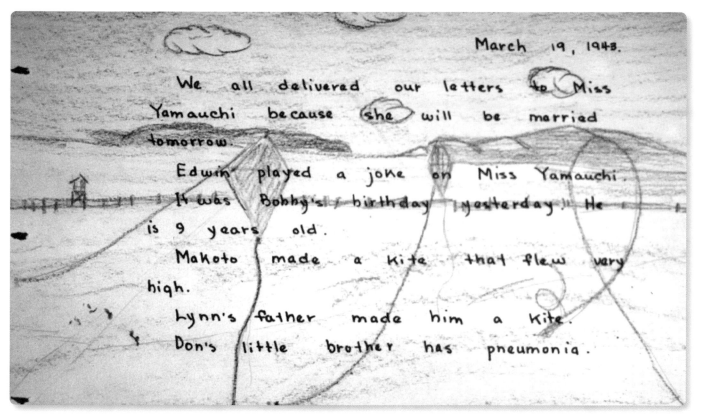

March 19, 1943.

We all delivered our letters to Miss Yamauchi because she will be married tomorrow.

Edwin played a joke on Miss Yamauchi. It was Bobby's birthday yesterday! He is 9 years old.

Makoto made a kite that flew very high.

Lynn's father made him a kite.

Don's little brother has pneumonia.

Because the War Relocation Authority wanted to show a positive image of camp life, there are virtually no government photos of camp guard towers. But in this drawing of kite flying, the young artist of the day included both the guard towers and the perimeter fence.

Spinning tops also caught on with the children that spring. *Our Daily Diary* confirms a top craze in Miss Yamauchi's class: "Makoto and Frankie are going to receive new tops. Richard's mother bought him a top in Delta." (Nikkei were eventually allowed limited trips into Delta to shop.) The third graders also report that Bobby Hirano acquired two tops—one from his dad and one from a classmate—and was trying to pick up more. In the popular game Crack Top, players spun their tops in a circle marked on the playground. Other players tried to hit the twirling tops with theirs. It was a demolition derby—tops getting chipped, scarred, and sometimes split—so it's no wonder Bobby wanted as many tops as he could get.

The Boy Scouts and Girl Scouts provided a marvelous diversion for the children of Topaz. After the first few months, the stricter security measures in Topaz were relaxed, which meant the children could leave their barbed-wire confines to hike and camp in the nearby mountains. In many ways the Utah mountains were a more exciting location for scouting than the cities of the Bay Area. The major camping destination was Antelope Springs, thirty-nine miles southwest of Topaz at the foot of Swasey Peak. On July 16 several of the boys in Miss Yamauchi's class were absent "because the Cub Scouts went to Antelope Springs."

Children swimming at Antelope Springs to beat the summer heat. Detainees were eventually allowed to hike, camp, and explore the mountain terrain around Topaz.

Not to be outdone, the Brownies took their turn on August 11. Swimming in the mountain spring water was a welcome escape from the dust and stifling summer heat.

"Several boys of our class went swimming in the bathtub. It is so hot now-a-days they just couldn't help it."

—*Our Daily Diary*, July 30, 1943

Boy Scouts lining up for an award ceremony.

In the fall of 1943, camp administrators began allowing detainees to hike the entire nineteen thousand acres of the Topaz project, which included the farms, cattle ranch, and other areas used to support the camp. Grace Hayashi's fondest camp memory was of the freedom "to wander around during summer vacation time." Children—along with their parents, teachers, and Scout leaders—fished in the irrigation ditches and searched the desert terrain for arrowheads, trilobite fossils, and other treasures. Sometimes school "field trips" included visits to the farms—or even the Topaz gravel pit, where *Our Daily Diary* reports that Don Adams found a genuine topaz gemstone.

Winter brought its own diversions. Several of Miss Yamauchi's students remember Topaz for its snow. "The most memorable camp experience," recalls Robert Suzuki, "was the coldness and seeing snow for the first time." Margaret Hamachi and Jane Kawaguchi particularly loved making snow angels—something they'd never done before. Margaret discovered she enjoyed skating, too, when detainees flooded a patch of ground to make an ice rink.

Indoors the children enjoyed watching movies, usually shown in the recreation halls, and shopping at the camp's general store or its smaller canteen. Ted Nagata, who was in kindergarten in 1942, later remembered

July 16, 1943

Several boys in our class are absent today because the Cub Scouts went to Antelope Springs.

A little boy suddenly had an attack of appendicitis while camping. He was rushed home with June's father and was operated at the Topaz Hospital. Jane's nurse sister came home with the patient too.

Tomorrow is Willie's birthday. He will be 9 years old. We are sorry it on Saturday.

The artist for July 16 depicted a campout scene at Antelope Springs.

being in heaven when he went to the canteen to buy a Coke and a Baby Ruth. Roy Takeuchi recalls hurrying to get tofu ice cream "before it ran out." Topaz Camp also had a good library that got its start with a donation of five thousand books from friends and schools in California.

A boy at Heart Mountain Camp, in Wyoming, ice-skates on a makeshift rink. Both children and adults in Topaz enjoyed skating in the winter. Many had never seen snow before.

Even the stress of wartime could not prevent such normal activities as storytelling.
Here young children gather outside a Topaz barrack to listen to a storyteller.

Yoshiko Uchida noted that reading helped keep her from being over-whelmed by the bleakness of the camp: "I read every book I could find."

When the Recreation Division at Topaz listed its responsibilities, which included supervising the golf course, playgrounds, picnic grounds, sports programs, festivals, and parties, it made Topaz sound like a resort rather than a prison camp. But these recreational activities were not those of resort guests. They were a necessary means of emotional survival for a group of people who would much rather have been back home.

Mae Yanagi holds a rabbit while a photographer from the camp's photo studio takes her picture.

Chapter 7

Creatures

FOR THE CHILDREN OF TOPAZ, leaving their homes behind was an unhappy, even traumatic event. Abandoning their pets made the forced move even worse. Detainees weren't allowed to bring animals. If they were fortunate, the family dog or cat found a new place with their non-Japanese friends. But the loss was still tragic for many children. For young Amy Iwasaki, turning her pet over to a neighbor was so disturbing that she repressed the memory. It was years later that she remembered—and only when her older sister began talking about how difficult that day had been for Amy.

A Topaz Junior High seventh grader wrote this about leaving a beloved collie, Spruce, behind: "He knew something was wrong. . . . He suspected because we were carrying our suitcases with us. When we were going down our garden . . . he followed us. I told him to go home he just sat and howled and cryed. My cousin and I got mad at him but we love him almost as if he were a human being. . . . When we drove away from the front of the house he was sitting inside the fence looking out."

Yoshiko Uchida and her sister had a pet dog but no friend who could take him. Yoshiko put an ad in the newspaper and "gave him to the first boy who called because he seemed kind and caring." The boy promised he would write to let the family know how the dog was doing. "Be a good boy now, Laddie," Yoshiko told her pet as the new owner led him away. "We'll come back for you someday." As she later recalled, "we could still hear Laddie's plaintive barking even after the car turned the corner."

Laddie died just a few weeks after Yoshiko's family left Berkeley. The boy never wrote, probably because he was too sad and embarrassed.

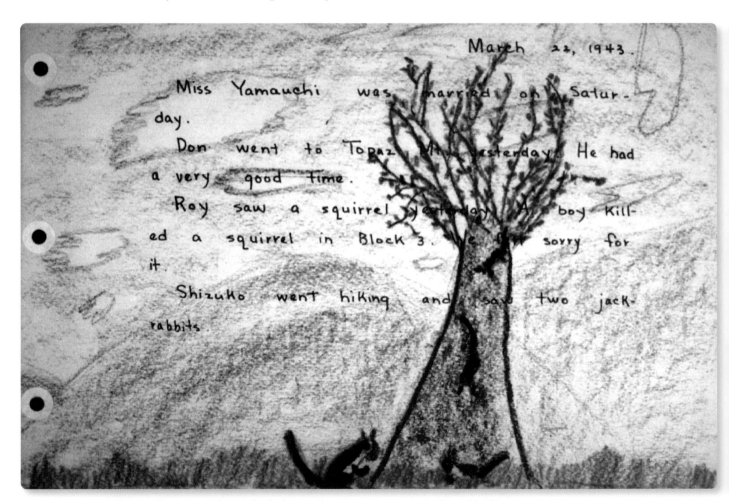

Squirrels apparently made their way into camp, as reported on this diary page:
"A boy killed a squirrel in Block 3." The class felt sorry for it.

When she found out, Yoshiko wrote, "I was sure [Laddie] had died of a broken heart, thinking we had abandoned him."

Even farm animals could be hard to leave behind. Tsuyako "Sox" Kitashima's family had to sell their farm equipment for a pittance, but the saddest event for her was putting down their faithful horse. "No one wanted an old horse," she later remembered.

Mae Yanagi doesn't recall having pets in California, but she remembers "hunting for critters" once she arrived at Topaz. Even though the camp guidebook stated, "Don't keep pet animals outside of dogs and cats," Mae and her friends rounded up lizards, insects, and other small creatures and kept them in bottles and other containers in their classroom and barrack homes. "We used to catch scorpions with ohashi [*oh-hah-shee*] [chopsticks] and put them in jars," Jane Kawaguchi remembers. "[We also] caught dragonflies and put thread around their bodies and let them fly like a kite."

"A man in Jane's block has 6 baby sparrows. He has promised her one just as soon as they are old enough to leave mother sparrow."

—*Our Daily Diary*, June 7, 1943

Of course, these wild pets did not always survive in captivity. On June 4 Edwin's horned toad became one of the casualties. "Some of the boys made a cross for it and buried it behind the barracks," the diary reports. Yoshiko Uchida also tells of the loss of Percy, a fish the class "loved . . . dearly." She found poor Percy floating lifelessly in its mayonnaise jar one morning. The class buried it in the sand outside the classroom door.

Grown-ups ignored the rule about animals, too. As revealed in *Our Daily Diary*, Makoto Oda's father bought a hen so the family could have fresh eggs in the morning. The oddest pet may have been "a big, fat badger." As Edwin and Bobby report in the diary, "a man was walking [the badger] with a rope tied around its stomach."

Pet dogs and cats became common in Topaz. Most of them were strays that wandered into camp. But one does wonder about the origin of the bloodhound that parked itself in Frankie's room and "would not move," as the third graders put it. The diary also reports that Edwin was

Despite the rule against farm animals in camp, many detainees kept hens so they could have fresh eggs. Here hens and eggs are on display at the Topaz harvest festival.

This diary illustration combines David's and Bobby's accounts of their separate hikes by showing a snake, a deer, and arrowheads (with a stone ax thrown in for good measure). Class members had plenty of encounters with desert animals, including poisonous rattlesnakes and scorpions.

gifted "a little dog named 'Tippy.'" Cats and dogs lead to kittens and puppies. Miss Yamauchi's class reports six kittens being born to a block cat on June 16. And when Ronnie Muramatsu lost his black kitten, his neighbors offered at least seven look-alikes as replacements. Eventually there were so many dogs and cats in camp that the administration demanded they be licensed.

The children also encountered animals when they visited Topaz's farms. Edwin Narahara was lucky enough to feed the pigs every day for a whole week. He remembers that it took him about two hours to walk home afterward. (Of course, the farm was only about three miles from camp, so Edwin may have taken a few detours along the way!) Shizuko Nishitani visited the pig farm, too, but was sorry she had. On May 31 she sadly reported witnessing "a big mother pig squash her two baby pigs to death."

A group of boys and their dog—most likely a stray that wandered into camp.

Taking care of a sow and her piglet at the Topaz pig farm.

Wild critters also invaded camp regularly. Besides the insects and lizards, the kids mention bats hanging from their windows and coyotes tangling with camp dogs. Perhaps the most dramatic battle came when a dog fought with a porcupine and lost. It had "quills all over its body," the diary reports.

March 24, 1943.

Makoto and Frankie are going to receive new tops. Richard's mother bought him a top in Delta.

This Sunday will be Don's birthday.

Bobby, Kiku and Frankie went on a truck ride yesterday.

Today we shall all go hunting for ants.

Yesterday Edwin caught two big fish.

The nurse fooled Lynn when she told him he had a new baby brother or sister. It was a false alarm.

Several boys of our class went swimming in the bathtub. It is so hot nowadays they just couldn't help it.

When Edwin went swimming at the pig farm he saw a baby shark. It probably swam from Sevier Lake.

For many of the imprisoned Nikkei, pets provided companionship and solace in a difficult time. But forming an attachment with a pet meant risking the possibility of having to leave an animal behind once again. When detainees were transferred to different camps and when Topaz Camp closed, people sometimes did take their pets with them. But for some, like Mae Yanagi, it was easier and safer to restrict pets to lizards and other such creatures—animals one could leave behind without heartbreak.

(Top) On March 24 Edwin Narahara reported that he caught a couple of big fish. The illustrator of the diary page chose to glorify the fishing expedition, showing a deep-sea fishing scene. Of course, Edwin was likely fishing in the irrigation ditches.

(Bottom) Edwin's fish stories continued on July 30, when he told his classmates that he went swimming at the pig farm and saw a baby shark. It's a wonder Miss Yamauchi took him at his word and put it in writing!

Nikkei in Topaz celebrated the new year with both American (above) and Japanese (below) customs. In the bottom photo, men pound steamed rice to make traditional New Year mochi (moh-chee) cakes.

Chapter 8

Holidays, Festivals, and Worship

MOST FIRST-GENERATION Japanese immigrants (Issei) were Buddhist, which was the predominant religion in Japan. But by the 1930s, the Nikkei in the Seattle and San Francisco areas were predominately Christian. In Topaz about 60 percent of the detainees were Christians and about 40 percent were Buddhist, with a small number practicing other religions. Virtually all the religious holidays and celebrations in camp centered on those two faiths, and Buddhists (like Mae Yanagi and her family) and Christians (like Yoshiko Uchida and her family) often enjoyed one another's celebrations.

The first Christmas in Topaz was a sad one for detainees, but it was brightened a little by an all-camp Christmas program. Miné Okubo recalled the mess halls being decorated with trees, but noted that "there was a lack of holiday spirit." Yoshiko Uchida's family received a gift in the mail that provided a bit of Christmas cheer: a big box of evergreen boughs from a friend. "I hadn't seen [my mother] so happy in a long time," Yoshiko later remembered. At school Yoshiko and her second-grade students decorated a little greasewood bush as a Christmas tree, held an open house for parents, and threw a party with apples and milk from the mess hall. On Christmas Eve carolers wended their way through the blocks. Christmas Day was bitterly cold and windy. The Uchidas braved the weather to call on friends, just as they'd done in Berkeley. Yoshiko's mother came bearing evergreen branches as gifts. After attending church and eating "a pleasant [Christmas] dinner at the mess hall,"

Detainees perform a Christmas Nativity pageant on a stage in a recreation hall.

Yoshiko's family settled down beside their glowing stove for a quiet evening together.

When Easter rolled around, both Christian and Buddhist children in Miss Yamauchi's classroom dyed eggs as a class activity. Then on Easter morning, the interfaith Christian churches held a large outdoor ceremony. Churchgoers arrived in their best Sunday finery, but as the last notes of "Hosanna" faded, a fierce wind shrieked through the camp. Worshippers scattered to find shelter from stinging clouds of dust!

Protestants, Catholics, Seventh-Day Adventists, and Buddhists shared a church building in Topaz. Services were typically held in both Japanese and English.

Our Daily Diary notes Buddhist holidays, too. On May 3 the children report a Buddhist parade celebrating Hanamatsuri (*hah-nah-mah-tsoo-ree*), an important flower festival honoring the birth of Buddha. The young diary artist for that day depicted a flower-bedecked shrine. Real flowers were difficult to grow in Topaz, but the detainees were masterful at creating beautiful copies out of paper.

In the summer Mae's family and other Buddhists observed Obon (*oh-bohn*), honoring the spirits of their ancestors. They began the festival by lighting lanterns or fires to welcome and guide the spirits to their homes. Then, at the family altar, they offered food, drink, and sweets to the spirits. Cleaning the graves of one's ancestors is a vital part of Obon, so it was painful for Mae's family to be so far away from their loved ones' gravesites. The festival also included Bon dances. In ancient times the dances were performed as prayers for the souls of fallen warriors, but they had become a joyful celebration by the 1940s. Mae remembers dressing in colorful kimonos and learning the moves for the festive dances.

"The only festival I remember is the Obon celebration because we learned the dances. . . . The music . . . was distinctive and played loudly so everyone could hear and join in the festivities."

—Mae Yanagi Ferral, February 14, 2017

Canada also incarcerated people of Japanese descent. Here a group of Japanese Canadian girls participates in an Obon festival at Greenwood Camp, in British Columbia.

The families of Topaz celebrated their children on Girls' Day and Boys' Day. Girls' Day, or Hinamatsuri (*hee-nah-mah-tsoo-ree*) (Doll Festival), was celebrated on March 3. In their homes, girls and their mothers traditionally displayed dolls of the Japanese emperor and empress and their court, but with the advent of the war, honoring the imperial court appeared treasonous. To avoid seeming loyal to the "enemy" emperor, families hid or even destroyed their dolls. In 1943 the festival was a

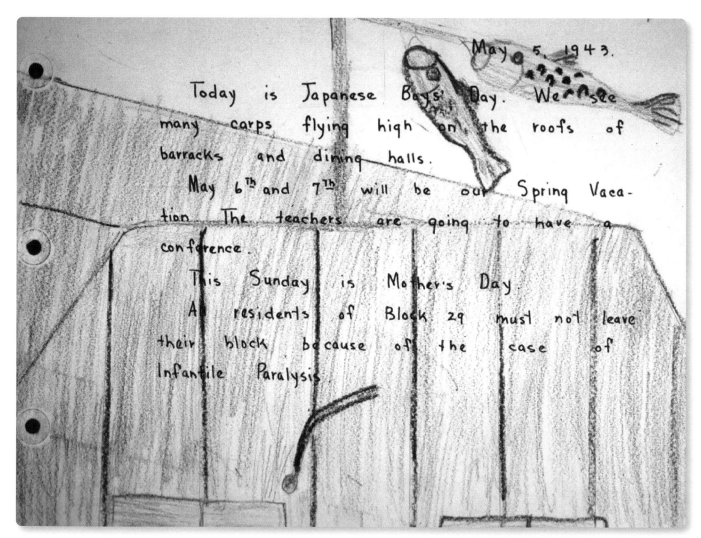

May 5, 1943.

Today is Japanese Boys' Day. We see many carps flying high on the roofs of barracks and dining halls.

May 6th and 7th will be our Spring Vacation. The teachers are going to have a conference.

This Sunday is Mother's Day.

All residents of Block 29 must not leave their block because of the case of Infantile Paralysis.

The artist for the May 5 diary page drew Boys' Day carp streamers, representing two sons, flying above a family's barrack apartment.

April 23, 1943.

Sunday, April 25ᵗʰ is Easter. We hope it will be a sunny Sunday.

Today is Good Friday.

Today we will color our Easter eggs. Last night Miss Yamauchi boiled our eggs and she cracked some of them.

David and Don high-jumped so much that their legs are very stiff this morning.

Last night another little boy was hit by a baseball.

Although this diary page focuses on Easter, both Christian and Buddhist holy days got equal billing in Miss Yamauchi's classroom. In 1944 Easter and Buddha's birthday fell on the same day, so worshippers held Easter services in the morning and Buddhist services in the afternoon.

campwide celebration that instead highlighted a doll-making competition for girls. Boys' Day, or Tango no Sekku (*tan-goh noh sek-koo*), a festival honoring the sons in each family, was held on May 5. Following tradition, Topaz households flew cloth or paper streamers shaped like carp from their barrack roofs. Swimming against the wind, the fish symbolized strength, courage, and determination.

Detainees also celebrated American holidays, such as Thanksgiving. For the first Thanksgiving in camp, Yoshiko Uchida and her second

Detainees at Tule Lake Relocation Center, in California, dressed up in Halloween costumes for the harvest festival parade.

graders made a little Pilgrim village out of old milk cartons. Workers from Yoshiko's mess hall hung a big sign that read "Thanksgiving Greetings from Your Mess 7 Crew." For Thanksgiving dinner, people wore their best clothes—high heels and dresses, suits and bow ties. The mess crew served the turkey dinner at the tables rather than having detainees pass through a cafeteria line.

Even Halloween found its way into camp, often coupled with a harvest festival. Although there doesn't seem to have been any trick-or-treating, kids dressed up in homemade Halloween costumes for the harvest festival parade. Adults and children also attended parties on All Hallows' Eve.

And what about American patriotic holidays? Few would have blamed the prisoners of Topaz if they had decided to ignore the Fourth of July in protest. Instead the captive population enthusiastically celebrated it. Sachi Kajiwara recalled the joy of making yards and yards of paper chains fashioned from strips of newspaper colored red, white, and blue. These were draped festively about her block's recreation hall. *Our Daily Diary* happily reports that "there was a camp-wide 4th of July carnival on the weekend of July 3rd and 4th." The children passed verdict on the event: "It was lots of fun." Ironically the Fourth of July was one of the most anticipated holidays in Topaz.

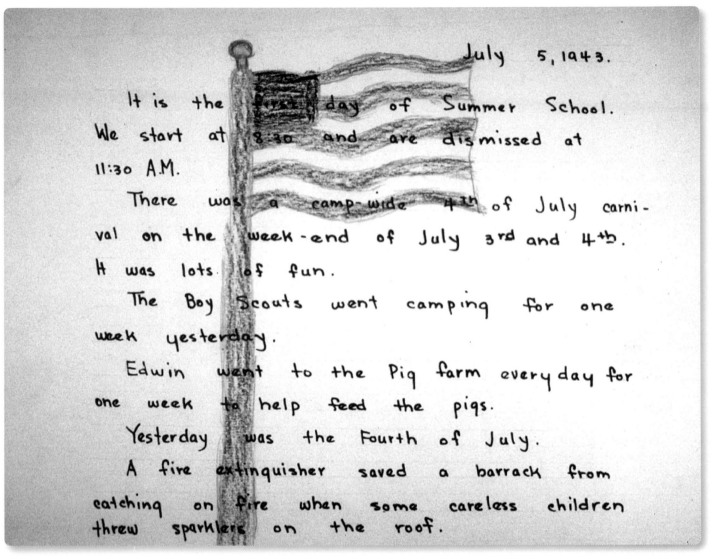

July 5, 1943.

It is the first day of Summer School. We start at 8:30 and are dismissed at 11:30 A.M.

There was a camp-wide 4th of July carnival on the week-end of July 3rd and 4th. It was lots of fun.

The Boy Scouts went camping for one week yesterday.

Edwin went to the Pig farm everyday for one week to help feed the pigs.

Yesterday was the Fourth of July.

A fire extinguisher saved a barrack from catching on fire when some careless children threw sparklers on the roof.

The imprisoned population of Topaz celebrated Independence Day with zeal.

Like children across the country, Miss Yamauchi's third graders celebrated Mother's Day and Father's Day—and even April Fools' Day. Their words and illustrations clearly show that holidays were as important in Topaz Camp as they had been before exile—perhaps more important because they helped create a sense of normality. Holidays also added a little spice to the children's lives.

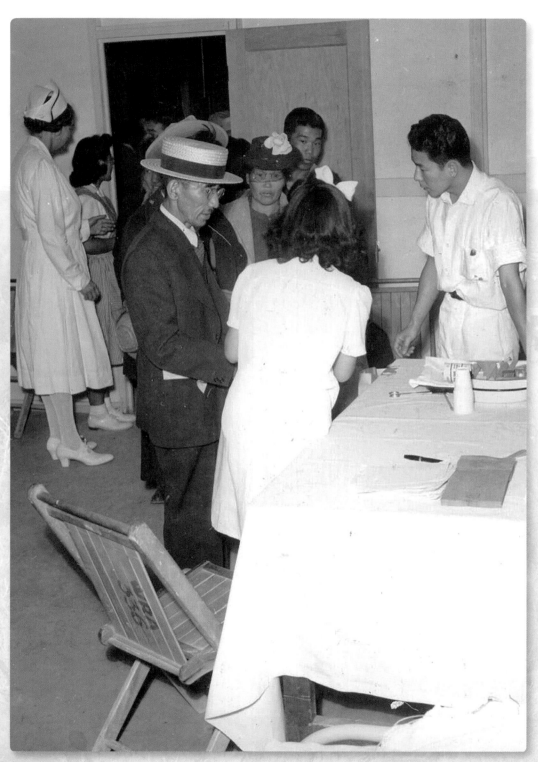

Doctors and nurses in the induction center at Topaz examine new arrivals from Tule Lake.

Chapter 9

Is There a Doctor in the House?

"JOHNNY AND JACKIE HAVE THE MUMPS."

"Last night a little boy was hit on the head by a baseball bat . . . and had to have six stitches."

"Kimiko's mother was burned very badly by hot water."

"Yesterday evening, Raymond's brother was hit by a truck." (He survived, luckily.)

Reports of illness and injury appear in more than a third of the entries in *Our Daily Diary*. Staying healthy was a challenge in Topaz Camp. With so many people crowded into so little space, diseases spread easily from person to person, especially when they were eating together in mess halls and using common latrines. Accidents were common in a place carved out of such a harsh environment. Poisonous insects and reptiles were a threat. And of course people also suffered from maladies they brought into camp—heart disease, cancer, diabetes, and the like. Eight-year-old Betty Sugiyama came to Topaz having had a severe concussion.

The white buildings in this photo are the Topaz Hospital complex.

When she was nine, she began suffering seizures. "Due to my condition, I was not physically able to participate in many activities," Betty remembers.

Topaz Camp did have what Miné Okubo called an "army-type hospital" with 175 beds. But supply shortages plagued the hospital, and it lacked important services such as a dietary kitchen and a care facility for the elderly. The hospital required sixty-six nurse's aides to function properly, but by 1944 only thirty-six were willing or able to come to work. Teenager Sachi Kajiwara was a nurse's aide trainee who tried to help relieve the shortage. "In Topaz, I took three weeks of instructions from one of the five Registered Nurses," she later recalled. "I didn't even know the names of the instruments—I felt terribly inadequate to take care of some very sick people." At one point there was such a shortage of doctors that Topaz had only three physicians on staff.

Halfway through 1944, the administration announced that the dental staff was to be reduced from seven to three, and the pharmacy staff from four to one. With dental work already six months behind, four of the camp dentists had to stop treating new patients. This led to undue suffering from common ailments like toothaches. When teenager Maya Nagata needed a tooth filled, she stood in line starting at 4:00 a.m. A dental assistant did the job, leaving decay under the filling; that tooth had to be removed later. Other sorts of dental care, like orthodontics, were also not well supported. Maya had braces—but no one in Topaz could adjust them.

Many detainees were reluctant to bother the "busy doctors," as was the case with Yoshiko Uchida's mother. She would not go in to have a troublesome wart removed. Another time she waited for hours to be examined for a persistent cough but finally left untreated.

As medical care became harder to access, detainees often turned to folk medicine to treat maladies. When Mae Yanagi lost some hair, her

The nursing staff of Topaz Hospital was mostly made up of detainees.

April 7, 1943.

On Saturday evening about 8:00 o'clock P.M. there was a dangerous accident in the high school grounds. Three boys were digging a cave and the dirt caved in. One boy was buried in the dirt. After many people saved him, he was rushed to the hospital.

Yesterday Don's dog had a fight with a cayote.

Kiku, Bobby, Frankie and Makoto had another truck ride.

Children met with all sorts of injuries living in the rough environment of Topaz Camp, but this diary entry reports one of the more unusual calamities: the collapse of a homemade cave. Fortunately the young excavator was rushed to the hospital and lived to dig another day.

mother treated the bald spot with vinegar. And when Yoshiko's older sister, Keiko, suffered from a prolonged illness, a neighbor brought over "a broth that she claimed could cure any ailment." As it happened, Keiko did feel better in a week's time, and the neighbor proudly announced that her earthworm broth had done the trick!

Sickness was a constant worry for Miss Yamauchi's students. "There are many people ill in Topaz with mumps, pneumonia, appendicitis and colds, so we must take very good care of ourselves," they declare in the diary in March. A week later Don's little brother came down with pneumonia. Margaret Himachi recalls being quarantined after contracting chicken pox. She also spent two days in the hospital while having her tonsils removed. She best remembers getting to eat ice cream to soothe her throat. Johnny Moritomo remembers a self-induced illness. He and his friends made a hideaway hole under his barrack so they "could get away." That's where he tried his first cigarette. "And did I ever get sick!"

Serious conditions, such as tuberculosis, also surfaced in Topaz. When Frankie Kawasaki's father sickened with meningitis, Frankie and his mother feared that he might never return from the hospital. Fortunately he recovered. Influenza outbreaks were common, too, as recorded in the diary: "There are many pupils absent lately due to an epidemic of the flu in Topaz." But for children one of the most feared contagious diseases was infantile paralysis, or poliomyelitis. Polio can cripple and kill, and it mostly affects the young. In the 1940s, unlike today, there was no vaccine or reliable cure. On May 4 the children reported "very sad and serious news. A little boy, James Yamasaki, aged eight years, has Infantile Paralysis." Such news must have been terrifying for Miss Yamauchi's third graders. The only way to avoid contracting the disease was to stay away from contact with the polio virus—hard to do in a place with eight thousand people crammed into one square mile. So it is understandable that James Yamasaki's block was put under quarantine; the next day, the children noted that "all residents of Block 29 must not leave their block because of the case of Infantile Paralysis." Fortunately for James, he was transported to Salt Lake City for treatment. Five days after the quarantine, the class reported with relief that James could "now move his hands to the back of his neck." Two months later James came home from Salt Lake Hospital, presumably doing much better.

Of course kids are also prone to injuries. Plenty of blood was spilled during sports and other recreational activities. *Our Daily Diary* mentions blackened eyes, broken bones, cut fingers, bruised knees, battered heads, and impaled feet—all from rough play. Richard Kaneko broke his little finger playing baseball, and Ben Morita missed a ball and ended up with a black eye. When Bobby Hirano and his friends played slingshot war, "one boy was hit in the eye so badly that it began to bleed." As the diary matter-of-factly reports, "It is a dangerous game."

May 25, 1943.

Many pupils in our class were flat on their stomachs working very hard on our frieze.

The Administration team will play against the Military Police in baseball tonight.

Bobby's friends were playing "sling-shot" war. One boy was hit in the eye so badly that it began to bleed. It is a dangerous game.

We feel very sorry for Miss Itashiki because her mother passed away. Miss Itashiki is the Low Third Grade teacher of the Mountain View School.

Kiku brought us a horned toad. Lynn lent us one of his father's beautiful lizards. Yesterday, Mae saw a girl carrying a snake.

It seems Bobby Hirano and other children sometimes played violent games such as slingshot war.

"A boy was playing with a knife and he stuck his little friend in the toe. We are going to be careful about playing with knives."

—*Our Daily Diary*, July 12, 1943

There were also work-related injuries and random accidents. Burns occurred frequently. As the diary mentions, Kimiko Tsutsui's mother and two little boys were burned by hot water and hot-water pipes. Heating with coal and potbellied stoves invited burns as well. And the combination of the stoves and tar-papered barracks resulted in fires and more burn victims.

Not all medical conditions in the camp meant illness and injury, though. Births outnumbered deaths almost three to one.

Mae's teacher, Lillian ("Anne") Yamauchi, and Saburo ("Sab") Hori on March 20, 1943, close to their wedding day.

Chapter 10

Congratulations and Condolences, Hellos and Goodbyes

"MISS YAMAUCHI WAS MARRIED on Saturday."

"A lady passed away in Mae's block. She had been ill for a long time."

"Today Johnny's sister left for Idaho to be with her fiancé."

"It is June's birthday today. She is nine years old. We sang to her."

Just as in life in the world outside Topaz Camp, the children and their families experienced happy times and sad times. People died, and children were born. Babies took their first steps, and people moved away.

Weddings are always cause for celebration, even though married life for detainees would begin inside a prison camp. Anne Yamauchi and her fiancé, Saburo ("Sab") Hori, were married in camp by a Buddhist reverend. Their honeymoon had to wait until years later. But Miss Yamauchi's class saw only the excitement when it came to the marriage of their teacher. *Our Daily Diary* notes the return of the new Mrs. Hori on March 29. Excited as they were, the children couldn't quite let go of the young unmarried teacher they loved. They voted for the name they liked best: "Miss Yamauchi" or "Mrs. Hori." "Miss Yamauchi" won twelve to ten, so the children declared, "We shall call her Miss Yamauchi just like before."

Welcoming a new baby, even into a world of captivity, was also a joyous occasion. On May 24 *Our Daily Diary* cheerfully reveals that Edwin acquired a new cousin when his auntie gave birth to one of those babies. In all, 384 babies were born in Topaz. Mae's little brother, Kenny, was also born in detention, while his family lived in a converted horse stall at Tanforan.

April 2, 1943.

Today is Lynn's birthday. We all sang "Happy Birthday" to him.

We were invited to a movie at Recreation Hall 8. The first film showed us that about ¾ of the earth is water.

The second showed us how nature protects her animals. The most interesting part of their protection was the camouflage of their skins and furs.

There was a fire at Block 38 about 10:30 o'clock P.M. yesterday.

Miss Yamauchi and her students always acknowledged one another's birthdays in their diary. Friends from back home also remembered birthdays. Yoshiko Uchida received a package with cupcakes, candles, chocolate frosting, an heirloom silver teaspoon, and a bouquet of flowers ("each stem wrapped carefully in wet cotton").

Memorial services for soldiers who died in the war were a way to honor them and their parents, even though the young men's bodies were most often buried in Europe or the Pacific islands.

One hundred forty-four people died in Topaz Camp. For some Issei, the prospect of dying in Topaz was unbearable. An elderly friend of the Uchidas wept as he told Yoshiko's father, "Uchida San, . . . I don't want to die and be buried in a place like this." Sometimes Topaz detainees lost loved ones living in other camps. Mae's grandfather died at Poston Camp, in Arizona. Her mother was given permission to travel by bus to attend the funeral, but Mae and the rest of the family were not allowed to go.

In their classroom diary, the third graders mention several deaths, mostly of older folks from their blocks. The diary also reports a dramatic death that unsettled the entire camp. On April 11, sixty-three-year-old James Wakasa was walking near the western stretch of the barbed-wire fence. A shot rang out from Watch Tower Number 8, striking his chest and killing him instantly. The army sentry in the tower claimed that he had called out several times to warn Mr. Wakasa away from the fence and then fired when he tried to climb under the wire. But Mr. Wakasa's body was found five feet inside the fence. The shooting caused an uproar among the detainees.

The army maintained a presence at Topaz, some eighty to ninety men who lived in a separate compound. Personnel were put on alert and armed with machine guns and gas masks. Because this was early in the history of Topaz, the detainees' mistrust and fear of the military guards was close to the surface. Tensions were high, which may explain why the diary page for April 14 simply states that "Mr. James H. Wakasa passed away," without saying he'd been shot from one of the guard towers. Miss Yamauchi may have been trying to protect her students and herself by not writing anything that might put them on the wrong side of camp officials.

Tensions rose when James Wakasa was killed by an army sentry on April 11, 1943. His funeral was attended by 1,500 to 2,000 detainees.

"Many people left Topaz this afternoon for the 'Tent City' in Provo, Utah. They will pick strawberries, cherries, apples and peaches. Grace's big brother was one of the workers."

—*Our Daily Diary*, May 24, 1943

Mae and her classmates witnessed plenty of hellos and goodbyes in Topaz. The imprisoned Nikkei were allowed to leave camp for a variety of reasons. Some were granted temporary leave to work at farms or canneries where they could earn more money. The classroom diary mentions that both Kiku's parents left camp to work—his father going to Idaho and his mother to Salt Lake City. (Kiku eventually left Topaz to join his

A "tent city" near Provo, Utah, housed seasonal field and orchard workers from Topaz. At first many stores and restaurants in Provo refused to serve the Nikkei, but when rifle shots were fired into the tents, local residents put a stop to the violence.

father.) People also could sometimes visit other camps. Yoshiko Uchida's mother and father were permitted to visit her ailing grandmother at Heart Mountain Relocation Center, in Wyoming. Yoshiko recalled that "it required weeks of paperwork and many teletypes to Washington" to gain permission. Occasionally detainees were allowed to relocate on a permanent basis to be with loved ones in other camps. In May, Kiku's auntie moved from a camp in Arkansas to join the family in Topaz.

The summer of 1943 saw a mass relocation that tore families apart. Everyone seventeen or older was required to take the same loyalty "test" as the Nisei who volunteered to be soldiers. Question 28 required swearing allegiance to the United States while disavowing allegiance to the Japanese emperor. Anyone answering no got a one-way ticket to Tule Lake Relocation Center, in Northern California. Tule Lake was a prison

A soldier (left) administers a loyalty "test" to a potential army recruit (right). Later the government required all Nikkei adults to take a similar "test" and profess loyalty to the United States. Those who refused were deemed a threat and shipped off to Tule Lake Center.

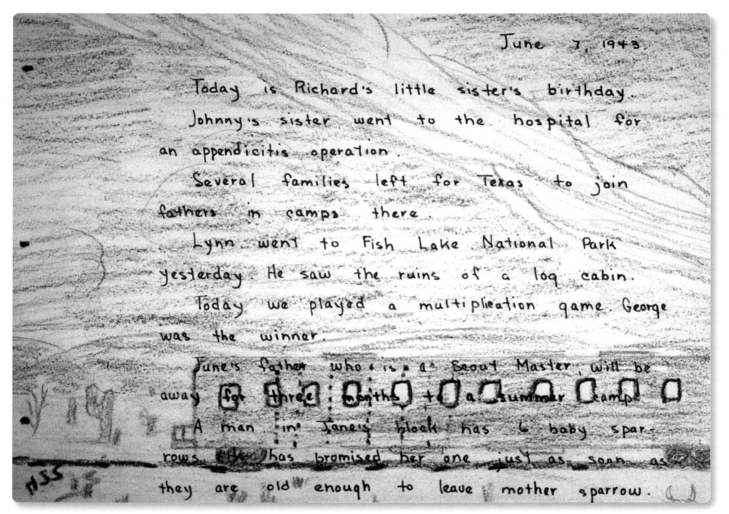

June 7, 1943.

Today is Richard's little sister's birthday.

Johnny's sister went to the hospital for an appendicitis operation.

Several families left for Texas to join fathers in camps there.

Lynn went to Fish Lake National Park yesterday. He saw the ruins of a log cabin.

Today we played a multiplication game. George was the winner.

June's father who is a Scout Master, will be away for three months to a summer camp. A man in Jane's block has 6 baby sparrows. He has promised her one just as soon as they are old enough to leave mother sparrow.

The art for this diary page is a reminder of the relocation of Topaz detainees, either willing or unwilling. Trains took Yoshiko Uchida to Massachusetts for graduate school, as well as Miss Yamauchi and six of Mae's classmates to Tule Lake Center.

camp guarded by a thousand soldiers, surrounded by an eight-foot fence, and ringed by six tanks. But if Issei answered yes, they'd be giving up Japanese citizenship without having US citizenship—they'd be people without a country.

In the end nearly 1,500 detainees from Topaz were sent to Tule Lake, switching places with people from that camp. On August 12 the third graders sadly reported in their last diary entry that Miss Yamauchi—

August 12, 1943.

Last night there was heavy rain, thunder and lightning.

All the Brownies had lots ~~and~~ lots of fun yesterday at Antelope Springs.

Johnny had a happy surprise yesterday. His mother came home from Provo where she was picking beans. She had been away for almost one month and a half.

Tomorrow, August 13th is the last day of school. We shall have a "last day of school" party.

This is the last page of our daily diary. We hope everyone has enjoyed it. It has been lots of fun for us.

Good-bye and good luck.

On the last page of the diary, the children wish their readers "good-bye and good luck."
The next day their first school year in Topaz ended.

along with class members Richard, Makoto, Raymond, Kaoru, George, and Shizuko—were leaving for Tule Lake. None of them had to leave; the children were too young to take the "test" and Miss Yamauchi answered yes to question 28. But naturally they wanted to be with their mothers and fathers and grandparents who were forced to go.

Once the detainees had passed the loyalty exam, they could leave camp for work or school in places other than the West Coast. Yoshiko

*In 1943 these college students left Topaz for schools
in the Midwest and on the East Coast.*

Uchida was granted leave to attend Smith College, in Massachusetts. Her sister Keiko landed a job in the Department of Education's nursery school at Mount Holyoke College, also in Massachusetts. Miné Okubo took a job in New York City at *Fortune* magazine, putting her artistic talents to use. Others took jobs wherever they could find them. This migration of the captive population—mostly Nisei young adults—to new lives outside the camp signaled the welcome beginning of the end. Topaz began to steadily decline in population.

A group, mostly of camp administrators and employees, gathers to say goodbye to former detainees leaving Delta on one of the last trains to depart for California.

Chapter 11

Going Home

THE WAR IN EUROPE ENDED on May 7, 1945, when Nazi Germany surrendered unconditionally to the Allied Forces. After the Americans dropped atomic bombs on the Japanese cities of Hiroshima and Nagasaki, causing horrendous devastation, Japan surrendered on August 14, 1945. World War II was over.

Months before, in December 1944, the US Supreme Court ruled that the War Relocation Authority could not detain loyal American citizens. President Roosevelt announced that Japanese American "relocation" would end on January 2, 1945. But by the end of January, there were still six thousand detainees in Topaz Camp. For many Issei, the thought of going home was frightening. How would they be treated by white Americans? "Here, there is little freedom; but we are not stared at," said one older man. "We don't get what we want here, but we live anyway and do not feel lonely."

The government worked furiously to push detainees out of the camp before October 31, 1945, the official closing date for Topaz. By the end of

Many Nikkei returned to the West Coast to discover their possessions ransacked, stolen, or damaged.

September, fewer than two thousand people remained. Block managers departed on October 18. By early November the camp was empty.

Going home was painful for many Nikkei. They faced housing and job shortages. Their stored belongings had often been stolen or vandalized. Some families were barely able to survive. Edwin Narahara, the boy who remembers Topaz as an extended campout, also remembers being truly hungry for the first time in his life when his family returned to California. Ted Nagata's family stayed in Utah after the camp closed, settling in Salt Lake City. But they were so poverty-stricken that Ted's father was forced to leave his children in an orphanage until he could get on his feet—it took a year. Others beside the Nagatas decided the

West Coast held little for them and opted to settle elsewhere in the United States.

Returning Nikkei feared that prejudice and bigotry would be waiting for them back home or wherever they decided to live—and in many cases, they were right. Mae remembers a sixth-grade classmate in Berkeley calling her a "Jap" and telling her "to go back to Japan." Even returning Nisei servicemen often faced a hostile reception from some white Americans, especially on the West Coast. Daniel Inouye, a captain in the

Daniel Inouye, a highly decorated officer with the 442nd Regimental Combat Team, later represented Hawaii in the US Congress for more than fifty years.

442nd Regimental Combat Team, lost his arm in battle and spent two years in a hospital. In 1947, while waiting for the troopship that would finally take him home to Hawaii, Captain Inouye entered a California barbershop for a haircut. He was in uniform, heavy with decorations for bravery, and wearing his newly fitted artificial arm. The barber stopped him with the words "We don't cut Jap hair."

Mae Yanagi's father and oldest brother left Topaz in August, before the rest of the family, to find housing in Berkeley. The Yanagi land and business in Hayward, California, were lost. "My father told us about losing the property," recalls Mae. "He had left [it] in the care of a Mr. King, [but] Mr. King was unable to maintain the property or pay the taxes. . . . When we returned to California, the house and property were occupied by strangers." Mae and her family had to find another place to live. Understandably Mae's father "had bitter feelings toward the government. He had lost his property, his pride and dignity, and witnessed the unfair treatment of his family."

Mae and the rest of her family left Topaz to join her father and brother on September 6. Mae was almost eleven years old. Upon arriving in Berkeley, the Yanagis stayed briefly in a place on University Avenue, then moved to a public housing complex, where they lived for several years. Mr. Yanagi found work as a gardener, and his wife cleaned houses. Finally the Yanagis bought a home on Sacramento Street. They were able to

Mrs. Sugimoto labels a crate of household goods for shipment to Redwood City, California. Both her husband and brother were away, serving in the US Army.

Not long after leaving Topaz, the Yanagi family sits
for a family photograph. Mae is on the far right, in the back row.

afford it only because Mae's oldest brother was drafted into the postwar army, which qualified him for a GI Bill loan.

The effects of captivity left lasting scars. "My parents and older siblings were under stress and faced an uncertain future," says Mae. "I was too young to comprehend what was happening." But as she grew older, she began to understand that the war years and its aftermath had taken more than a financial toll on her family. Mae's parents "seldom spoke of the camp or of the experience." Looking back, Mae says, "I have come to believe that was a way to shield us from the events."

Not all returning Nikkei faced hostility. When Torao Mori and his wife returned to their chrysanthemum farm in Redwood, California, local white, Filipino, and Chinese growers gave them chrysanthemum cuttings for reestablishing their gardens.

Most surprising to Mae was discovering the repressed memories and feelings she harbored about Topaz. "My sister Jane and I are unable to talk about 'Camp' without welling up in tears," she says. "It is disconcerting. I must have long held feelings regarding internment." Sadness. Bitterness. Anger. Shame. The effects of incarceration are difficult for her to express, but she does know that the experience caused her to go "through a period of rejecting my Japanese ancestry." It was only many years later that she was able to reconcile those confused feelings and embrace her heritage, which she credits in part to "the interest in the internment experience in books, TV, and films."

"Although some Issei were shattered and broken by the experience, those I knew and observed personally, endured the hardship of the evacuation with dignity, stoic composure, disciplined patience, and an amazing resiliency of spirit. I think they displayed a level of strength, grace, and courage that is truly remarkable."

—Yoshiko Uchida

With Pearl Harbor and the camps decades behind us, there are those who may wonder about the lasting personal effects of "internment" on the people incarcerated. The devastation of personal property, wealth, and dignity was more than some Nikkei, especially the elderly, could overcome. Many survivors still struggle with the terrible consequences of their captivity. But many of them also proved what they always had known about themselves: they are productive, creative, and responsible citizens. And they are resilient.

Issei taking the citizenship oath after finally becoming eligible for US citizenship in 1952.

Epilogue

Moving Forward

THE CLASSROOM DIARY kept by Miss Yamauchi and her third-grade students is housed in the Utah State Historical Society, in Salt Lake City. The pages are somewhat yellowed with age but still retain the bright colors of the children's drawings. Today *Our Daily Diary* stands as a poignant reminder of the price bigotry and fear exacted from everyday American families. The injustices of what was misleadingly called Japanese American relocation were not fully acknowledged by the US government until forty-five years after Topaz and the other camps closed their doors.

In the wake of World War II, President Harry Truman began the long road to a full acknowledgment by granting Nisei draft resisters full pardons in 1947. A year later he issued Executive Order 9981, which desegregated the US military—there would be no more single-race combat teams like the 442nd. The president also approved the Japanese American Evacuation Claims Act, which was meant to compensate

Japanese Americans for financial losses due to resettlement. However, the law was flawed and didn't provide nearly enough funds to compensate for individual losses. Unless one chose to sue the government for more money, each claimant was allowed a maximum of only $2,500. Still, it was a step in the right direction. Then, in an effort to prevent similar sorts of discrimination, the US Congress passed the Immigration and Nationality Act of 1952. Against President Truman's wishes, the bill retained discriminatory quotas limiting immigrants of Asian descent. (These quotas were not removed until 1965.) But the law at least protected people from ever again being denied US citizenship based on race. The Issei took full advantage of the new law; forty thousand of them became citizens between 1952 and 1965.

Those who had suffered the indignation of forced removal mostly remained silent about their mistreatment. Then the third-generation Sansei (*sahn-say*), the children of the imprisoned Nisei, pushed their parents to open up about what had happened. This "opening up" resulted in the redress movement—a concerted effort, mostly by the Sansei and former Issei and Nisei detainees, to get the US government to formally admit wrongdoing. Though these activists called for more adequate compensation for financial losses, their primary goal was an official acknowledgment of wrongdoing—and an apology.

Due in part to the redress movement, Congress finally created, in 1980, the Commission on Wartime Relocation and Internment of Civilians to examine the injustices. In 1983 the commission announced its findings: it concluded that the decision to imprison Japanese Americans was not based on military necessity but rather on "race prejudice, war hysteria and a failure of political leadership." The commission estimated the forced Japanese American loss of income and property at about $370 million—or, adjusting for 1983 values, about $2 billion! It also recommended a

President Ronald Reagan signs the Civil Liberties Act of 1988. At last Japanese Americans incarcerated during the war would receive an official apology from the US government.

one-time compensation of $20,000 per survivor (still a relatively paltry amount considering all the Nikkei had lost). It wasn't until five years later that Congress passed the Civil Liberties Act of 1988, turning the commission's recommendations into law. At last, in October 1990, President George H. W. Bush signed and sent the first letters of apology, along with redress payments. Unfortunately most Issei and some Nisei were no longer alive to receive the long-awaited expression of regret from their country.

"We can never fully right the wrongs of the past. But we can take a clear stand for justice and recognize that serious injustices were done to Japanese Americans during World War II."

—George H. W. Bush, 1990

Miss Yamauchi's husband, Saburo Hori, examines Our Daily Diary *for the first time. My colleague George Chilcoat located Saburo and helped with research for our earlier book,* The Children of Topaz.

Author's Note

MISS YAMAUCHI'S third grade class of 1942–1943 features prominently in this recounting of Topaz Camp's story through the eyes of its children. In the process of writing this book (and its predecessor, *The Children of Topaz*), I had the pleasure of meeting and interviewing several of those children—now grown up—and making numerous visits to the former site of the desert camp. I also met, interviewed, and befriended Saburo Hori, Miss Yamauchi's husband. Sadly I missed meeting Lillian Yamauchi Hori herself, as she died a year before I began to research Topaz.

I first encountered *Our Daily Diary* when I walked into a colleague's office at the university where I taught. There was an old, worn brick on his bookshelf, and when I inquired about its significance, he told me it came from the sewer system at Topaz Camp. Then he showed me something else: a photocopy of the diary. A sense of awe overwhelmed me as I combed through the pages, and I knew I wanted to help share these children's story. It could not be forgotten. The original diary, I learned, was in the archives of the Utah State Historical Society. When I finally

Class clown Edwin Narahara holds a reproduction of a page from Our Daily Diary.

held it in my hands for the first time, I felt as if I had stepped back in time.

That was in 1994. In those days, the internet was relatively new. Tracking down the students, then in their early sixties, was difficult. At first only boys surfaced. One of those boys was Edwin Narahara, the student whose name seems to appear in the diary more often than any other. He lived in the Los Angeles area, and I was fortunate that he was excited to talk about Topaz. The girls were harder to find because many had married and changed their last names.

Finding Miss Yamauchi was also a challenge. I knew her husband was Saburo Hori, but his Michigan phone number was no longer in service. There were 220 Horis listed in Michigan, and the only recourse was to call them all. The thirty-third call hit pay dirt. Saburo wasn't on the other end of the line, but rather his best friend, who happened to have the same last name. Takeo Hori knew where to find "Sab," who had moved to Houston, Texas, to live with his married daughter. Sadly Takeo also told me that Lillian ("Anne") wasn't with Sab. She had lost her battle with cancer.

Until I contacted Sab, I had no idea which class photograph in the Utah State Historical Society archives was Miss Yamauchi's—if it was even there at all. Sab saved the day by providing me with the correct photo, which appears in chapter 4. What a thrill it was to at last lay eyes on those kids and their teacher who had kept the classroom diary!

The Topaz site fifty years after the camp closed its doors. The rubble at the center was the backstop for a Topaz baseball field. Notice that there are still no trees.

Sab didn't know (or remember) anything about the diary. He was excited to make the drive from the Los Angeles area, where he'd moved after Anne died, to see it and to visit the Topaz site again after fifty years. It was a singular and moving experience to watch Sab touch the diary pages and leaf through his dear one's handiwork. And it was equally moving to meander down the dirt streets of the Topaz site with him— and to find the spot where Mountain View School had been. The former prison city of eight thousand was so empty and lonely. Sewer manholes and the weathered foundations of administration buildings were the only hint of its former structures, which had been moved from the site after the camp closed. We stumbled onto a baseball backstop made of boards and bedsprings, as well as the remains of a Japanese garden pool that had graced someone's barrack. A piece of electric wire, an old-fashioned shoe, a bit of broken crockery—the place still seemed strangely alive to us. Thankfully, since our visit, the site has become a National Historic Landmark, preserved for future generations.

mae Yanagi

Here is the photocopied picture I received from Mae Yanagi Ferral, along with a letter asking if my research had turned up any of her classmates. She circled herself in the picture.

Another important experience happened to me after *The Children of Topaz* was published—one that led to the writing of this book. Mae Yanagi was one of the girls that I could not find. Instead, she found me! Just before publication, I gave Sab a manuscript of *The Children of Topaz*, complete with the diary images and other photographs. He shared it with his community of friends, who in turn shared it with others. One day I received a letter with the name Mae Yanagi Ferral in the return address.

The fourteen classmates present at the Berkeley reunion tried to take the same places as in the 1943 class photo. Mae (red jacket) is second from the right in the first row. Edwin (black jacket, blue shirt) should have been at the top right, but he is second from the right instead. Sab Hori (blue sweater) is standing in for his wife.

In the envelope I found not only a letter but also a photocopy of the class picture with a circle drawn around a little girl in the bottom row. Somehow the manuscript had come across Mae's desk, and now she wanted to know which of her classmates I'd located. I happily shared the few names I had, including Sab's, along with contact information. She promptly went to work locating as many of those third graders as possible.

In October of 1996, I traveled to Berkeley, California, to attend a Children of Topaz reunion. Fifteen of the class members and their families were present, as well as Sab and his family. This event proved to be

Sixty-two years after she and her classmates completed Our Daily Diary, *Mae posed for this picture holding a facsimile of a diary page. I snapped this photo during a Topaz reunion in Delta, Utah, in 2005.*

one of the highlights of my writing career. Like Mae, many of the former "internees" had repressed memories of Topaz or simply forgotten them. When I showed slides of the entire diary, I was amazed to hear those memories resurface in their responses. "My pet lizard! Oh, I had forgotten about my pet lizard." "I hadn't remembered that Mr. Wakasa was killed." But when Edwin Narahara tried to deny what the diary repeatedly confirmed—that he was the class clown and life of the party (he claimed to have been shy)—his classmates hooted with laughter. Apparently they hadn't repressed memories of Edwin!

"Edwin played a joke on Miss Yamauchi."

—*Our Daily Diary*, August 19, 1943

I was impressed by how happy and successful these fifteen "children" were. Edwin was an architect in Los Angeles. Mae had just retired after teaching elementary school for thirty-one years.

Since that reunion, the members of Miss Yamauchi's class have moved into their eighties. Some have passed on. During the intervening time, I have crossed paths again with some of them, as well as Sab, most notably during a reunion for Topaz detainees held at the Topaz Museum in Delta and at the Topaz site. Saburo Hori died in 2015, having lived well into his nineties and remaining active until the end. Mae Yanagi Ferral lives in Sacramento, California, and was kind enough to take time from her busy life to be an ongoing resource for the writing of *Desert Diary*. Many thanks to Saburo Hori. And untold thanks to Mae, Edwin, and the whole of Miss Yamauchi's class for leaving behind that historical gem, *Our Daily Diary*.

Glossary

geta (*gay-tah*): wooden clogs worn outdoors

go (*goh*): a game of strategy played with black and white stones on a grid. Two players compete to capture as much territory as possible.

Hanamatsuri (*hah-nah-mah-tsoo-ree*): a flower festival honoring the birth of Buddha

Hinamatsuri (*hee-na-mah-tsoo-ree*): Doll Festival or Girls' Day; a celebration of girls on March 3

Issei (*ees-say*): first-generation Japanese immigrants

jintori (*jeen-toh-ree*): a game that resembles Capture the Flag. Two teams compete to capture each other's base.

mochi (*moh-chee*): cakes made from steamed sticky rice. Traditionally people pounded the rice with heavy mallets, but nowadays most use machines.

Nikkei (*neek-kay*): people of Japanese ancestry; Japanese emigrants and their descendants

Nisei (*nee-say*): second-generation Americans of Japanese descent; children of the Issei. Since Nisei were born in the United States, they are American citizens.

Obon (*oh-bohn*): a Buddhist festival honoring the spirits of one's ancestors

ohashi (*oh-hah-shee*): chopsticks

Sansei (*sahn-say*): third-generation Americans of Japanese descent; children of the Nisei

shōgi (*shoh-gee*): a chess-like game of strategy in which two players try to capture each other's king

Tango no Sekku (*tan-goh noh sek-koo*): Boys' Day; traditionally a celebration of boys on May 5. Boys' Day is now called Children's Day in Japan.

Editor's Note on Terminology

This book avoids using the terms *internment* and *internment camp*. This may come as a surprise to some readers, as people commonly refer to the "internment" of Japanese Americans during World War II. As a Yonsei, or fourth-generation Japanese American, I used this language for most of my life.

As Michael Tunnell and I worked on editing the text, though, we realized we had to make decisions about the terminology of so-called "internment." We did so with as much thought and care as we could. When Mike asked me to write this note because of my Japanese American heritage, I felt honored but a little apprehensive about clearly and fairly addressing the issue. I'll try my best to explain why we made the choices we did.

There is a long-standing controversy surrounding the language of "internment." *Internment* refers to the legal confinement of enemy aliens (citizens of an enemy nation) during wartime. It does *not* refer to the imprisonment of a nation's own citizens, which is what happened to the Japanese American population during World War II.

Due to bigotry and fear, as many as 120,000 people of Japanese descent were rounded up and forced to leave their homes. Two-thirds of them were American citizens. The government called the forced removal "relocation" or "evacuation," which made it sound less devastating than it was. "Evacuation" implies that people are being moved for their own safety, which clearly was not the case.

The expelled Nikkei were imprisoned in harsh camps, such as Topaz, fenced in by barbed wire and guarded by armed soldiers. The government called these prisons "internment camps" and the prisoners "internees," "residents," or "campers." Euphemisms like these helped make a dehumanizing, unconstitutional situation seem acceptable. As historian Roger Daniels puts it, "carefully chosen words" helped "blind Americans to the fact that their government was systematically stripping some American citizens of their most basic rights."

In this book we have tried to be as accurate as possible with terminology. Instead of saying that Japanese Americans were "relocated," we show how they were removed from their homes by force. Instead of calling them "internees," we refer to them as "prisoners" or "detainees." Finally, we call Topaz what it was: a prison, not an "internment camp." According to some historians, the most accurate term is "concentration camp" (a place where people are imprisoned without fair trial, based solely on their ethnicity or political beliefs). While this term is accurate, Mike and I chose not to use it because of its close association with the Nazi death camps of World War II.

When we talk about history, accurate language is key. We need to face the truth, no matter how ugly. Hiding behind euphemisms hinders our ability to learn from our mistakes.

As a country, we're still struggling with these issues. Mass incarceration based on racism and fear is not something confined to the past; it's happening right now. If we can learn from history and talk about it using accurate, honest language, there's hope.

Alyssa Mito Pusey
Executive Editor

Special thanks to Dr. Paul Watanabe, professor of political science and director of the Institute for Asian American Studies at the University of Massachusetts Boston, for his invaluable expertise and advice.

For more information:

Daniels, Roger. "Words Do Matter: A Note on Inappropriate Terminology and the Incarceration of the Japanese Americans." Originally published in *Nikkei in the Pacific Northwest: Japanese Americans and Japanese Canadians in the Twentieth Century*, Louis Fiset and Gail Nomura, eds., Seattle: University of Washington Press, 2005, pp. 183–207. Online at https://www.nps.gov/tule/learn/education/upload/RDaniels_euphemisms.pdf.

Denshō. "Terminology." https://densho.org/terminology/.

National JACL Power of Words II Committee. "Power of Words Handbook: A Guide to Language About Japanese Americans in World War II: Understanding Euphemisms and Preferred Terminology." San Francisco: Japanese American Citizens League, 2013. https://jacl.org/wordpress/wp-content/uploads/2015/08/Power-of-Words-Rev.-Term.-Handbook.pdf.

A Note on the Photos

Most of the photos in this book were taken by photographers from the federal War Relocation Agency (WRA). These photographers were tasked with presenting the so-called evacuation and internment in a positive light, to make the injustice seem more acceptable to the public. The WRA photos usually show smiling prisoners and avoid the unpleasant sight of guard towers and barbed wire.

Most Nikkei in Topaz did not have photography equipment, as their cameras had been confiscated in California. One of the few exceptions was Kaneo Kido, who took the photo of the guard tower on page 8. Dave Tatsuno secretly filmed scenes from daily life with his home movie camera. Clips from his color films are on the Discover Nikkei website: http://www.discovernikkei.org/en/nikkeialbum/albums/270/.

Author and artist Miné Okubo's honest and personal drawings of the Topaz experience can be seen in her book *Citizen 13660* or on the Japanese American National Museum's website: http://www.janm.org/collections/mine-okubo-collection/.

Photo Credits

Front Cover

Michael O. Tunnell (background)

Used by permission, Benjamin Thomas, www.facebook.com/coloursofyesterday |
  @coloursofyesterday (colorized photo of Mae Yanagi)

Used by permission, Utah State Historical Society (diary cover)

Back Cover

Michael O. Tunnell (background)

Used by permission, Utah State Historical Society (foreground)

Front Matter

Michael O. Tunnell: pages ii–iii (background)

Used by permission, Utah State Historical Society: pages i, ii–iii (foreground)

Prologue: "I Pledge Allegiance"

Michael O. Tunnell: pages vi–vii (background)

Used by permission, Utah State Historical Society: pages vi (foreground), viii–ix

Chapter 1: Unwanted

Courtesy of Mae Yanagi Ferral: page 5

Michael O. Tunnell: pages x–1 (background)

National Archives and Records Administration: page 3

Special Collections Research Center, California State University, Fresno: page 4

Used by permission, Benjamin Thomas, www.facebook.com/coloursofyesterday |
  @coloursofyesterday: page x (foreground)

Used by permission, Utah State Historical Society: pages 6, 7

Chapter 2: A Square Mile of Desert

Michael O. Tunnell: pages 8–9 (background)

Photo by Kaneo Kido from the Miné Okubo Collection of the Topaz Museum, Delta, Utah:
  page 8 (bottom)

Used by permission, Utah State Historical Society: pages 8 (top), 11, 12, 13

War Relocation Authority photographs: Japanese-American evacuation and resettlement,
  BANC PIC 1967.014, The Bancroft Library, University of California, Berkeley: page 10

Chapter 3: Barracks, Mess Halls, and Latrines

Michael O. Tunnell: pages 14–15 (background), 18

Special Collections, J. Willard Marriott Library, The University of Utah: page 24

Used by permission, Utah State Historical Society: pages 17, 19, 20, 21, 23, 25

War Relocation Authority photographs: Japanese-American evacuation and resettlement, BANC PIC 1986.059, The Bancroft Library, University of California, Berkeley: pages 14 (foreground), 22

Chapter 4: School Days

From the Emil and Eleanor Gerard Sekerak collection of the Topaz Museum, Delta, Utah: page 29

Michael O. Tunnell: pages 26–27 (background)

Used by permission, Utah State Historical Society: pages 26 (top and bottom), 28, 30–31, 32, 33, 34

Chapter 5: The War

Gerth Special Collections and University Archives. University Library. California State University, Sacramento: page 40

Michael O. Tunnell: pages 36–37 (background)

Used by permission, Utah State Historical Society: pages 36 (top and bottom), 38, 41, 42, 44, 45

War Relocation Authority photographs: Japanese-American evacuation and resettlement, BANC PIC 1967.014, The Bancroft Library, University of California, Berkeley: pages 39, 43

Chapter 6: Take Me Out to the Ball Game

Michael O. Tunnell: pages 46–47 (background)

Special Collections Research Center, California State University, Fresno: page 46 (foreground)

Used by permission, Utah State Historical Society: pages 48, 50, 51, 54, 55, 57

War Relocation Authority photographs: Japanese-American evacuation and resettlement, BANC PIC 1967.014, The Bancroft Library, University of California, Berkeley: pages 49 (all), 52–53, 56

Chapter 7: Creatures

Courtesy of Mae Yanagi Ferral: page 58 (foreground)

Michael O. Tunnell: pages 58–59 (background)

Used by permission, Utah State Historical Society: pages 60, 62, 63, 64, 66 (top and bottom)

War Relocation Authority photographs: Japanese-American evacuation and resettlement, BANC PIC 1967.014, The Bancroft Library, University of California, Berkeley: page 65

Chapter 8: Holidays, Festivals, and Worship

From the Emil and Eleanor Gerard Sekerak collection of the Topaz Museum, Delta, Utah: page 72

Michael O. Tunnell: pages 68–69 (background)

National Archives and Records Administration: page 76

Rare Books and Special Collections, University of British Columbia Library: page 73

Used by permission, Utah State Historical Society: pages 68 (top and bottom), 70–71, 74, 75, 77

Chapter 9: Is There a Doctor in the House?

Michael O. Tunnell: pages 78–79 (background)

Used by permission, Utah State Historical Society: pages 80, 81, 82, 84

War Relocation Authority photographs: Japanese-American evacuation and resettlement, BANC PIC 1967.014, The Bancroft Library, University of California, Berkeley: page 78 (foreground)

Chapter 10: Congratulations and Condolences, Hellos and Goodbyes

Courtesy of Saburo Hori: page 86 (foreground)

Michael O. Tunnell: pages 86–87 (background)

Used by permission, Utah State Historical Society: pages 88, 89, 90, 91, 92, 93, 94, 95

Chapter 11: Going Home

Courtesy of Mae Yanagi Ferral: page 101

Michael O. Tunnell: pages 96–97 (background)

US Army: page 99

Used by permission, Utah State Historical Society: pages 96 (foreground), 98

War Relocation Authority photographs: Japanese-American evacuation and resettlement, BANC PIC 1967.014, The Bancroft Library, University of California, Berkeley: pages 100, 102

Epilogue: Moving Forward

Courtesy of Denshō, Scene and Nisei Vue Collection, Mr. and Mrs. Joe Hamanaka: page 104 (foreground)

Michael O. Tunnell: pages 104–105 (background)

Ronald Reagan Presidential Library & Museum: page 107

Author's Note

Michael O. Tunnell: pages 108–109 (foreground and background), 110, 111, 112, 113, 114

Source Notes

Please see the bibliography on pages 129–130 for more information about the cited works.

Chapter 1: Unwanted

Page 2: "Japanese are not . . . be made": James Duval Phelan quoted in Sandler, p. 9.

Page 4: "I am for . . . all of them": Henry McLemore quoted in Daniels, Taylor, and Kitano, p. 80.

Page 5: "How can we . . . fifteen years!": Iku Uchida quoted in Uchida, *Invisible Thread*, p. 70.

Page 7: "Mommy, let's go back to America": Unidentified six-year-old child quoted in Sandler, p. 60.

Chapter 2: A Square Mile of Desert

Page 8: "the diarrhea train": Ken Fujii quoted in Taylor, p. 89.

Page 9: "Houses, gardens, . . . wonderful to us": Uchida, *Invisible Thread*, p. 90.

Page 10: "pound[ing] the heel of [his] boot": Raymond Akashi, Children of Topaz reunion questionnaire, October 26, 1996.

Page 10: "the fine alkali . . . covered everything": Mae Yanagi Ferral, interview with author, January 19, 2016.

Page 11: "the wind . . . strength," "swirling masses of sand," "eclipsed barracks . . . away," and "Fear gave . . . fight": Uchida, *Desert Exile*, pp. 112–113.

Page 12: "Yesterday there. . . around and around": *Our Daily Diary*, May 13, 1943.

Page 13: "until they put . . . for help": Sato Hashizume quoted in Sandler, p. 73.

Page 13: "Jewel of the Desert": *Topaz Times*, September 17, 1942, p. 1.

Page 13: "As time passed, . . . appreciate [it]": Edwin Narahara, Children of Topaz reunion questionnaire, October 26, 1996.

Chapter 3: Barracks, Mess Halls, and Latrines

Page 15: "The sheeting . . . they survived": Roger Walker quoted in Taylor, pp. 93–94.

Page 16: "Running to . . . barracks": Roy Takeuchi, Children of Topaz reunion questionnaire, October 26, 1996.

Page 17: "some careless children . . . the roof": *Our Daily Diary*, July 5, 1943.

Page 17: "was absent . . . to school": *Our Daily Diary*, March 16, 1943.

Page 17: "signs were. . . of Topaz": *Our Daily Diary*, May 17, 1943.

Page 17: "While waiting . . . of my life!": Jane Kawaguchi Imura, Children of Topaz reunion questionnaire, October 26, 1996.

Pages 17–18: "they lived . . . equipped kitchen" and "filled with . . . resentment": Uchida, *Desert Exile*, p. 117.

Page 18: "Lynn will . . . refrigerator today": *Our Daily Diary*, March 11, 1943.

Page 18: "dirty": Margaret Hamachi as reported by Mae Yanagi Ferral, interview with author, February 18, 2016.

Page 19: "When the water . . . and shout": Uchida, *Desert Exile*, p. 114.

Page 23: "liver, liver, liver (ugg)!!!": Roy Takeuchi, Children of Topaz reunion questionnaire, October 26, 1996.

Page 25: "I couldn't . . . spoil rice": Frankie Kawasaki, Children of Topaz reunion questionnaire, October 26, 1996.

Page 25: "pronounced themselves . . . they saw": Taylor, p. 164.

Chapter 4: School Days

Page 27: "as cold . . . a refrigerator": Uchida, *Invisible Thread*, p. 102.

Page 28: "I really don't . . . education": Robert Utsumi quoted in Taylor, p. 131.

Page 28: "When we made . . . fun to me": Betty Sugiyama Tsukamoto, Children of Topaz reunion questionnaire, October 26, 1996.

Page 32: "Our ants . . . sweet things": *Our Daily Diary*, March 26, 1943.

Page 33: "many pupils . . . our frieze": *Our Daily Diary*, May 25, 1943.

Page 35: "cardboard box . . . an oven": Roy Takeuchi, Children of Topaz reunion questionnaire, October 26, 1996.

Page 35: "they were . . . we were": *Our Daily Diary*, June 3, 1943.

Page 35: "I was touched . . . reach school": Uchida, *Desert Exile*, p. 119.

Chapter 5: The War

Page 37: "Please remember . . . stamps" and "not to kill spiders . . . the war": *Our Daily Diary*, March 11, 1943.

Pages 37–38: "We have a . . . Uncle Sam": *Our Daily Diary*, May 18, 1943.

Page 38: "rubber, money, . . . Uncle Sam": *Our Daily Diary*, March 12, 1943.

Page 38: "After we finish . . . Red Cross": *Our Daily Diary*, July 20, 1943.

Page 38: "practically everyone . . . victory garden": Okubo, p. 192.

Page 40: "This afternoon . . . volunteer too": *Our Daily Diary*, May 21, 1943.

Page 42: "the most decorated . . . United States": Quoted in Sandler, p. 112.

Page 43: approximately 150 dead and 1,800 wounded: Abbie Salyers Grubb, "Rescue of the Lost Battalion," Denshō Encyclopedia, 2019, http://encyclopedia.densho.org/Rescue_of_the_Lost_Battalion/.

Page 44: "Why don't you . . . over with?" and "We are liberators . . . We are American Japanese": Efron, Sonni, "Japanese-American GIs Are Focus of Dachau Memories: World War II: Nisei Veterans Are Reunited with Some People They Rescued from Horror of Nazi Death Camp," *Los Angeles Times*, December 1, 1991, https://www.latimes.com/archives/la-xpm-1991-12-01-mn-872-story.html.

Page 45: "shortened the . . . two years": Major General Charles Willoughby quoted in Sandler, p. 126.

Chapter 6: Take Me Out to the Ball Game

Page 47: "Military Police . . . score of 11–5" and "the little boys . . . old men": *Our Daily Diary*, May 26, 1943.

Page 50: "when the sun . . . opposing team": Roy Takeuchi, Children of Topaz reunion questionnaire, October 26, 1996.

Page 51: "Makoto and Frankie . . . Delta": *Our Daily Diary*, March 24, 1943.

Page 52: "because the . . . Antelope Springs": *Our Daily Diary*, July 16, 1943.

Page 53: "Several boys . . . couldn't help it": *Our Daily Diary*, July 30, 1943.

Page 54: "to wander . . . vacation time": Grace Hayashi Okamoto, Children of Topaz reunion questionnaire, October 26, 1996.

Pages 54–55: "The most memorable . . . first time": Robert Suzuki, Children of Topaz reunion questionnaire, October 26, 1996.

Page 56: "before it ran out": Roy Takeuchi, Children of Topaz reunion questionnaire, October 26, 1996.

Page 57: "I read every book I could find": Uchida, *Invisible Thread*, p. 110.

Chapter 7: Creatures

Page 59: "He knew something . . . looking out": Unidentified seventh-grade student quoted in War Relocation Authority, p. 9.

Page 60: "gave him to . . . caring," "Be a good boy now, Laddie," "We'll come back for you someday," and "we could still . . . the corner": Uchida, *Invisible Thread*, p. 71.

Page 61: "I was sure . . . abandoned him": Uchida, *Invisible Thread*, p. 87.

Page 61: "No one wanted an old horse": Tsuyako "Sox" Kitashima quoted in Taylor, p. 243.

Page 61: "hunting for critters": Mae Yanagi Ferral, interview with author, February 18, 2016.

Page 61: "Don't keep . . . and cats": Central Utah Relocation Project, p. 27.

Page 61: "We used to . . . in jars" and "[We also] caught . . . a kite": Jane Kawaguchi Imura, Children of Topaz reunion questionnaire, October 26, 1996.

Page 61: "A man in . . . mother sparrow": *Our Daily Diary*, June 7, 1943.

Page 61: "Some of . . . the barracks": *Our Daily Diary*, June 4, 1943.

Page 61: "loved . . . dearly": Uchida, *Invisible Thread*, p. 104.

Page 62: "a big, fat badger" and "a man was . . . stomach": *Our Daily Diary*, June 3, 1943.

Page 62: "would not move": *Our Daily Diary*, March 23, 1943.

Page 63: "a little dog named 'Tippy'": *Our Daily Diary*, April 20, 1943.

Page 64: "a big mother . . . to death": *Our Daily Diary*, May 31, 1943.

Page 65: "quills all over its body": *Our Daily Diary*, May 24, 1943.

Chapter 8: Holidays, Festivals, and Worship

Page 69: "there was . . . holiday spirit": Okubo, p. 156.

Pages 69–70: "I hadn't seen . . . long time": Uchida, *Invisible Thread*, p. 106.

Pages 70–71: "a pleasant [Christmas] . . . mess hall": Uchida, *Desert Exile*, p. 130.

Page 73: "The only festival . . . the festivities": Mae Yanagi Ferral, interview with author, February 14, 2017.

Page 76: "Thanksgiving Greetings . . . Crew": Uchida, *Desert Exile*, p. 126.

Page 76: "there was . . . lots of fun": *Our Daily Diary*, July 5, 1943.

Chapter 9: Is There a Doctor in the House?

Page 79: "Johnny and Jackie have the mumps": *Our Daily Diary*, March 15, 1943.

Page 79: "Last night . . . six stitches": *Our Daily Diary*, April 23, 1943.

Page 79: "Kimiko's mother . . . hot water": *Our Daily Diary*, May 18, 1943.

Page 79: "Yesterday evening, . . . truck": *Our Daily Diary*, March 17, 1943.

Page 80: "Due to my condition, . . . many activities": Betty Sugiyama Tsukamoto, Children of Topaz reunion questionnaire, October 26, 1996.

Page 80: "army-type hospital": Okubo, p. 162.

Page 80: "In Topaz, . . . Registered Nurses" and "I didn't even . . . sick people": Sachi Kajiwara quoted in Sandler, pp. 74–75.

Page 81: "busy doctors": Iku Uchida quoted in Uchida, *Desert Exile*, p. 133.

Page 82: "a broth . . . any ailment": Uchida, *Invisible Thread*, p. 99.

Pages 82–83: "There are many . . . ourselves": *Our Daily Diary*, March 12, 1943.

Page 83: "could get away" and "And did I ever get sick!": Johnny Moritomo, Children of Topaz reunion questionnaire, October 26, 1996.

Page 83: "There are many . . . flu in Topaz": *Our Daily Diary*, May 3, 1943.

Page 83: "very sad . . . Infantile Paralysis": *Our Daily Diary*, May 4, 1943.

Page 83: "all residents . . . Infantile Paralysis": *Our Daily Diary*, May 5, 1943.

Page 83: "now move . . . his neck": *Our Daily Diary*, May 10, 1943.

Page 84: "one boy . . . to bleed" and "It is a dangerous game": *Our Daily Diary*, May 25, 1943.

Page 85: "A boy was . . . with knives": *Our Daily Diary*, July 12, 1943.

Chapter 10: Congratulations and Condolences, Hellos and Goodbyes

Page 87: "Miss Yamauchi . . . Saturday": *Our Daily Diary*, March 22, 1943.

Page 87: "A lady passed . . . long time": *Our Daily Diary*, May 27, 1943.

Page 87: "Today Johnny's sister . . . her fiancé": *Our Daily Diary*, May 26, 1943.

Page 87: "It is June's birthday . . . sang to her": *Our Daily Diary*, June 22, 1943.

Page 88: "We shall call . . . like before": *Our Daily Diary*, March 29, 1943.

Page 88: "each stem . . . cotton": Uchida, *Desert Exile*, p. 123.

Page 89: "Uchida San, . . . place like this": Unidentified elderly Issei man quoted in Uchida, *Desert Exile*, p. 123.

Page 90: "Mr. James H. Wakasa passed away": *Our Daily Diary*, April 14, 1943.

Page 91: "Many people . . . workers": *Our Daily Diary*, May 24, 1943.

Page 92: "it required weeks . . . Washington": Uchida, *Desert Exile*, p. 131.

Chapter 11: Going Home

Page 97: "Here, there . . . stared at" and "We don't get . . . lonely": Unidentified Topaz detainee quoted in Taylor, p. 118.

Page 99: "Jap" and "to go back to Japan": Mae Yanagi Ferral, interview with author, December 28, 2016.

Page 99: "We don't cut Jap hair": Unidentified barber quoted in Inouye, p. 208.

Pages 99–100: "My father told . . . by strangers": Mae Yanagi Ferral, interview with author, February 10, 2016.

Page 100: "had bitter feelings . . . his family": Mae Yanagi Ferral, interview with author, January 19, 2016.

Page 101: "My parents . . . was happening" and "seldom spoke . . . the experience": Mae Yanagi Ferral, interview with author, January 19, 2016.

Page 101: "I have come . . . events": Mae Yanagi Ferral, interview with author, February 10, 2016.

Page 102: "My sister Jane . . . regarding internment": Mae Yanagi Ferral, interview with author, February 10, 2016.

Page 102: "through a . . . Japanese ancestry": Mae Yanagi Ferral, interview with author, January 19, 2016.

Pages 102–103: "the interest . . . films": Mae Yanagi Ferral, interview with author, October 28, 2017.

Page 103: "Although some Issei . . . remarkable": Uchida, *Desert Exile*, p. 148.

Epilogue: Moving Forward

Page 106: "race prejudice . . . political leadership": Commission on Wartime Relocation and Internment of Civilians, p. 18

Page 106: forced Japanese American loss of income and property estimated at about $370 million ($2 billion in 1983 values): Daniels, Taylor, and Kitano, p. 166.

Author's Note

Page 115: "Edwin played . . . Yamauchi": *Our Daily Diary*, August 19, 1943.

Selected Bibliography

My most important primary sources for this book were *Our Daily Diary*, housed in the Utah State Historical Society, and interviews with Mae Yanagi Ferral, Saburo Hori, Edwin Narahara, other members of Miss Yamauchi's class, Ted Nagata, Grace Oshita, Jane Beckwith, and Takeo Hori. I also relied on many books, historical documents, and websites, the most helpful of which are listed below.

Books

An asterisk indicates a title for young readers.

Daniels, Roger, Sandra C. Taylor, and Harry H. L. Kitano, eds. *Japanese Americans: From Relocation to Redress.* Rev. ed. Seattle: University of Washington Press, 1991.

Hoobler, Dorothy, and Thomas Hoobler. *The Japanese American Family Album.* New York: Oxford University Press, 1995.

Inouye, Daniel K., with Lawrence Elliott. *Journey to Washington.* Englewood Cliffs, NJ: Prentice-Hall, 1967.

* Levine, Ellen. *A Fence Away from Freedom: Japanese Americans and World War II.* New York: Putnam, 1995.

* Marrin, Albert. *Uprooted: The Japanese American Experience During World War II.* New York: Knopf, 2016.

* Mochizuki, Ken. *Baseball Saved Us.* New York: Lee & Low, 1993.

Okubo, Miné. *Citizen 13660.* New York: Columbia University Press, 1946. Reprint, Seattle: University of Washington Press, 1983.

* Sandler, Martin W. *Imprisoned: The Betrayal of Japanese Americans During World War II.* New York: Walker, 2013.

Sosnoski, Daniel, ed. *Introduction to Japanese Culture.* Rutland, VT: Tuttle, 1996.

* Stanley, Jerry. *I Am an American: A True Story of Japanese Internment.* New York: Crown, 1994.

Sterner, C. Douglas. *Go For Broke: The Nisei Warriors of World War II Who Conquered Germany, Japan and American Bigotry.* Clearfield, UT: American Legacy Historical Press, 2008.

Tanaka, Chester. *Go For Broke: A Pictorial History of the Japanese American 100th Infantry Battalion and the 442d Regimental Combat Team.* Novato, CA: Presidio, 1997.

Taylor, Sandra C. *Jewel of the Desert: Japanese American Internment at Topaz.* Berkeley: University of California Press, 1993.

* Tunnell, Michael O., and George W. Chilcoat. *Children of Topaz: The Story of a Japanese-American Internment Camp.* New York: Holiday House, 1996.

Uchida, Yoshiko. *Desert Exile: The Uprooting of a Japanese American Family.* Seattle: University of Washington Press, 1982.

* Uchida, Yoshiko. *The Invisible Thread.* New York: Simon & Schuster, 1991.

Documents

Central Utah Relocation Project, Topaz, Utah, Project Reports Division. "Guidebook of the Center." September 1943.

Commission on Wartime Relocation and Internment of Civilians. "Personal Justice Denied." December 1982. https://www.archives.gov/research/japanese-americans/justice-denied.

Topaz Times. 1942–1945. Available online through Utah Digital Newspapers. https://newspapers.lib.utah.edu/search?facet_paper=%22Topaz+Times%22&q=topaz+times.

United States Department of the Interior, National Park Service. "National Historic Landmark Nomination: Central Utah Relocation Center Site (Topaz)." February 26, 2006. www.nps.gov/nhl/find/statelists/ut/CentralUtah.pdf.

War Relocation Authority, Central Utah Project (Topaz, Utah), Historical Section of the Project Reports Division. "Citizens of the Seventh Grade." April 14, 1943.

Websites

Calisphere, University of California. Japanese American Relocation Digital Archive. https://calisphere.org/exhibitions/t11/jarda/.
Contains thousands of personal diaries, letters, photographs, drawings, WRA materials, camp newsletters, photographs, and personal histories.

Denshō Encyclopedia. https://encyclopedia.densho.org.
Focuses on the exclusion and incarceration of Japanese Americans during World War II. Includes links to still and moving images, documents, databases, and oral histories.

Japanese American National Museum. www.janm.org.
Collections of materials from Japanese American prison camps, such as Miné Okubo's artwork from Topaz Camp and Mori Shimada's photographs from Heart Mountain Camp.

National Archives. Japanese Americans. https://www.archives.gov/research/japanese-americans.
Includes photographs, documents, and WRA records related to Topaz Camp.

National Park Service. Japanese American Internment. https://www.nps.gov/subjects/internment/index.htm.
Photos, documents, maps, and other information dealing with Japanese American prison camps, including Topaz.

Telling Their Stories, Oral History Archives Project. Japanese Americans Interned During World War II. www.tellingstories.org/internment/.
An oral-history archive of interviews with people of Japanese descent who were incarcerated during World War II.

Topaz Museum. www.topazmuseum.org.
Includes photos, maps, and a full list of all 11,212 Nikkei who were imprisoned at Topaz.

Utah Department of Heritage & Arts. Digital Collections. https://heritage.utah.gov/history/utah-state-history-digital-collections.
Includes a digitized reproduction of *Our Daily Diary*, as well as photos, maps, and other information about Topaz Camp.

Utah Digital Newspapers. *Topaz Times*. https://digitalnewspapers.org/newspaper/?paper=Topaz%20Times.
Digital copies of all issues of the camp newspaper, the *Topaz Times*.

Index

THE LORE OF THE TRAIN

THE LORE OF
THE TRAIN

BY C. HAMILTON ELLIS

CRESCENT BOOKS
New York

This edition published by CRESCENT BOOKS
distributed by Crown Publishers, Inc.,
by arrangement with AB Nordbok.

c d e f g h

Printed in Spain, 1987, by Heraclio Fournier S.A. Vitoria.

Library of Congress Cataloging in Publication Data

Ellis, Cuthbert Hamilton, 1909-
  The lore of the train.

  Bibliography: p. 238.
  Includes index.
  Summary: A history of the train as it developed from
early steam engines to today's high-speed electric and
diesel powered ones.
    1. Locomotives—History.   2. Railroads—History.
[1. Locomotives—History.   2. Railroads—History]
I. Title.
TJ603.E398   1981   385'.09   79-156326
ISBN 0-517-18348-X   AACR2

THE LORE OF THE TRAIN

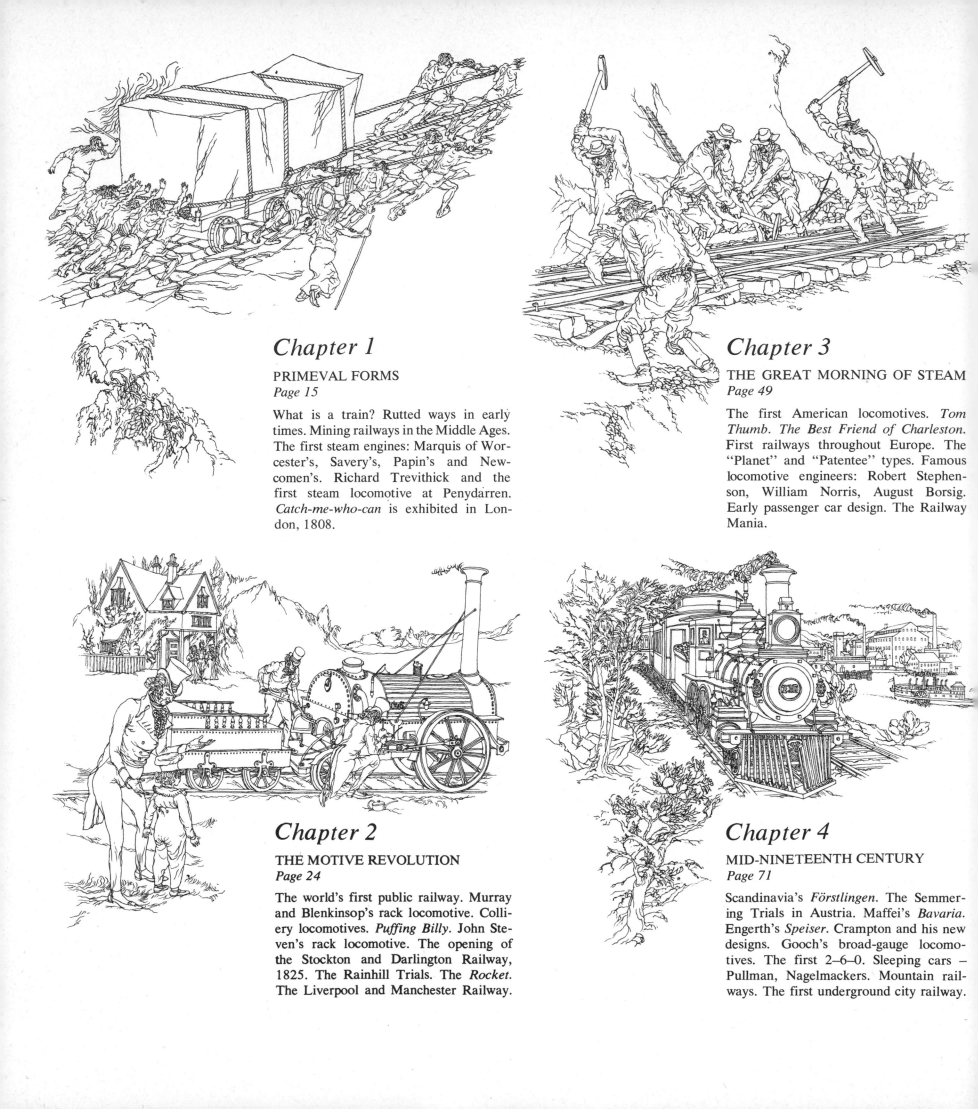

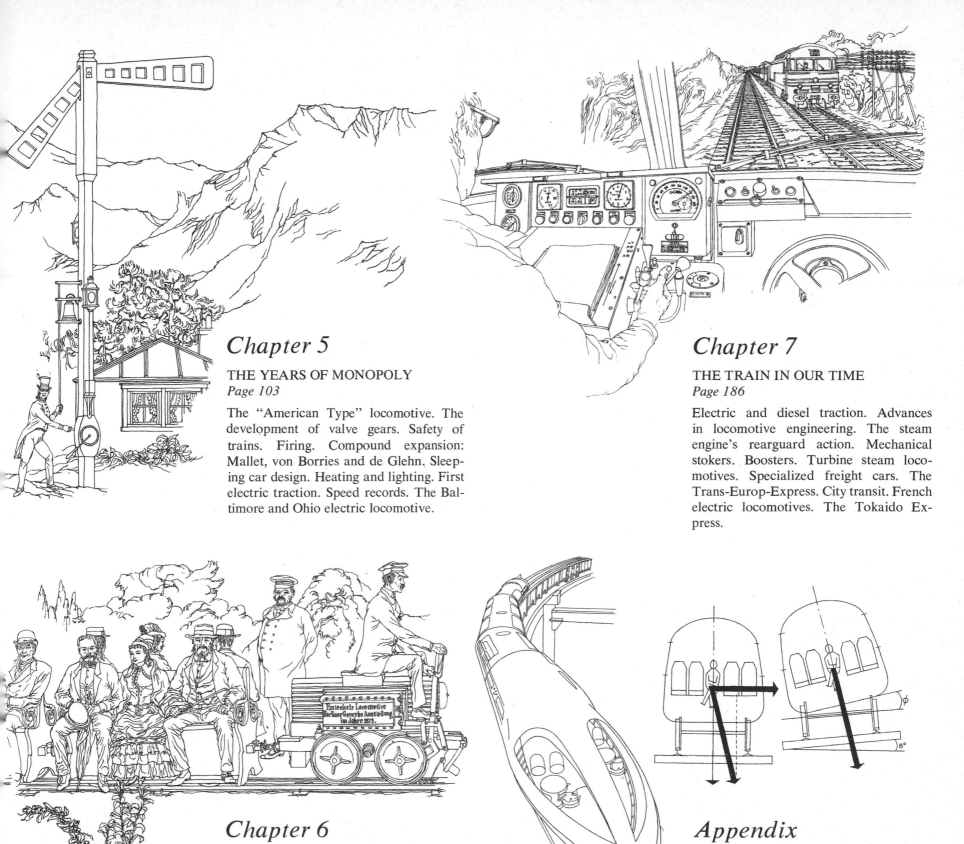

Chapter 5

THE YEARS OF MONOPOLY

The "American Type" locomotive. The development of valve gears. Safety of trains. Firing. Compound expansion: Mallet, von Borries and de Glehn. Sleeping car design. Heating and lighting. First electric traction. Speed records. The Baltimore and Ohio electric locomotive.

Chapter 7

THE TRAIN IN OUR TIME

Electric and diesel traction. Advances in locomotive engineering. The steam engine's rearguard action. Mechanical stokers. Boosters. Turbine steam locomotives. Specialized freight cars. The Trans-Europ-Express. City transit. French electric locomotives. The Tokaido Express.

Chapter 6

STEAM CHALLENGED

The 1875 Jubilee. Schmidt's superheater. Gauge variations and its problems. Electric traction in Europe. The "Pacific" type. Passenger classes. Travelling in comfort. Freight engines. The Beyer-Garrat. Snow-plows. The first Diesel engines. Monorails.

Appendix

THE FUTURE OF THE TRAIN

A special section written by P. M. Kalla-Bishop for this book. Present developments are described: automatic railways, high speed on steel railways, unorthodox railways. The linear electric locomotive. The tracked hovercraft system. The "tilting body" train. The magnetic levitation train.

With a life-long experience of working on trains behind me I feel qualified to express my admiration for the way in which the author and the Tre Tryckare team have dealt with The Lore of the Train.

"Lore", meaning knowledge gained by study, symbolises the author's thoroughness in dealing with his subject and it is quite obvious that it must have grown up with him from boyhood. The vast amount of knowledge and information he has imparted, relating to travel in so many parts of the world, is truly remarkable. This I can substantiate from my own personal experiences. The illustrations are excellent and portray the atmosphere that covers so many climates.

Hamilton Ellis proposed that the preface should be written by one of the family that started the whole business of powered railroad traction, namely the Trevithicks. It was agreed, and he wrote to me: "The Americans will not mind that you are not descended from Oliver Evans."

As the reader will discover, all this began with strong steam which was pioneered by Richard Trevithick before 1800. This high-pressure steam enabled the steam engine to move about under its own power, and it thus became a prime mover. Steam engines have served the world of travel on both land and sea in very good stead for a matter of 150 years and although the steam locomotive is practically extinct, it is not so with strong steam as it is now being used in ever-increasing quantities for the generation of electricity, which in turn propels so many of the world's electric trains.

I believe that those interested in trains – past, present and future – will find a mine of information in this book.

RICHARD TREVITHICK
Dorset, England

The Lackawanna Valley by George Inness, 1825–1894. This oil painting, which we reproduce with the kind permission of the National Gallery of Art, Washington, beautifully conveys the impact of the railroad on a new, ex-colonial country at the beginning of its expansion. With the coming of the train, the small town will rapidly grow. Already, beyond the locomotive roundhouse, there is growing up a quarter which will be socially the wrong side of the tracks, the right side being marked by the older, more solid buildings and dominated by the church steeple. Inness is an interesting figure in the history of American painting, his work having developed from the colonial vernacular styles through European study. His lighting is masterly.

THE LORE OF THE TRAIN is the result of international co-operation over several years. Experts from a number of countries have collaborated with the author and the Tre Tryckare team, of whom Turlough Johnston was the supervising editor and Åke Gustavsson drew the main illustrations. The artwork was done in the Tre Tryckare studios.

C. HAMILTON ELLIS,
the author, has written over thirty books on trains and railways. He is also an acknowledged painter of train scenes and has provided two of his own paintings for this book. He is an Associate of the Institution of Locomotive Engineers, a Fellow of the Royal Society of Arts, and a Vice President of the Historical Model Railway Society.

C. Hamilton Ellis was advised and assisted by the following international experts:

MARIE-ANNE ASSELBERGHS
Holland. Director of the Netherlands Railway Museum, Utrecht.

YNGVE HOLMGREN
Sweden. Author and keeper of the railway history departments of the Kristianstads and Trelleborgs Museums.

P. M. KALLA-BISHOP
Italy. Locomotive engineer and well-known author, he has written the final section "The Future of the Train" especially for this book.

KARL-ERNST MAEDEL
Germany. Author and editor of *Lok Magazine.*

DAVID P. MORGAN
U.S.A. Editor of *Trains Magazine,* he has a number of books on trains to his credit.

SABURO MOTOJIMA
Japan. Author and Official Historian of the Japanese National Railways.

KONRAD PFAHL
Germany. Author and locomotive engineer.

GUSTAVO REDER
Spain. Author and locomotive engineer. Permanent contributor to *Via Libre.*

JEAN SALIN
France. Editor-in-Chief of *La Vie du Rail.*

Gratitude is due to the following for advice, material and permission to reproduce:

Alsthom of France
ASEA of Sweden
British Railways
Civica Raccolta di Stampe Bertarelli
Danish State Railways
Finnish State Railways
General Electric of America
German State Railways
Galleria d'Arte Moderna, Milano
Japanese National Railways
Locomotive and Allied Manufacturers' Association
National Gallery of Art, Washington
National Museum of Wales
Norwegian State Railways
Railway Museum, Gävle, Sweden
RENFE (Spanish Railways)
Science Museum, London
SKF
SNCF (French Railways)
Swedish Railway Club
Swedish State Railways
Swiss Federal Railways
Transport Museum, Tokyo
Verkehrsmuseum, Nürnberg

東京繁榮圖 氣車馬車及力車

In South-west Asia manpower was used for hauling huge stones from quarries to towns for the construction of temples and monumental graves. In the scene reconstructed here lay, perhaps, the first inkling of the Railway Idea.

(previous page)
In 1872 the first Imperial Government Railway was opened over 18 miles between Shinbashi, Tokyo and Yokohama. The print shows a 2-4-0 engine from the Vulcan Foundry in England pulling a train near the Shinagawa beach close to Tokyo. The artist was Kuniteru.

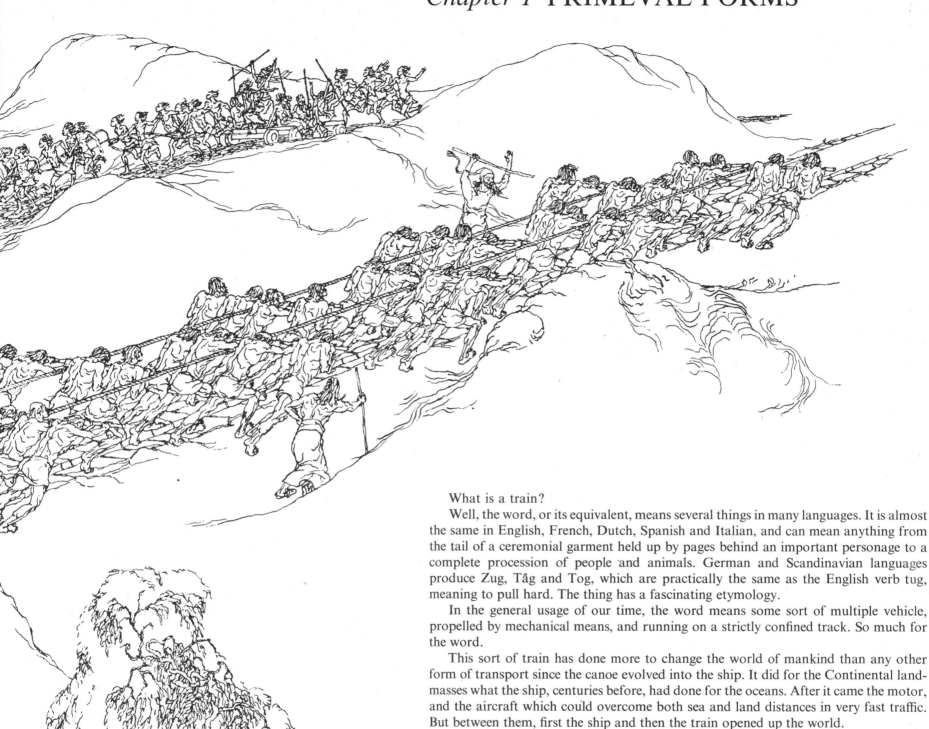

Chapter 1 PRIMEVAL FORMS

What is a train?

Well, the word, or its equivalent, means several things in many languages. It is almost the same in English, French, Dutch, Spanish and Italian, and can mean anything from the tail of a ceremonial garment held up by pages behind an important personage to a complete procession of people and animals. German and Scandinavian languages produce Zug, Tåg and Tog, which are practically the same as the English verb tug, meaning to pull hard. The thing has a fascinating etymology.

In the general usage of our time, the word means some sort of multiple vehicle, propelled by mechanical means, and running on a strictly confined track. So much for the word.

This sort of train has done more to change the world of mankind than any other form of transport since the canoe evolved into the ship. It did for the Continental land-masses what the ship, centuries before, had done for the oceans. After it came the motor, and the aircraft which could overcome both sea and land distances in very fast traffic. But between them, first the ship and then the train opened up the world.

At a remote time, someone invented the wheel. At a later time, but still remote, someone else invented the guided vehicle. Both events probably took place somewhere in Western Asia, in Mesopotamia, the country of the great rivers.

The guided vehicle?

That was the wheeled vehicle whose course was determined by the ruts it originally ran in. Ancient vehicles had gouged out those ruts in the streets of Ur, of Babylon, and in the ancient cities of Assyria. Men soon saw that the ruts, once they had formed, kept the vehicles to a fixed path, so that they damaged neither themselves nor the corners of the buildings round which they passed in the close-built riverside cities of Tigris and Euphrates. Then paving succeeded the mud roads and in that paving, ruts were made deliberately by measure, so that the carts still should follow a disciplined course. When the four-wheeled cart was a new invention, there were no swinging front axles!

It was not the beginning of railways, but it was the beginning of the Railway Idea. The Prophet Isaiah, who was a very discerning man with things as well as people, knew more than a thing or two about the Assyrians and their ways, when back in the Eighth

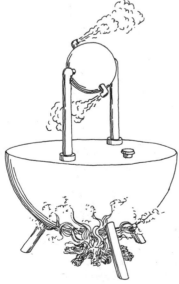

Century B.C. he wrote about the crooked being made straight and the rough places plain. He had seen their marvellous stone-ways, and he looked into the future, when every valley should be exalted and every mountain and hill laid low.

Those stone-ways, as suggested, were not railways, but they were tramways of a sort. They were invaluable for the movement of huge blocks of stone from quarry to city, or of religious monuments from quarry or city to some holy place, and for these things they were used by the Greeks, who took the idea with them when they colonized Sicily, whence the Romans copied them. One can still see stone rut-ways in the quarries of Syracuse, which served Dionysius Tyrannus both for building material and as a place to keep political prisoners and captured soldiers out of mischief. One can see them in the relatively modern paved streets of Pompeii, volcanically overwhelmed and thus by the irony of history preserved, in 79 A.D.

The Greeks seem to have got as far as making turnouts and passing loops, the remote precursors of the points or switches in a modern railway. The Greek word for them was *ektropoi*. But there was no mechanical agent beyond that of the lever and the pulley. Motive power was furnished by men (probably poor devils of slaves or convicts), by horses, asses, mules, or possibly camels in some places.

Yet the thing—the Railway Thing—almost might have happened even then. Hero, an Alexandrian Greek, devised a primitive reaction turbine—a steam-filled whirling ball with opposed escape-jets—about this time. It was simply a scientific toy, though something like it is said to have been used for turning spits in medieval kitchens, notably in the great monasteries where learning was kept alive in the Dark Ages.

The Romans, like the Minoans of Crete before them, were great plumbers and domestic engineers, and one of their appliances was an internally-fired boiler, heated by burning charcoal in an extraordinarily advanced water-tube firebox. But its service was only that of the bathroom in the houses of the rich. Nobody bothered about motive power for industrial machines and transport. As suggested, there were plenty of slaves and prisoners-of-war around, as well as animals, for such power as people thought they needed.

Classic Greece declined into a Roman satellite state, ultimately to fall to the Turks. What we now call the Middle-East, with the past glories of Sargon, King of Kings, buried in the sand, furnished outposts for the Roman Empire. Nor did Imperial Rome complete her civilization of Europe and Western Asia, though, to be sure, her stone-ways as well as her ordinary roads stretched far and wide, to be regarded and then forgotten, by invading Celt, Goth, Frank, Saxon, Hun and Turk. For Imperial Rome died as Assyria and Persia and Macedon had died, and the Dark Ages set in for many countries over many centuries.

They were ages so dark that only in the Nineteenth Century did people of Western Europe unearth the remains not only of well-planned cities and garrison towns, but of splendid country houses, centrally heated and admirably drained; of beautifully paved roads deep down below muddy pack-horse lanes, and, rather significantly, those rutted stoneways whereon wagons could pass with heavy loads yet without need of steering. One of these turned up in the British Isles, with quite curious significance, on the site of Abbeydore Railway Station on the border of England and Wales.

That, then, was the beginning of the guided vehicle, but not of the railroad proper. Whence came that? The most facile explanation is that on rutted roads in wet months, men laid split tree-trunks in the bottoms of the muddy ruts to sustain the wheels, and that these constituted the first real rails. No doubt this was done in many places where there was little stone and plenty of mud. But the essence of the railway was the use of flanges, either in the track or on the wheels themselves. The stoneways had provided flanges in the form of their track. But what about the flanged wheel on the plain rail?

In its most primitive form, this was produced by an arrangement of great grooved bobbins to act as wheels for the wagons, while smoothly-trimmed tree-trunks—spruce or larch for example—laid on and secured to much shorter sections at right-angles, formed the track. Thus there were rails on sleepers or cross-ties, and there were even primitive switches. Just who first made such a track, no man dare say, but early in the sixteenth century it was certainly being used by the miners in the gold-diggings of Transylvania, and specimens of both track and vehicle have almost miraculously survived the centuries.

We find illustrations of early wooden wagon-ways in several sixteenth-century treatises, of which perhaps the best-known is the *De Re Metallica* of Georgius Agricola

A Graeco-Roman rutway near Syracuse, Sicily. It is one of the earliest forms of the permanent way and probably saved the walls of the houses on either side from being damaged by swaying or badly driven carts. (Charcoal sketch by Hamilton Ellis.)

(opposite) Trevithick's Tramroad Locomotive, on the Penydarren Tramroad, Merthyr Tydfil to Abercynon, Wales, February 1804. This was the beginning of mechanical transport by rail. Richard Trevithick, spanner in hand in case of trouble, runs alongside the mother of all railway locomotive engines, which according to the painter, Terence Cuneo, had already a red-hot patch where her smokebox ought to be. So she probably had; there was a wager to be won, and Trevithick was a sporting Cornishman as well as a great original inventor. The painting is reproduced by courtesy of the National Museum of Wales.

The Aelopile, a primitive form of steam reaction turbine ascribed to Hero of Alexandria. He probably considered it to be nothing more than an amusing plaything.

(alias Georg Bauer). It was published in 1556. Six years before, a mining railway in Alsace was illustrated by Sebastian Münster in his *Cosmographiae Universalis*. Mining railways in Eastern Europe, and also in the Tyrol, probably had been in use for quite a time before these publications.

One can only write "probably", noting that as far as we know the idea of the confined track occurred to some unrecorded Mesopotamian, and the use of flanged wheel on plain rail to some forgotten German, not necessarily in the countries we now call Iraq and Germany. The wagons were called in Old German *Hunte* (dogs).

In the eighteenth century, there were two rival systems; that of the flanged wheel on the plain rail—the present form—and that of the plain wheel on the flanged rail, the latter being formed of L-shaped iron plates extending from stone to stone; a rough but workable road so long as loads were not too heavy. In that century, very extensive mining railways were built in Europe, most notably in South Wales and North Eastern England, where collieries were booming. In Scotland, too, they had arrived sufficiently soon for a battle to be fought over one (at Prestonpans near Edinburgh in 1745) during the last British dynastic war. One may read of these and many other things in Charles Edward Lee's scholarly book *The Evolution of Railways,* which quite properly leaves off where most railway books begin.

What, one may ask, has all this to do with trains? A horse pulling a wagon over rails did not make a train. But while, on a common road, that horse could pull but one wagon, on rails he could pull several. So there was your train!

Still, it could not be our idea of a train until it had a propulsive engine of some sort. In the sixteenth and seventeenth centuries there were no engines apart from very simple and quite academic models. What in later years was to be called Civil Engineering (that was, not military as in the building of fortifications) was a much older science than that of mechanical engineering. The Roman aqueducts built under the Emperor Claudius were quite "modern".

In eighteenth century Europe, particularly in North Eastern England, there were tremendous earthworks to support the archaic mining railways. The mines were often in the hills, and the railways went down to the nearest waterway where ships could come in to collect the coal. Going uphill, the horse or horses pulled the wagons. Downhill they rode in a "dandy-cart" attached at one end. So used to the drill were the horses that they would trot round and mount the dandy-cart without being led. For the rest, movement was controlled by brake levers and blocks on the wheels.

There still stands in County Durham, England, what is probably the first railway viaduct in the world. It is the magnificent Tanfield Arch, built in 1727. The mines it served were probably worked out by the end of the century, but like the Roman aqueducts it still stands, and under British Government today, it is scheduled as an ancient monument.

Mechanical engineering also had much to do with military matters. It is not absurd to suggest that the first spring was the bow, and that the most primitive internal-combustion engine was the cannon. But just as mining produced the first railed tracks, so did mining produce the first steam engines. Their work was to pump out the water that was always flooding the workings. In the seventeenth century, the Marquis of Worcester in England and Denis Papin and Thomas Savery in both France and England (Papin lived for some years in Kassel) made various applications of steam power through displacement.

Early in the eighteenth century, in England, Thomas Newcomen made the first commercially practical reciprocating steam engines, for pumping water from mines. The real power was that of the atmosphere, for steam was admitted simply to create a vacuum in the bottom of the cylinder by condensation. James Watt, a Scot (1736–1819) improved on Newcomen's system by providing a separate condenser, greatly speeding the action of the engine, and also produced the first practical rotary motion by crank and flywheel (initially with a "sun-and-planet" gear, as the crank was covered by another man's patent.) Watt's engine could drive machines as well as work a pump. Pressure was still very low.

Now long ago, Papin had produced a high-pressure boiler, though simply as what we could call a pressure-cooker ("Papin's Digester").

At the end of the eighteenth century came Richard Trevithick, a Celt from Cornwall where he was an official and engineer in one of the tin mines. He it was who applied high-pressure steam to the driving of a double-acting reciprocating engine. The slide valve for steam admission and exhaust had been invented by one of James Watt's young men,

A

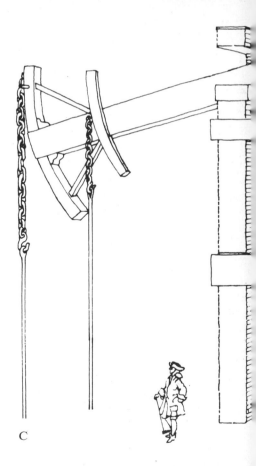

C

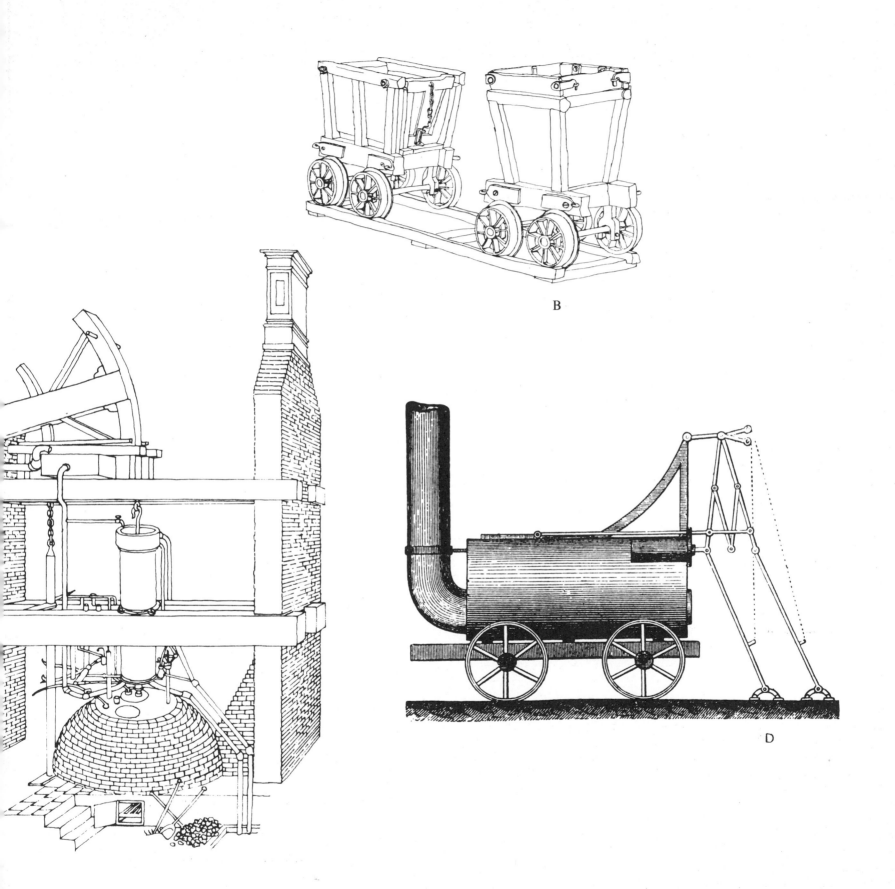

B

D

A *Mining railway illustration of about 1519 from* Der Ursprung gemeynner.

B *These wagons were used in the Höganäs mines in the South of Sweden in the 18th century.*

C *Newcomen's low-pressure steam engine for pumping water out of mines. It was built in the early 18th century and was the first commercial use of steam.*

D *Brunton's locomotive, 1813. This strange-looking object was supposed to push itself along by its "hind legs".*

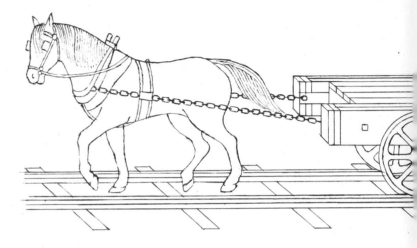

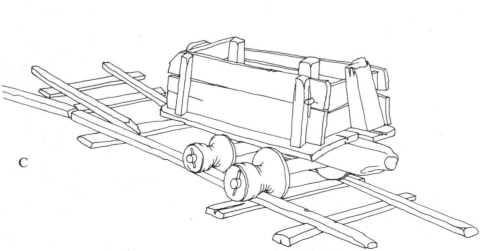

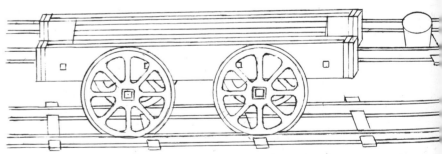

A

B

C

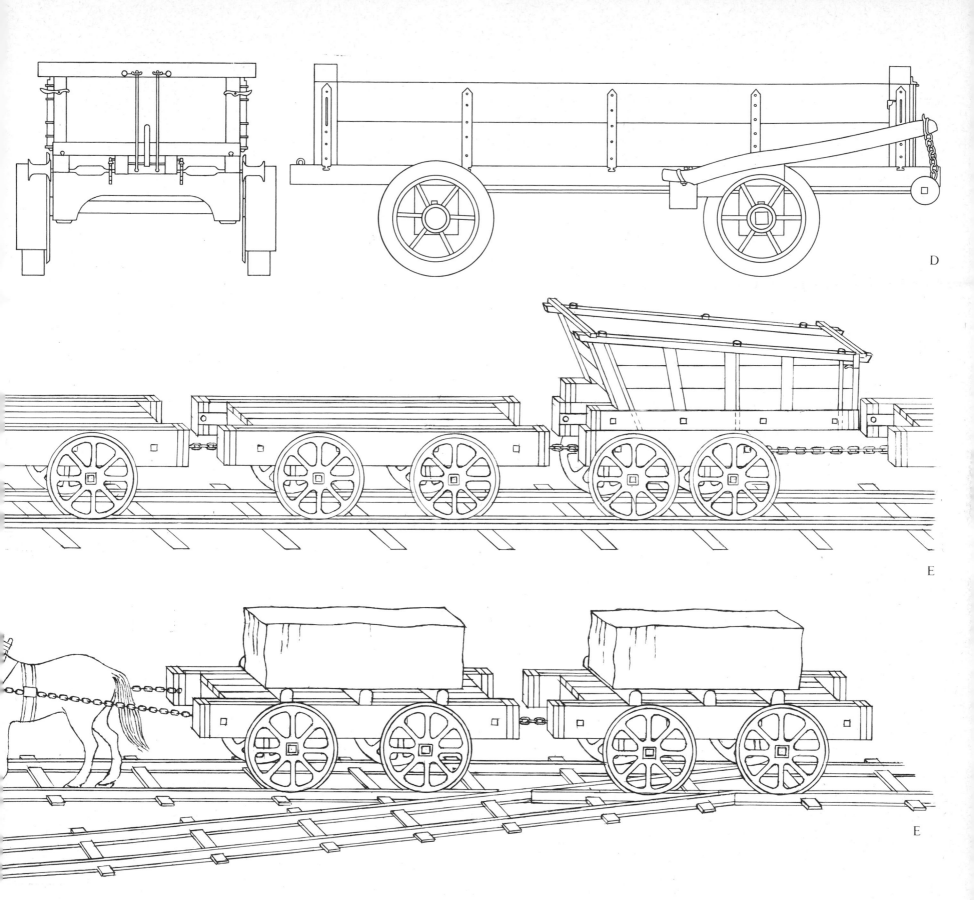

A *This print, from Sebastian Münster's* Cosmographiae Universalis *(1550), shows a mining truck with iron wheels on a track at the Leberthal silver mines in Alsace.*

B *This drawing, from Gabriel Jars'* Voyages Metallurgiques *(1765), shows a colliery tram-wagon being pulled by a horse in the mines near Durham, England. The wagon had flanged iron wheels and ran on a four-foot wagonway*

C *Wooden mining tramway with its wagon on flanged rollers was in use in South East Europe in the early 16th century. The drawing is taken from an actual relic preserved in Germany. Note the single-tongue switch.*

D *Perspective and elevation drawings of one of the wagons used by Ralph Allen for hauling stone from his quarries at Combe Down, near Bath, England. It had cast iron wheels. From a drawing by Desaguliers in* A Course in Experimental Philosophy *(1734).*

E *The "train" at Alltwen Quarry showing one of the early switches used.*

William Murdoch. The Trevithick engine was small, compact, and immensely powerful for its size. It was the answer to the industrialists' prayer. The huge low-pressure engines of Watt had needed a large building to house them, but one could put a Trevithick engine almost anywhere.

Watt was much annoyed, and playing on the idea that the use of high-pressure steam was very dangerous, publicly remarked that his rival ought to be hanged. But at last there was a steam engine sufficiently compact to make the locomotive a practical possibility.

Attempts there had been already. At the turn of the seventeen-sixties to 'seventies, Nicolas Cugnot, a French artillery officer, had produced a steam-wagon for gun traction on roads, propelled by a kettle-shaped boiler supplying steam to a pair of single-acting cylinders which drove a single front wheel through ratchet and cog. It did move itself, but was unmanageable as well as being able only to steam for a short while.

Murdoch, too, had experimented with a very small model locomotive (again not for rails) fired by a spirit lamp. This ran quite well; it was a most engaging steam toy. Murdoch's chief, James Watt, was not amused.

Trevithick, however, approached steam locomotion very seriously, first with a model, and then with full-size road locomotives, basing them on his existing stationary engine which had been put already to commercial use. With his partner Vivian in Cornwall, he built a steam road carriage which they drove along the roads from Redruth to Plymouth in 1802, there shipping it to London where it was demonstrated to an unenthusiastic public. It was in fact the first practical motor-car, and people were not yet ready for motor-cars. Further, it got damaged, and now became apparent a fatal defect of Trevithick's character.

He was a giant among original inventors and mechanical engineers. He was on the other hand about as poor a businessman as ever hoped to exploit an invention. If anything broke, or otherwise went wrong, he lost interest in it and went after something else, like an artist burning an unsuccessful picture. But though the steam carriage was lost, all was not lost. The world's first railway locomotive was about to be born.

In the winter of 1803–4, Trevithick was in South Wales, and it was there that this engine was built, to be demonstrated on the Penydarren mining railway—or tramroad as it was called, near Merthyr Tydfil. On February 21, 1804, it was publicly steamed. Even in stern, evangelical Wales, it was a time of heavy betting. The owner of Penydarren Ironworks wagered a neighbouring ironmaster that the "travelling engine" would haul ten English tons of iron on the tramroad from Penydarren to Abercynon, a distance of 9¾ miles. The stakes were 500 guineas (£525 sterling in gold). Trevithick's locomotive made the journey in four hours, five minutes, with the stipulated load of pig-iron, on top of which about seventy men had climbed to enjoy such a novel experience, that of being the first people to travel by a mechanically powered railway train. The track was of flanged iron rails on stone blocks, the common form of the period.

Original drawings have not survived, at any rate entire, but from certain very old drawings contemporary with Trevithick, we know enough to make a very close reconstruction of the engine.

It was in all important features a locomotive version of the Trevithick stationary engine, with a single cylinder driving a transverse shaft with a very large flywheel. The boiler was internally fired, with a return flue. Our drawing (p. 33) is sufficiently explanatory of the way in which the power was transmitted from this shaft, through spur wheels, to the four wheels on which the engine was carried. The single cylinder was embedded in the boiler above the furnace and flue, with the piston rod issuing at one end to drive a crosshead on two parallel slidebars, whence the connecting rods went back to cranks on the transverse shaft at the other end. With little doubt, the crosshead and slidebars were a contribution of William Symington, the Scots pioneer of steam navigation (1763–1831).

Not only is the actual performance of Trevithick's locomotive on record; so is her fuel consumption. Two hundredweight of coal sufficed on the famous trial run.

Did Richard Trevithick press home this advantage with a rich patron who had backed his engine with such a princely wager?

Well he might have done, but the wonder was a thing of a few months only. For the first time, but not for the last, it was seen how an iron locomotive smashed to pieces the flanged cast-iron plates which formed the early rails. A sufficiently substantial wooden way, even, would have answered better.

Yet Richard Trevithick—"Captain Dick" as his Cornish friends called him—had

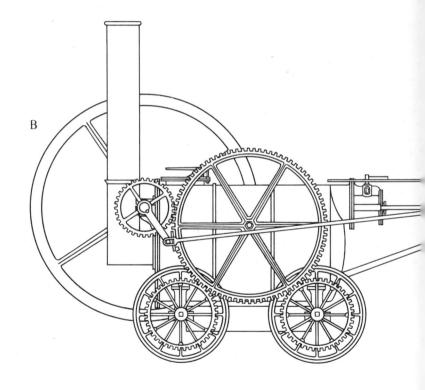

A   *Richard Trevithick, 1771-1833. A truly original inventor, by 1801 he had produced the first high-pressure stationary steam engines and in 1804 he built the first steam locomotive to run on rails. It was successfully tested with a heavy train of coal wagons on the Penydarren*

Tramroad, Merthyr Tydfil, Wales, on February 21, 1804. Despite his greatness as an inventor, he died in poverty.

B   *Trevithick's* Black Billy *was in use in the collieries of Northumberland, England, for many years.*

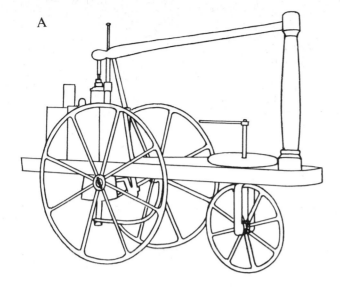

A

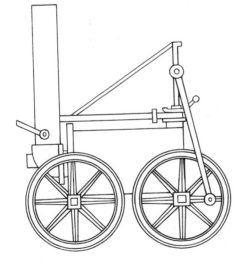

B

made a contribution to technological history anticipating, in magnitude, the first flights of the Wright Brothers in the United States, ninety-nine years after. Here and there an odd Trevithick locomotive cropped up. There was one, locally known as *Black Billy,* in the Northumbrian coalfields of North-Eastern England, which seems to have been an unfortunate venture. It was doubtless seen there by George Stephenson and other torch-bearers of steam locomotion.

In London again, Trevithick showed yet another steam locomotive he had built, called *Catch-me-who-can,* on a circular track in the northern suburbs of that time (1808) near the present Euston Road. Round the circle was a high fence, to guard the thing against becoming a free show. The curious were admitted at a shilling a head, which covered a ride for the more adventurous ones in an adapted carriage drawn by the little locomotive. The latter appears, from an old drawing, to have been smaller than the Penydarren engine, without the big flywheel and complex gears; a sort of mechanical horse on rails. The outfit was indeed a sort of circus, but be it remembered that the visitors were truly the first fare-paying passengers ever to have been hauled on the rail by any sort of locomotive.

There was no high-powered advertising in those days; the newspapers were scornfully indifferent. Before long, there was a derailment. It does not seem to have been serious, with anybody badly hurt, or we should have heard more of it from people who detested the mere existence of any sort of engine. But it was enough for the ingenious inventor once more to lose interest. Very possibly he was too hard-up to repair the damage. He was often so.

Thus the true father of the powered railway train passes out of its history. Yet not only is that to be claimed for him. He was the father of all mechanical land transport, for his steam road carriage of 1802, unlike Cugnot's courageous but quite unmanageable machine, was the first of its kind to carry people on a real journey.

A *Murdoch's steam carriage, 1784. William Murdoch was an apprentice of James Watt, who wrote of him "I fear his amazing genius will drive him too far". Unfortunately, he did not continue with his experiments.*

B Catch-me-who-can *was exhibited by Trevithick and his* *partner near Euston Square, London between July and September, 1808 in an attempt to attract financial backing. The engine weighed 8 tons and ran at 12 m.p.h. round a circular track. Unfortunately, it was regarded more as an entertaining toy than as a worthwhile investment.*

Chapter 2 THE MOTIVE REVOLUTION

So far we have seen the coming of the three essentials; firstly, the principle of the guided vehicle going back to remote times; then the industrial use of vehicles on raised rails, which certainly was known at the end of the Middle Ages; and thirdly the dawn of the powered vehicle, which preceded by one year the defeat of Napoleonic sea-power off Cape Trafalgar. Indeed, the Napoleonic phase of Western politics just about coincides with the first rise of industrial mechanism and the application of the engine to transport.

One should remark that the steam ship and the locomotive appeared *almost* simultaneously, but owing to the confined dimensions imposed by conditions of land movement, the steam ship made the more rapid start, just as the stationary steam engine had been in advance of both. Regarding a locomotive of the late eighteen-twenties, and then a mill engine of the same time, we find the latter almost "modern" by comparison. There are many "almosts" in this, as in many other phases of mechanical history.

In 1804, the year in which Trevithick had produced the world's first railway locomotive of any sort, Oliver Evans in the United States made America's first locomotive vehicle which, though it had no connection with railroads, strangely anticipated the amphibious motor vehicles which were to serve military purposes nearly a century-and-a-half later. Evans was a gifted and ingenious character who significantly plied the trades of both boatbuilder and blacksmith in Philadelphia, Pennsylvania. There he built a remarkable punt-like craft which he named *Oructor Amphibolis*. Not for him the quite skittish nomenclature of his contemporary Trevithick! In America, however, the machine was more generally remembered as "Evans' Scow". In the big punt he mounted a small steam beam-engine, geared to a little paddle-wheel astern. But to get it down to the Schuylkill River, Evans mounted his boat on four large iron wheels and improvised a form of belt drive to the after axle. Thus equipped, the machine majestically waddled down Walnut Street to the riverside and took the water like a gigantic mechanical duck. That done, it was no longer a locomotive but a craft, but thus America took her honourable place with the pioneering nations of mechanical locomotion.

The trouble with the incipient steam railroad at that time was not so much in the infantile ailments of the locomotive as in the hopeless inadequacy of the existing tracks. Iron plateways were really even worse than the ancient wooden baulk road when it came to supporting a heavy engine and receiving the shocks it gave when in motion. It is not surprising, therefore, that the railway seemed for a while to develop more than the locomotive.

As we have seen, in certain parts of Europe, and certainly in England, mineral railways with horse traction were well established. One needs special mention here, for we shall hear about it again in a rather important connection. It was the Middleton Colliery Railway near the rising industrial city of Leeds in the North of England. Its initial claim on history is that, although it was an ancillary undertaking and not a public railway, it was the first line ever to have been built under an Act of Parliament (June 9, 1758, exactly twenty-three years before the birth of George Stephenson).

Two more of these pre-steam lines must be mentioned. At the beginning of the century, England was much troubled by the great Napoleon's Continental System, and railroads were being considered for by-passing the Straits of Dover. On May 21, 1801, the Surrey Iron Railway was incorporated by the British Parliament, and it was opened from wharfs on the Thames at Wandsworth to Croydon in the South of England on July 26, 1803. This was *the world's first public railway*. It had double track for continuous traffic in both directions; it was laid with flanged iron plates spiked to stone blocks; its traffic was in freight and minerals, and the trains were drawn by horses. Its traffic continued until the coming of modern steam railways, which partly followed its course.

This scene shows the Stephensons working on the Northumbrian *shortly before the opening of the Liverpool and Manchester Railway. Robert is firing while his father is oiling. The top hat was regarded as appropriate dress for such work. After a drawing by Alexander Nasmyth.*

An extension called the Croydon, Merstham and Godstone Railway, incorporated in March, 1803, was opened on July 24, 1805. Parts of its course have long been concurrent with the main line from London to the English South Coast, which, electrified since 1933, has long had one of the highest train frequencies in the world apart from underground lines in big cities.

Meanwhile, on June 29, 1804, there was incorporated the Oystermouth Railway Company which opened its line along the coast from Swansea in South Wales in the spring of 1806, though the precise date is not known. This was *the first public railway to carry fare-paying passengers,* who rode in single horse-drawn cars. To later notions it was a tramway rather than a railway, and it went on using horse traction for many years. (Steam was introduced in 1877; electric cars in 1929, and the line was at last closed in favour of buses in 1960.)

COLLIERY LOCOMOTIVES

So we come to the first commercial use of steam power on railways, and it brings us back to that old-established Middleton Railway in Yorkshire. It brings us also to a very famous partnership in design, the more remarkable in that at that time, pioneering mechanical engineers usually went alone, as Trevithick, Watt and Newcomen had done.

In spite of the obvious workability of Trevithick's locomotives—apart from their distressing habit of smashing up light iron rails—there was a strong school of thought that for practical purposes, traction through the adhesion of a smooth wheel upon a smooth rail never would succeed. People believed in cog-wheels, which could not slip, and since the oldest example of mechanical engineering known to most was clock-work, that is scarcely surprising. Surely, if one put a Trevithick-type engine, however much improved in power and reliability, to hauling really heavy loads simply by its adhesion to a smooth surface, it would slip hopelessly!

Now in those early eighteen-hundreds, one of the most formidable minds in the improvement of steam engines was Matthew Murray, whose name makes his Scots descent patently obvious. Only a Northern Englishman could have had a name like John Blenkinsop. Murray had invented the short D-shaped slide valve in 1806, greatly improving admission and exhaust events. Blenkinsop's contribution was propulsion by rack and pinion. The rack consisted of a closely regular set of teeth or lugs on the outside of the left-hand rail, and with these engaged a large cog which was the engine's driving wheel.

Our representation of the Murray-Blenkinsop locomotive (p. 33) is made from a beautiful model in London's Science Museum, South Kensington. It is fairly self-explanatory, but the following points should be noted. The boiler, with a central furnace leading to a flue at the opposite end, had the two cylinders mounted vertically in the top of its shell. Power was transmitted through transverse cross-head beams to spur wheels both driving the main pinion axle. The exhaust led not to the chimney, as in Trevithick's first locomotive, but to an outlet between the cylinders. Possibilities of making the exhaust produce draught in the firebox had not occurred to Murray. But the open exhaust must have created abominable din, especially for people who had not been previously accustomed to engines moving about the country. Hence the large wooden silencer which occurs on the model and in the present drawing. Just when this was fitted cannot be accurately recorded; it is lacking in many of the old drawings.

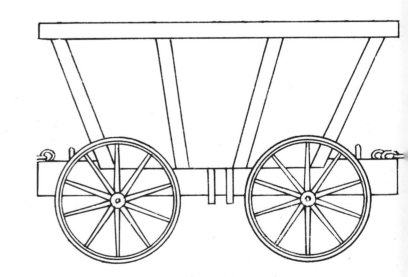

Construction of the first Murray-Blenkinsop locomotive probably began during 1811, and it was certainly in regular traffic at Middleton in 1812, the year in which, be it added, James Fenton produced the spring-loaded safety-valve, a very desirable and important accessory which, however, did not prevent boilers from bursting now and then, usually because of the unsystematic inspection tolerated in early days.

Steam traction is recorded as having been inaugurated on August 12, 1812 with two locomotives named *Salamanca* and *Prince Regent.* This as suggested, was the world's first commercial use of steam haulage by locomotives on rails. Two more locomotives were added in the following year; *Lord Wellington* on August 4 and *Marquis Wellington* on November 23. The names of the engines reflect European power politics of the time, apart from the tribute to His Rather Rascally Royal Highness who later became George IV of the United Kingdom. The general, it will be noted, was not yet a duke, but was rising rapidly in aristocratic status. He had won at Salamanca, but not yet at Waterloo!

Matthew Murray, 1765–1826. He collaborated with John Blenkinsop in the building of the rack locomotives for the Middleton Colliery.

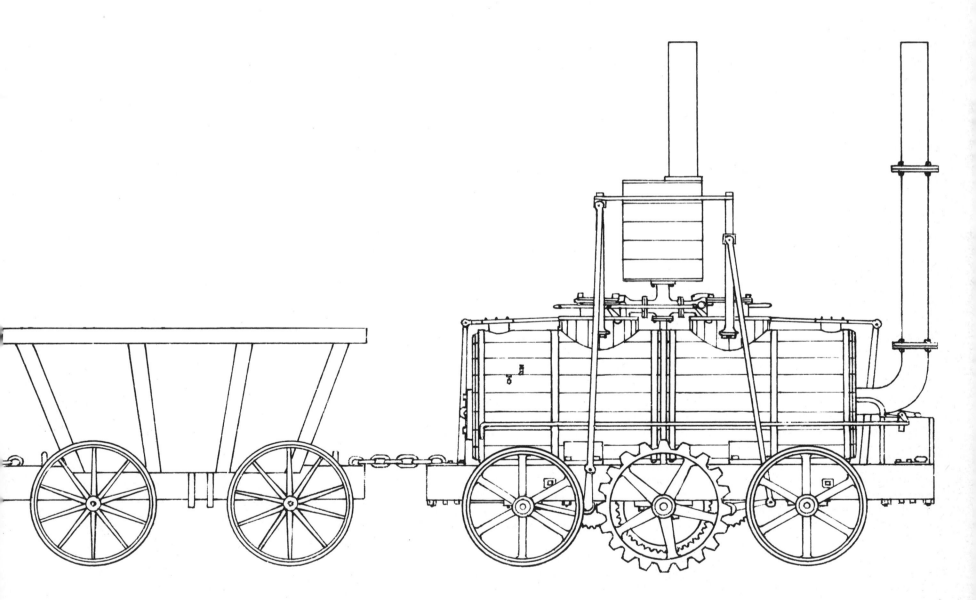

This rack-rail locomotive hauled coal from the Middleton Colliery to Leeds in the North of England, 1812.

Rack-and-pinion propulsion was to continue on the Middleton Railway until 1835, by which time steam lines of orthodox sort were entirely established and appearing all over Europe and in many parts of North America. The principle then became dormant until it was revived, in less primitive form for steep-grade mountain railways, as on Mount Washington in the United States and very soon after on the Rigi in Switzerland.

The Middleton trains were scarcely rapid things. The famous English engineer David Joy saw one in infancy. Having been told that it would come by "like a flash of lightning", the little boy was somewhat disappointed that "it only came lumbering on like a cart".

Still in England, our scene shifts now from Yorkshire to the real North-East, to that Northumbria which once was a kingdom in its own right, and more recently had become the stage for railway development. Wylam Colliery, near Newcastle, had had a wooden railway for many years. Beside it, George Stephenson had been born. But it was not he, but a partnership again, that brought locomotives to Wylam. In spite of Blenkinsop's rack-and-pinion, faith in the smooth wheel on the smooth rail did not die. After all, Trevithick had shown that locomotives *could* run by adhesion. William Hedley at Wylam was of like persuasion, and for him in 1813, Christopher Blackett built some very famous old locomotives. No high-sounding names from the Napoleonic wars here! The local people called them *Puffing Billy* and *Wylam Dilly,* and the names stuck. There was a third, nearly forgotten one, named *Lady Mary.*

The first two engines are still in existence, treasured relics in London and Edinburgh. That in London is generally assumed to be "Billy" while the one in Scotland is "Dilly". There is a splendid replica of the former in Munich, built many years later by the Bavarian State Railway Works. It must be said straight-away that these relics do not show the engines in their original condition. As built, they had flangeless wheels and ran on flanged cast-iron rails which they inevitably smashed to pieces, as Trevithick's engines had done before.

To distribute the weight more easily (even empty, each engine weighed about seven tons) new frames were made, giving the engines eight wheels instead of four, the axles being grouped in pairs of supplementary frames resembling bogies, though flexibility on curves was not the object in this case.

In later years both engines were altered back to the original two-axle arrangement, but with flanged iron wheels to run on iron edge-rails. It was not until 1820 (October 23) that a patent was granted to John Birkinshaw of Bedlington Iron Works, in North-Eastern England, for the making of rolled malleable iron rails. Only then did the rail-road—as we understand the term, meaning a complex system of heavy transportation at reasonably high speeds—become possible. The term "railroad", indeed, is the old English word for such a system, distinguishing it from the much lighter, and more primitive "railway". Unfortunately, it was dropped in British usage though America most happily perpetuated this splendid, sonorous word.

To revert to "Billy" and "Dilly". They had boilers of wrought iron plates, each containing furnace and return flue so that firedoor and chimney were at the same end, as in the original Trevithick type. (Generations of museum cats in London's Science Museum at South Kensington have had their kittens in *Puffing Billy*'s inaccessible stomach!) The cylinders were vertical, as in Matthew Murray's Middleton engines, but they were outside, a progressive step long ignored by other pioneer designers. They exhausted into the chimney. Transmission was by beams and spur-wheels, and the valve gear was overhead. A four-wheel tender carried coal and water.

What a distant world was that of 1813! Great Britain and the United States were having a second, and futile, war. Napoleon still straddled much of Europe, but had lost the adoration of Beethoven, who had yet to compose his Ninth Symphony. Up in the extreme North of England, *Puffing Billy* was moving coal, except when derailed, which was not seldom.

At that same time George Stephenson, son of a colliery fireman, was Enginewright at Killingworth Colliery, while the smith at Wylam, Stephenson's birthplace, was Timothy Hackworth, of whom also much more was to be heard. Stephenson was self-educated in a very hard world, that of poverty. Hackworth was an intellectual mechanic of the period, a worker for six long days and a lay preacher on Sundays.

Stephenson moved into locomotive work. Not an entirely original inventor, he was a great improver, a perseverer, and a shrewd business man; which qualities made him one of the historic immortals of applied technology. In his early locomotives he copied Murray's arrangement of boiler and overhead cylinders with their motion and gear, but

A curiosity is shown here; one believes for the first time since it was published in the 1827 edition of Thomas Tredgold's The Steam Engine. *Modestly presented as a "steam carriage", the design seems to have been Tredgold's own, and in it he disregarded nearly every conventional feature of the period except Murray's top-embedded cylinders which Stephenson had also used. There was what Tredgold called a "fireplace" at each end, and the main heating surface was provided by an internal hot-water-and-steam drum surrounded by flue, as in the Smithies boiler for model steam locomotives nearly a century after. The central chimney with two-way cowling is amusing. More interesting is the hopper feed to each "fireplace", which, at least in appearance, suggests the automatic Krauss-Helmholtz bunker on certain very small Bavarian locomotives some eighty years later. We present the design now for its quaintness and extreme rarity. And did it go? One doubts that it could have done so, or even that it was ever made unless as a small model.*

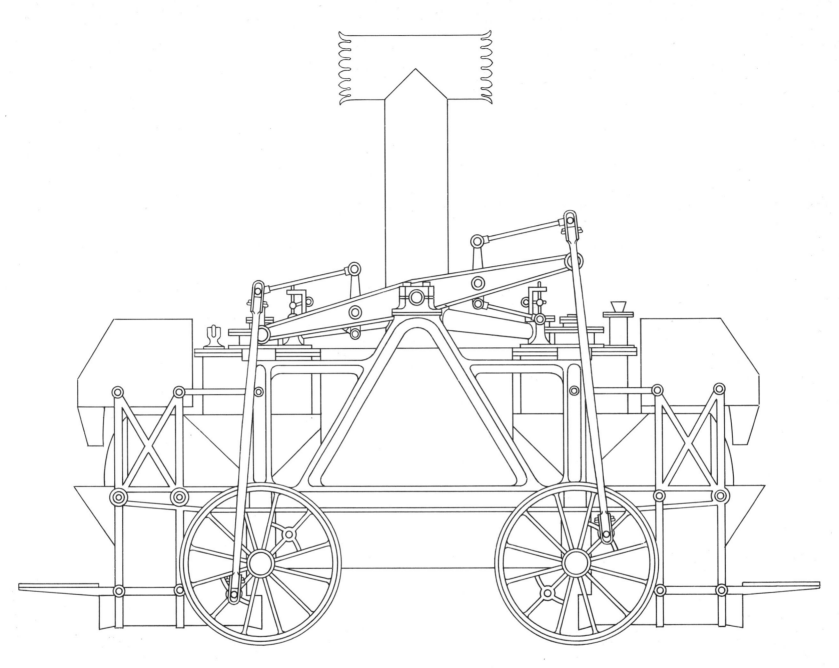

he would have nothing to do with rack-and-pinion propulsion. It was adhesion from the first. In 1814 he built for Killingworth Colliery *My Lord* (named for the proprietor, Lord Ravensworth) whose two cylinders drove the two axles through gears and countershafts. Next year he discarded this arrangement for direct drive, with the axles coupled by chain and sprockets, and in 1816 he was using a valve gear worked by loose excentric. The chain coupling was apt to break and was very noisy. It was fairly soon to be succeeded by coupling the wheels by side rods and cranks, which would persist throughout the history of the orthodox steam locomotive and in the design of earlier electric locomotives also.

Various Stephenson locomotives were built for industrial lines in the English North-East over the next ten years, though cable-haulage with stationary engines came into considerable use, and was indeed essential on any appreciable gradient. George Stephenson had been given charge of such an engine when he married, as far back as 1802 when he was twenty-one. Two very old Stephensonian locomotives lasted in service for an immense time, one for some eighty years, and have survived, one at Newcastle and the longest-lasting, from Hetton Colliery, at York.

Suspension was an important matter, especially with the uneven tracks of the time. All wheels had to be sprung and there was a short phase in which the springs consisted of plungers contained by cylindrical "legs" in the bottom of the boiler shell, open to the water space, so that the actual boiler pressure provided the necessary resilience. When not in steam, the engine sat down on its axles. It was an ingenious but fallible arrangement.

Stephenson of course was not alone. Hackworth, as suggested, was in the running, with honest, dogged, and sometimes ingenious work. Some others designed, and even built, locomotives of more fantastic sort. Perhaps the most absurd was Brunton's, which rested on two free axles and was expected to push itself and its load along by mechanical legs in the rear. It did succeed in exploding its own boiler, with bloody results for some people.

That term "steam carriage" reminds us that in these years there was intense interest in steam propulsion, *especially for passengers*, on ordinary main roads; indeed the steam motor-car very nearly arrived with the train. It is one of the tragedies of mechanical history that the two did not develop simultaneously on a proper commercial scale. One of the steam carriage pioneers, Sir Goldsworthy Gurney, must be mentioned in our present connection. In 1826 he produced three most important inventions; a firebox fusible plug which, by melting, flooded the furnace with steam if the boiler water-level fell dangerously; a valve gear designed to use steam expansively instead of by a primitive sequence of admission and exhaust; and a multiple-jet blast-pipe to give even draught from the engine exhaust turned into the chimney.

THE STOCKTON AND DARLINGTON RAILWAY

George Stephenson was now in his forties. His son Robert was grown up, and through some toil and privation had been given the advanced technical education his father had never enjoyed. The inevitable European depression after the Napoleonic Wars was righting itself in heavy industrial expansion; in England, France; even in feudal Germany and impoverished Scotland. The last-named had tried steam on its Kilmarnock and Troon Railway as far back as 1817, with the then usual results; cast-iron rails smashed to atoms and the engine discarded as a destructive machine. The Germans had tried, and even built for themselves in the Royal Foundry, Berlin, two Murray-Blenkinsop type of rack-rail locomotive, with tragi-comic results.

But, as noted, Birkinshaw's rolled iron rails had arrived, and were to work a great magic. The River Tees was the natural outlet of the Durham coalfield in the English North East. Between Darlington inland, and Stockton on Tees, there was need for a railway on a more ambitious scale than before. The great Quaker family of Pease was behind the enterprise. The Peases consulted George Stephenson, who was now locally famous. The Stockton and Darlington Railway was incorporated in 1821. Its Act of Incorporation allowed for its working by "men, horses or otherwise". Stephenson suggested (probably with some force, being himself) that "otherwise" could and ought to mean "by steam locomotion". Edward Pease was cautious, as Quaker people are, with much silent comment after their manner, but he was a man of his word, after their kind. The end of it was that the Stephensons, father and son now, produced the first steam locomotive to work public traffic regularly on a company-owned right of way.

(*above*) *Brandreth's Cyclopede of 1829, drawn after the plan preserved in the Science Museum, London. It was never taken really seriously — except by its inventor.*

(*below*) *Andraud and Tessié du Motay were experimenting with this "compressed air" engine during the earliest years of the locomotive in France.*

We show here the quaint experiment of Colonel John Stevens, who had been working in vain for years to implant the railroad idea on the American awareness at a time when, as in England, canal construction was at its height. The Colonel produced in 1825 a little rack-rail locomotive which was demonstrated on a circular track. It may be regarded as a scientific toy, but it was America's first railway locomotive. Colonel Stevens did not labour in vain, though. One may laugh at his essay in mechanical engineering (if one is a Philistine) but he was to be the first President of the Camden and Amboy Railroad which received its charter in 1830. His vision materialized!

It will be seen that *Locomotion* was still of the primeval Stephenson type, with her cylinders and "works" on top, the former driving cranks set at ninety degrees front and rear on each side. Coupling rods were arranged by means of a return crank on each driving crankpin on the rear wheels, the front bearings of the rods being of course coincident with those of the forward connecting rods. The boiler, lagged with wooden strips over its upper portion both to retain heat and to spare the enginemen, had the old medial and furnace-and-flue arrangement, with no smokebox. The wheel centres were built up of perforated iron segments with iron tyres shrunk on. The tender was simple. On a frame resembling that of the traditional English *chaldron* coal wagons it supported a cistern for the feedwater, with space for fuel below.

Late in 1824, the Stephensons' *Locomotion* was under construction in their Forth Street workshops at Newcastle-upon-Tyne. She was ready in the following year, but ere the railway was ready for opening, the young Robert Stephenson was far away on a mining survey in northern South America. (There, incidentally, he was to find the impoverished Richard Trevithick, and to help him home.) The final irony may be added here; for Trevithick was to die in England, poor and distressed in 1833, having often petitioned the British Government for some sort of civil pension, which was always refused. Robert Stephenson (and again without Government assistance) was to become the first millionaire engineer (sterling, in gold) and, when he died at the age of fifty-six, he was buried with the kings and the great soldiers in Westminster Abbey. Quaint!

Now, there was another thing about this Stockton and Darlington Railway; it was to take passengers as well as goods traffic. With this in view a solitary passenger coach was built and included in the make-up when the inaugural train, headed by *Locomotion*, ran over the line on September 27, 1825. Its exact form cannot be reproduced. For many years there was current a drawing of a sort of shed-on-wheels, but it seems to have been an ingenious adaptation of the road coach of the period, judged by J. R. Brown's beautiful pencil drawing, recently discovered and believed to have been made at the time.

It was marshalled in the middle of a train of coal wagons, with the important personages sitting in it while as many as could climb on to the wagons did so. Crowds had come to see the prodigy, some at least because they thought *Locomotion* would explode and thus give them a nice kick. But all went off without a hitch. All the same, in regular traffic, for some time passengers were conveyed by horse-drawn rail coach in between the steam coal trains. People were still rather nervous about riding behind a ferocious, fire-breathing machine which, they had been credibly told, could blow both itself and them to bits if it suffered from mechanical indigestion.

Still, the thing was done. The steam railroad, which previously had been regarded as a sort of industrial machinery, as we today regard mining equipment and telpherage, was at last present as a means of mechanical public conveyance. It was not an entirely happy occasion. George Stephenson was still without his son Robert, who had done so much with him in the improvement of the engine. Edward Pease, the faithful backer and sponsor, had just lost a son, and was full of the sorrow that he had been trained never to show. Still the majority of the British aristocracy had little awareness of what was going on, though later it was to improve their fortunes quite considerably.

The revolution (and, thinking of France, they did not quite recognize the term in this connection) had really begun.

Revolution indeed was a word conveying different meanings to different people. To the French it meant Reform. To the Americans it meant Glorious Independence. To the English landed aristocracy it meant social upheaval that none of them wanted; and, at worst, all the excesses of the French Terror under Robespierre. They wished no revolution, mechanical or political, and believed that the one would lead to the other. Where railways might adventure out into the country from the industrial districts, wherein they might be tolerated as a necessary evil, all schemes were fiercely opposed, both by political pressure and by actual violence against parties of surveyors. The great northern commercial and industrial families, on what was then the political Left, were of course greatly in favour of this magnificent invention, and that is how, during the eighteen-twenties and early 'thirties the thing became a party issue in Parliament.

In the early days of the railway signalling was done manually using either flags or semaphore.

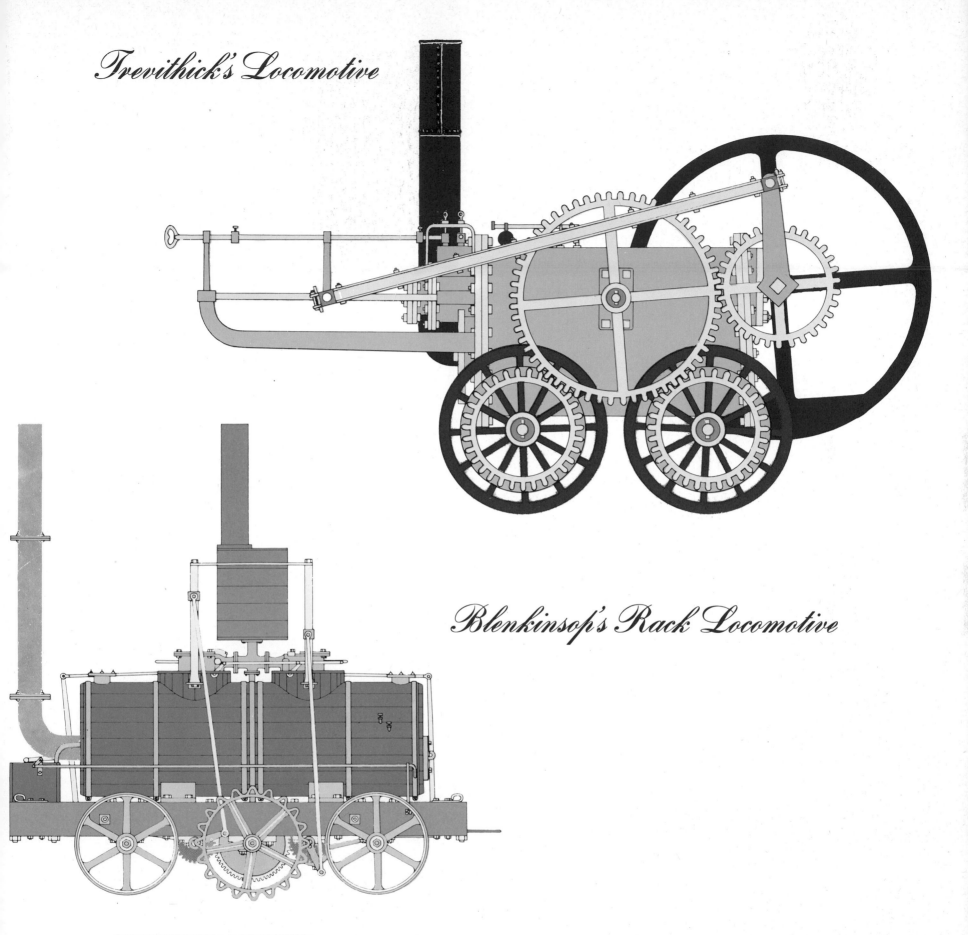

Trevithick's Locomotive

Blenkinsop's Rack Locomotive

TREVITHICK'S LOCOMOTIVE WAS THE FIRST STEAM LOCOMOTIVE ENGINE EVER RUN ON RAILS. IT WAS DESIGNED AND BUILT BY RICHARD TREVITHICK IN 1803–1804.

BLENKINSOP'S RACK LOCOMOTIVE WAS DESIGNED AND BUILT BY JOHN BLENKINSOP AND MATTHEW MURRAY. THE FIRST LOCOMOTIVE TO BE COMMERCIALLY USED.

Stourbridge Lion

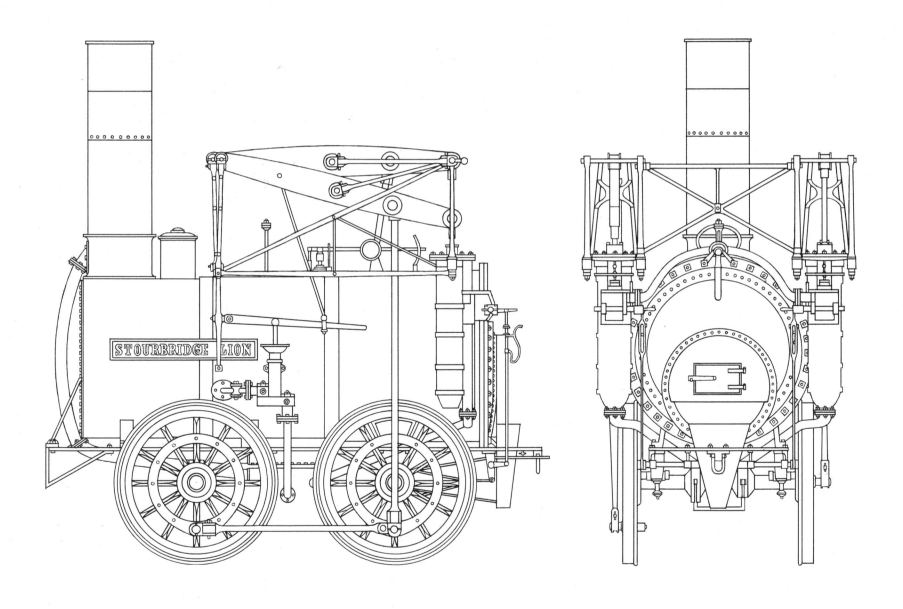

THE STOURBRIDGE LION WAS ORDERED FROM THE ENGLISH FIRM OF FOSTER, RASTRICK & COMPANY FOR THE DELAWARE AND HUDSON CANAL COMPANY IN 1829. IT WAS THE FIRST ACTUAL LOCOMOTIVE TO RUN IN AMERICA.

ROBERT STEPHENSON BUILT THE LANCASHIRE WITCH IN 1828 FOR THE BOLTON & LEIGH RAILWAY, ENGLAND. TWO OUTSIDE CYLINDERS DROVE THE FRONT WHEELS, BOTH AXLES WERE MOUNTED ON SPRINGS.

Seguin's Engine

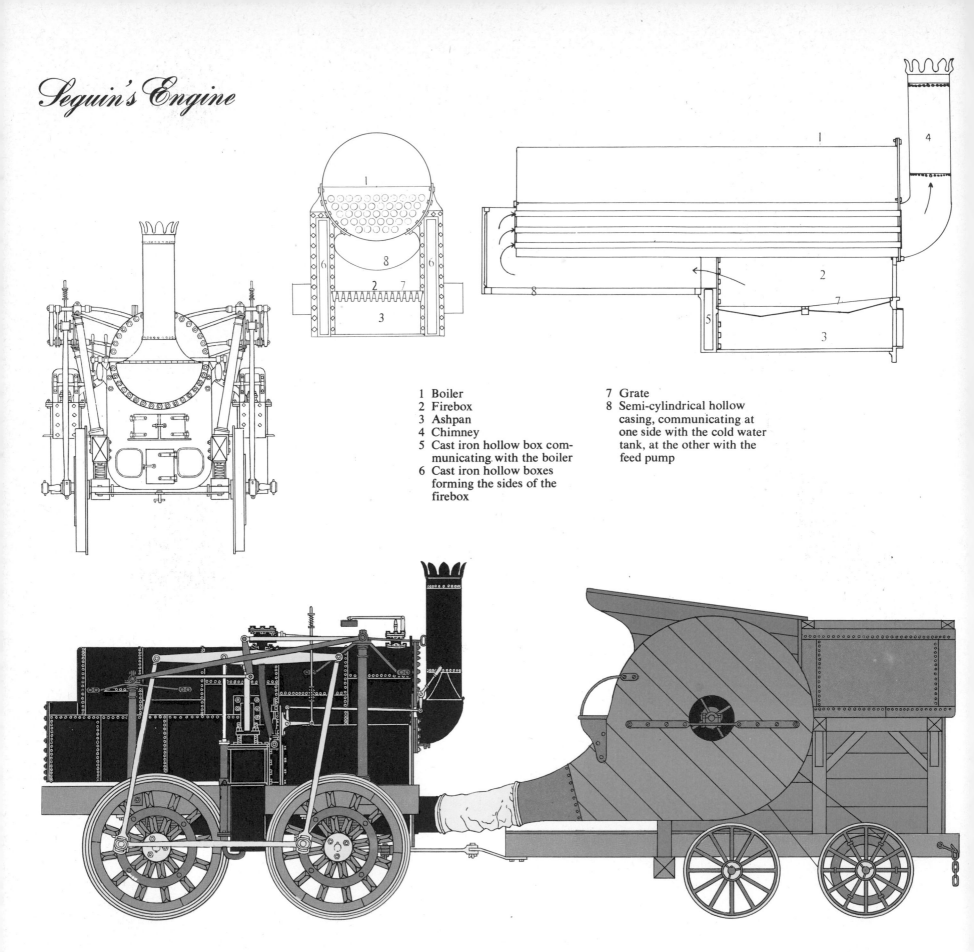

1 Boiler
2 Firebox
3 Ashpan
4 Chimney
5 Cast iron hollow box communicating with the boiler
6 Cast iron hollow boxes forming the sides of the firebox

7 Grate
8 Semi-cylindrical hollow casing, communicating at one side with the cold water tank, at the other with the feed pump

THE FRENCHMAN, MARC SEGUIN, BUILT THIS ENGINE FOR THE ST. ETIENNE–LYONS RAILWAY IN 1829. IT HAD A MULTITUBULAR BOILER WHICH WAS MUCH MORE EFFICIENT THAN THE OLD SINGLE-FLUE OR RETURN-FLUE TYPE.

PUFFING BILLY WAS DESIGNED AND BUILT BY CHRISTOPHER BLACKETT, THE PROPRIETOR OF WYLAM COLLIERY IN ENGLAND, AND WILLIAM HEDLEY, IN 1814.

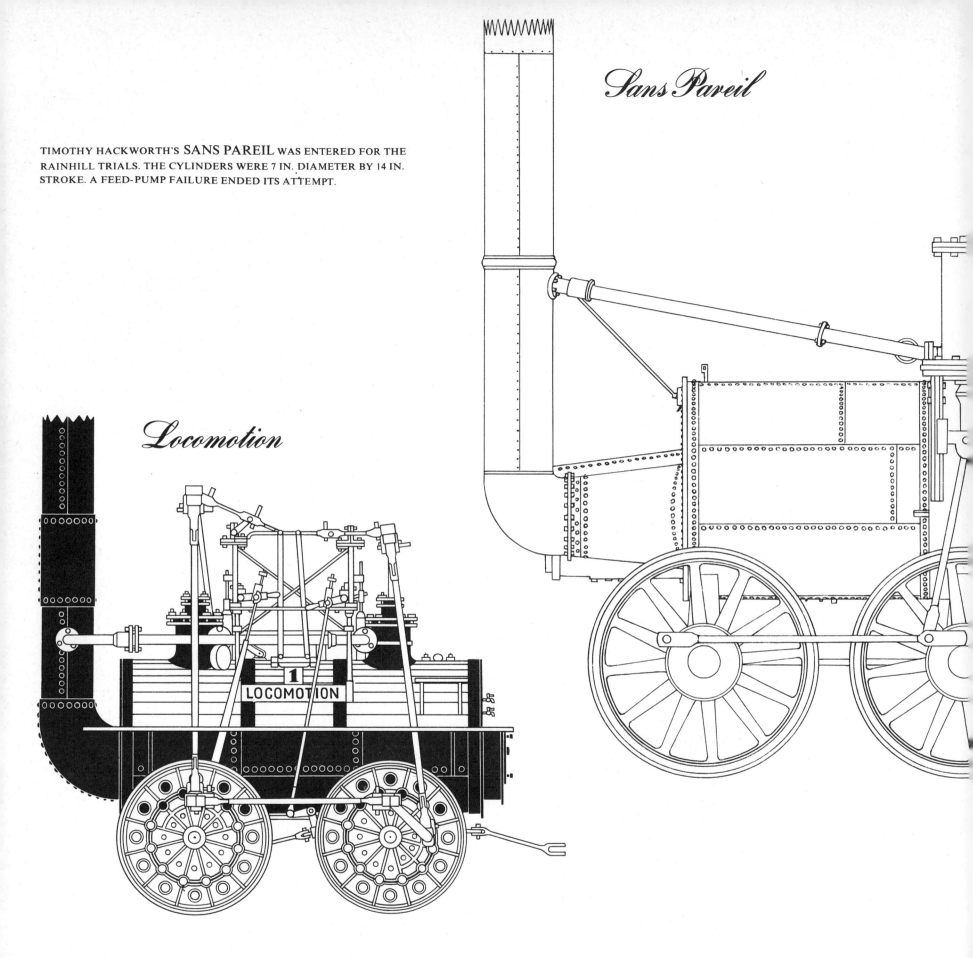

Sans Pareil

TIMOTHY HACKWORTH'S SANS PAREIL WAS ENTERED FOR THE
RAINHILL TRIALS. THE CYLINDERS WERE 7 IN. DIAMETER BY 14 IN.
STROKE. A FEED-PUMP FAILURE ENDED ITS ATTEMPT.

Locomotion

GEORGE STEPHENSON'S LOCOMOTION WAS BUILT FOR THE STOCKTON AND DARLINGTON
RAILWAY IN 1825.

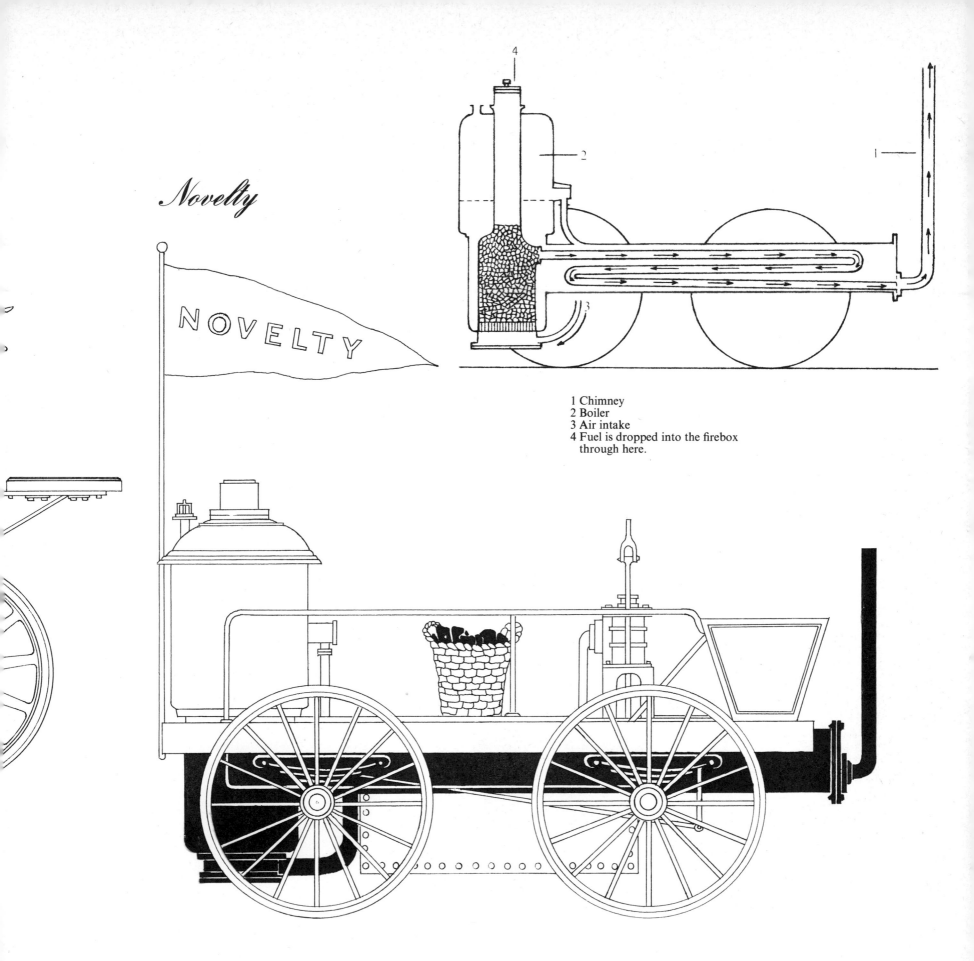

Novelty

NOVELTY

1 Chimney
2 Boiler
3 Air intake
4 Fuel is dropped into the firebox
   through here.

ERICSSON AND BRAITHWAITE'S NOVELTY WAS ONE OF THE ENTRANTS FOR THE RAINHILL TRIALS. IT WAS THE POPULAR FAVOURITE ON ACCOUNT OF ITS ELEGANT APPEARANCE AND SPEED.

Rocket

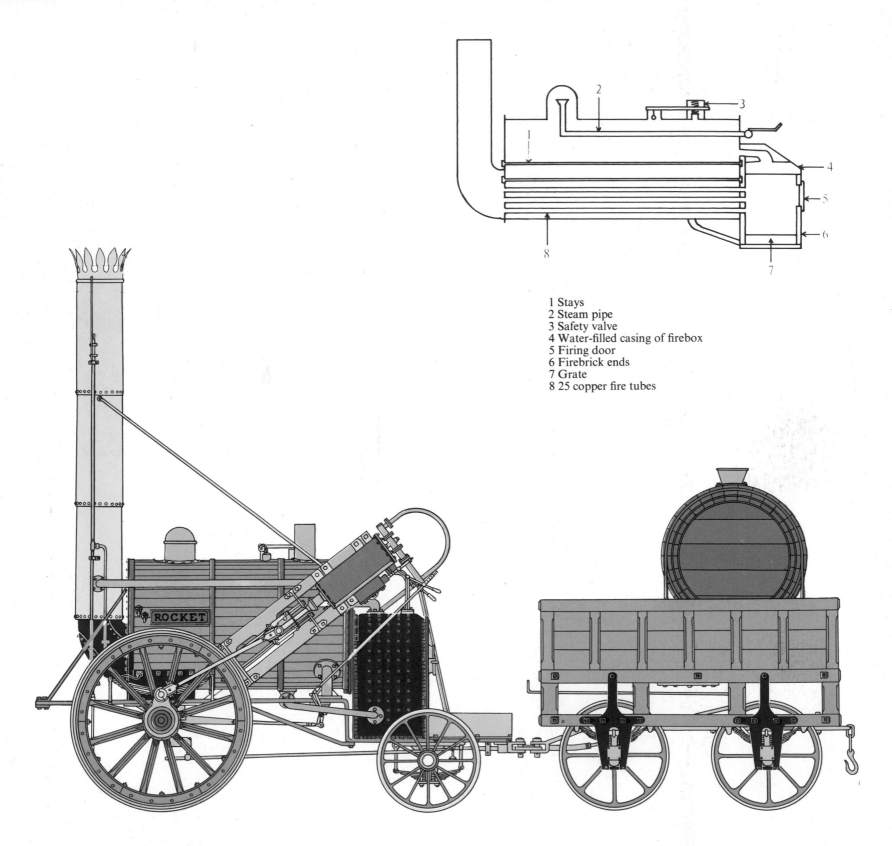

1 Stays
2 Steam pipe
3 Safety valve
4 Water-filled casing of firebox
5 Firing door
6 Firebrick ends
7 Grate
8 25 copper fire tubes

THE STEPHENSONS' ROCKET WAS THE WINNER OF THE RAINHILL TRIALS. IT ALONE COMPLETED ALL THE JOURNEYS AND
FULFILLED ALL THE CONDITIONS.

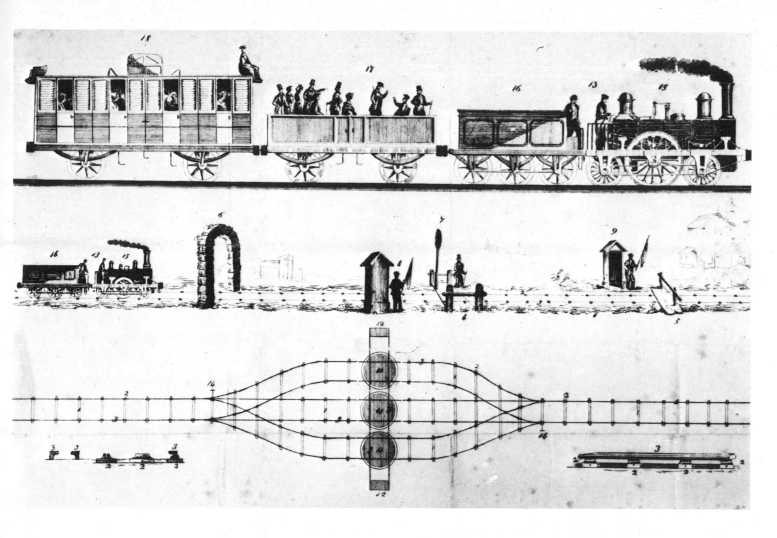

These two prints illustrate early days on the railway in Italy. Courtesy of Civica Raccolta di Stampe Bertarelli, Milano.

EARLY DESIGNS

Visionary Englishmen like Thomas Gray and William James foresaw, and backed even to bankruptcy, a national railway network with steam traction. But ere that could happen, not only must Government be influenced, great improvements were still necessary in motive power itself, before it could be adequate for scheduled passenger and freight movements. At this stage, George Stephenson was passing rather out of the locomotive picture into that of Civil Engineering. In the late 'twenties he was busy with the survey and construction of a real trunk railroad between cities, the historic Liverpool and Manchester Railway. Robert Stephenson was home again (with the tragic Trevithick) but now two very important men enter our stage.

One was the sober-sided Timothy Hackworth, who had taken charge of the Stockton and Darlington Railway's engine-works at Shildon. The other was Marc Séguin in France. Hackworth was the more practical and Séguin the more academic, as one might have expected with a puritan Englishman and an intellectual Frenchman. Let us take Hackworth first.

Most important of his work at this time was the locomotive *Royal George*, which he built for the Stockton and Darlington Railway in 1827. Its origin was odd. Previously, a man named Robert Wilson of Gateshead in the same county had built an engine with a long boiler and four cylinders, two to each axle. Desire outran performance, though the idea was bold. The Stockton and Darlington company bought the engine simply for the sake of its large return-flue boiler. This Hackworth mounted on a six-wheel frame with two vertical cylinders high up, driving the same cranks as those which served the side coupling rods. He had previously made a model to see how this six-coupled, direct-drive arrangement answered. The model had worked well. So did the *Royal George*. Though slow, she was a heavy puller such as none had known before, admirable for Durham coal traffic. In the formulae of much later years, her wheel arrangement was describable as 0-6-0 (Anglo-American), 0-3-0 (French) or C (German, in which an alphabetical sequence was and still is used for counting powered axles).

Railways for coal haulage came to Central France at this time. Beaunier's horse railway from St. Etienne to Andrézieux had come in May, 1827, and in 1829 trials were being made with steam on the Givors to Rive-de-Gier section of the St. Etienne and Lyons Railway. For this, Marc Séguin had already obtained some rather odd engines from the Stephensons, but in 1828 he patented a multitubular (fire-tube) boiler which he had incorporated in a locomotive late in the following year. Models have survived. It was altogether a more advanced boiler than anything in previous Stephenson or Hackworth practice. The draught arrangements, however, were clumsy, consisting of immense rotary fans mounted on a tender and feeding air to the furnace through bellows-like leather pipes.

Marc Séguin, unlike his British contemporaries, was rather a practical scientist than an advanced enginewright. Ingenuity ran in the family. Joseph and Etienne Montgolfier, the pioneers of ballooning and makers of the first airborne craft, were his uncles. The idea he had incorporated, that of providing heating surface by a large number of small flues passing through the water in the boiler, had been patented by James Neville in England, in March, 1826. Marc Séguin and his brother were engaged in many notable projects, including early steam navigation on the Rhône.

Before going on to its next applications we must notice some other landmarks. The first railway in the old Austro-Hungarian Empire, generally called Linz-Budweis, was interesting in that from the beginning it was a passenger line, but only horse traction was used when its first section was opened from Budweis (Ceské Budejovice) to Trojanov in what is now Czecho-Slovakia, on September 7, 1827. It was chiefly the work of Franz Zola, father of the Emile Zola of French literature.

The advent of steam locomotion on rails in the United States was tragi-comic; a pity, seeing how its use was to make possible the ocean-to-ocean form of the great republic. Important canals had already been built in the Eastern States, and in the summer of 1829 the Delaware and Hudson Canal Company obtained a steam locomotive from Foster, Rastrick and Company in England, for use on an auxiliary railway which it was building between Carbondale and Honesdale. The engine was named *Lion,* but since there were many *Lions* in the course of time, and in view of her English Midland origin, she is generally called the "Stourbridge Lion". She was one of four ordered by Horatio Allen of the Delaware and Hudson Company; two more from Foster Rastrick, and one,

Timothy Hackworth, the blacksmith at Wylam Colliery who helped to build Puffing Billy *in 1813, later went on to build his own engines. His* Sans Pareil *was an entry in the Rainhill Trials. Hackworth did much of the locomotive work on the Stockton and Darlington Railway and in 1827 produced the* Royal George, *the first engine with six-coupled wheels.*

of which more later, from Robert Stephenson.

Allen had been to England to see what was going on there, when he made the order. On her arrival at Honesdale, *Lion* was deemed too heavy for service. True, the road was laid with quite respectable iron rails, but people were anxious about a wooden trestle over Lackawaxen Creek. To justify his purchase, Mr. Allen drove her over the trestle and back, without any fearsome results, but the Board was not convinced, and the unfortunate engine was laid by, eventually to be broken up. The other two Rastricks and the Stephenson never reached Honesdale. Some limbo in New York claimed them.

On October 9, the railway inclines and levels of the canal were opened, but they were worked by cables and gravity. None could guess that, as well as coal, some day the Delaware and Hudson Company would be handling not only millions of tons of freight, but lifting passengers on overnight plush between New York and Montreal.

That the "Stourbridge Lion", as an engine, was quite all-right, even though by then she was slightly archaic, is suggested not only by Horatio Allen's doughty championship of her on that trestle, but by the record of an almost identical engine called *Agenoria* which never left England but worked usefully for some thirty years on the Earl of Dudley's colliery line, the Shutt End Railway, in her native West Midlands. Some bits of the *Lion* were later unearthed, and *Agenoria* has long been preserved. Horatio Allen's brave but sad adventure with the *Lion* ended his connection with the Delaware and Hudson Company. He went south to Charleston, and that was to have very important results. At the time, however, his prospects may well have seemed hazardous.

There was this difference from a similar situation in Europe. America received any new machine, if it were seen to be practical and likely to further the interests of a new and rapidly growing nation, with delighted enthusiasm. In Europe, substantially powerful classes viewed it with distrust, alarm and even dismay.

We must return awhile to England. A rather important type of locomotive was just being essayed by the Stephenson firm. It still ran on four wheels, all coupled. But it had inclined outside cylinders, instead of vertical ones whether outside or embedded in the boiler-top as in the ancient Murray form. One such was the *Lancashire Witch* built in 1828 for the freight-hauling Bolton and Leigh Railway. The boiler was still old-fashioned, though instead of a single or return flue, it had two furnace-flues side by side, leading into a common chimney. Akin to the "Witch" was the *America*, the engine which Stephensons built for the Delaware and Hudson Company, but which never got nearer to it than New York. A third was called *Invicta*, which went into service in the South of England on the Canterbury and Whitstable Railway, opened on May 3, 1830, and for which may be claimed that it was the world's first line to carry both freight and passengers entirely by steam power. But the little locomotive was a relatively feeble thing, confined to one short level section of the single-track line, stationary engines and cables doing the rest of the work.

It was between Liverpool and Manchester in the English North-West that the world was first to see a railroad as succeeding generations would understand it, with all sorts of traffic hauled by locomotives, on two separate roads for opposite directions, with real stations, proper schedules, and trains of reasonably respectable rolling-stock. Behind the enterprise was a group of rich Lancashire capitalists who later became so powerful that the business world called them simply *The Liverpool Party*.

They had a long and bitter fight. Several lines were surveyed before that of George Stephenson was adopted, with its imposing rock cutting and tunnelling in Liverpool, and its magnificent multi-arch viaduct across the Sankey Valley. Much could be written about its vicissitudes from the time of its incorporation on May 15, 1826; of landowner-trouble, of the way in which the elder Stephenson laid his solid road across Chat Moss, a moor which had been regarded from time immemorial as a bottomless bog wherein a horse and his rider could be engulfed, to vanish for ever. This, however, is a chronicle of the train, not of railroad building.

With the line at length authorised, the company showed itself suddenly shy of locomotive traction, favouring cable haulage by stationary engines. George Stephenson, who had a ferocious tongue when roused, fluent with four-letter and other words, demanded that they should recognize the ability of the conqueror of Chat Moss to provide traction. He had been building locomotives for over a decade now.

The Directors so far relented as to offer a prize of £500 sterling for a locomotive which should fulfil certain very stringent conditions as to weight, power and speed. Nor did they simply challenge Stephenson to produce such an engine. They made it an open

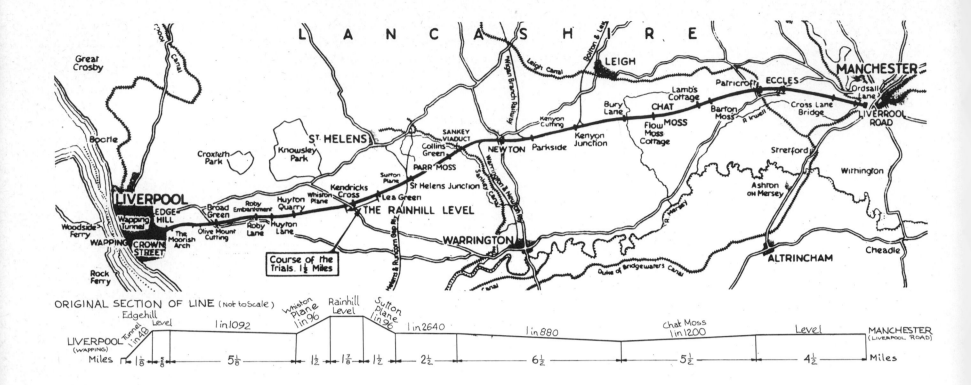

competition, and whoever produced the most satisfactory locomotive would clearly land a contract worth a fortune.

THE RAINHILL TRIALS

There were plenty of competitors, some of them, indeed, from the lunatic fringe of their profession. The serious ones were George and Robert Stephenson in partnership with Henry Booth; Timothy Hackworth on his dogged own; the ingenious Swede Captain John Ericsson in a rather unfortunate partnership with the Englishman John Braithwaite; Timothy Burstall, of Leith in Scotland, who had designed a steam road carriage (an aversion of George Stephenson, be it remarked); and Edward Bury of Liverpool.

The last-named, though later of some eminence in locomotive engineering, could not produce an engine in time for the trials, which were held on the Rainhill Level of the Liverpool and Manchester line, from October 6 to October 14, 1829.

Getting the engines from factory to Rainhill presented plenty of problems. Burstall's engine from Scotland was damaged in transit, though it is reported to have made a short run or two. It was an effete little thing with a small upright boiler between large wheels, an adaptation of its designer's steam carriage engine.

Hackworth's engine, *Sans Pareil*, was perhaps describable as a shortened, four-wheeled version of his *Royal George*. She did not strictly fulfil the conditions as to the weight allowable on two axles only, but she certainly *went*, if rather ponderously, consuming an inordinate amount of fuel. One of the conditions was that the engines *should effectively consume their own smoke*. All the entrants got round that one by firing with coke instead of coal. But the unfortunate *Sans Pareil* had bad luck apart from her astonishing appetite. She broke down on the eighth trip over the course; her water-level fell and she dropped her fusible plug, filling the firebox with steam. For what it is worth one must in fairness remark that her cylinders had been cast by Stephensons, and were not faultless.

That left Ericsson's *Novelty* and the Stephensons' *Rocket,* with the former a hot favourite.

Captain John Ericsson, sometime of the Swedish Army, was then twenty-six years old, and not yet a legendary figure. Those who liked him least regarded him as a mechanically minded mountebank, and there were to be long and bitter years before he was to achieve worldwide fame and fortune in the United States with the *Monitor* warship. He had come to London in 1826, and had met that lesser figure, John Braithwaite, who

This map and gradient profile of the Liverpool and Manchester Railway shows where the Rainhill Trials took place. The railway line was laid by George Stephenson. His magnificent viaduct across the Sankey Valley and his achievement in laying the line across the treacherous and supposedly impassable bog of Chat Moss made him famous.

in later years was to be a singularly inept engineer of the Eastern Counties Railway. The locomotive *Novelty* bore all the marks of Ericsson's genius and she was to suffer from the failings of ingenuity without practical trial. She was a four-wheeler with vertical cylinders, most beautifully designed and made, a prototype for a light locomotive which really would have been much better suited to road transport. She carried her fuel and water-supply on the main frames, the latter in a big tank below and a smaller one aft. Her weak points were in her boiler.

Now this was a very ingenious boiler. But it had serious weaknesses, as we shall see. Its main portion was vertical, with a copper casing, fired through a funnel in the top. From this, a much narrower portion went horizontally to the rear, so that the whole steam-generator was something like a T laid on one side. From the furnace, a back-and-forth flue led ultimately to a tall chimney in the rear. It was a clever way of obtaining heating surface; also the greater proportion of this was in the firebox, an important virtue as later experience was to show. It was the engine's light and very elegant appearance which chiefly endeared her to the spectators. When she skimmed along at thirty miles an hour their enthusiasm was intense. Draught was induced by bellows, always a weak point, so the sharp puffing of Hackworth's and the Stephensons' engines was absent; she went more like a steam motor-car, which was ever a pleasantly silent thing, and that pleased the crowd still more.

Indeed, the alarming aspect of a steam locomotive had been much argued by its angry opponents. During one of his constant catechisms in Parliamentary Committee and elsewhere, George Stephenson had had it suggested that the spectacle of a loco-motive engine working hard, with a red-hot chimney, would terrify cattle, with disastrous results of all sorts.

Now old George, as a boy, had once herded cows, and knew something about them. He said that the cow was not the most intelligent of beasts. The cows would doubtless think that the engine had merely had its chimney painted red, and would not bother themselves further. But perhaps to show that a properly-driven locomotive never would have a red-hot chimney, he painted the tall stack of the *Rocket* white.

The *Rocket,* one believes, was largely Robert Stephenson's work. She had a multi-tubular boiler like Séguin's, fired by a water-jacketed firebox at the rear, believed to have been the work of Henry Booth, the Stephensons' co-entrant in the competition. She had the inclined outside cylinders of the *Lancashire Witch*, *America* and *Invicta*. As a curiosity, by the way, we give a tracing from an ancient Robert Stephenson drawing which shows such an engine with James Watt's "sun-and-planet" drive instead of the by-then-normal cranks. No prizes are offered for solution of this historical mystery!

The *Rocket* needs little further introduction and her beautiful simplicity is evident from the drawing. The colours are authentic. The tender (still with a water-barrel instead of a proper tank) was built by Nathaniel Worsdell, a noted English coachbuilder of the time. After many vicissitudes, the engine's worn-out shell still exists in the Science Museum, London. There are several full-size replicas, one in the same place, sectioned for display, and more in America, the first of which was commissioned from Robert Stephenson and Company by Henry Ford. We have seen the Ford engine working under steam.

Now for the Rainhill contest! Each engine was required to run seventy miles continuously (that was in fact back-and-forth over the relatively short course) at not less than an average speed of ten miles an hour. *Novelty,* as we have seen, managed a *maximum speed* of thirty miles an hour. ("It seemed to fly . . ." wrote one spectator, and it must be remembered that never had anybody seen anything going so fast, apart from eagles, swallows, ducks and some other birds!)

Other conditions must be mentioned. The accepted engine must not weigh more than six tons on six wheels, or 4·5 tons on four wheels; its working pressure must not be more than fifty pounds a.d.p. per sq. in., its boiler having been previously subjected to a water test equal to thrice that pressure; it must have two safety-valves and a mercurial pressure gauge; it must be able to pull a twenty-ton train at ten miles an hour. The *Rocket* and the *Novelty* both fulfilled conditions, but the latter's ingenious yet dicey boiler was her undoing. There were two failures, and then she was withdrawn; collapsed though not indeed exploded.

So poor little *Novelty*, as well as Hackworth's massive *Sans Pareil*, was out of the contest, leaving only the Stephenson engine *Rocket*. At that, one wonders less that some parties had brought forward machines without benefit of artificial power. Brandreth's *Cyclopede,* for example, was worked by a horse trotting on something like an escalator

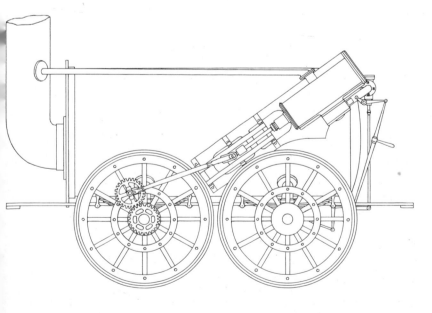

Watt's "sun-and-planet" drive as proposed for a Stephenson locomotive, c. 1828.

or *trottoir roulant* connected by gears to the axle below, and there was even a "manu-motive" approximating to the hand-car of later years.

But the *Rocket* stayed the course, completing all her trips, loaded, without any accident. To the Stephensons and to Booth went the £500 prize, and to the former went the contract for supplying locomotive power to the Liverpool and Manchester Railway. The *Rocket's* maximum speed was twenty-nine miles an hour, and her average was sixteen. She was sold to the company for another £500, the stipulated maximum price having been £550. Up in Newcastle-upon-Tyne, eight more "Rockets" were put in hand for the opening of the railway in the following year. Improvements were made from engine to engine. Firstly, and in the *Rocket* herself before she went into service, the angle of the inclined cylinders was greatly decreased. The original high angle had resulted in very alarming oscillation. Then the boilers were given proper smokeboxes. The blast-pipes in these were much improved to create adequate vacuum at the ends of the flues. The engine *Northumbrian* (August, 1830) had a much advanced firebox, completely within the boiler barrel as to its upper part, and she also had a proper tender instead of a coal-truck with a water-barrel on top.

Of the other contestants, Hackworth's *Sans Pareil* was found useful, and still survives at the Science Museum in London, in her original state as far as one can tell. Braithwaite and Ericsson made two more locomotives of "Novelty" type, but larger, and with fan drive instead of bellows, which were to work on the St. Helens and Runcorn Gap Railway. *Novelty's* wheels and cylinders were unearthed many years later. There is a handsome replica, containing original parts, permanently exhibited beside her two rivals.

Thus was answered the question of how this Liverpool and Manchester Railway, the first inter-city main line for passengers and freight, should be worked. It was to be done by locomotive, with no more nonsense about stationary engines and cables. The locomotive, as a machine in constant public service, had *arrived*. It is wrong to call George Stephenson the *Father of the Locomotive*. He was not; though many people were to call him so—quite angrily when disputed—for many years. But one may safely remember him as the *Father of the Steam Passenger Train*, indeed of all trains as we have known them. When he was old, he told a young man that a time would come when electricity would be the great motive power of the world. He would not see it, he said, but the young man might. Be it added that at that time the power of electricity was generally unknown, or at most regarded as a sort of laboratory magic. Alessandro Volta (1745–1827) was fresh in the memory; Michael Faraday (1791–1867) was in his prime. To most people who had ever heard of him outside American revolutionary politics, Benjamin Franklin (1706–1790) was a crackpot character who had flown a kite to catch

This engraving of the Novelty—*probably with Captain John Ericsson driving—is by Vignoles. This shows how private coaches, landaus, etc., were attached to wagons.*

the lightning! For the present, it was Steam's Day. For a long time steam had been pumping water out of mines, then hauling mine-shaft cages, tip-wagons, and working machines in mills. Now it was shown able to move freight and passengers with some speed over apparently illimitable distances. To some, those speeds of twenty-to-thirty miles an hour were against Nature and therefore quite blasphemous. With this new machine, mankind was clearly infected with the madness of the Gadarene swine, and thus doomed to a miserable end in double-quick time. In England that old general, the Duke of Wellington, feared that such rapid mechanical progress would enable fierce revolutionary mobs to capture the country, while less politically-minded critics foresaw a dangerous ability to circulate among the criminal classes (a situation which was indeed to come to pass, over a century later, with the advent of the cheap motor-car!). The general, by now a rather unsuccessful Prime Minister, need not have worried so much. A revolutionary mob *might* capture a train, but it was even more easy for Government to requisition a few, load them up with soldiers, and rush them to wherever they might expect trouble.

With that irony which is so peculiarly English, the Duke of Wellington formally opened the Liverpool and Manchester Railway, on September 15, 1830.

Really, it was a most inauspicious function! For one thing, Wellington was cordially detested by the mass of the people in North-Western England, which was extremely Radical. Then the weather was fearsome, with terrific thunder showers. During a leg-stretching halt at Parkside, on the way from Liverpool to Manchester the *Rocket* ran over William Huskisson, sometime President of the Board of Trade, who had lately quarrelled with Wellington, and crushed his legs so that he died the same night. Festivities were abandoned, but Wellington proceeded to Manchester in the ducal train, and was there received with screams of hatred and even brickbats.

Late in the evening came what may have been the world's first serious attempt at train wrecking. Some angry young man—or it may have been even a squire's under-gardener—put a wheelbarrow on the line as the trains returned. The wheelbarrow was damaged beyond repair, but the trains continued to run.

Such was the beginning of public, power-hauled, passenger and freight railroads which were to cover much of the world's land masses before the century was done. The rail was to have its tragedies, and many of them, but its history was to be less sinister and less gory than those of other agents which were to come later. It was left to the automobile to spawn the tank; to the aeroplane to produce the bombing aircraft. The ghosts of those mild and peace-loving Quakers, the Pease Family, might well console themselves.

George Stephenson, 1781–1848. Almost entirely self-taught, he rose from being engine-wright at the Killingworth Colliery to become the leading locomotive and railway engineer of the first half of the 19th century.

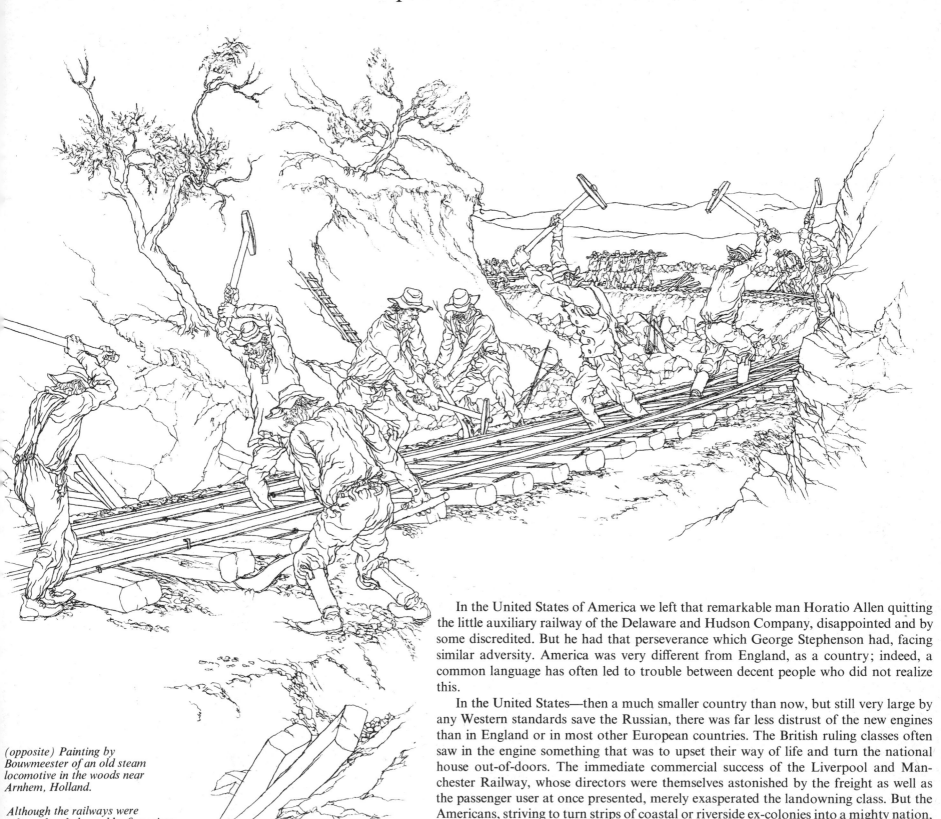

Chapter 3 THE GREAT MORNING OF STEAM

(opposite) Painting by Bouwmeester of an old steam locomotive in the woods near Arnhem, Holland.

Although the railways were schemed and planned by financiers and engineers, it was the muscle and bone of the "navvy" which actually built them. Many thousands of men were employed as labourers on the railroads in the 19th century. The work was hard, slow and ill-paid, but the conditions of the times were such that a never-failing source of manpower was always available.

In the United States of America we left that remarkable man Horatio Allen quitting the little auxiliary railway of the Delaware and Hudson Company, disappointed and by some discredited. But he had that perseverance which George Stephenson had, facing similar adversity. America was very different from England, as a country; indeed, a common language has often led to trouble between decent people who did not realize this.

In the United States—then a much smaller country than now, but still very large by any Western standards save the Russian, there was far less distrust of the new engines than in England or in most other European countries. The British ruling classes often saw in the engine something that was to upset their way of life and turn the national house out-of-doors. The immediate commercial success of the Liverpool and Manchester Railway, whose directors were themselves astonished by the freight as well as the passenger user at once presented, merely exasperated the landowning class. But the Americans, striving to turn strips of coastal or riverside ex-colonies into a mighty nation, saw in the infant railway train a tremendous peaceful weapon which could do just that, and they received the steam railroad with delight.

To be sure, there was to be plenty of real fighting in the States thereafter, and not yet was the time when trains would run (in relays) from Atlantic to Pacific. But the great waters could be linked; even the Atlantic with the Mississippi Basin. It was not easy. By European notions the country was incredibly wild. There was little native mechanical engineering; a village blacksmith was quite a personage, cf. Henry Wadsworth Longfellow, one of the greatest of earlier American poets, and an enlightened man in several

other ways. The sole seat of mechanical knowledge was in the engineering faculty of the United States Military Academy, West Point, New York State.

On February 28, 1827, the State of Maryland granted a Charter to the promoters of what was to be called the Baltimore and Ohio Railroad. In the survey, the United States Army greatly helped. The original route included the splendid Carollton Viaduct, built of Maryland stone and begun in 1828. The foundation stone of this was laid by Charles Caroll who had given his name to the place and was even then the last survivor of those who had signed the American Declaration of Independence. By half a decade this remarkable structure anticipated the much-more trumpeted Thomas Viaduct at Relay, Maryland, which was completed in 1835. Between them, among great arched railway structures came the Sankey Viaduct in England (1829–30) though none of them came near, in antiquity, to the Causey Arch in Northumberland, which was out of useful service before they were built.

But back to *The Train*! By the beginning of 1830 the Baltimore and Ohio Railroad (which was not to reach the Ohio until 1863) mustered fourteen miles of route on double track from Baltimore to Ellicot's Mills, worked by horse-cars, on wooden road with iron straps a-top.

Peter Cooper, a rich and ingenious New Yorker of the period, made a very small experimental locomotive, the *Tom Thumb*, for demonstration on this new railway. She had a vertical multitubular boiler with its flues made from sawn-off musket barrels, geared drive and draught induced by belt-driven fans. In 1830, with benefit of double track, Cooper raced *Tom Thumb* against one of the horse cars. The great horse went off at a fast trot. Then the little engine overhauled him. But the belt driving the fan began to slip. Cooper tried hard and heroically to keep belt on wheel, but only got his hand sawn, as one does when trying tricks with rapidly moving belts. So the Horse won that race. But still Peter Cooper had shown some people something that otherwise they would not have believed.

More heroic notions were being realized in the South. What was to become the South Carolina Railroad was surveyed to connect the Atlantic Coast at Charleston with the township of Hamburg, on the banks of the Savannah River opposite the modest but rising city of Augusta, Georgia.

Thither went Horatio Allen, recovering, like a good American, from certain disappointments with the Delaware and Hudson Company in the North. He was made Chief Engineer of the new railroad in the second half of 1829, about the time the Stephensons, Hackworth, Ericsson and lesser people were busy convincing cautious Lancashire business people about the desirability of steam locomotives, up in the English North-West. Allen in his turn, early next year, convinced his Directors that steam should be used exclusively. He had an able mechanical engineer in E. L. Miller of Charleston. West Point Foundry undertook to build four engines, so this time there was no need for recourse to British manufacturers, as at Honesdale. The first engine, happily named *The Best Friend of Charleston,* was ordered in March, 1830, was safely shipped to Charleston where she was safely erected by Julius Petsch and Nicholas Darrell, and steamed for the first time on November 2.

Peter Cooper's Tom Thumb *in its famous race with the horse-drawn car. A little engine of about one horsepower, it weighed only a little more than a ton and had musket barrels for tubes. Its one cylinder was only 3½ inches in diameter and had a 14-inch stroke. The race was held on August 28, 1830 when the engine pulled a car-load of the directors of the Baltimore and Ohio Railroad. Although the* Tom Thumb *lost the race the directors were impressed and Peter Cooper had proved the practicability of steam motive power. It was the first locomotive in America to pull a load of passengers.*

During December she ran several trips, just exceeding twenty miles an hour with upwards of forty passengers (about ten to a light four-wheel car). Public service began on January 15, 1831, inaugurating America's first railroad to work a regular service under steam power. The initial section was six miles long, out of the pleasant city of Charleston. Though the present venture was more modest, as yet, than the previous one between Liverpool and Manchester in England, the event was certainly happier and nobody was damaged, not even an ex-Cabinet Minister. The first of the little cars carried soldiers with a very light field gun, with which they joyously fired rounds of blanks as they drifted past the live-oaks and cottonwoods. Next came one with a brass band, and safely in rear came the proprietors and their friends.

A modest beginning, perhaps; but in 1833 the line reached Hamburg, across the river from Augusta, Georgia. The distance of 135 miles made this the longest railroad yet.

Someone called the "Best Friend" the "Rocket of America", with adequate reason. But like the *Rocket* in England (which was later in two bad derailments) she was accident-prone. Her fireman was a Negro boy not sufficiently aware of the power of steam. When the safety-valve annoyed him with its din, he tied it down on one unlucky day, which happened to be June 17, 1831. The little hock-bottle boiler exploded. Darrell, who was in charge and might have seen his fireman's fatal prank, was badly scalded. The fireman died.

The "Best Friend" resembled none of the engines at the Rainhill Trials in England, save that like *Sans Pareil* she had her four wheels coupled. The cylinders were inclined, and between the frames, driving a crank-axle at the rear. These, and a water-tank below, balanced the vertical boiler, or were supposed to do so. After the accident, the engine was rebuilt and appropriately renamed *Phoenix*. In this form, the boiler was between the axles. It was still bottle-shaped, but this time suggestive of gin rather than German wine.

By then, other engines had come from West Point Foundry, mechanically similar but different as to their boilers. The second, the *West Point*, had a more-or-less English-style horizontal boiler, which was eventually to become the standard form in spite of American liking for the vertical type.

Here let it be said, with no intended insult, that early American locomotives were often very roughly made compared with those in England; but still they went. They were sturdy, indeed, and arranged as far as possible so that in the event of breakdown, repairs could be adequately carried out in a remote place by Basil the Blacksmith (cf. Longfellow, again!).

Back to England for a while! Edward Bury, as we have seen, was too late to produce a satisfactory locomotive for the Rainhill Trials, and just what his first engine, the *Liverpool*, was really like, we cannot show here, not knowing for certain. Probably she was not entered for the competition simply because she would not go in her original, mysterious form. But in partnership with James Kennedy (he who, most unhappily, ran down and killed Huskisson at Parkside in 1830) he rebuilt his engine in the form shown on p. 58. The locomotive certainly ran on the Liverpool and Manchester Railway, but is much more important as an international prototype.

The Best Friend of Charleston *was the first locomotive in America to pull a train. It was built at the West Point Foundry of New York for the Charleston and Hamburg Railroad (which later became the South Carolina Railroad). It had to be sent to Charleston by ship and it was set up there by Julius Petsch and Nicholas Darrell (who was the engineer the day the boiler exploded, killing the fireman). After the accident Julius Petsch rebuilt the engine and it was renamed* Phoenix.

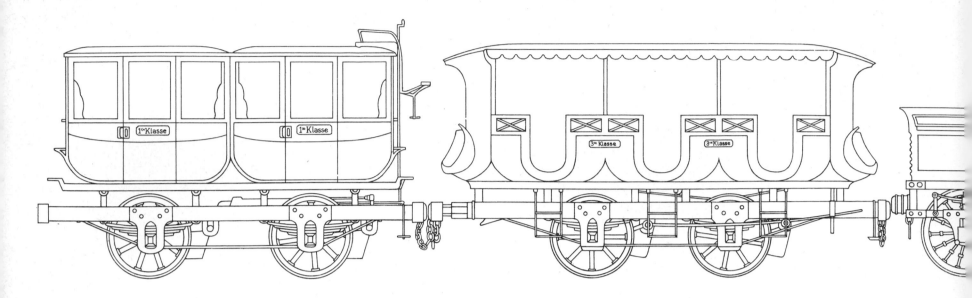

Passing over her relatively enormous coupled wheels (quite freakish for 1830, though a great precedent) we see most prominently her inside bar frames of iron as well as her inclined cylinders below the smokebox, also inside. We see a horizontal boiler with a D-shaped firebox below a domed outer casing. Compared with either the *Rocket* or the *Best Friend of Charleston*, she is almost familiar! (A note in passing; the ornate red crown on the top of her stack was a cut-out procession of *liver birds*—mythical winged creatures who formed the insignia of that great and terrible city of Liverpool. The *liver*, in this connection, had nothing to do with an important organ of all the vertebrata, including ourselves!)

The *Liverpool* is extremely important in the development of locomotive design. Those bar frames were to be universal in America for as long as the steam locomotive lasted, while Continental and Eastern Europe, with much of the rest of the world, were to take them up sooner or later. The D-shaped, dome-topped firebox also was taken up by America, and was still to be seen in the eighteen-sixties, though not much later. All this arose out of some engines which Bury made for the Philadelphia and Reading Railroad (one of them was named *Rocket*!) in the eighteen-thirties. But the development of the Bury locomotive can keep a-while, while we look back at the Stephensons.

We left them building "Rockets", making some improvements within the limits of that very limited design. But—still in 1830—they produced the *Planet*. Her boiler was something like those of *Northumbria* and *Majestic*, the last of the Rocket class on the Liverpool and Manchester Railway. But the cylinders were inside and horizontal. The frames were outside, making a very strong and sturdy engine.

Very quickly, improvements were made in this Planet type, the first of which was the use of four-coupled wheels for a freight variety. Various "Planets" were sent to America, where Matthias Baldwin copied it in a rather famous engine called *Old Ironsides*, which he built for the Philadelphia, Germantown and Norristown Railroad in 1832. So much trouble did he have in at last getting $3,500 of the $4,000 previously agreed that he is reported to have said in despair: "That is our last locomotive." It was not so, of course; Baldwin Locomotive Works of Philadelphia was to become one of the greatest and most famous locomotive makers in the world.

A four-coupled "Planet" named *John Bull* was made by the Stephensons for the Camden and Amboy Railroad in Pennsylvania (a Stevens enterprise) and assembled by Isaac Dripps in 1831. A drawing shows a dome-cased firebox in the Edward Bury style. Later, Dripps furnished a pilot, running on an axle of its own in front, which both steadied the engine and saved it, one supposes, from derailment if it encountered some absent-minded cow; hence the widely used, if un-academic term *cowcatcher* for a locomotive

The first public railway to be opened in the German States was the Nuremburg–Fürth Railway on December 7, 1835. Our drawing shows the Adler, *the inaugural engine, with first and third class carriages. It exemplifies Stephenson's* Patentee *type, which was basically an elongation of the Planet type, with the addition of a trailing axle.*

pilot, current over about a century. Though the pilot was to become universal in America, it was ever rare in Europe except in the East and North. *John Bull* survived to become the oldest original locomotive in the Americas, and is treasured to this day.

THE PATENTEE TYPE

"Planets" were unsteady at any speed, and their firebox capacity was limited. Stephensons rectified these by adding a trailing axle behind the firebox, which then could be made considerably bigger, in the early eighteen thirties. From the first engine of the type, it was known as the "Patentee" class. The extra axle could be a free one on a passenger engine, or coupled for goods. Alternatively, the leading axle, or all three, could be coupled. "Patentees" of one sort and another were freely built for European service, as, one-by-one, the Continental countries essayed the new form of conveyance. The first locomotives for public service in Belgium (*La Flèche, Stephenson* and *L'Eléphant,* Brussels-Mechlin State Railway, 1835), in the German States (*Adler,* Nuremberg-Fürth Railway, 1835), in Russia (Pavlovsk-Tsarskoye Selo, 1837), the Netherlands (*De Snelheid* and *De Arend,* Holland Iron Railway, 1839) and the Italian States (*Bayard,* Naples-Portici Railway, 1839) were all "Patentees". In its native England, the type abounded, and direct derivatives, still with wood-and-iron sandwich frames, were to be found there even in the early years of the next century.

An extremely fine example is the *North Star,* built by Robert Stephenson for the Great Western Railway in England in 1837. This splendid line was engineered by Isambard Kingdom Brunel, son of an emigré French father and an English mother, who conceived railroads on the grand scale. By this time, railway construction was having its first boom and lines were being promoted and built in many parts of the Western World. The commonest rail-gauge was 4 ft. $8\frac{1}{2}$ in., or 1·435 metres, which was not only that of the old colliery lines in North Eastern England, but was even approximate to the wheel-width of the Roman roads in the days of the Caesars. Brunel alone thought that very inadequate to such an advanced conveyance as the train, and fixed his gauge at seven English feet, 7 ft. $0\frac{1}{4}$ in. to be exact or 2·14 m. It is one of the tragedies of world railway construction that this did not become a generally-used gauge, bearing magnificently spacious trains, though to be sure it would have been unwieldy in the narrow places of mountain country. As it was, it remained confined to the Western portions of Great Britain, and the last of it vanished in 1892. Stephenson's old gauge became widespread in Europe from the Russian borders to the Pyrenees, and ultimately throughout North America. We shall meet with wider gauges, though not on Brunel's

Two Daumier prints show how signals were given in the early days on the railways in France.

grand scale, and many narrower ones. The Holland Iron Railway began with two metres (measured from centre of rail-head). Important broad-gauge countries today include the U.S.S.R., India, several South American republics, and Spain and Portugal.

Quite apart from its broad gauge, *North Star* was a large example of a "Patentee" (as *Adler* in Germany was a small one) indeed she was a big engine by any standards of the late eighteen thirties. Originally built for the 5 ft. 6 in. gauge New Orleans Railway in the U.S.A., a broken contract was the cause of her being altered to seven-foot gauge and going to the Great Western instead. She had driving wheels 7 ft. in diameter and the inside cylinders were 16 in., both diameter and stroke; total heating surface was about 711 sq. ft. Obsolescence was rapid in those days, but the *North Star* was rebuilt with new cylinders and a larger boiler in 1854, and was in service for over thirty-three years, a prodigy of that period. She had taken the first Great Western train out of London, on June 4, 1838. She was preserved by the Great Western company for many years. A barbarian mixture of indifference and vandalism brought her to the scrap-heap in 1906, since when many specious excuses have been made, and a partly wooden replica constructed.

Much happier in such respect was the story of the *Lion*, a front-coupled "Patentee" with a square Gothic-arched firebox casing, built as their first engine by Kitsons of Leeds (Todd, Kitson and Laird) during the winter of 1837–38 and bought by the Liverpool and Manchester Railway for freight traffic. The L. and M.R. was amalgamated into the Grand Junction Railway which had come to connect it with Birmingham, and these in turn, by amalgamation with the London and Birmingham Railway, the first great line out of the capital, became parts of the mighty London and North Western Railway, which in turn inherited the *Lion*. The L.N.W.R. sold her for docks service in Liverpool, where she latterly (indeed for many years) worked a dock pump. From this she was rescued in the nineteen twenties, and was fully restored by Robert Stephenson and Company in 1929, under the direction of A. C. W. Lowe. She steamed again at the Liverpool and Manchester Railway Centenary celebrations in 1930. Perfectly sound, she has appeared in various films since then.

As remarked, the wheel arrangement of a "Patentee" was varied in Europe from 2-2-2 (1-A-1) for passenger haulage to 0-4-2 or 2-4-0 (B-1 or 1-B) for heavier work requiring more adhesion. Also remarked previously was the early incidence of its predecessor, the "Planet" type, in North America. It was here that certain very interesting, non-European, variations took place in the basic "Planet/Patentee" form. While wrought-iron rails, at first chaired on stone blocks and then on timber sleepers or crossties, were general in Europe, America clung doggedly for a long time, on certain lines, to the wooden road with iron straps on top of the baulks; also these early American roads were often laid very roughly on a road-bed scarcely worth the name. At the same time be it added that proper English iron rails were extremely expensive. In an expanding country, the thing was to get the railroads down as quickly as possible so that new towns and plantations could blossom beside them. That roughness demanded a much more flexible locomotive if the daily train was not to spend much of its time off the rails and possibly axle-deep in good earth.

One way to this end was the use of a flexible leading truck on two axles, not so much as a pivoting agent on curves as to give three-point suspension to four wheels. Its origin has been argued. The invention has been claimed for the Stephensons (the English word "bogie" is a North-Eastern one for a truck). Certainly the appliance was first made in the United States, wherever it was invented. In fairness be it remarked that a deputation of American engineers visited the Stephensons as early as 1828, and that Robert Stephenson spoke to them about the arrangement, which he had not yet built.

In 1832 John B. Jervis designed, and had built by West Point Foundry for the Mohawk and Hudson Railroad, an engine which he called *Experiment*, but which has gone down to history as *Brother Jonathan*; (at that time the rather quarrelsome Anglo-Saxon cousins were known respectively as John Bull and Brother Jonathan; Uncle Sam and Wilhelm Busch's Mister Beef had not yet arrived properly).

This engine's likeness (p. 82) shows her arrangement sufficiently well. Basically, she was a "Planet" but she had the leading truck replacing the old rigid axle behind the smokebox, while the driving axle, instead of being close behind it, was in rear of the firebox, anticipating patents later granted in England to T. R. Crampton, of whom we shall see more later. She was a *very* small engine, but—probably with little load—she was regarded as a flyer. Few of the early speed records can be regarded as authentic, and

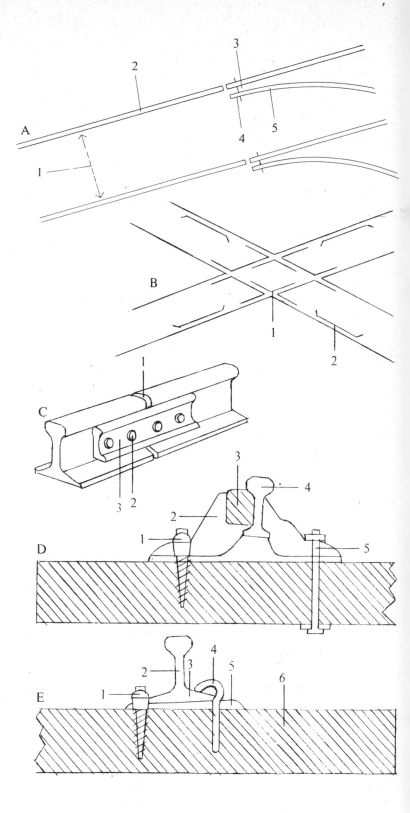

The railway tracks (or permanent way) is shown here in detail:

A Points	D Bull-headed rail
1 Gauge	1 Screw
2 Stock rail	2 Chair
3 Throw of point	3 Key
4 Point	4 Head
5 Tongue	5 Bolt
B Crossing	E Flat-bottomed rail
1 Frog	1 Screw
2 Check rail	2 Web
C Method of joining rail	3 Base
1 Gap	4 Spike
2 Fish bolt	5 Base plate
3 Fish-plate	6 Sleeper

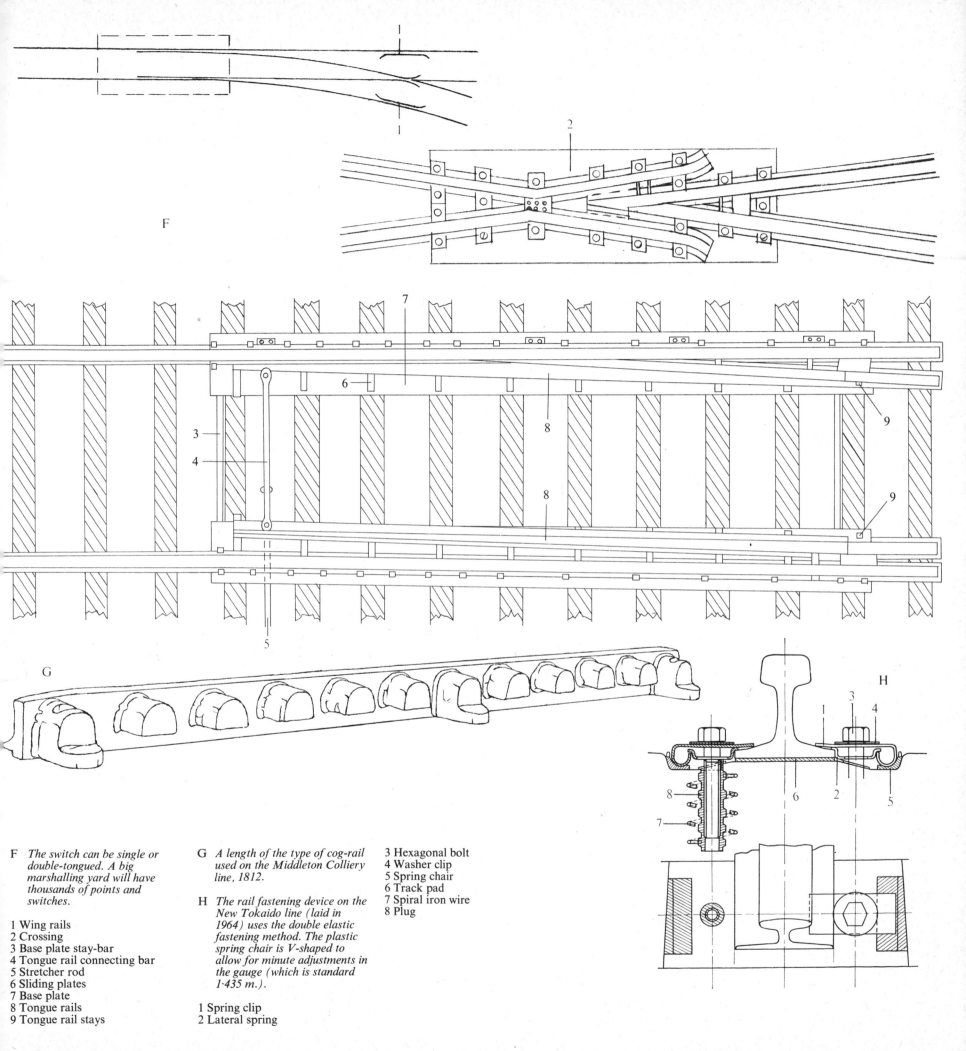

F The switch can be single or double-tongued. A big marshalling yard will have thousands of points and switches.

1 Wing rails
2 Crossing
3 Base plate stay-bar
4 Tongue rail connecting bar
5 Stretcher rod
6 Sliding plates
7 Base plate
8 Tongue rails
9 Tongue rail stays

G A length of the type of cog-rail used on the Middleton Colliery line, 1812.

H The rail fastening device on the New Tokaido line (laid in 1964) uses the double elastic fastening method. The plastic spring chair is V-shaped to allow for minute adjustments in the gauge (which is standard 1·435 m.).

1 Spring clip
2 Lateral spring

3 Hexagonal bolt
4 Washer clip
5 Spring chair
6 Track pad
7 Spiral iron wire
8 Plug

Brother Jonathan's (or *Experiment's*) mile-a-minute must stand in the apocrypha. It *might* have been so. England built a similar engine for the Camden and Woodbury Rail-road in the United States in the following year of 1833, when, also, J. and C. Carmichael in Scotland built a freakish one (0-2-4 with side-lever drive) for the Dundee and Newtyle Railway.

A much more interesting American development of the basic Stephenson type was that of Henry Campbell in 1836. For the Philadelphia, Germantown and Norristown Railroad in Pennsylvania he built a locomotive which had the general arrangement of a "Planet" but with the Stephenson-Jervis truck in front, and an extra axle in rear of the firebox (also Jervis) which was coupled to the driving axle by outside cranks and rods. The engine was not very successful, by some trustworthy accounts, and for years was somewhat forgotten. Certainly she did not become a great American prototype. But she was the first of the widely used 4-4-0 type as to wheel arrangement, and she had such mighty European descendants as the French "Outrance" bogie class in the 'seventies and even the very advanced English "Cities" of the nineteen-hundreds (Northern, and Great Western Railways respectively). In these, of course, there was no timber in the frames.

Henry Cambell's eight-wheel bogie locomotive was built in 1836 by James Brooks of Philadelphia for the Philadelphia, Germantown and Norristown Railroad. The type was more copied in England than America.

THE BLACK HAWK WAS THE FIRST LOCOMOTIVE BUILT BY BALDWIN TO HAVE OUTSIDE CYLINDERS. IT WAS DELIVERED TO THE PHILADELPHIA AND TRENTON RAILROAD IN 1835.

Liverpool

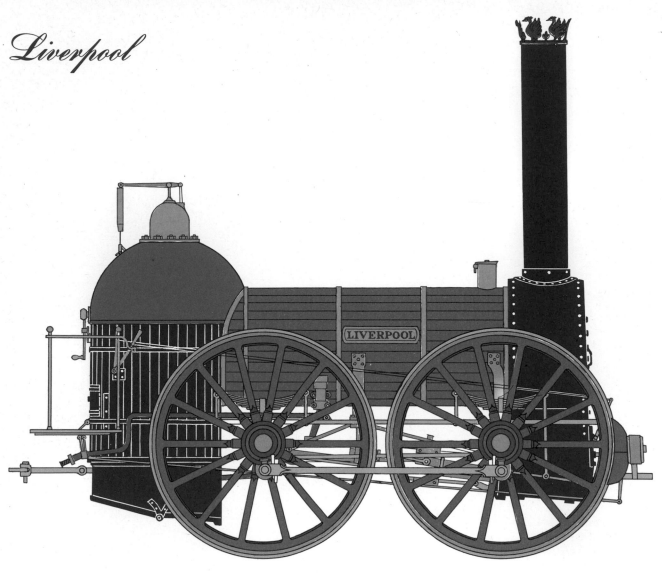

EDWARD BURY'S LIVERPOOL FOR THE LIVERPOOL AND MANCHESTER RAILWAY, 1830. UNIQUE FEATURES WERE THE MULTITUBULAR BOILER, D-SHAPED FIREBOX WITH DOMED CASING AND SUPPLEMENTARY STEAM DOME.

Planet

North Star

THE **NORTH STAR** WAS BUILT IN 1837 BY ROBERT STEPHENSON AND COMPANY. ORIGINALLY INTENDED FOR THE NEW ORLEANS RAILWAY IN AMERICA, IT WAS ALTERED TO RUN ON THE 7 FT. GAUGE OF THE GREAT WESTERN RAILWAY IN ENGLAND.

THE **PLANET** WAS CONSTRUCTED BY ROBERT STEPHENSON IN 1830 AND USED ON THE LIVERPOOL AND MANCHESTER RAILWAY. IT IS REGARDED AS THE FORERUNNER OF THE TRADITIONAL ENGLISH LOCOMOTIVE.

Royal George

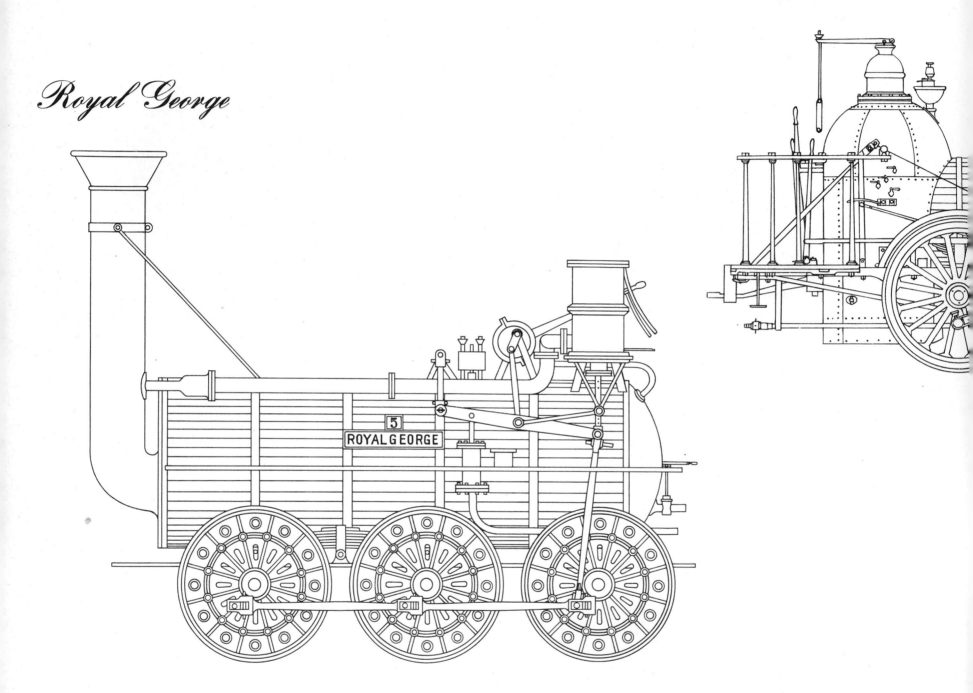

5

ROYAL GEORGE

TIMOTHY HACKWORTH'S ROYAL GEORGE WAS PRODUCED FOR THE STOCKTON AND DARLINGTON RAILWAY IN 1827. IT WAS THE FIRST ENGINE WITH SIX-COUPLED WHEELS.

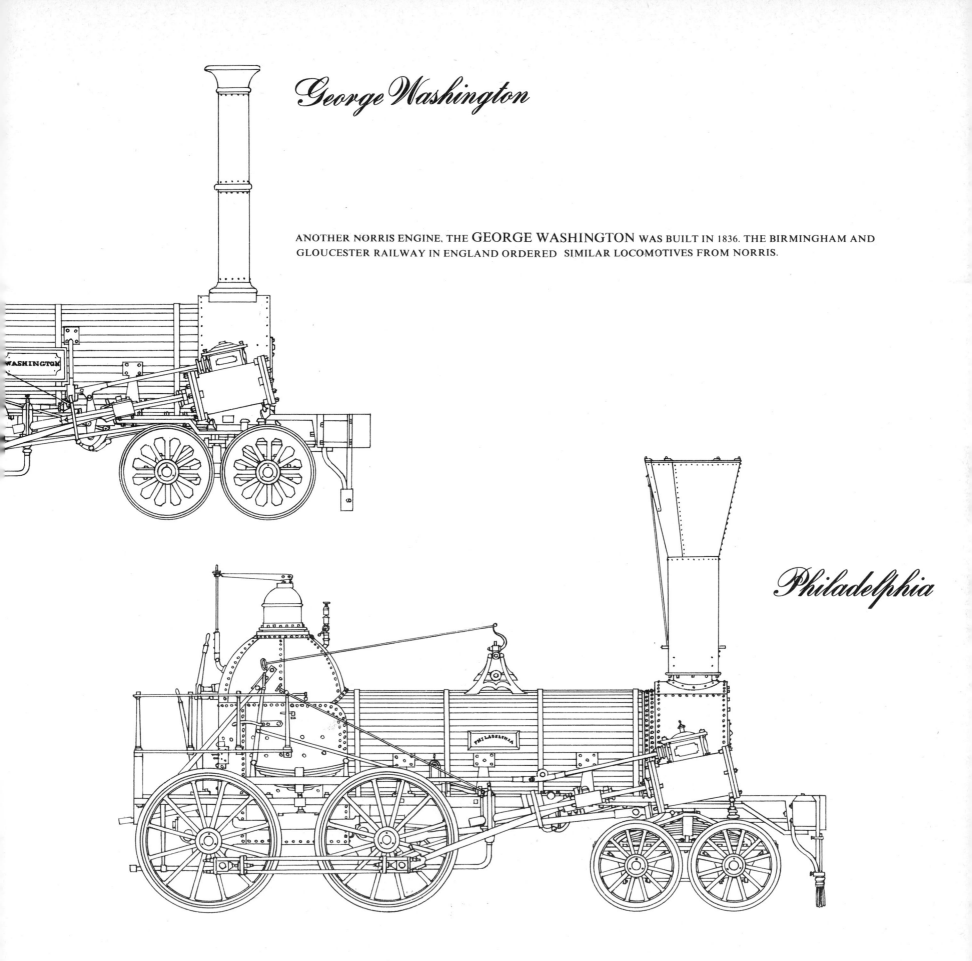

George Washington

ANOTHER NORRIS ENGINE, THE GEORGE WASHINGTON WAS BUILT IN 1836. THE BIRMINGHAM AND GLOUCESTER RAILWAY IN ENGLAND ORDERED SIMILAR LOCOMOTIVES FROM NORRIS.

Philadelphia

THE 1843 PHILADELPHIA EXEMPLIFIES WILLIAM NORRIS'S "IMPROVED EIGHT-WHEEL LOCOMOTIVE" WHICH HAD THE BURY BOILER AND BAR FRAMES FROM ENGLAND, PLUS THE AMERICAN LEADING TRUCK AND TRAILING COUPLED AXLE.

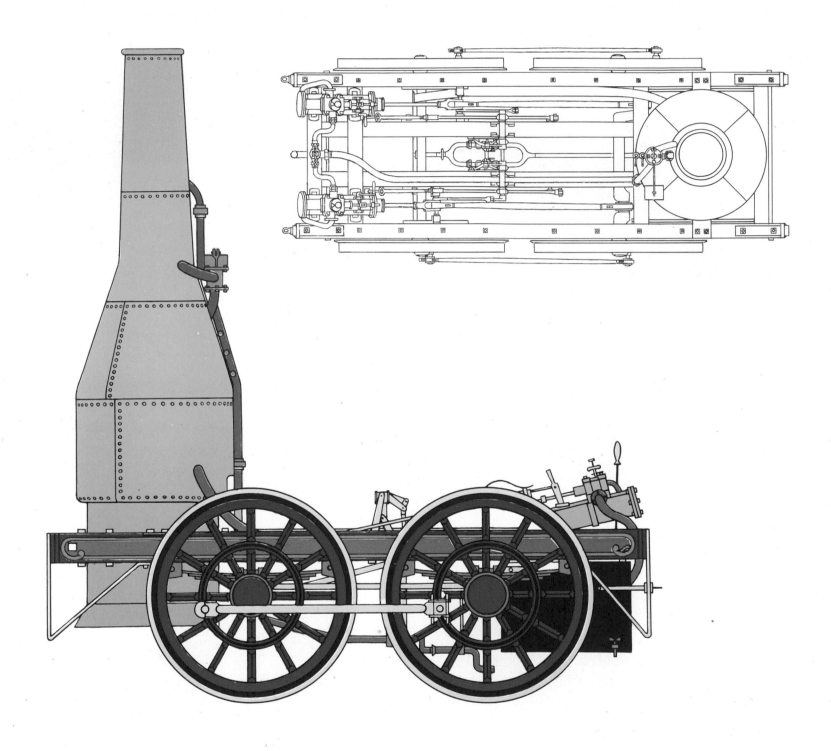

THE FIRST ALL-AMERICAN STEAM RAILWAY LOCOMOTIVE TO GO INTO COMMERCIAL SERVICE ON THE SOUTH CAROLINA RAILROAD, 1830.

Experience

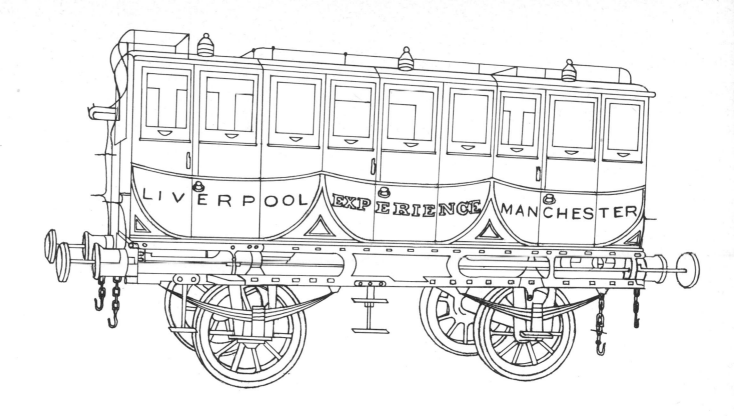

BUILT IN 1834 FOR THE LIVERPOOL AND MANCHESTER RAILWAY, THE EXPERIENCE HAD THREE "STAGE-COACH" COMPARTMENTS SIDE BY SIDE.

Lion

THE IMMORTAL LION WAS BUILT FOR THE LIVERPOOL AND MANCHESTER RAILWAY OVER 130 YEARS AGO AND IS STILL IN WORKING ORDER.

Monster

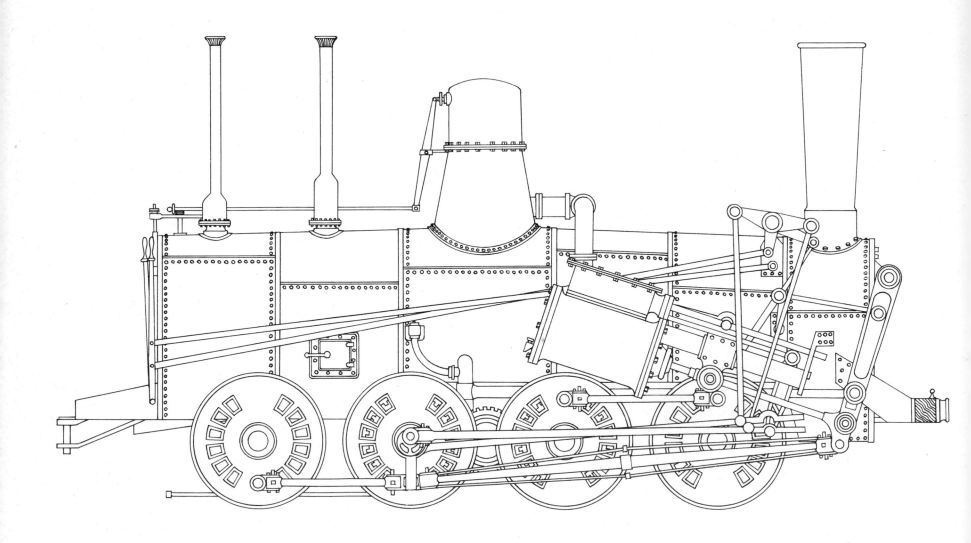

THE MONSTER WAS BUILT BY ISAAC DRIPPS AND ROBERT STEVENS FOR THE CAMDEN AND AMBOY RAILROAD, *c*. 1834. DEPENDENT ON BOTH LEVER DRIVE AND INTERMEDIATE GEARS, THIS INDEED MONSTROUS ENGINE STILL WORKED.

THE PASSENGER CAR

Before we go on to the development of the other early classic types such as the Bury with its bar-frames, let us look at car design. At the very first, the wagon or freight-car was simply a larger version of the old *chaldrons*, the primeval mining vehicles, while ancient passenger coaches were flanged-wheel adaptations of the stage and private coaches on the roads. There were indeed some fantastic experiments, but in general the better class of passenger coach in Western Europe was for many years composed of compartments with side-doors—stage-coach bodies combined, three, four, or more at a time, on a single railway frame. This type made its appearance with the opening of the Liverpool and Manchester Railway, and probably originated with Nathaniel Worsdell, the eminent coachbuilder who had made the *Rocket*'s tender. Each compartment, or "body", held six passengers on heavily padded but very upright seats (we have ridden in a replica!). Cheaper fares were charged for riding in an open-sided *char-à-banc*. Both types are shown in the drawing of the Nuremberg-Fürth train, as well as in the famous Ackermann "Long Prints" of the Liverpool and Manchester Railway.

On the latter, for an extra charge, people might ride in compartments belonging to the mail carriage, providing corner seats only. The cheapest passengers rode in box-like wagons which were often without seats and known in England as "Stanhopes" (a very bad pun on "Stand-ups"). The Stanhopes were an old and honoured family, so presumably their name was borrowed to lend these frightful vehicles a spurious sort of respectability. One doubts that it had anything to do with the Stanhope and Tyne Railway, which had no monopoly of this mean sort of "carriage".

The side-door-compartment type of coach, however, answered well for many years. Before very long it was being used—with proportionately narrower compartments and harder seats—for second- and third-class passengers. A century later, it was still being built for suburban trains around the big cities of Great Britain on account of its high capacity and its ease of entry and exit, though of course it was by then a very much larger thing than its remote precursors had been.

A favourite arrangement among the richer English families of those early days was to ride in their own private coaches chained to flat wagons. It was "exclusive"; ladies and gentlemen needed not to soil their skirts and pantaloons by sitting on public cushions; but the dust, fumes and cinders were the devil to pay when the conveyance was an open landau in summer. The Duke of Wellington was recorded as having travelled thus when he was over eighty, though the South Eastern Railway had thoughtfully made a special railway carriage for him. Probably the last person to travel so was a most unpleasant English eccentric, Mrs. Caroline Prodgers, who was observed *en route*, covered with dust, at Chesterfield in the English Midlands as late as the eighteen-eighties, but there is a sort of revival in our own time, where motorists and their cars are ferried by train through certain Alpine tunnels.

The cheaper passengers had an awful time in the "Stanhopes" and other abominations. Throughout Europe it was much the same. An old French cartoon (by Daumier) shows the third-class passengers being lifted out by porters, stiff as frozen codfish.

Though all European countries at that time regarded the American way of life as rough and horrid, to America railroad history owed some considerable debts for introducing, at one time and another, passenger cars that were at once more practical, and occasionally more comfortable, for long journeys. Once again the stage-coach furnished an early model, but even here there were differences. The American stage-coach was a longer, more substantial vehicle than the sporty British article, though less refined than the sometimes massive French *diligence*. It had to negotiate frightful roads without too many upsets. Adapted to railroad service, it might have seats on top, as in Imlay's coaches for the Baltimore and Ohio Railroad, or have an almost boat-shaped body, as in our drawing of *Old Ironsides* with her train. Both these and the early British railway carriages suffered from their short wheelbase, which gave them a nasty fore-and-aft motion, called with some reason, by children, "sick-making". As might have been expected, one of the first improvements was in mounting each on eight wheels.

A very early example of a railroad coach on pivoted trucks or bogies was one called *Victory* built by Imlay for the Philadelphia and Columbia Railroad in 1834. (Before this, there had been one on the St. Etienne–Lyon Railway in France.) An old model of *Victory* survived the years. Between the trucks, the body was of Imlay's boat-shaped form. An apparent clerestory deck on the roof may have been a sort of box-truss to

(above) One of the carriages drawn by the Atlantic in 1832 for the Baltimore and Ohio Railroad.

prevent sagging. There has been speculation about apparently blind compartments over the trucks, even so optimistic as to suggest that one contained a bar and the other a water-closet. The likelihood seems remote. But eight-wheelers appeared generally in the 'forties under the influence of John Stevens on the Camden and Amboy Railroad, and Ross Winans on the Baltimore and Ohio. By the time Charles Dickens came to the United States in 1841, he was already able to describe their coaches as resembling a *shabby omnibus*, with a passage down the middle. His hosts, who had welcomed him as a distinguished English Liberal, were annoyed when they read his *American Notes*.

By then there were even sleeping cars of a sort. On the Cumberland Valley Railroad in the United States they put on bunk-cars which enabled people to lie down by night, though not, possibly, to sleep. Even at the speeds of the day, the journey was short. The time was 1836.

Two years later, in England, there was the *bed-carriage* on the night service from London to the North West. It was of the usual compartment type with, at one end, a boot such as the road coaches had had for carrying the mails. But in this case, the end passenger partition was hinged; padded boards were put between the seats, and for a supplement first-class passengers could lie down with their feet in the extra space. If they

A *The* Experiment *carriage was built for the Stockton and Darlington Railway in 1825. It was merely a stage coach body placed on a wagon underframe. Luggage was placed on top and the guard probably sat outside.*

B *This second-class coach belonging to the Lancashire and Yorkshire Railway*

Company was in use in 1839 on the Manchester–Leeds line.

C *The* DeWitt Clinton, *designed by John B. Jervis for the Mohawk and Hudson Railroad and built in 1831 by the West Point Foundry, used stage-coach type cars also. The bottom part of the tender held water—probably the first "water-bottom tank" tender.*

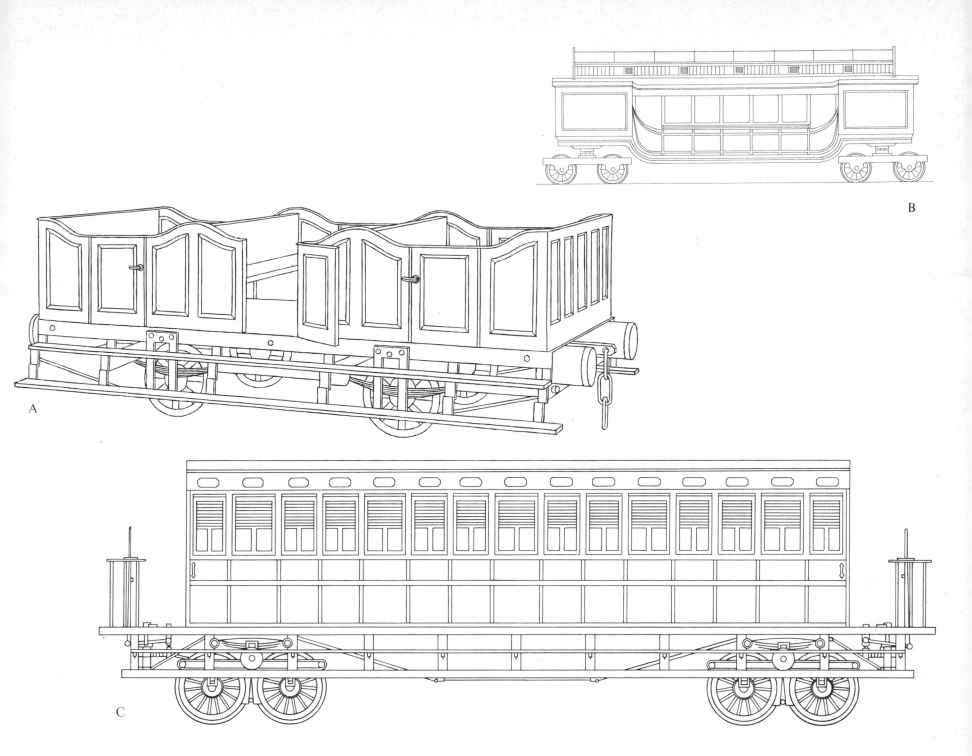

A Third-class carriages were introduced in 1838. They were not much different from goods wagons in that they had no seats or roof. In 1844 Parliament decreed that at least one train each way per day should have protected third-class seating. These coaches were called "Parliamentaries".

B This was the first passenger car with a raised roof. Named "Victory", it was designed by Imlay and built in 1836 for the Philadelphia and Columbia Railroad.

C This American passenger car was designed and built by Ross Winans. His double truck cars first appeared in the mid-1830s. This example is probably from the early 1840s.

did not literally go to bed in their boots, two or three might do so with their feet in a collective one.

"First-class!" The term arrived early, as did "second-class" and "third-class" where Europe was concerned, to denote excellence or inferiority according to the fare paid. But in America then, as in communist countries much later, "class" was a dirty word. So old American railroad advertisements advised patrons that the fare would be so-many dollars in the *best cars* and so-many-less in the *accommodation cars*. Even under Louis-Philippe, that uneasy French king, egalitarian feelings were soothed by the terms *diligence, omnibus* and *wagon*. That must do for passenger cars for the present. Except in America, they were quite singularly unimaginative; on the other hand the European first-class soon became very comfortable within the limitations of tradition, especially on the broad-gauge trains of the Great Western Railway in England, whose standard first-class compartments could seat eight assorted stout men and fat women—John and Joan Bulls—with room to spare on the best hair-stuffed morocco leather. But there was no winter heating for them, no applied sanitation, while the vegetable-oil lamps dropped through holes in the roof at night were of the dimmest sort. These appeared in the late eighteen-thirties.

ENGINEERING PROGRESS

From these passenger-miseries, let us turn to the more heroic progress of locomotion, and at this point we come to some singular equations of English, American and German practice. In England, the firm of Bury, Curtis and Kennedy in the late thirties was building Bury's little bar-framed locomotives, for both the London and Birmingham, and other English railways, and for the American market. In America, indeed, they did quite well, though the Baltimore and Ohio Railroad was sticking to the old vertical type engines with bottle boilers, exemplified by the "Grasshoppers" of Phineas Davis (so-called because their overhead levers suggested the hind-legs of those agile insects).

But the Bury engine was still a rigid thing for American track of the time. Matthias Baldwin's eleventh locomotive, the *Black Hawk* of 1835, had a Bury boiler combined with inclined outside cylinders at the front, which was supported on a four-wheel truck, while the driving axle was in rear of the firebox, as in *Brother Jonathan*. There were no main frames; the boiler barrel held the engine together, as with the steam road rollers of much later years.

Even more successfully, William Norris of Philadelphia took the Bury locomotive, retaining the bar frames and the driving axle in front of the firebox, but using the leading four-wheel truck and inclined outside cylinders as in the Baldwin *Black Hawk*. Norris's *The Washington Farmer* of 1836 distinguished herself by hauling a load up a gradient of 1 in 14. The secret of her success was doubtless in the high proportion of her modest weight being on the driving wheels. The Norris locomotive of this type was extremely successful in its day; even the Birmingham and Gloucester Railway in England invested in a set, and had more built in British works.

Development became rapid. In the *Hercules*, built for the Beaver Meadow Railroad in 1836, two coupled axles, fore-and-aft of the firebox, replaced the single one. Garrett and Eastwick of Philadelphia were the builders; their foreman was Joseph Harrison, who had been one of Norris's men. He became a partner, and in 1839 Eastwick and Harrison produced the *Gowan and Marx* for the Philadelphia and Reading Railroad. This was of pure Bury-Norris type, but with both coupled axles ahead of the firebox. There was a steam-jet blower for maintaining draught while standing. Hackworth had first used this, but it was hitherto unknown in the States. Though she weighed but eleven tons, the little *Gowan and Marx* succeeded in hauling 423 tons on a slightly falling grade from Reading to Philadelphia at nearly ten miles an hour. It was a prodigy!

Norris's famous design had developed, by 1839, into the form exemplified by his No. 25, named *Pegasus*, for the Baltimore and Ohio Railroad. This was to be the basic form of the ordinary American locomotive for half a century, though progressively enlarged and improved. Indeed, it became cosmopolitan.

A most interesting development of the Bury-Norris form belongs to Germany. August Borsig founded locomotive works first at Moabit and then at Tegel, Berlin, and then his own foundry at Moabit. He took Norris's six-wheel type, but to steady it he added a trailing carrying axle. Higher speeds were intended, without coupling the axles. This, and many succeeding engines, were built for German service; initially for the Berlin-Anhalt Railway and later for the Cologne-Minden Railway and others. Now German railways at the time were closely modelled on the British, with a fairly solid *permanent way* compared with the happy-go-lucky American *track*. While that leading truck had been designed to cope with the inequalities of the latter, it showed on the former, at higher speeds, a fearsome tendency to waggle about. At worst it could completely derail and get itself at right-angles to the engine frames. In later designs, Borsig substituted a single rigid axle in rear of the cylinders, and on the solid road all was well again. This form may be studied in a splendid replica of Borsig's *Beuth* (named affectionately after his old professor) in the Deutsches Museum, Munich. *Beuth* was altogether a more finished, more robust and indeed very beautiful engine compared with the original *Borsig*.

A few notes are deserved on early German railways generally. Germany was still a sprawl of independent states ranging from kingdoms to tiny principalities, not yet welded into an empire by Prince Bismarck and the King of Prussia. They ordered things very much their own way, with dozens of separate railway undertakings under company ownership. Soon after Queen Victoria had succeeded to the British throne and married Prince Albert of Saxe-Coburg-Gotha, there was a family squabble with Ernest-Augustus, King of Hanover and Duke of Cumberland. Under the Salic Law, Victoria could not

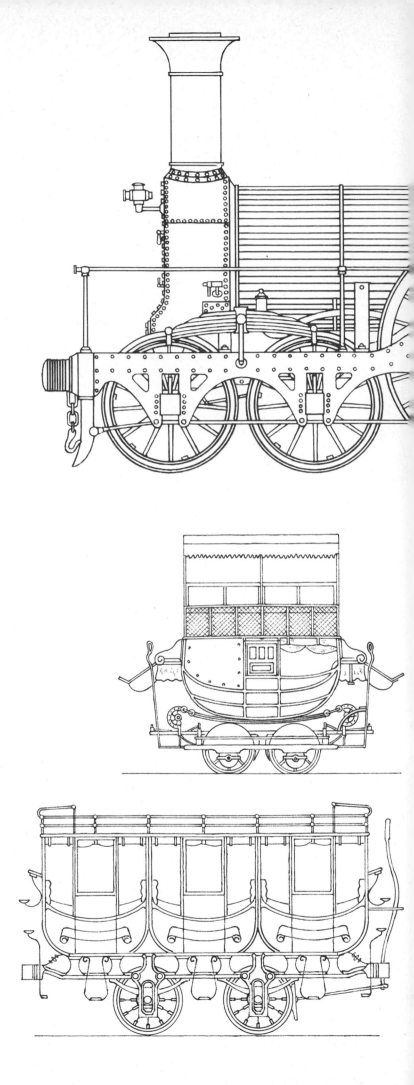

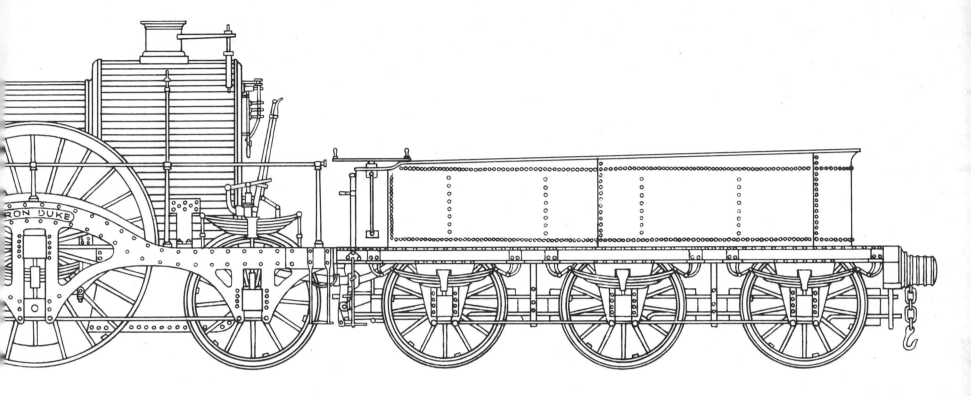

Daniel Gooch of the Great Western Railway built the Iron Duke *in 1847. It was a broadgauge engine with an outside sandwich frame. The heating surface was 1944·8 sq. ft. and boiler pressure was 100 lb. per sq. inch. It was later increased to 115 lb. per sq. inch. The cylinders were 18 by 24 inches and the Gooch valve gear was used. The engine weighed 35½ tons of which 12·3 tons were on the driving wheels.*

Two early stage-coach type American cars.

succeed to the Hanoverian throne (as the Queen delicately put it ; "Hanover is no longer a British possession!"). But Ernest-Augustus equally could not succeed to the British throne, and one retains an impression of a king with a chip on his shoulder. According to a persistent story, within his kingdom he decreed that trains entering Hanover should *never connect* with trains going to a further destination. There was business, however, in his cantankerosity. It meant that travellers from West to East, kicking their heels in his capital, were bound to spend money there.

In a previously distrustful world, railways enjoyed in the eighteen-thirties a business boom. In the middle eighteen-forties, there was a second, far greater one, known in England with some reason as the Railway Mania, which was reflected on a rather less lunatic scale in other countries. Sanity prevailed in Belgium, already quite highly industrial and densely populated, where railway construction from the first was under State enterprise and planned for the national advantage. Whether the promoters were acquisitive or State-minded, it resulted in important railways being built between principal cities and out to other places. The steam railway became a part of modern life.

Under such conditions, it flourished, and ironically it advanced mechanically, most admirably, where people believed in cut-throat competition, the Law of the Jungle, and all that. As to the train, therefore, let us turn back to that magnificent Great Western Railway in England (which was to be speedily at war with its neighbours, the London and North Western and the London and South Western). The three had the first main lines out of London, and for years they were to fight bitterly for traffic in overlapping areas and often between the same cities.

The Great Western, as remarked, had the advantage of a most generous broad gauge, allowing its trains to be much faster and very much more comfortable for its passengers. On the other hand it was sandwiched by the two rivals named. Even in practical America, there were at first variations in gauge, and a competing company would virtuously advertise itself as being "opposed to all monopolies".

So to the Great Western Railway in England let us go for what might be called the *Apotheosis of the Patentee*, though it was not quite that. It was the transformation of a little basic design (e.g. Bavaria's *Adler*) into what for many years would be a *very big* locomotive.

Daniel Gooch, a North-Eastern Englishman, was still under 21 when I. K. Brunel placed him in charge of the Great Western locomotives, which apart from *North Star* and *Morning Star* were a frightful outfit of mechanical monsters. The young Gooch wisely standardized on the Stephenson Patentee type with its solidity and what one might call its mechanical integrity. His brother John assumed a similar position on the rival South Western line. As far as we know, the brothers, though under business rivals, between them produced a valve gear which, through variation in the position of a link between excentrics and valve rods, could use steam expansively instead of simply admitting and exhausting it, as in the old "gab" gear which survives to this day in Kitson's *Lion*. Almost simultaneously, Robert Stephenson and Company, and Alexander Allan on the Grand Junction Railway, also in England, were working on similar gears, all of which were to be used for many years all over the world.

As to straight locomotive design, by the late eighteen forties Gooch had produced the first of many splendid eight-wheel engines—still basically "Patentees"—but incomparably bigger, more powerful, and faster. We show the *Iron Duke* of 1847 (p. 69) traced from a plate in the 1851 edition of Tredgold's *The Steam Engine*. This engine had 8 ft. driving wheels, 18 in. by 24 in. cylinders, 100 lb./sq. in. boiler pressure (later 115 lb.) and 1,944·8 sq. ft. of heating surface, so she was indeed a giant of her day. Corresponding vital statistics of the original *Patentee* were 5 ft., 12 in. by 18 in. and 50 lb./sq. in.

The *Iron Duke* was named for Wellington, that eminent general of whom it was written that *the more one reads of Wellington, the more one respects him and the less one likes him.* He was a military hero in the same company as Leonidas, Pompey, William Wallace and Gustavus Adolphus, and it was not through his own fault that, unlike them, he died in his bed. As to the engine, many like her were built, with but minor alteration, for forty-one years after.

One of the class, the *Great Britain*, made in May, 1848, one of the earliest record runs, fully authenticated by instruments on a dynamometer car (also Gooch's invention). She took a train of ordinary coaches plus the dynamometer-car from the original Paddington terminus in London to Didcot, 53 miles, in 47·5 minutes. The train probably weighed about 75 tons at most, but the average speed, start-to-stop, was just over 67 miles an hour, against a slight but constant gradient. Ordinary Great Western fast trains at the time averaged rather more than 50 miles an hour, start-to-stop, with usual maxima in the 'sixties. These speeds were much faster than anything else in the British Isles; indeed the Great Western, with its great engines on broad gauge and an extremely solid road, was by far the fastest railway in the world at that time. It extended from London to Bristol, with broad-gauge connection by allied companies to Exeter and even to the outskirts of Plymouth at Laira. It was indeed a majestic railway.

Robert Stephenson, 1803–1859, was the only son of George Stephenson who made sure that Robert received the education which he missed. In 1821 he was assisting his father in surveying the Stockton and Darlington Railway and from then on he became more and more his partner rather than assistant. He became manager of his father's locomotive works and was appointed the sole engineer for the Birmingham– London line which, when it was completed in 1839, was the first railway into London. Although maintaining his interest in locomotive engineering, he began to specialize in bridge-building— among his most famous achievements are the Conway Bridge, the Britannia Bridge over the Menai Straits and the Victoria Bridge over the St. Lawrence river. He refused a knighthood for his contributions to engineering and continued working until his death at the age of 56.

The railroad brought prosperity to many isolated towns and it was common to see factories springing up in its wake. Better communications meant easier access to markets. The railroad was faster and could carry more freight than the canal which quickly fell into disuse.

From the railroading point of view, this term means the years 1850 to 1875, rather than from 1840 to 1860. The commercial side of the industry set during those twenty-five years from 1850. It was not to change much until well on in the twentieth century, and more was the pity from the practical railwayman's point of view, for it was based on the idea of a mechanical monopoly.

In those years, wherever the rails advanced, the carriers and coaching firms retreated. To be sure, the river steamboats fought a rearguard action up and down the great rivers of both America and Europe. They could hold their own on bulk but not on speed, as indeed they continued to do on the great European waterways. As for transport by rail, the lines had spread through the land of their birth from south-western Cornwall (Trevithick's country) to Caithness (the extreme north-eastern corner of Watt's Scotland) while the narrow British waterways languished and sometimes died. The only real fighting was between rival railway companies where the local brand of democracy demanded what it called *unfettered competition*, as in North America, and to a lesser extent in Great Britain. There were several large-scale brawls between company-hired ruffians in the latter; in America there was sometimes not only battle but murder and sudden death, with charging locomotives striking on disputed rights-of-way and guns being fired in anger.

Assisted by such various agents as American gunmen and that Emperor of All the Russias who is supposed to have decided a disputed survey by using his sword as a ruler for the line from St. Petersburg to Moscow, the lines spread rapidly. They were all over Western Europe, even over the Semmering and under the Col de Frejus. They spanned European Russia, even in the deep south. They were opening up Scandinavia where, ever since 1798, they had been linking waterways and mines, though steam did not appear until Munktell of Eskiltuna produced the grotesque little *Förstlingen* (*The Pioneer*) in 1853. Most spectacularly they crossed North America from Atlantic to Pacific (1869).

Such tremendous geographical development meant corresponding mechanical improvement and variations. Railways across mountains needed locomotives very different from those on fast service between cities; more akin to those for heavy coal and iron haulage. One cannot easily divide mechanical history by arbitrary dates, and here we must look back a little. From early Victorian England, with the astonishing flight of that auspiciously named engine *Great Britain*, we must turn first to America and then to Austria.

Something odd was not unexpected on the old Camden and Amboy Railroad in Pennsylvania with Isaac Dripps in action. His *Monster*, 1836, had been a monster indeed. The drawing (p. 64) is fairly explanatory, when one recovers from astonishment. Points to be noted are the drive through side-levers by reversed cylinders, and the effect of eight coupled axles achieved by coupling two pairs and putting gears between Nos. 2 and 3. Very notable was the use of tapering in the boiler shell, which was to be regarded as "modern" a century later, at any rate in the English-speaking countries, and for long in Austria too.

Again among eight-coupled coal engines, there were the "Mud-diggers" of the Baltimore and Ohio Railroad. The second one, with a Bury boiler, is shown here. She was built by Ross Winans in 1844, and her predecessor had a large version of the old upright gin-bottle boiler which was hopelessly inadequate for any but a very small engine. Both had simple coupled axles, though drive was through jackshaft and spur wheels.

Both these types, with their rigid wheel-bases, were prone to derailment on the light tracks of the time. The nickname of the Winans engines describes their habits only too well, while Dripps' *Monster* was later rebuilt as 4-6-0 or 2-C. But long before that, the idea of a really flexible engine had engaged engineers. Even Blackett and Hedley had tried it, and in 1832, for the South Carolina Railroad, West Point Foundry built an experimental engine with twin chassis supporting a double-barrelled boiler, the firebox in the middle. The design is usually credited to Horatio Allen. It was a very early example of an articulated locomotive, assuming *Puffing Billy's* metamorphosis to have furnished the first.

THE SEMMERING TRIALS

Our scene shifts to the old Habsburg Empire, where between Vienna and Trieste was built the first great main-line railway across a major mountain range. The Semmering Pass went back in transport history to the Middle Ages. It was the lowest of the Alpine passes, but still, for a railroad, involved a summit level of 2,880 ft., much tunnelling, and a ruling gradient of 1 in 40. The line was begun in 1848, by Carlo Ghega, who favoured locomotive traction from the first, though State bigwigs suggested both atmospheric and cable traction as being the only ones possible. Atmospheric traction, be it added, was a mechanical aberration of the middle 'forties. It involved a continuous vacuum pipe with a slot in the top, closed, or supposed to be closed, by a flap-valve of greased leather. Trains were connected to pistons running inside the pipe, and while stationary pumps at intervals exhausted the air in front of the train piston, atmospheric pressure in its rear pushed the cars along at very considerable speed. The cumbersome locomotive engine, said its promoters (among whom one is sorry to count I. K. Brunel) was doomed. Four such lines were in public service: London-Croydon, and South Devon, in England; Le Pecq-St. Germain in France, and Dublin-Kingstown (Dun Laoghaire) in Ireland. Apart from absurd junction complications, the thing was a frightful fiasco after a very short time. Wear-and-tear was fearsome. Rats ate the greased leather valves with great relish. It came and it went, most fortunately before people could take it and play pranks on that magnificent Austrian Southern Railway over the Semmering.

A prize of 20,000 Florins was offered for a powerful and flexible locomotive capable of working such a line. The competition has been called, with retrospect to that between Liverpool and Manchester in 1829, the "Rainhill of the Alps". Joseph Anton Maffei of Munich, whose locomotive genius was Joseph Hall, an emigré Englishman, entered the *Bavaria*, shown on p. 85. She was the winning engine, and managed 132 tons behind the tender at 11·34 miles an hour on the rising gradient of 1 in 40. But she was really a box of tricks. Her second and driving axles were chain-coupled as in ancient Stephenson practice, and so were her trailing axle and the leading tender axle. Side rods coupled the leading and second axles. The chains constantly broke; the engine did no regular work, and her big boiler was used to drive the machines in the workshops at Maribor (now in Yugo-Slavia) until 1870.

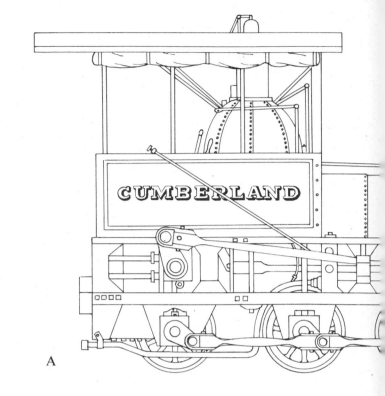

A

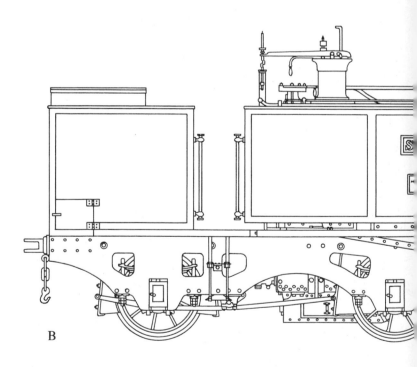

B

A *Ross Winans' "Mud-digger" type derived its name from the way in which it pounded up the dirt from the light track then in use, but* *each engine had its own name. That illustrated is the* Cumberland. *They were excellent engines and some were in use as late as 1865.*

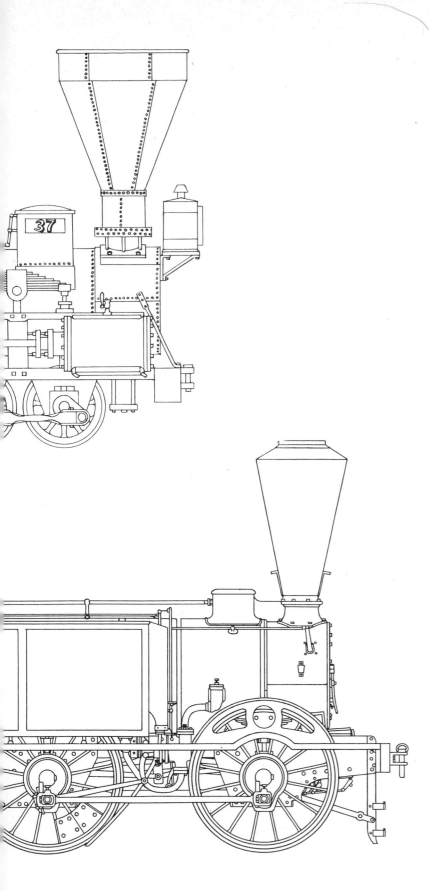

From John Cockerill of Seraing, Belgium, came the interesting little double engine *Seraing*. Here was a relatively modern development of Horatio Allen's *South Carolina*, with two motor-bogies and a centrally-fired, double barrelled boiler. In its turn, this design anticipated the double-bogie engines built in quite considerable numbers by British works from the middle-sixties onwards under patents granted—with rather dubious justification—to Robert Fairlie. Fairlie used outside cylinders, which made his engines much more accessible than Cockerill's.

John Haswell was a Scot, born near Glasgow in 1812. He went to Austria about 1837 and soon became engineer of the Vienna-Raab Railway and Director of the Imperial-Royal Austrian State Railway Works. We have seen Haswell locomotives at work and in good shape when they were over a century old, on the Graz-Köflach Railway in Styria. That outrageous fraud of our own time, which some rascal called "built-in obsolescence" —meaning jerry-built to wear out quickly—was unthinkable in the great old days.

For the Semmering trials, Haswell built an engine called *Vindobona*. Our drawing shows her as she appeared during the trials; the first European locomotive with four coupled axles, and the forerunner of many thousands. One notes the firebox, which had a flat crown-plate and a rectangular casing, anticipating the later form of Alfred Belpaire, that eminent Belgian. Though her Semmering performance was rather feeble, she was quite the most practical engine of those entered, with few troublesome gadgets.

Günther of Wiener-Neustadt entered another articulated engine with two motor bogies like Cockerill's, but with a single long boiler. It had outside cylinders, being thus better than the *Seraing,* though the Stephenson link motion remained dreadfully inaccessible. It rather anticipated the Mallet and Meyer types of locomotive built in more recent times.

The Austrian Southern Railway bought all these engines, but one doubts that any were of much more use than the winner, the all-too-complex *Bavaria* which showed the best trial performance. All could do the job, provided that they did not break down, but they often did so. Late in 1851 Wilhelm Engerth made for the Austrian Ministry of Transport yet another design. In this, the rear of the engine was partly supported by the tender through a radial connection ahead of the firebox, this coming between the two tender axles. The latter in turn were coupled by side rods, and a set of three gear wheels conveyed tractive power from the driving axle to the leading tender axle. This flexible drive to the tender was indeed the only weak point of the design. Though ingenious, it gave trouble like the other people's complex drives. Without it, the Engerth locomotive made an excellent mountain engine of its day, and in France the Eastern, Northern, Midi and Dauphiné Railways found it useful also for heavy coal haulage. There were even Engerth express passenger locomotives in France and Switzerland, and from the latter we show one of a once numerous class on the Swiss Central Railway. The *Speiser* was built in 1857 and ran until 1902, afterwards being kept as a relic. We recall seeing a six-coupled Swiss "Engerth" still in service as late as 1927, and a French one worked on the La Bastide-Mende line up to World War II. The Engerth principle was applied to narrow-gauge locomotives for Spain right into relatively modern times, and in a modified form. As we write, we know of quite advanced examples still at work in that country.

Austrian practice, however, discarded the supporting-tender principle fairly early, finding that a long-boilered eight-coupled locomotive (0-8-0, or D) served perfectly well the purposes of the Semmering, and later of the Arlberg, Brenner and Tauern lines.

Several funny things happened in British locomotive engineering at mid-century. We have seen Joseph Hall, the Englishman going to Munich and producing *Bavaria*, we have seen Haswell the Scot becoming an eminent Austrian. Next we have the case of Thomas Russell Crampton who was another Englishman being cold-shouldered in his own country but honoured and rewarded by both the Germans and the French.

He had been one of Daniel Gooch's young men on the Great Western Railway, and his experience with broad-gauge engines convinced him that, subject to some mechanical tricks of his, an ordinary "narrow" locomotive could go just as fast, and even be as powerful, as Gooch's splendid examples. Some of his earlier patents and designs look fantastic, but by the late eighteen-forties he had produced a most interesting type of locomotive (p. 74).

As will be seen, he placed his driving axle in rear of the firebox, to keep the centre of gravity down. (Low centre-of-gravity was a shibboleth of the period; it was supposed to prevent trains from tipping over on curves, but in fact it caused much rough riding and disturbance of the still flimsy tracks.)

B *Wilhelm Engerth's express tank locomotive, the* Speiser, *built in 1857 for the Swiss Central Railway.*

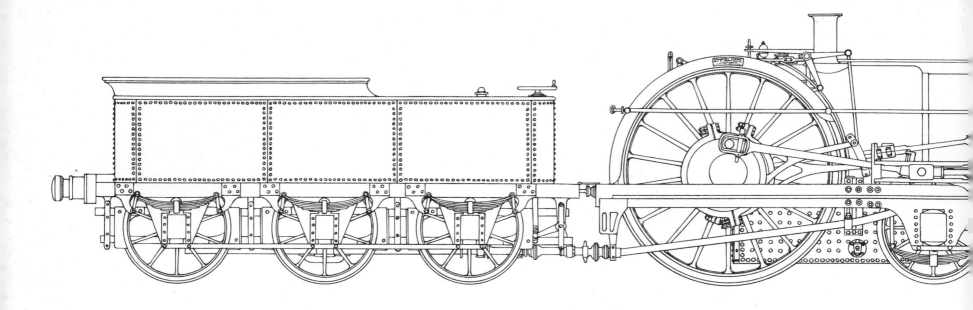

THE CRAMPTON

Crampton's first practical locomotives were six built during 1847. Two, named *Liége* and *Namur*, went to Belgium. One, named *Kinnaird*, went to the Dundee and Perth Junction Railway in Scotland. The others became Nos. 81, 83 and 85 of the South Eastern Railway in England, where Charles Dickens may have been familiar with them, he knowing the South Eastern well. (It killed Mr. Carker, very properly, in *Dombey and Son*.)

Apart from its huge driving wheels right at the rear, the design had other features very important for the future. Cylinders, connecting rods and valve gear were all completely outside with the platforms raised to make them entirely accessible. Years after, this was to be invariable practice in both Continental Europe and North America, while ironically England was very late in adopting it.

Two rather similar engines to these were built; one generally larger and called *London* for the London and North Western Railway, and the last with a longer boiler barrel, for the Maryport and Carlisle Railway in the extreme North of England. In all cases the tenders seem to have closely resembled the standard form on the Great Western Railway, recalling T. R. Crampton's office under Daniel Gooch. These early Crampton engines were not entirely successful. Their boilers were inadequate, especially as to firebox heating surface: indeed the original Crampton firebox was an odd thing, with the grate longer than the distance between back-plate and tube-plate. The Scottish engine *Kinnaird*, however, lasted long enough to be photographed in service by R. E. Bleasdale, the first photographer to make a systematic collection, recording locomotives all over the British Isles during the second half of last century.

Crampton's patents were many, and he was responsible for several distinct types of locomotive, some with drive through jackshaft or "dummy crank-axle".

By far the most successful was that generally called the "French Crampton", which had very strong outside frames, the cylinders being supported between these and the inside frames, together with the driving and valve motion. *Le Continent* of the Eastern Railway of France, was built in 1852 by Derosne, Cail and Company of Paris, who had first taken up the design in 1848 with an order of twelve engines for the French Northern

A *T. R. Crampton's giant,* Liverpool, *built for the London and North Western Railway in 1848.*

B *Two railway policemen slowing down trains with flag signals (1840s).*

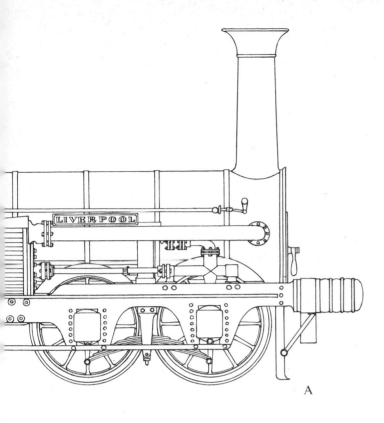

A

B

Railway. With a light express train of first-class carriages—forerunner of the "limited" of later years, a "French Crampton" was an extremely fast runner. Though rather rough-riding, with their low centre of gravity and relatively long rigid wheelbase, the engines were steady runners, and were much liked both in France and in the German States. That named above was in service until 1919 on light work, any locomotive being useful in wartime! The old thing had been in the retreat after Sedan, back in 1870. She can still steam, and occurs in films from time to time.

Ironically, though even the "French Crampton" was initiated with several engines on the English Eastern Counties Railway, and one on the North British Railway which was painted all over in Royal Stuart tartan to please Queen Victoria, T. R. Crampton was without honour in British railway circles. For one thing, Gooch's great broad-gauge engines on the Great Western Railway stole their thunder, and when Crampton produced an engine (of "French Crampton" type) called *Liverpool*, which equalled the best of Gooch's in power and speed potential, she simply tore to pieces the much lighter track of the London and North Western Railway which had invested in her. Apart from this one, most of the British Crampton engines were quite deficient in boiler power. Directors were very much afraid of high boiler pressures. On the Great Western, Gooch went his own way in this respect, and being a wise man, did not advertise his pressures to those who, in his opinion, had no business to know about such things.

In America at that time, the Crampton type was likewise a failure, for the same reasons, only, in respect of track destruction, more so. For John Stevens on the Camden and Amboy Railroad, Isaac Dripps built several chiefly notable for their 8 ft. driving wheels and for their nightmare appearance. (Some of the French and German engines were of great elegance.) For an example of an American Crampton engine we show (p. 76) the rather more shapely *Lightning*, built by Norris for the Utica and Schenectady Railroad in 1849. She was to be sure much more "English" in appearance and arrangement than other American locomotives of the time, even down to the stuffed leather side buffers, which were very rarely used in the States, even then. She had, however, Norris's bogie or leading truck. Apparent weak points were in the extreme lightness of the outside frames. She was also much too small, but had she been bigger, it is doubtful that she ever would have held the road at all.

In France, as remarked, the Crampton engine was a great success in the sort of work for which it had been designed; for nearly thirty years it worked all the fastest passenger trains between Paris and Strasbourg, and in the cadets' slang of the Military Academy of St. Cyr, *prendre le Crampton* meant to take the train, to go on leave, to have a night out, long after Crampton locomotives had finally vanished from French railways. Two Crampton engines have survived the years; *Le Continent* as mentioned, and in Germany, the Badenese *Phoenix*, which for many years was kept for instruction in mechanical engineering at *Karlsruhe*. There is also a beautiful replica of *Die Pfalz*, one built by Maffei of Munich in Joseph Hall's time for the Palatinate Railway. Both these German Cramptons had Hall's arrangement of cranks, which mounted all the motion—connecting rods and valve gear, outside the external frames, giving splendid accessibility with less likelihood of running hot, at the expense of making the engine somewhat wide. Lineside structures had to be kept at their distance. A solitary English engine with a similar arrangement, by J. E. McConnell of the London and North Western, was so destructive in this way that the men named her *Mac's Mangle*.

In Central Europe, Hall's cranks with outside frames were much used. Maffei built them in engines for the Bavarian State and Bavarian Eastern Railways. Thousands of Austrian locomotives had them; consequently they were to be seen, during the middle and later years of the nineteenth century, fairly continuously on a journey from the French frontier of Baden to the Bosphorus. For an engine of this type and period we show p. 86 the *Erzsébet* on the Royal Hungarian State Railways. Though not a particularly distinguished example, she was typical of the eighteen-sixties in the Danubian countries, and was notable as being the thousandth locomotive built by G. Sigl of Wiener-Neustadt. In the drawing we have shown the ceremonial decorations bestowed on her to celebrate the fact.

Sigl's works produced many bogie engines during this time, unlike most European builders, for the several Austro-Hungarian State Railways and for the Austrian Southern Railway. We show one of these (p. 77) with large driving wheels for passenger train haulage on the more level lines both north and south of the Alps. This particular engine dates from the late 'seventies but is best exemplified here. Like *Erzsébet* she typifies the Hall/

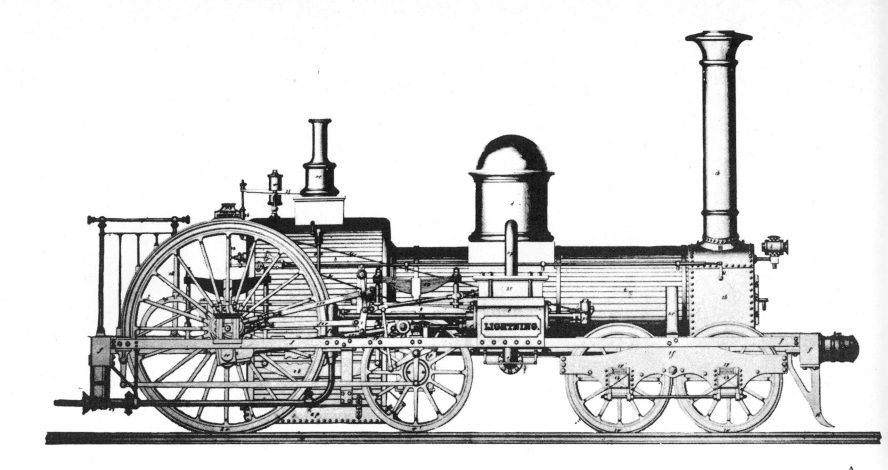

A

Haswell locomotive of the Danubian countries, with her deep, slotted, outside frames taking much of her weight and, through the bearings, most of the strains of a heavy engine in motion. The drawings show also how the excentric sheaves and rods were between the bearings and the main cranks. Common French and Italian practice of the time was to mount the valve gear *outside* these, which was T. R. Crampton's arrangement.

PIONEER RAILROADING IN RUSSIA

Neither such arrangements enjoyed any popularity in North America, nor yet in the British Isles, in spite of the fact of Crampton and Hall having been Englishmen and Haswell a Scot. There were many migrant engineers at this time, not least in Russia, which had at first absolutely no mechanical engineering tradition of her own. Harrison and Eastwick from the United States, and Ross Winans also, moved in on the design of Russian locomotives and vehicles. One of Russia's pioneer railroad builders was Major George Washington Whistler, a most memorable American, although to a few he is vaguely known as the father of a great artist and by the rest forgotten either by default, or by design for reasons of political prestige. When he went to Russia, it was virgin railroading land, with the Americans and the British both riding hard for the first jump and the Germans watching for the fall of either or both. The British had got in first, as noted before, with the "Patentee" locomotive, though a Uralsk engineer Tcherpinov had produced, as far back as 1833 what appears from a model to have been a "Planet" of sorts, but with the wheels outside instead of within the timber outside frames. It was Whistler who invited the Winans clan and the Eastwick and Harrison outfit to move in on Russia. Whistler was not without cause for honour in his own land; he had built, *inter alia,* the Boston and Albany Railroad over the Berkshires; further when it comes to Russia, he is believed to have been the most interested person present when the Tsar Nicholas I made that alleged ruling in the map with his imperial sword, (or ruler?).

Imperial Russian officials had visited the United States and watched the performance of that remarkable *Gowan and Marx* which we have already encountered. Joseph Harrison was the practical engineer of what had become the firm of Eastwick and Harrison. Both partners were invited to St. Petersburg (Leningrad, as we now know it). A contract

B

A *The* Lightning *was built by E. S. Norris for the Utica and Schenectady Railroad in 1849. Although attractive to look at, she was not too successful and stayed in service hauling express trains for little more than a year.*

B *Joseph Harrison, who helped to set up a locomotive works in Russia where he produced many locomotives.*

A

B

was drawn up, so handsome that Eastwick and Harrison quitted the United States to set up works in Russia.

During the eighteen-forties they produced thoroughly businesslike locomotives; four wheels coupled for passenger work and six for freight. We illustrate here one of the freight engines, usually accepted to have been the first 2-6-0 type ever built. The type had been built already for the St. Etienne-Lyons Railway in 1841. In later years the type was to be very popular, first in the United States and then over most of Western Europe as well as Russia. One of the later American locomotives was named *Mogul* and this became the strict type-name for 2-6-0 or 1-C engines. In common parlance, it was used for all sorts of large steam locomotives in the United States over many years. Looking at this Russian-American design, we notice several differences from what had already become recognised American practice. She had inside slab or plate frames, like many British engines. The arrangement of the cross-heads and slide bars was also very British. The spark-arrester at the base of the smokestack suggested certain old German designs and, although square in plan instead of round, rather anticipated a form very popular in later years on many railways in Sweden. Contemplating the complete lack of any sort of a cab for the enginemen, one wonders how they survived long hauls across Northern Russia in winter.

Eastwick and Harrison's first Russian passenger engines were much more in the American style, though the mounting of the valves inside instead of on top of the cylinders was also distinctly European. These old Eastwick and Harrison locomotives were rebuilt in the eighteen-sixties with new boilers and proper cabs (possibly improvised at an earlier date!).

THE CLASSIC AMERICAN

As remarked, the 4-4-0 engine with outside cylinders and a single-pivoted leading truck early became the American national type, though there remained also a vogue in the States for a somewhat similar engine with the cylinder centre-lines much closer together, driving crank axles instead of cranks outside the driving wheels. It was not quite the same as a later arrangement with inside cylinders, for a long time typical of the British Isles, India, parts of Australia and certain Swedish railways such as the Ber-

A *Sigl's bogie engine for the Semmering Railway; a great prototype.*

B *This Eastwick and Harrison locomotive was built at the Alexandrovsk Works in St. Petersburg in the 1840s.*

Originally it was an 0-6-0 engine but later it was fitted with a leading truck in order to reduce axle loadings, and thus it became the first 2-6-0 in the world. It ran on the St. Petersburg–Moscow Railway.

gslagernas. For a specimen of the old American "inside-connected" locomotive we have chosen the *New York* of the Boston and Providence Railroad (p. 84). She was delivered to the company by George S. Griggs in December, 1854, and had a remarkable double firebox divided by a longitudinal water-filled partition and fed through two firedoors. Above the twin firebox was a combustion chamber receiving the flames through two short flues in a water-bridge.

The same sort of thing was being tried in England at that time, in the interests of burning coal instead of coke without passing most of it blackly out of the chimney as wasteful and nuisance-valuable smoke. For the rest of this very interesting old locomotive, we should notice the still very short and old fashioned leading truck, the early form of the chimney always known in America as a "diamond stack" and the irregular spacing of the rigid axles on the six-wheel tender. This was quite peculiarly an old New England engine.

Much more typical of the expanding United States was the outside-connected 4-4-0 locomotive with inside link valve-motion, working through rockers the slide valves on top of the cylinders which, in turn, were becoming horizontal instead of inclined.

A classic example of the late eighteen-fifties and, most typically, of the war years in the early 'sixties, is shown in the engine by Thomas Rogers of Paterson, New Jersey. The drawing (p. 105) almost identically represents the "war engine", the *General*, which was built in 1855, and on a rainy day of 1862 was captured by a Northern raiding party and driven on a wild tour of sabotage from near Marietta, Georgia, almost to Chattanooga, Tennessee. The story has often been told, sometimes with doubtful "improvements". The *General*, somewhat altered in later years, and narrowed from the old Southern broad gauge is still preserved as a treasured relic.

The Rogers design of this time, and many others generally like it, was both simpler and much more accessible than the type exemplified in Griggs' *New York*. A very great improvement was in the long wheelbase of the leading truck, though this still had a rigid central pivot, without any sideplay. The tender was on two generally similar trucks.

Thousands of such engines were built over many years, gradually increasing in size until, at the end of the century, the largest of them were distinctly adequate. We show (p. 80) an example by the Grant Locomotive Works in 1873; a coal-burner with a diamond stack. The enormous balloon stack on the Rogers engine bespoke wood burning. Both engines have the coned gusset-ring to the boiler-barrel, forming what Americans called the "wagon-top" boiler. Such locomotives were to span the Continent. When this was ceremonially done for the first time, at Promontory Point, Utah, on May 10, 1869, the Central Pacific Railroad's engine from Sacramento was the *Jupiter*, a wood-burner, while the Union Pacific company's No. 119 from Omaha was a coal-burner with an extended smokebox. Otherwise they were very similar engines which the untrained eye might distinguish only by the very differently-shaped smokestacks (the Union Pacific one was straight, with a slightly bulbous cap).

This was the engine of post-war America, as much a part of the American landscape as white wooden frame houses and majestic river steamers. Their enormous headlamps cast night beams far across the prairies, or through vast northern woods, or upon the vertiginous curves of the mountain-rights-of-way. Their music was, to strangers, most melancholy—the soft *choo-choo* of their great stacks, the deep hoots of their whistles and the dolorous clanging of their ornately mounted bells—but to Americans from Atlantic to Pacific these were well-loved sounds, breaking the loneliness of remote places and heralding a nation's advance. By comparison the European locomotive screamed and roared, and to older people especially was often regarded as an intruder. But European youth loved her too, especially in Great Britain where a great coterie of amateurs grew up.

Back to the serious business of design: "Mogul" engines have been mentioned already. The classic form became that shown on p. 106 by an engine built by the Baldwin Locomotive Works about 1870. It is obviously first-cousin to the four-coupled American type but with an extra pair of coupled wheels occupying the space which had previously belonged to the trailing truck wheels, while the four-wheel pivoted truck itself was replaced by a radial one with a single axle—the Bissell truck, for long much favoured in North America. Such locomotives were generally for freight service, but were useful enough for passenger trains in mountain country. It should be remarked that as yet, in spite of many wild claims for record speeds, regular trains were nowhere very fast apart from a few favoured services in Great Britain and France.

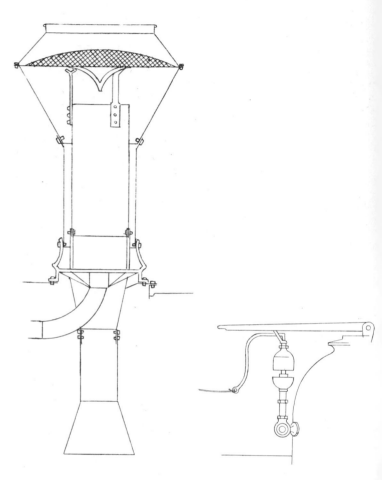

Section of the American "diamond-stack". This arrangement was supposed to prevent cinders flying up from the wood-burning engines.

This is a typical American-type steam whistle. The cord stretched from the whistle into the driver's cab.

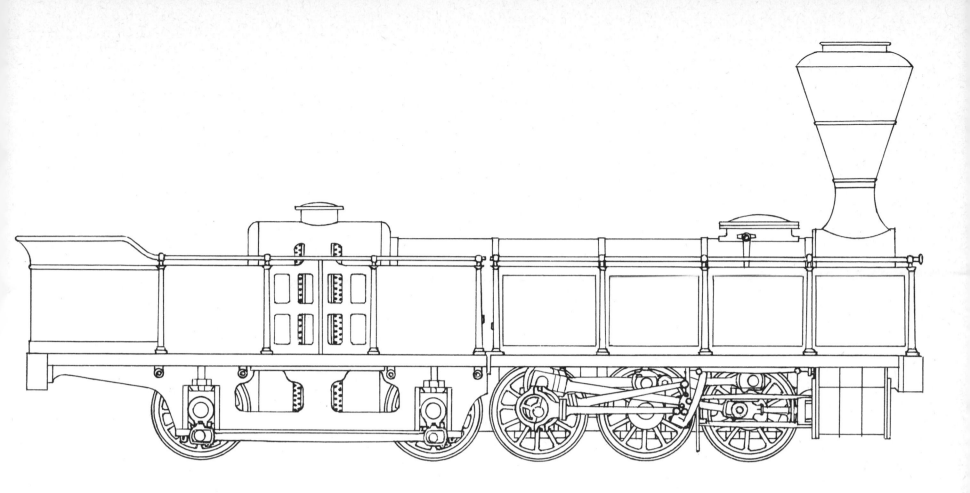

Wilhelm Engerth's 1851 design for the Austrian Ministry of Transport. It was an excellent mountain locomotive.

For one thing; in most places the track would not stand it. Where rail-ends were simply spiked close together on sleeper or cross-tie, without any proper joint, there was bound to be trouble. The English Great Western company and a few others overcame that at the expense of being over-rigid and difficult to relay when that became necessary. The *fish-joint*—the bolting together of rail-ends by lateral plates—was the invention of William Bridges Adams in England. Its use became world-wide, but, Adams being more inventive than businesslike, he never reaped his royalties. After the perfection of Sir Henry Bessemer's process in making steel, by the primary removal of carbon from pig-iron by air blast, and the subsequent re-introduction of a predetermined amount of carbon (*Spiegeleisen*) and ferro-manganese, in 1856, the way was clear for the use of steel instead of iron rails. Two forms of rail were to be used for the best part of a century thereafter; the bull-head rail keyed into iron chairs, much used in Great Britain, India, Western France, the high Alps and for a while in New South Wales, and the flat-footed rail invented by John Stevens in the States, introduced to Europe by Sir Charles Vignoles, which is now generally used throughout the world. Thereafter, up to the use of long welded rail-lengths in our own time, development of the *permanent way* (delightful English expression!) was simply a matter of heavier rails and superior road-bed. Qualities varied from country to country, and from railway to railway. By the end of the century the Pennsylvania Railroad, the London and North Western Railway and some others were immeasurably superior to the—— but even after all these years, that would be insulting! But as tracks improved, locomotives could become heavier and faster, passenger haulage more comfortable, and freight-handling more expeditious and more capacious. So it was.

This standard American Type was
built in 1873 by the Grant
Locomotive Works, Paterson, New
Jersey. By the middle of the 1850s,
the form of the American
locomotive for all ordinary traffic
had set. It was the four-coupled

engine with a leading bogie truck
supporting outside cylinders, later
described as a "4-4-0" in the
American Whyte formula. This
particular engine was a coal-
burner.

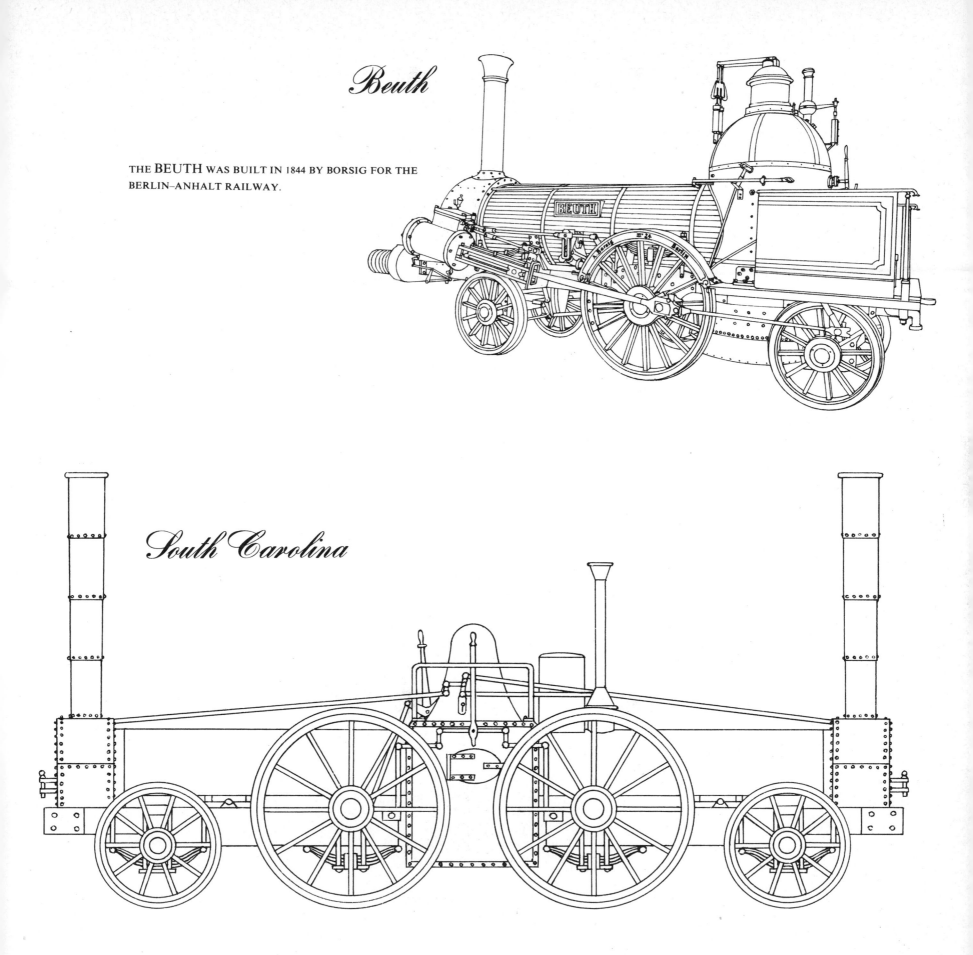

Beuth

THE BEUTH WAS BUILT IN 1844 BY BORSIG FOR THE BERLIN–ANHALT RAILWAY.

South Carolina

THE SOUTH CAROLINA, BUILT IN 1832, WAS THE WORLD'S FIRST ARTICULATED LOCOMOTIVE.

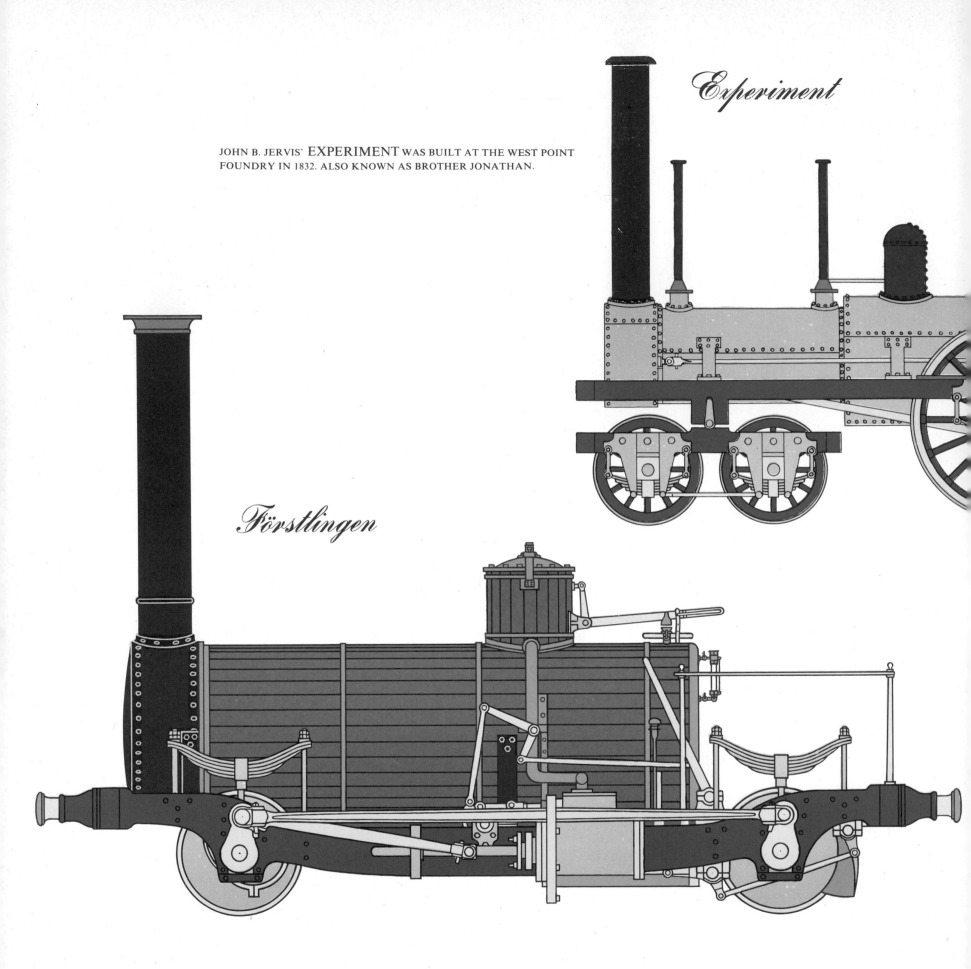

Experiment

JOHN B. JERVIS' EXPERIMENT WAS BUILT AT THE WEST POINT FOUNDRY IN 1832. ALSO KNOWN AS BROTHER JONATHAN.

Förstlingen

THE FÖRSTLINGEN WAS THE FIRST LOCOMOTIVE TO BE BUILT IN SWEDEN, 1848.

Borsig no.1

AUGUST BORSIG'S FIRST LOCOMOTIVE, 1841, TOOK THE AMERICAN NORRIS TYPE AS ITS MODEL.

New York

GRIGGS' INSIDE CONNECTED ENGINE, 1854, ON THE NEW YORK AND PROVIDENCE RAILROAD.
THIS TYPE WERE NICKNAMED "DUTCH WAGONS" FOR THEIR APPARENT SIMPLICITY.

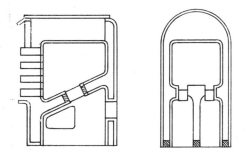

O. W. Bayley's double-barrelled firebox was tested on the New York by Alexander Holly, Siperintendent of Locomotive Engineering on the Boston and Providence Railroad.

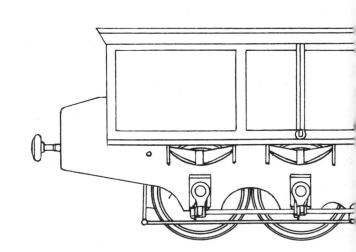

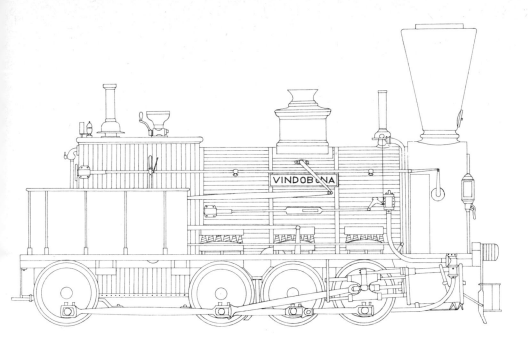

BUILT BY JOHN HASWELL FOR THE SEMMERING TRIALS.

Bavaria

WINNER OF THE SEMMERING TRIALS, THE BAVARIA WAS DESIGNED BY JOSEPH HALL AND BUILT BY J. A. MAFFEI OF MUNICH.

Erzsebet

SIGL'S THOUSANDTH LOCOMOTIVE, THE ERZSEBÈT WAS BUILT IN 1870. SHE IS SHOWN IN HER DECORATIONS FOR THE OCCASION.

T. R. CRAMPTON'S FAMOUS DESIGN, BUILT IN 1846 FOR THE LIÈGE AND NAMUR, SOUTH EASTERN (ENGLAND) AND THE DUNDEE AND PERTH RAILWAYS.

French Crampton

THIS 4-2-0 WAS BUILT BY CAIL OF LILLE IN 1859 FOR THE CHEMIN DE FER DU NORD. DESIGNED BY T. R. CRAMPTON.

FIRING AND FIREBOXES

The heaviest haulage, from the first, was that of minerals; chiefly coal and iron-ore, and later heavy machinery. In coal-bearing country, there was great desirability of the locomotives burning low-grade anthracite, instead of the homely cordwood which fed so many American trains—nicely aromatic and thermally inefficient. England and Scotland, by comparison, were positively luxurious: at first coke, and then the finest hard steam-coal, were the only things worthy of a locomotive! England was rich, though headed for a depression later, and even Scotland was picking-up!

In the United States, Ross Winans was a pioneer in the economic firing of loco-motives, and looking back to the 'forties we see his once-famous "Camel" type of locomotive (so called because of its sloping stern containing a long narrow firebox, plus the placing of the engineer in a cab on top of the boiler, like an Arab traveller on top of the animal's hump). The first of the Winans "Camels" went into service on the Baltimore and Ohio Railroad in 1848, and was indeed named after that disagreeable beast. Winans built about 200 altogether; our drawing shows a specimen of 1852.

Winans had Confederate sympathies in the Civil War, but he had already closed his works in Baltimore. Like Eastwick and Harrison, he found another good market in Russia, where, more than locomotive work, he was strongly to influence car design. In America, however, the Winans type was quickly revived by Samuel Hayes, who most importantly suppressed the leading coupled axle and added a leading four-wheel truck, centred under the cylinders as in the classic American Type. We show a Hayes "Camel" of 1854. Hayes was Master of Machinery on the Baltimore and Ohio Railroad from late in 1851 to the spring of 1856, and the last of his engines, of this type, ran until 1901, after which it was preserved at Purdue University.

A very eminent American designer of those days was James Millholland, who in extreme youth had helped with the building of Peter Cooper's *Tom Thumb*. He became Master of Machinery on the Philadelphia and Reading Railroad in 1848, and almost at once applied himself to getting the last ounce of steam out of low-grade anthracite, in a capacious—and ultimately very wide—firebox whose final form is generally known as the Wootten firebox, named after the President of the "Philly" (the P. and R. Railroad). Millholland's express passenger engines such as *Hiawatha*, *Minnehaha* and *Kosciusco* were famous in their day, and of their kind very beautiful and unusual examples of the usual American type. We illustrate here his *Pennsylvania* of 1863, the first locomotive to have twelve coupled axles. It was in many ways Winans' *Camel* greatly enlarged and modernized by the standards of the time.

In England at this time, even using such beautiful steam coal as that of South Wales, there were problems about any sort of coal burning. Americans might watch affec-tionately a belching of thick black smoke from the advancing stack, but in all Great Britain there were not entirely-dormant penalties for such emission. Yet coke was abominably expensive, and in any case, no locomotive engineer there liked to see all that unburnt stuff being wasted on the fresh air. Joseph Beattie, an ingenious Irishman on the London and South Western Railway, James McConnell, another Celt on the London and North Western, and James I'Anson Cudworth, a northern Englishman on the South Eastern Railway, all set about securing complete combustion by elaborate double firebox arrangements, with midfeathers and water-bridges—and in Beattie's case thermic syphons and complex combustion chambers. We have already seen something of the kind in the little *New York* of the Boston and Providence Railroad. Beside some of Beattie's weird arrangements, her firebox was a simple kitchen kettle!

For the record we show here an outline of Beattie's London and South Western locomotive *Ironsides*, built in 1855. Very briefly she had a single driving axle, but a coupled trailer was quickly incorporated. The drawing shows the engine as she was in 1881, for she had a long life of thirty years. Her firebox was divided into front and back compartments, divided by a water-filled half arch. Heavy firing was in the rear part, the forward fire being kept as far as possible incandescent all the time. Further, at one stage, there was a combustion chamber in the boiler barrel, containing a thermic syphon, so at the expense of some fairly heavy maintenance, a Beattie boiler could be relied on to get very much more than a pound of steam out of an ounce of coal, and so it did. A century ago these engines—for many were built—were not to be beaten at this game. Mechan-ically, the design was one schemed by Sir John Hawkshaw in the 'forties. For years it was very popular in Europe, and steady too, in spite of all that overhang at the front. The first

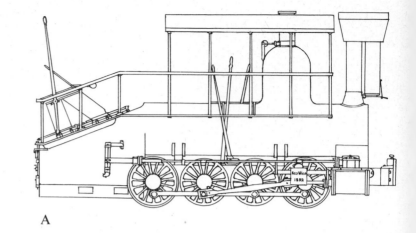

A

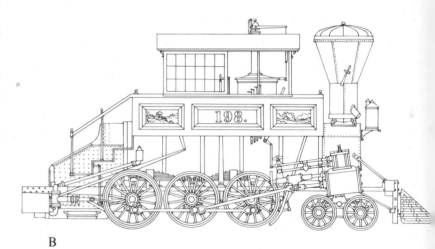

B

(previous page)
Milan Railway Station by Angelo Morbelli, 1863–1919. This painting gives a grand impression of space under the great roof of the station and the lighting through the glass is finely done. The engines and cars of the old S.F. Meridionale are a pretty accurate representation. Note the gas-lamps hanging from the ceiling and on the platform. Courtesy of the Galleria d'Arte Moderna, Milano.

A *The Camel was built by Ross Winans in 1848 for the Baltimore and Ohio Railroad for freight haulage. It marked a great advance in motive power. More than 200 of them were built.*

B *The Hayes's ten-wheeler was designed by the master of machinery at the Baltimore and Ohio Railroad, Samuel Hayes. Similar in outline to the Winans Camel-type, it was used for passenger and freight service. The last of the type was still in service in 1901.*

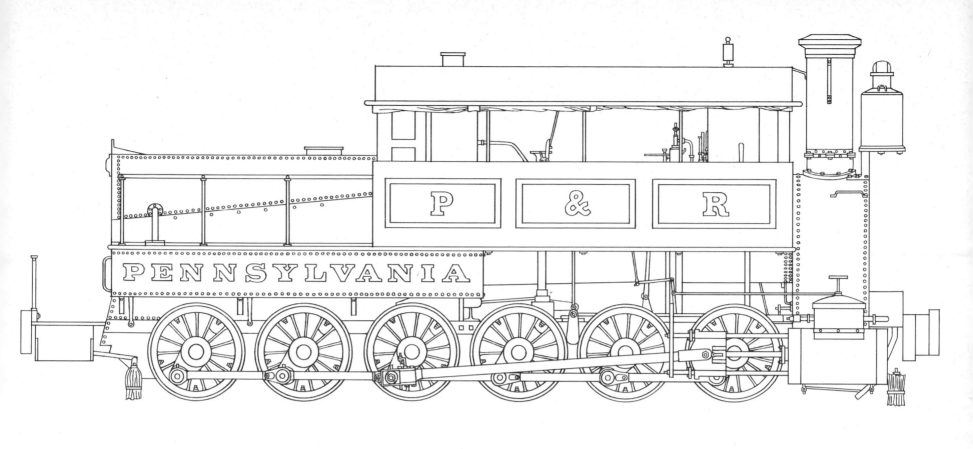

(above) James Millholland designed the Pennsylvania in 1863. It was the first locomotive to have six pairs of driving wheels. It is shown here as it was originally built, with the fuel and water being carried on the engine. However, it had to be rebuilt in 1870 because it had difficulty on the curves, and the rear pair of drivers were taken out with a separate tender being added.

(below) Joseph Beattie's Ironsides was built in June, 1855 at the Nine Elms Works as an express engine for the London and South Western Railway. This drawing shows it after its conversion to four-coupled wheels. It was in use for thirty years, being sold in June 1885.

locomotives of the Swedish State Railways in 1856; built by Beyer Peacock and Company of Manchester, were of this type, though without Joseph Beattie's weird and wondrous fireboxes which probably lost on maintenance what they won on fuel economy, but certainly made their designer nicely rich by patent royalties. The Netherlands State Railways Company (lovely mixture of interests!) had some very fine examples in the late 'seventies, and so did certain Prussian lines such as the Bergisch-Märkische Eisenbahn. On the latter, be it remarked here, a Wagner other than the one who composed *Den Ring* mounted water purifiers in an extra dome on the boiler, the feedwater being allowed in this dome to drop through a series of trays and so, under steam temperature, to deposit its mineral content before this could settle on the boiler plates and do cumulative mischief as the boiler grew older.

All these were extremely elegant engines in the European style; they seemed to breast their head-winds like great swans rising, though to American eyes, in absence of that leading truck, they seemed likely to become airborne in a less desirable way than that of the noble bird. They were in fact remarkably steady, and fast too. On the London and South Western they could *average* their mile-a-minute, *by schedule*, with a favourable gradient.

Another archaic type of British locomotive which lasted for a very long time and was to be used in many other countries was one which had originated in the late 'forties. It was generally known as the "Jenny Lind" type, a famous early example having been named after that sweet singer from Sweden who, incidentally, was to number among her later lovers one James Staats Forbes, for many years Managing Director of the London Chatham and Dover Railway. The drawing (p. 112) is reasonably explanatory. The type was describable as a "Patentee" with only inside bearings to the driving axle. Thanks partly to increased boiler pressure, "Jenny" was a very successful engine. A famous later example of the type is the *Dom Luiz*, built by Beyer, Peacock and Company of Manchester for the South Eastern Railway of Portugal in 1862, which has survived as a beautiful relic. Her domeless boiler (which remained unchanged though doubtless renewed) exemplified an old argument as to whether a dome really provided valuable steam space to the boilers as well as a convenient place to house the regulator and steam-pipe opening, or whether it merely weakened the boiler shell. The argument never was resolved. Looking back to Gooch's *Great Britain* on the Great Western Railway, and to certain very efficient little engines known as the "Eddy Clocks" in New England, and forward to the last steam engines built by that same Great Western, and to the last—giant—steam engines built for the Canadian Pacific Railway, we note that all these were domeless, while most engines in the rest of the world had as much dome as the loading gauge would allow.

Another curiosity! Carl Friedrich Beyer, joint founder of the Manchester firm, was a German from Plauen in Saxony. His migration is comparable to the nearly opposite one of Haswell to Vienna. Their designs were to be regarded, respectively, as typically British and typically Central European.

CAR DEVELOPMENT

At this point, motive power can rest awhile, and as freight and mineral handling was as yet in fairly primitive vehicles, let us turn to passengers. Their conveyance across the North American Continent naturally demanded something fairly superior to carry them, and there were similar, if more regional, demands from Biscay to the Urals. Two starting points: America tended to base her passenger cars on the canal boats which had preceded them; Europe still stuck to the stage-coach idea, with increasing modifications.

America produced the first really spectacular improvements. The long "shabby omnibus" which had scarcely pleased Charles Dickens became gradually refined. People might still use its central passage as what someone called an *elongated spittoon*, but it had many good points. Its little two-by-two seats with reversible backs were adequate enough by day. A pot-bellied stove kept people warm in winter. Near this was a little annexe with a bottomless can to serve natural calls. There were candle-lanterns at night. In the middle sixties these were replaced by quite good kerosene lamps with Argand burners, slung in clerestory decks which not only raised them above the passengers' heads but gave better daytime lighting and better ventilation at all times, as well as rather more head-room than the old, nearly flat, coach roof. Such was the dust on old-time journeys that people thought twice about opening the windows even in summer

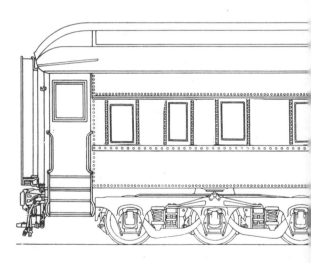

(above) The Prins August *was the first passenger locomotive used by the Swedish State Railways. Bought from Beyer Peacock of Manchester in 1856, it had a speed of 75 km/h and is now preserved at the Swedish Railways Museum.*

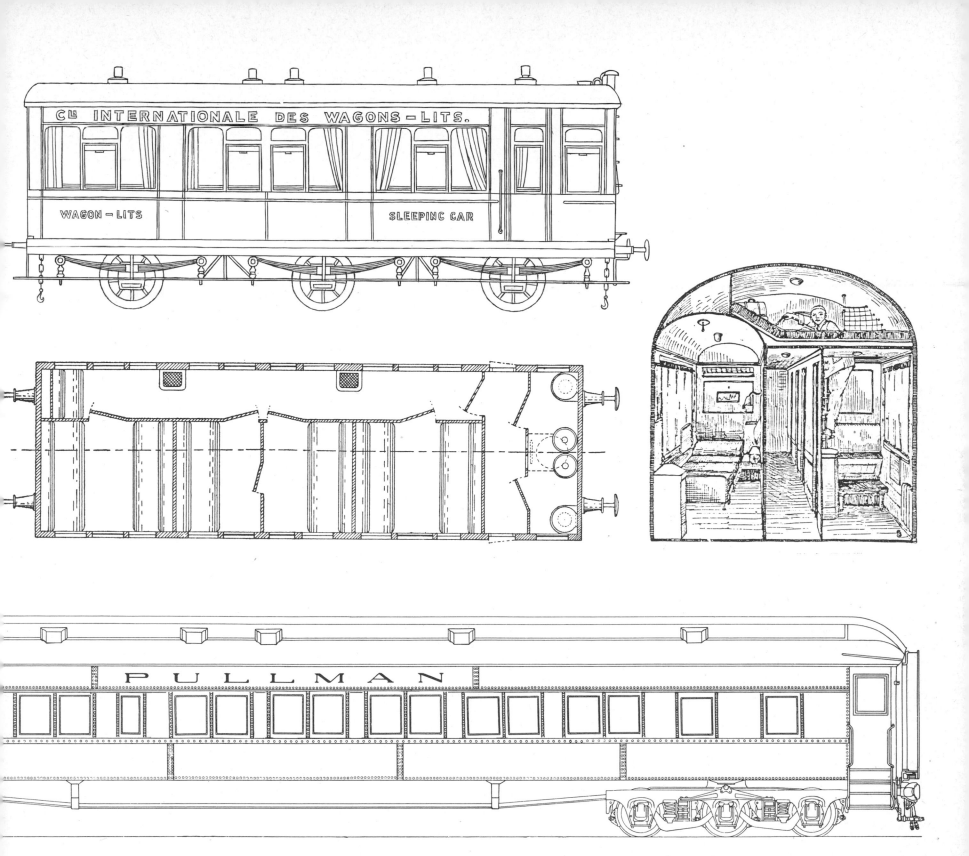

Variety in Sleeping Cars. Georges Nagelmackers' six-wheel car (top left), shown at the Paris Exhibition of 1868, had two four-berth compartments and two doubles which could be converted for family use. The great steel

Pullman car (bottom), characteristic of North America in the 1908–28, had ten open two-berth sections, one drawing-room with adjacent lavatory, and one compartment with contained lavatory fixtures. The men's

general lavatory was also for smokers. In the cross-section (top right) we have a German anticipation (1924) of the later Pullman roomette. Its second-class passengers slept in the roof.

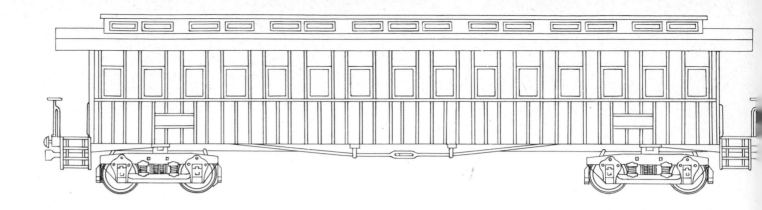

even if they could. *Sticks like a car window!* ran an ancient American advertisement for some adhesive. By that time, such windows were slid upwards into a hollow top quarter in America, and lowered ("drop-lights") into the hollow of the primeval carriage door of Western Europe.

Here we show a drawing of a characteristic American railroad car of 1865. It was quite spacious, though cramped as to seating, giving a foretaste of large passenger aircraft just a century later. There were small seats with reversible backs, often quite parlorly trimmed in the best available red plush. In the words of Mark Twain: *Uncomfortable, but stylish.*

Travel in such a car could be tolerable enough in the daytime, but it was penitential at night. Many attempts, as briefly noted, had been made to produce a reasonable sleeping car. George Mortimer Pullman, a cabinet-maker, had the idea of making the daytime seats pull out flat to meet in the foot-space, while folding berths were brought down from the ceilings each side of the aisle, beds being made up on both levels. During 1858–59 he converted three ordinary day cars of the Chicago and Alton Railroad. They were a success, but war interfered with his plans and, not being interested in the hostilities, he went west until the four awful years were over. In 1865 he produced the *Pioneer*, the first real, sleeping car. The roof was altogether higher, with a liberal clerestory in the middle, and sliding boards prevented the recumbent passengers from kicking each other's heads. It was an instant success, and became an American prototype that was to be followed for several generations. The classic Pullman sleeper had arrived, and though funny stories have been told about the business of undressing in those berths behind buttoned curtains, and embarrassing mistakes (the main portion of the car formed a dormitory for two-dozen assorted men and women) the Pullman sleeper could be adequate enough, and reasonably comfortable, even on a transcontinental journey of several days and nights.

In Europe, quite a different approach was made. The compartment arrangement was kept. (For that matter, a Pullman sleeper would offer, at a price, a couple of private compartments, each with two berths, at one end.) In the 'sixties, Russia provided four-berth compartments reached by side corridor, which were nice enough for family parties or two couples travelling together. Some were quite luxurious. Russian railroads had been very spaciously built, unlike those of the pioneer lines in Great Britain which paid the penalty of so many pioneers. A Russian sleeper of 1867 had five four-berth compartments, a small middle saloon, and above this an overhead observation compartment reached by a stair, anticipating the "Vista Dome" of America, some ninety years after. The arrangement made an intermediate appearance on the Canadian Pacific Railway in the early nineteen-hundreds. For the rest of this Russian sleeper, it was entered by open platforms each end, as in America at that time, and had some sort of water-closet beside each entrance. The car has been several times illustrated, even recently.

Less familiar to posterity has been the neat little Austrian sleeping car shown on p. 108, which combined the compartment idea favoured by Georges Nagelmackers, a Belgian, with the Pullman arrangement of seats and berths. It was evidently designed for international travel as from Vienna to Berlin or Munich. Something rather like it was to be found in Scotland, on the slow night trains between Glasgow and Inverness, regularly until 1907 and occasionally thereafter.

Our drawing of the Austrian car is quite sufficiently self-explanatory. One notes the under-floor stoves for heating through gratings. Steam heating from the locomotive

This 1865 American car was in general use on most railroads. I was 50 feet in length and weighe just under 16 tons.

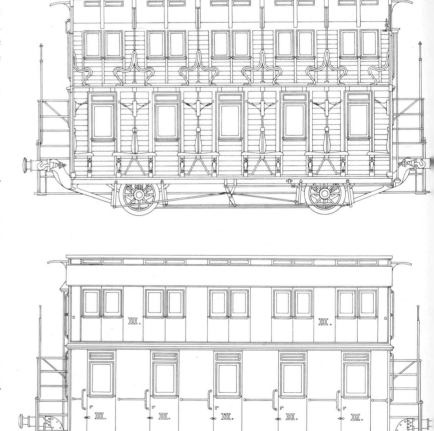

An Austrian third-class double decked car.

George Mortimer Pullman, 1831–1897. Founder of the Pullman Palace Car Company in 1867 after the success of his first sleeping cars. He built the Pioneer in 1864. It had folding upper berths and extensible seat cushions for the lower berths. He became a millionaire through his company and founded the model town of Pullman for employees of his company. In 1894 he achieved a *different sort of fame when he reduced employees wages by 25% while maintaining the rents for the houses in Pullman. The employees went on strike and were supported by the American Railway Union. The strike spread and troops were sent in to suppress it. Officials of the union were imprisoned and the strike was lost. Pullman thus wrote his name in labour as well as railway history.*

was still in the academic stage, which means that nobody had ever seen—or felt—it. In the Austrian sleeper, the shape of the clerestory deck was markedly un-American. Its arrangement of windows and ventilators followed the convention of the side- and door-windows of the old English side-door coach, and in this form it was soon to become very popular in Prussia and on certain English railways, notably the Great Western which built it thus from 1874 to 1903.

European sleeping cars took their form from that memorable Belgian, Georges Nagelmackers, father of the famous International Sleeping Car Company. After some struggling, he teamed-up with an ingenious if rascally American, Colonel William D'Alton Mann, who had got hold of some British capital. The Compagnie Internationale des Wagons-Lits became, briefly, Mann's Railway Sleeping Carriage Company, Limited. The Nagelmackers cars were divided into compartments with transverse berths and short side corridors leading to lavatories. Colonel Mann called them *boudoirs*.

Supplementary to sleeping berths giving passengers a fully recumbent position, there was a limited vogue in Central and Eastern Europe for a carriage furnished with *chaises-longues*. The accompanying sketch (p. 97) shows what was available in the eighteen-sixties to those willing to pay for it on such various lines as those between Vienna and Trieste (this example) and between Kiev and Odessa. It was certainly better than no sleeping berth at all, and less disquieting than certain coffin-like berths of the pre-Pullman period in North America. The specimen shown was at one end of an otherwise ordinary first-class coach, and was approached by an end-balcony which also gave access to a very small water-closet. A stove with a primitive vapour-heater was mounted under the carriage frame.

French designers at first favoured a sleeping berth formed by tipping forward a very high-back seat. The seat proper folded underneath while the reverse side of its upholstered back, now horizontal, became the bed. The first real sleeping car in Great Britain, built by the North British Railway in Scotland for the Glasgow-Edinburgh-London night trains in 1873 was of this sort. It did not last long on the British railways, but was still to be seen in France in the nineteen-twenties. The official term was *lits-salon*.

From America, George Mortimer Pullman made a move towards European user, beginning with the Midland Railway in England (1874). The cars were of pure American type, very gorgeously decorated, but made rather smaller to suit the British loading-gauge, dictated by those numerous long tunnels built rather too small in the dawn of the railway industry. Several British railways invested in Pullman sleepers, and so did Italy. They were prefabricated in the States and assembled at Derby and at Turin. But just as the Pullman became the standard American form, so did the Nagelmackers type become characteristic of Europe. Colonel Mann certainly made a few cars in his own country, but his chief interests there seem to have been in blackmail, in conjunction with a scandalous newspaper, which made him a lot of money. He really *was* a colonel, be it added!

Apart from sleeping cars and special cars for eminent personages, the West European coach remained in its classic side-door-compartment form. Australian railways, unlike those of Canada, were very English in style, and we show (p. 97) a second-class carriage with a central guard's-brake compartment, built for the New South Wales Government Railway in 1867. It was notable, for a British carriage of that time, in having eight wheels, the axles having a certain amount of side-play though no bogies were employed. As a coach, it was a comfortless thing; its very narrow compartments had low-backed wooden seats. The guard had a view either way along the train from the raised lantern roof, and could also keep an eye on his passengers through two peep-holes.

Already by the eighteen-sixties, there was heavy movement by railway, of daily workers in and out of the greater cities, both labourers and more and more office workers, the former at special very-cheap rates. Their trains grew longer and longer; too long for many of the stations in areas already built-up. If possible then, the passengers must be carried on two decks. From very early days certain French railways had mounted roof seats on carriages and so had certain pioneer American lines, as we have seen.

At the Vienna Exhibition of 1873 there was shown—along with the Hernalser sleeping carriage already noticed—the double-deck third-class carriage now illustrated. Really, it was a masterpiece of reasonably liberal accommodation within a short body, seating fifty persons in the lower compartments and forty in the gang-wayed upstairs portion. The latter had a clerestory, perhaps against claustrophobia, though this feature was lacking in similar vehicles which subsequently appeared, in large numbers, on the lines of Paris, Berlin and Copenhagen. The well-construction of the iron underframes will be

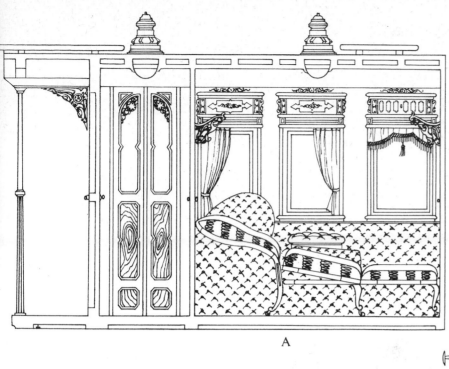

A   *This Austrian compartment could be turned into a sleeper by use of the extensible seats.*

B   *Colonel Mann's sleeping boudoir.*

C   *Fraser's broad-gauge family saloon, Great Western Railway, 1866. As was then proper, the servants were segregated from the family.*

D   *This second-class coach was built for the New South Wales Government in 1867. It had a central guard's brake-compartment.*

1 Saloon
2 Lobby
3 W.C.
4 Hand-basin
5 Servants' compartment

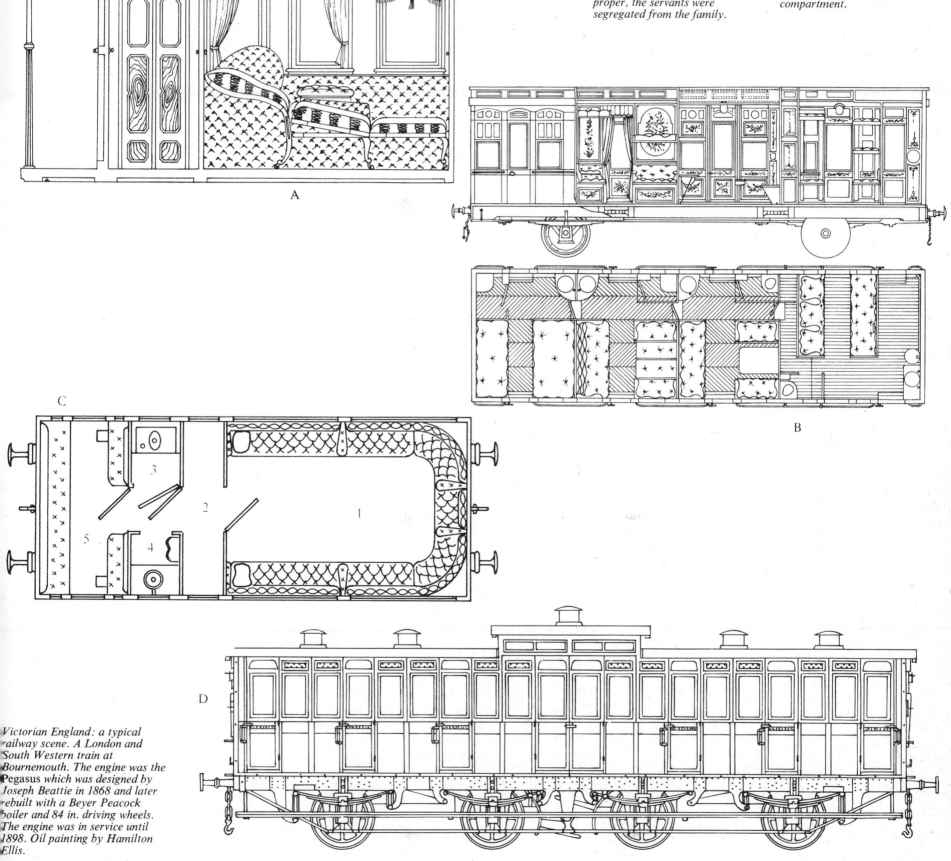

A

B

C

D

Victorian England: a typical railway scene. A London and South Western train at Bournemouth. The engine was the Pegasus which was designed by Joseph Beattie in 1868 and later rebuilt with a Beyer Peacock boiler and 84 in. driving wheels. The engine was in service until 1898. Oil painting by Hamilton Ellis.

noted, allowing for the maximum possible head-room in the passenger space. Again, England's unfortunately small tunnels made such a vehicle impracticable in London, where it would have been very useful, but even during the unpleasant nineteen-forties, Paris could muster suburban cars very similar to this old Austrian specimen, on both the Eastern and the Western lines. On the latter, too, a more disagreeable sort with open sides to the top deck lasted for nearly as long. *Impériale* was the French term. They were terrible things in cold weather, and dangerous too: also nasty when there happened to be some drunk and disorderly character on the top deck. Spain still has some old double-deckers at the time of writing.

From these Spartan vehicles, let us turn to a much more distinguished sort. Royal and other great personages had commanded luxurious railway carriages from the time when Queen Victoria made her first English journeys by rail in 1842. She, and the Russian, French and Austrian Emperors, all had sumptuous vehicles built for their long journeys, and so did the numerous German kings and many others. Many of these vehicles have survived the years in European museums. Very noteworthy examples are those of Queen Victoria, built by the London and North Western Railway in 1869 and now at Clapham Museum, and of Maximilian II of Bavaria, now at Nuremberg. This, somewhat older than Victoria's, is an almost incredible specimen of ornate Wittelsbach-Rococo, outside as well as within. It is more generally associated with King Max's successor, Ludwig II ("Mad Ludwig" to people who were not Bavarians) whom it must have suited admirably.

These two, as remarked, may still be looked at, and marvelled at; and they have been fairly often illustrated. More likely, therefore, to satisfy retrospective curiosity is the example on p. 109, which was made for the Tsar.

The carriage was extremely spacious and most luxuriously arranged. Its flat roof and consequent lack of headroom may have helped to solve the problem of keeping Imperial Majesty warm on long winter journeys. The body was very efficiently insulated and heavily upholstered to the same end. The closed receivers to the lavatory fixtures will be noted. Open drains could let in the intense cold, or alternatively ice-up. (An unhappy experience of Queen Victoria on a wintry journey from Scotland to the South. Everybody suffered!) The Russian arrangements curiously anticipated those of the passenger aircraft in our time.

That will do for cars, for the time being. The worst of them were very awful indeed, but the best were handsome, elegant, and even luxurious. It depended on one's purse or bank.

Wheatley's bogie engine, no.224, for the North British Railway, Scotland, 1871. It fell with the first Tay Bridge in 1879, but was rescued, rebuilt and in service until 1919.

George Forrester of Liverpool designed and built this 2-2-0 outside cylinder engine, Vauxhall, *for the Dublin and Kingstown Railway in 1834.*

Velocipede, *Alexander Allan's 2-2-2 passenger locomotive for the London and North Western Railway 1847. Outside cylinder, it had a 7-ft. driving wheel. This was an experimental engine, only one being built.*

PROGRESS IN DESIGN

Reverting to traction, the coupling of driving wheels on locomotives was fairly general by 1870, even on the fastest express passenger service, but two notable exceptions were Great Britain and France, on certain railways having a demand for fairly light, high-speed trains making but limited stops. We have not yet noticed a sort of locomotive known in England as the Allan type, and in France as *le Buddicom.* (Allan, incidentally, was a Scotsman and Buddicom an Englishman!) Its origins were ancient. The *Vauxhall* of the Dublin and Kingstown Railway, here shown, was built by C. and S. Forrester in 1834. Noteworthy are the outside cylinders and drive, the former supported by the inner and outer frames with slots in the latter over the piston rods and cross-heads. Otherwise the engine was a "Planet" with inside bearings only. At the end of the 'thirties, the Grand Junction Railway (Birmingham to Liverpool and Manchester) was having terrible trouble through the breakage of the early crank axles. Conversion of the engines to an outside-cylinder arrangement was rapidly carried out on Forrester's plan. The credit has been given variously to Joseph Locke (builder of the line), to Alexander Allan, to W. B. Buddicom, and to Francis Trevithick who was in charge of the locomotives for the railway company. Anyway, they lengthened the Forrester design, which had been Allan's work, into a six-wheel engine. All these men were closely associated at the time. Locke, a civil engineer, went to France to build the railway from Paris to Rouen, Dieppe and Le Havre. Buddicom went also, to build engines at Rouen. New engines of the Allan-Buddicom type appeared almost simultaneously on what became respectively the Western Railway of France and the London and North Western Railway. The first in fact appeared at Rouen in 1844, and early in 1845 the *Columbine* was the first locomotive to be built at Crewe in the English Midlands, one of the world's most famous locomotive towns. Both engines worked into the present century, and both *Columbine* and one of the Frenchmen are still in existence and capable of being steamed.

Our present drawing of this type shows the *Velocipede,* built at Crewe in 1847, and is based on one of Alexander Allan's own drawings. She had 7 ft. driving wheels and the high pressure, for those days, of 120 lb./sq. in. This type of engine was very widely used. It abounded in Scotland, whither Allan later returned, on the North Western line in England, on the Western Railway of France, and for a while in Canada. Early examples were to be found on the Spanish Barcelona-Mataro Railway, on the Roman Railways in pre-Victor-Emanuel Italy, and in India. The Great Western of Canada and the Grand Trunk Railway in the same country added leading four-wheel bogies to allow for the usual North American track standards of the period, and this feature, already adopted by the Tudela and Bilbao Railway in Spain, though with little record now, was adopted by David Jones on the Highland Railway, in Scotland—a steep and curvaceous line—from 1873 onwards. By that time the engines almost invariably had coupled wheels. Jones of the Highland built the type—very much enlarged—right up to 1892. Survivors of these were still at work in 1930, so the type lasted the best part of a century.

A very famous British design, with single driving wheels 8 ft. in diameter, was that of the Scots engineer Patrick Stirling for the Great Northern Railway, 1870; so famous indeed that artists of last century were inclined to use it as a "stock railway engine" where a train had to be portrayed. Uruguay put its likeness on a five-cent stamp, though there were no engines much like this at Montevideo. The design had forerunners, the oldest going back to days at the Stirling family's foundry at Dundee in the eighteen-thirties. A rigid-pin bogie supported the front end. The idea was not that of following curves (the rigid pin was against that) but, to use Stirling's own expression, of *rolling out the road.* They were indeed very steady engines; fast, too, and more powerful than their long-legged aspect might suggest to strangers. The class was built over twenty years to the beginning of the 'nineties, with very little alteration. During intense competitive running on the East and West Coast routes from London to Scotland, during 1888 and 1895, such engines made start-to-stop average speeds exceeding sixty miles an hour from London to Grantham and thence to York. Probably their best run was one of 181 minutes for the 188·25 miles, with a four minute stop for changing engines at Grantham. That was in 1895, when the design was already half a century old. A typical load was of two vans or baggage cars, three coaches and a sleeping car.

But what was to be a highly characteristic passenger locomotive on British lines for the best part of half a century, in despite of a liking for single driving wheels on express engines, was that with four coupled wheels, a leading bogie with controlled sideplay to

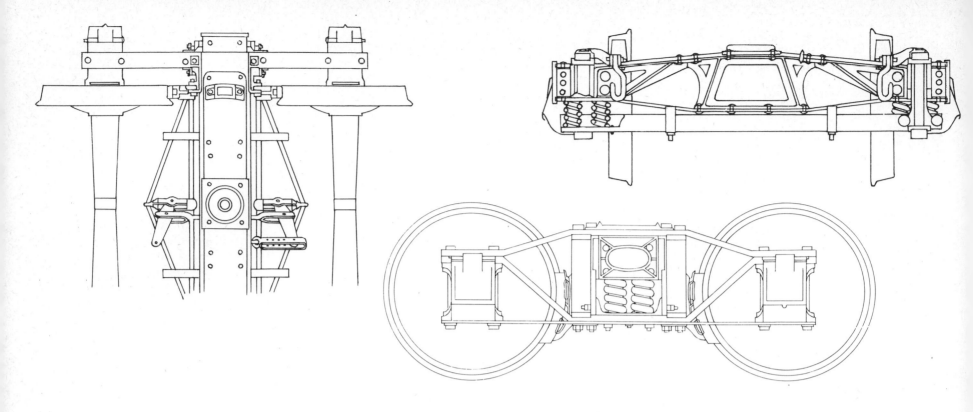

the pin, inside frames and inside cylinders. It really belongs to our next period, but we show (p. 98) North British Railway No. 224, built in 1871, designed by Thomas Wheatley (a rare specimen of an English locomotive engineer serving a Scottish railway; David Jones of the Highland Railway was another). The bogie has been mentioned. What was to become the standard form of the world had been invented by William Adams of the North London Railway (sometime of Victor-Emanuel's Sardinian Navy) in the late 'sixties. Lateral movement of the pivot was controlled in early examples by inclined planes and later by springs on each side of a slot in which the central pin moved. It was a perfect "truck" in American parlance, both steadying the engine and making her amenable to quite sharp curves at high speed.

North British engine No. 224 must have been one of the very first real express engines to have such an appliance. It must be admitted that she was, compared with many in Europe and America by then, somewhat undersized, but many pioneer designs have been modest enough. She had a frightful misfortune in 1879 when she went down, with the northbound mail train, in the collapse of the first Tay Bridge on December 28. There were about seventy-eight persons involved when bridge and train were blown over together. None survived. It was a national disaster without precedent. After three months the engine was recovered from that great river, there nearly two-miles wide, and repaired. Twice rebuilt, she lasted for forty years longer. In view of her early ordeal, North British enginemen rather callously called her "The Diver", a name which stuck.

Turning to less orthodox types of locomotive it was not only on the Semmering that there was interest in engines with paired motor units, as in Cockerill's *Seraing* and the *Wiener-Neustadt*. In France there was Jules Petiet, a very memorable locomotive man whose reputation abroad suffered from British and German indifference and, one regrets to say, public sneers in America. We show (p. 129) one of a series of tank engines for heavy freight, built for the Northern Railway of France in 1863, with four cylinders, paired at opposite ends of the frame. The lateral bending of the two sets of wheels, which we might term motor-units, was allowed for by the use of Beugniot's balancing levers, with the very long copper steam-pipes and exhaust pipes running fore-and-aft from the locomotive's mechanical fulcrum. But more interesting to the eyes of later years was the apparatus on top. This combined the functions of feedwater-heater and steam dryer, a long flue passing right through it from the smokebox while right on the summit was a steam collector and regulator box of the sort T. R. Crampton has already introduced to French railroads. He had first made this arrangement in rebuilding one of Cail's Cramp-

The Adams Bogie, introduced in 1865 by William Adams for the North London Railways. The wheel-base was lengthened to ensure steady running, and the pivot moved in a transverse slot. The design made a superb bogie and became the standard throughout the world.

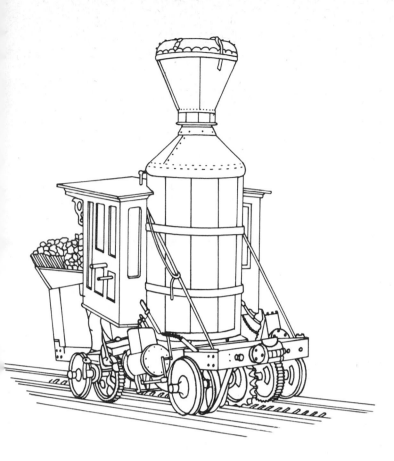

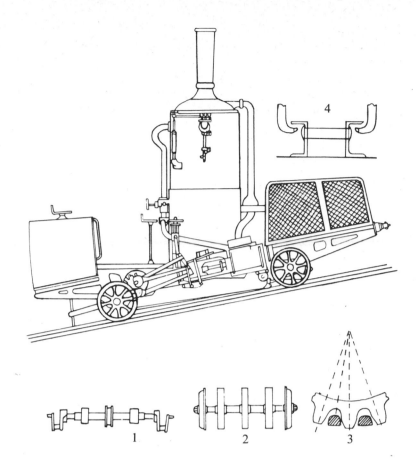

(left) Old Peppersass *on the rack railway on Mount Washington, 1869. The line had a maximum gradient of 1 in 3.*

(right) *In 1870 Nicholas Riggenbach constructed the Rigi Railway in Switzerland, which had a maximum gradient of 1 in 4. His rack locomotive above was used on it.*
1 Driving axle
2 Crank shaft
3 Clearance between the driving cogged wheel and the rack
4 Safety arrangement against derailment

ton locomotives on the same railway. Thus equipped, the transformed "Crampton" resembled nothing else on earth, but the economiser evidently worked. Petiet built some passenger engines arranged in much the same way, but with a set of cylinders and single driving axles at each end, separated by three carrying axles. These too were tank engines, without separate tenders, and were perhaps the most fantastic-looking locomotives in regular public traffic for many a long year. One of them, we were told by the late J. C. Cosgrave, a very senior colleague, took the last train out of Paris before the siege of 1870.

Steep-grade mountain railways made their first appearance in the eighteen-sixties, almost simultaneously in America and Europe. Rack and pinion propulsion, as we have seen, was one of the oldest things in steam traction, but its use had long been dormant. In the States, Sylvester Marsh made a model locomotive for very steep grades, using a geared engine and a pinion wheel engaged in a ladder-shaped rack between the running rails. Nicholas Riggenbach of the Swiss Central Railway patented a very similar form in 1863 and applied it on the Kahlenberg Railway, Austria, in 1866. In that year, Marsh gave a similar demonstration in the States. Both were successful, and both resulted in the building of full-scale mountain railways. In 1867 construction began on the Mount Washington Cog Railway in New Hampshire. It was opened to the summit in the summer of 1869, preceding by two years the partial opening of the Swiss line from Vitznau to the summit of the Rigi, as far as Staffelhohe. Rigi-Kulm was reached in July, 1873. Riggenbach's first Rigi locomotive, named *Stadt Luzern*, and Marsh's, which went down in history as "Old Peppersass", both had vertical boilers, hence the skittish nickname of the American engine, whose boiler reminded people of a savoury sauce bottle. Later boilers were of ordinary locomotive type, but at an angle to the frames to suit water-level on the very steep gradient, and were used on both lines. "Old Peppersass" was preserved, but a well-meaning celebration trip comparatively recently ended in a sad and very destructive accident. Portions of the engine were retrieved. A Vitznau-Rigi locomotive, in original form, is preserved in the famous Verkehrshaus, Lucerne. These two lines were the real pioneers of steep-grade tourist railways to the tops of popular mountains in holiday country. The maximum gradient on the Rigi line was 1 in 4. Both lines are still doing well. The Vitznau-Rigi line has long been electrified.

James Barraclough Fell, an Englishman, used instead of rack-and-pinion a central rail laid on its side and gripped by horizontal driving wheels on the locomotive. A line on this system was built on Napoleon's military road over the Mont Cenis pass between

France and Italy in 1867, with a life-expectation of a quarter-century while a tunnel was being built under the Col de Frejus but mechanical advance dashed people's hopes. Thanks to Sommeiller's compressed-air rock drills, the tunnel was ready by the autumn of 1871 instead of the early 'nineties. In those few years, however, the Fell railway carried passengers and also the Indian Mail from London to Brindisi. Fell was a disagreeable character, so one feels less sorry about his disappointment. Even the "Fell System" went back to a joint patent of Vignoles and Ericsson, respectively masters of track techniques and mechanical invention. It was used in France on the Puy de Dôme Railway.

A virtue of both the rack and the centre-rail was that they made extremely efficient braking systems possible at a time when this was one of the weakest points of railway mechanical engineering. The most celebrated Fell line was that of Rimutaka in New Zealand (1885–1955) which also, ultimately, was replaced by a great tunnel. The arrangement is still used for braking on the Snaefell Mountain Line in the Isle of Man.

In 1863, the world's first underground city railway was opened in London, between Paddington in the west and Farringdon Street in the city proper. All sorts of substitutes for the orthodox locomotive were proposed, including that old fraud the Atmospheric System and more normal machines which are supposed to maintain steam chiefly on a range of white-hot bricks in an enormous combustion chamber along the inside of the boiler barrel. One such locomotive was built, quite imposing, but a hopeless failure.

The line was first built on broad gauge (7 ft.) and briefly worked by the Great Western company. For it, Daniel Gooch built locomotives with surface condensers, the steam being turned into the water-tanks during passage underground while the smoke was kept as clean as possible and left to look after itself.

Chapter 5 THE YEARS OF MONOPOLY

In the last quarter of the nineteenth century, many people believed that the steam railway train had reached perfection. It came to span the world in its journeys. One could live in a train for several days and nights and be none the worse. The train handled freight by land on a scale which even its pioneers had scarcely forseen. By 1900, locomotives were already so large that many considered that they had reached their limit in size. Electric traction and internal-combustion engines were both over the horizon, though pooh-poohed by the old school of engineers.

Still the steam locomotive maintained its classic form and certain recognized varieties, one of the commonest of which was that faithful old "American Type", the 4-4-0 engine with outside cylinders supported by a bogie. In Europe it almost invariably had plate- or slab-frames, first applied to the type in Eastwick and Harrison's locomotives for Russia and by Haswell in Vienna (1844). We show two beautiful and efficient examples with much in common, though serving very different country. The Finland State Railways' No. 11 (p. 111) was one of a series built in Scotland by Dübs and Company of Glasgow as far back as 1869. More were built by Sigl in Austria in 1875–76 and, with little variation, again by Dübs in 1893 and 1898, and by the Swiss Locomotive Works, Winterthur, also in the latter year. Twenty were still running in 1927, the oldest dating back to 1875 (five Sigl engines). The design was entirely that of the Scottish firm, and in early days the engines were wood-burners, with the Russian form of spark-arresting smokestack. There was a reasonably liberal cab for the enginemen, who needed it in Northern Europe!

Speeds were low in Finland, as in the old Russian Empire generally. The engines were both strong and flexible, with the Adams bogie, and their long life is a sufficient certificate of their usefulness.

This type—the slab-framed "American" which America proper scarcely knew—came to abound in many places, especially those under powerful British influence in railways such as the South American republics, and to some extent in China. Austria, Prussia and Italy all built it; to it belonged the handsome Class CC on the Swedish State Railways, which last had a remarkable bogie arrangement.

For an English example we show No. 471 of the London and South Western Railway (p. 199), designed by that William Adams who produced the modern locomotive bogie. This particular engine, built in 1884, was one of many generally similar, and built over the years 1880–87. They were strong, powerful and fast. In their prime they competed with the mighty Great Western Railway, then still on broad gauge. Over forty years later we

had a sprightly run with this very engine, No. 471, following a late arrival at Okehampton
in the West of England. The colour scheme shown is the original one; later greens were
much lighter, right up to the end in the middle nineteen-twenties.

About contemporary with these were some express passenger locomotives which to
American eyes were almost incredible, for they had the coupled wheels on the leading
axle; no bogie—no other axle in front of it. The type had originated for freight haulage
right back in the beginning. The English variety had inside cylinders; the old Scottish
goods engine had them outside, giving a very head-heavy appearance. In 1873, Emil
Kessler of Esslingen produced a large-wheeled express engine of the latter sort for the
Galician Carl-Ludwig Railway in the north-eastern part of the old Austrian Empire,
and this we show first. Hartmann of Chemnitz built the type for Spain. One doubts that
any really high speeds were attempted. The outside reciprocating masses, while all right
on an old Scottish coal train, would have made a fast-running locomotive very unsteady.
The arrangement allowed, however, for a good long firebox extending well back into
the cab. One must say that it was rather a courageous design on the part of Kesslers!

The English version with inside cylinders, designed by William Stroudley for the
London, Brighton and South Coast Railway, is exemplified by *Gladstone* (p. 157), first of
a series of thirty-six built at Brighton from 1882 to 1891. Six very similar engines were
older (1878–80). The "Gladstones"—though Americans might shudder to look at them—
were not only extraordinarily powerful for their modest size; they were perfectly steady
at seventy-five miles an hour, and for many years they worked the heaviest Pullman car
trains between London and the South Coast of England. *Gladstone* herself is lovingly
preserved, and the last of the class to remain in service steamed until the autumn of 1933.
In both design and workmanship they were superb examples of old English practice.

No other railway dared to build fast passenger locomotives with 6 ft. 6 in. coupled
wheels leading, but only once was a "Gladstone" in a serious derailment, and that was
through failure of an old iron bridge, and no engine fault. The Northern Railway of
France tried the type as an experiment, but no more, subsequently substituting a four-
wheel truck for the leading big wheels. Its track was below English standards in those
days, and there may have been trouble.

*This passenger locomotive for the
Carl-Ludwigsbahn was built by
Kessler of Esslingen and
exhibited at the Vienna
Exhibition.*

THE CLASSIC AMERICAN TYPE USED ALL OVER NORTH AMERICA. THIS EXAMPLE WAS BUILT BY ROGERS OF PATERSON, N.J., ABOUT 1855.

Baldwin's Mogul

THIS BALDWIN-BUILT MOGUL IS A FINE EXAMPLE OF THE FREIGHT LOCOMOTIVE OF THE 1870s IN NORTH AMERICA.

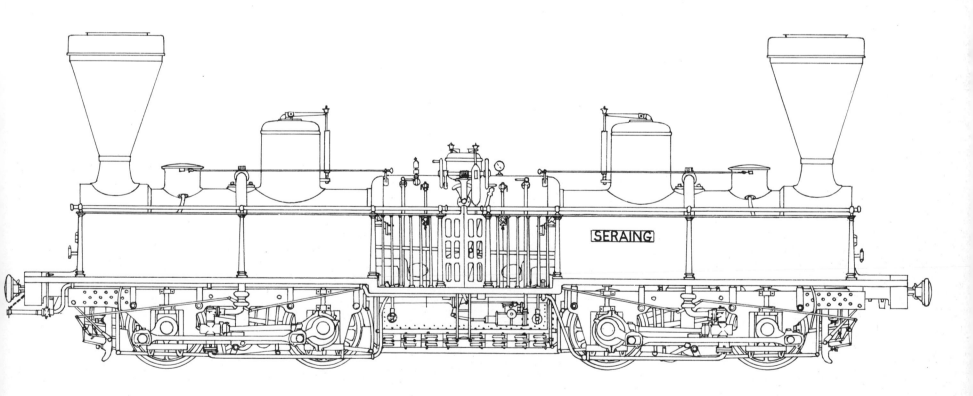

BELGIUM'S CONTESTANT AT THE SEMMERING TRIALS WAS DESIGNED BY JOHN COCKERILL. IT ANTICIPATED THE FAIRLIE PATENT.

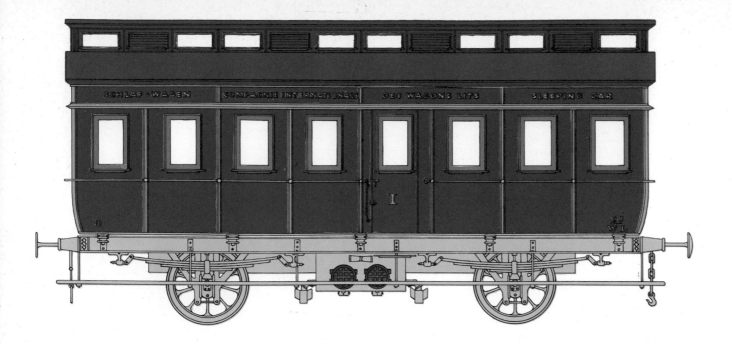

Hernalser Sleeper

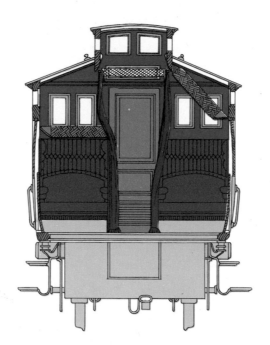

THIS AUSTRIAN SLEEPING CAR WAS BUILT BY HERNALSER
AND COMPANY OF VIENNA AND EXHIBITED AT THE VIENNA
EXHIBITION IN 1873.

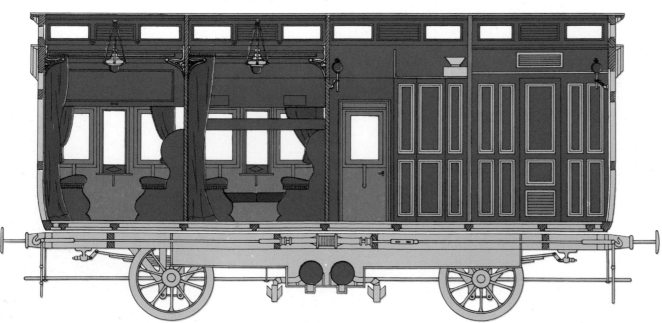

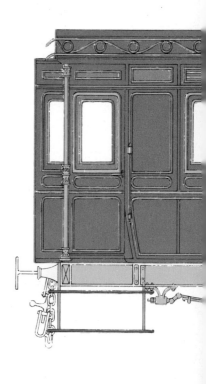

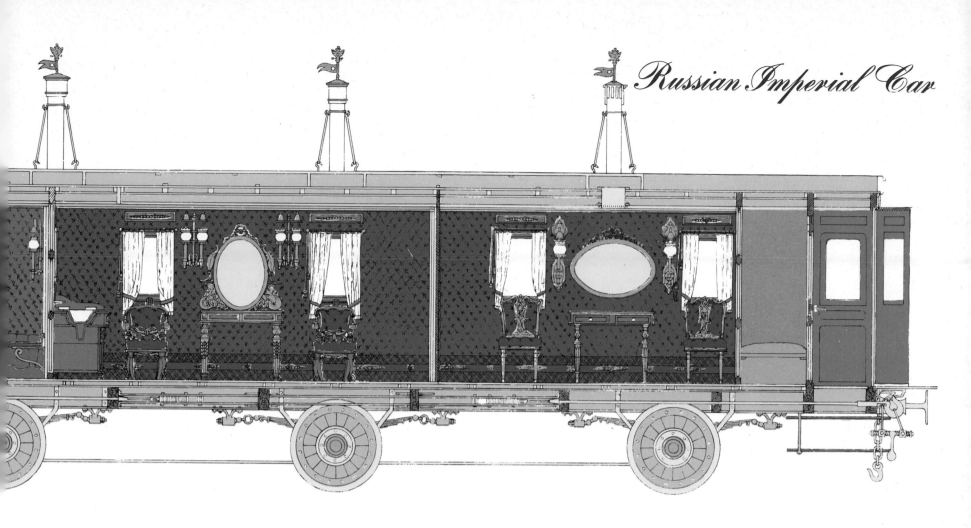

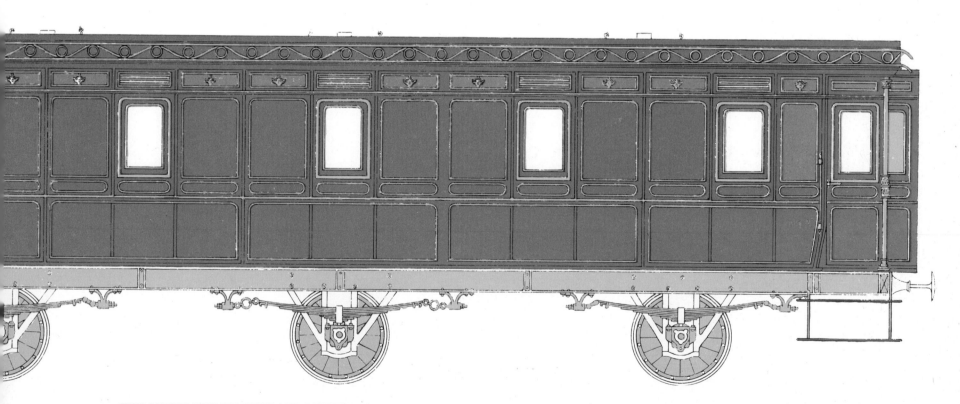

THIS EXTREMELY SPACIOUS AND LUXURIOUS CAR WAS BUILT FOR THE RUSSIAN TSAR. UPHOLSTERED AND INSULATED WALLS KEPT THE HEAT FROM THE STOVE INSIDE THE CAR. IT WAS USED ON THE MOSCOW–KURSK RAILWAY.

Van Borries Compound

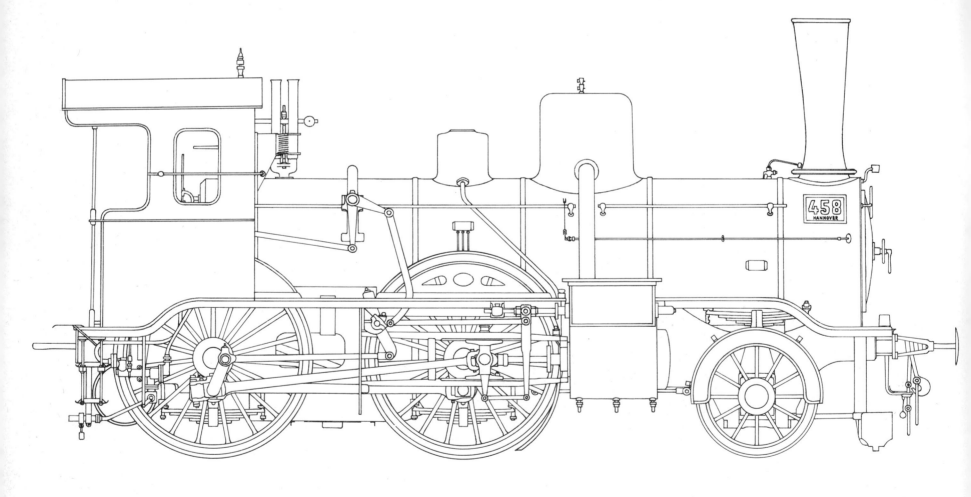

VAN BORRIES COMPOUND LOCOMOTIVE WAS USED FOR PULLING PASSENGER TRAINS ON THE HANNOVER LINE OF THE PRUSSIAN STATE RAILWAYS.

THE FINLAND STATE RAILWAYS NO. 11 LOCOMOTIVE WAS BUILT BY DÜBS OF GLASGOW IN 1869.

Jenny Lind

DESIGNED BY DAVID JOY AND BUILT BY LEEDS ENGINE FOUNDRY IN 1847 FOR THE LONDON, BRIGHTON AND SOUTH COAST RAILWAY, THIS ENGINE WAS A CLASSIC OF ITS DAY.

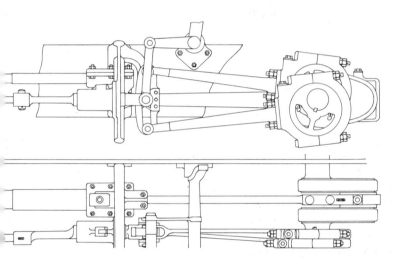

LOCOMOTIVE ACCESSORIES

Some notes are needed on locomotive accessories. Evolution of valve-gear makes a fascinating study, and has been the subject of various learned papers. As we have seen, the expansive use of steam dated back to the days of Gooch and Robert Stephenson's firm in the eighteen-forties, while a primitive form of expansive motion had been used even on the American experimental engine by James in 1831. The object of these new gears, apart from admission, exhaust and reversal, was to make all the valve events—cut-off, exhaust, compression and admission—occur earlier in the cycle by *linking up*. Through use of the link (curved in Gooch's and Stephenson's, straight in Alexander Allan's), moving the reversing lever nearer to its central (neutral) position, steam could be economized while running fast. From the early use of these gears dated the first real express-running over long distances. With the old non-expansive gears, engines would have lost their steam.

Radial valve gears, ultimately general in steam locomotive practice, had their origin in mid-western Europe. Egide Walschaerts was one of the three Belgian giants. (The others were Alfred Belpaire and—relatively much more recently—J. B. Flamme.) Walschaerts' first patent was one of 1844, but more important was his improvement of 1848, (p. 114). Quite independently, in Germany, Edmund Heusinger produced in the following year the radial gear on p. 116. The use of a return crank instead of an excentric was Heusinger's work, and the same sort of gear, in after years, was named for both men, according to the habit of people in this place or that. Neither reaped any patent royalties, but neither fell, like poor Richard Trevithick, into seedy poverty. Several much more recent American valve-gears have been of the Walschaerts/Heusinger family. An English gear of some interest, widely used in the late nineteenth century, was that of David Joy (probable chief designer of the engine *Jenny Lind*, opposite). From our drawing of the gear (p. 116) it will be seen there was neither excentric nor return-crank actuation. But this simplification was at the expense of perforating the connecting rod, which was all very well while locomotives remained fairly small, but apt to lead to bad breakages on big engines at high speed. It had quite a vogue in England on certain lines, notably the North Eastern and the London and North Western Railways. The Western Railway of France used it in a very British-looking 4-4-0 design (Series 900). In the early 'eighties, it was being installed at Altoona Works on the Pennsylvania Railroad, but already American locomotives were beginning to grow bigger than other people's, and making holes in their connecting rods was correspondingly less desirable.

At this time, slide valves were still practically universal, though ultimately, with the use of much higher pressures, the use of piston-valves became essential. As far back as the middle 'seventies piston-valves were being made and installed on some London and South Western locomotives by William George Beattie, son of the man who was so clever with fireboxes and feedwater-heaters. But he was too eager. Metallurgical knowledge was still behind mechanical experience. There were some shocking failures, and as far as the South Western company was concerned, W. G. Beattie was "out", to be succeeded by W. Adams, sometime Italian Naval officer. Advanced theories can be expensive to a man. Fortunately Joseph Beattie had left his infant-prodigy well-off.

Boiler pressures rose, cautiously-gradual through the half-century 1850–1900. By the end of the century, 160 lb./sq. in., once prodigious, was common; 200 lb., later to be common, was prodigious.

Pressures suggest safety-valves. The old weight-loaded safety-valve was not very suitable for locomotives, though it was used by both Kessler and Maffei in the German States for some years (e.g. in the Galician Carl-Ludwig engine just shown). Going over rough track or uneven points, such an engine would bump up the big weight, losing a lot of useful steam through the valve. Weighting the lever by a Salter spring-balance was much better, and a common practice over many years. But the safety-valve could be *doctored,* and accidents through such wicked operations led to the invention of other forms.' Naylor's side-lever type, shown on Finland engine No. 11 still allowed interferance, and also had a habit of sticking and then going off with a roar that shortened one's life.

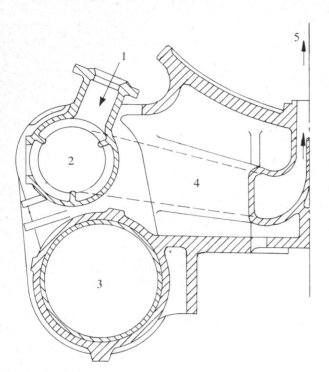

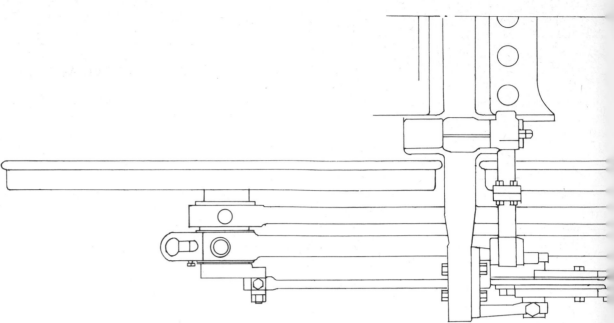

WALSCHAERTS' VALVE GEAR

*Invented in 1844, it was quite
different in arrangement from
established link-motions and many
English engineers, suspicious of
such a radical change, were
cautious of it. However, other
countries adopted it and it turned
out to be most satisfactory. It soon
became the standard form on
railways all over the world,
including British Railways.*

1 Live steam inlet
2 Valve chamber
3 Cylinder
4 Exhaust passage
5 Steam to exhaust nozzle
6 Exhaust steam
7 Live steam enters at centre
   of valve chamber
8 Piston
9 Exhaust steam passes out at
   ends of valve chambers
10 Steam passage between valve
   and cylinder
11 Piston rod extension not used
   on many locomotives
12 Piston
13 Cylinder cocks
14 Crosshead link
15 Crosshead (Laird type)
16 Crosshead guides
17 Valve stem
18 Radius rod
19 Combination lever
20 Lifting link
21 Main rod
22 Side rod
23 Drivers
24 Eccentric crank
25 Main crank
26 Reverse shaft arm
27 Reverse shaft
28 Reverse shaft lever
29 Rod to power reverse or to
   control in cab
30 Piston rod
31 Eccentric rod
32 Reverse link

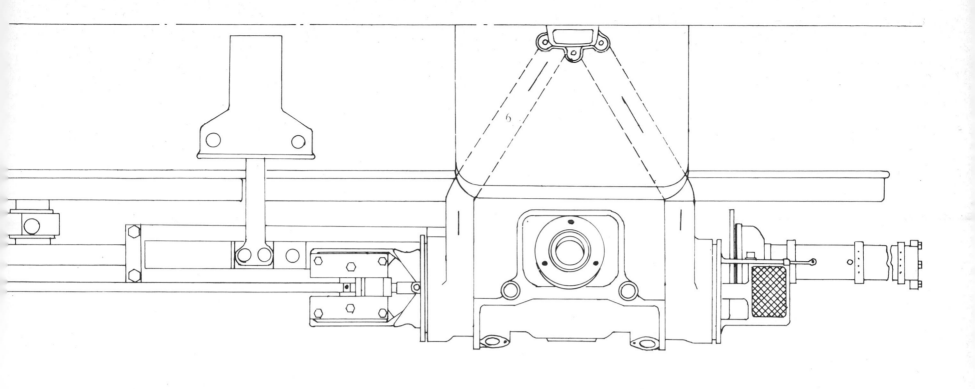

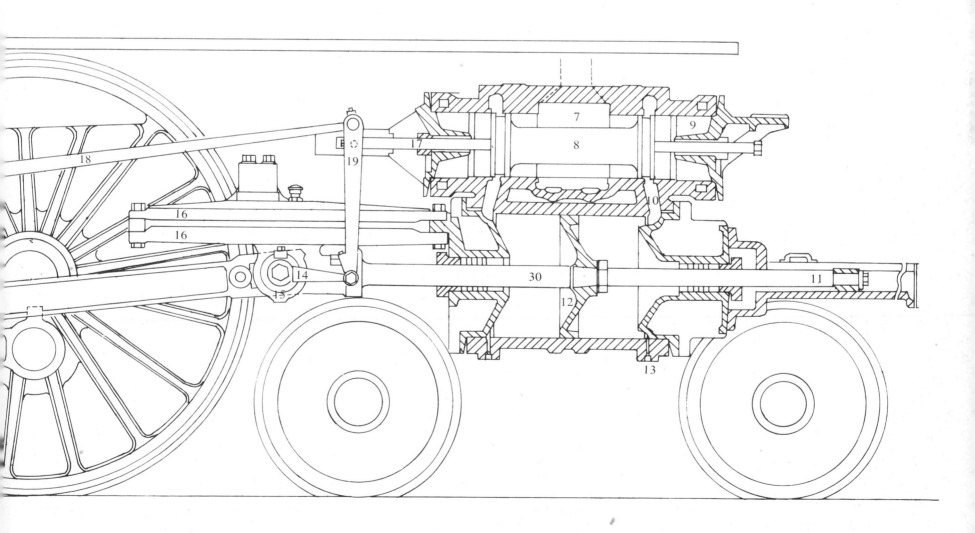

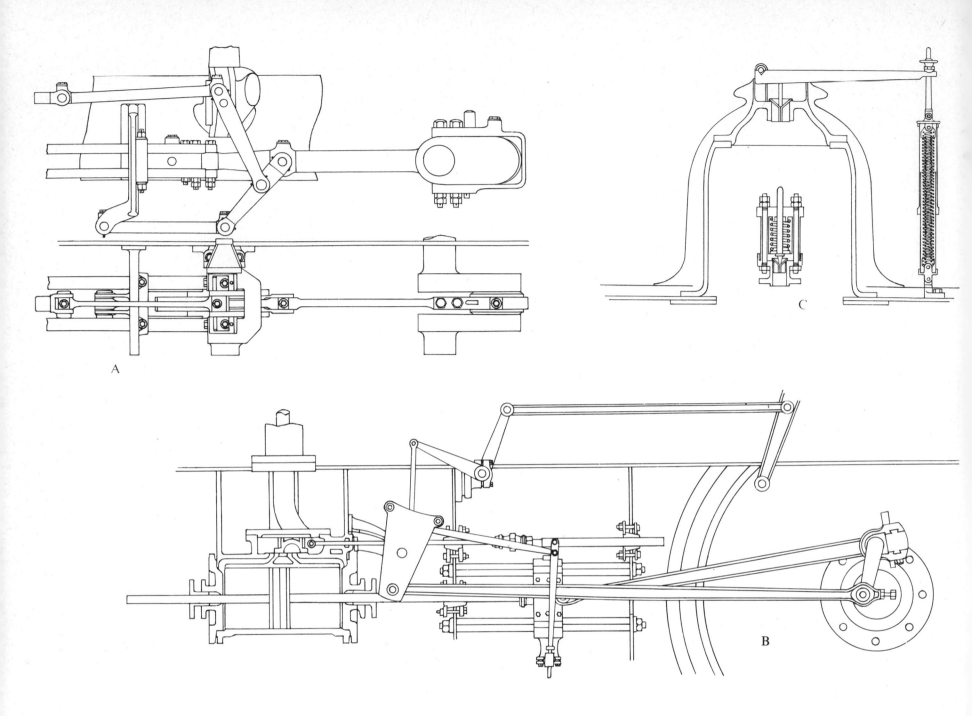

One of the very earliest incorruptible safety valves was that patented by John Ramsbottom of the London and North Western Railway in the late eighteen-fifties, exemplified in the London and South Western engine No. 471. Its *modus operandi*, like those of the valve-gears, is obvious, and it was much used everywhere but in North America, which in the eighteen-nineties speedily adopted direct-loaded safety-valves, in columns or cowlings which defied interfering enginemen seeking a little extra pressure. An admirable example was the Ashton safety-valve. Others included the Lethuillier-Pinel valve in France and the Richardson valve, much used in Northern Europe, especially Sweden and Finland. Neat little direct-loaded valves, locked-up in brass columns, were for long very popular in Scotland, on England's South Western line, and in Queensland, Australia, usually mounted on the dome. It was almost impossible to monkey about with any of these, or with the Wilson valve, once much favoured in Belgium, which superficially resembled the Ramsbottom valve but had the springs inside the columns, rising first against compression instead of by tension, and then by tension as it lifted conical caps on those columns. The excellent Ross "pop" safety valve originated in Ireland.

Pressure was at first measured by a scale on the Salter spring balance at safety-valve. Bourdon's pressure gauge, which was to withstand the test of a century, had its index figure moved on a dial by the straightening tendency, under direct internal steam pressure, of a curved, flattened tube.

A *Joy's Valve Gear.*

B *Heusinger's Valve Gear, 1849.*

C *Safety Valve.*

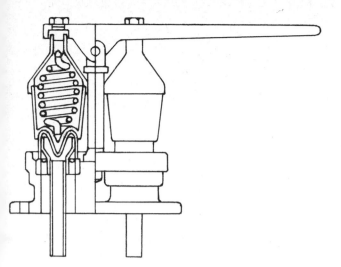

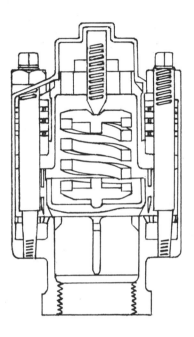

Two types of safety valves.

Hear the train blow! ran an old American ballad. There has been much argument as to the origin of the steam whistle, which later was to work just as well under air pressure on electric trains. The first steam whistle was invented by Adrian Stephens, a Cornishman, who went to South Wales like Trevithick, and possibly as early as 1826, applied such a whistle on a stationary boiler to the safety-valve, which also was equipped with a float against falling water level. It was certainly in use by 1833. The noise was produced by the impinging of an annular steam jet on an inverted brass bell or cup. In 1835 it seems to have turned up as a warning device for locomotives, and in the same year, quite independently, an English locomotive on the old Leicester and Swannington Railway was given a "steam trumpet" after an accident at a road crossing. The whistle was better than the trumpet, and since then has taken many forms and emitted many sorts of sound, from the joyous scream of England and Central Europe to the melancholy *whoo-hoo* chord of North America and Russia; from the frightened-lady squeals of French express engines to the deep majestic hoot—achieved by a miniature organ-pipe—remembered by many Scotsmen. French freight engines also sounded a deep note. There were such variations all over the world, according to influence by makers.

At first, locomotive boilers were fed by force-pumps worked off the engine proper, which meant that she had to move about to keep up the water-level in her boiler; sometimes an awkward business, if the subject were bottled up in some terminal station. The injector, whereby the operation was carried out by a jet of live steam from the boiler itself, was the invention of Henri Giffard, that most illustrious Frenchman who also produced the first navigable power-driven aircraft as early as 1852, (a steam-driven, hydrogen-filled airship). The principle was that the steam first exhausted all air from the appliance then naturally achieved suction of the cold feed-water. The steam condensed and the resultant mixture, passing between opposed cones, had sufficient force to pass through a valve (the clack) into the boiler against the latter's pressure. The Giffard apparatus, first applied to locomotives in 1859, was the prototype of many later forms, though the earlier ones would work with cold water only. Hot-water injectors are relatively modern. Locomotives with early feed-water heaters, like Beattie's in the South of England, mounted steam donkey-pumps instead.

A prominent feature of locomotives in lands of wood fuel or difficult coal was the spark arrester. The old American "balloon" and "diamond" stacks have been already mentioned. An internal cone, inverted, and plenty of wire mesh, formed their business parts. An ingenious Scandinavian arrangement comprised a sort of fixed spiral turbine in a big collar at the base of the stack with the blast-pipe orifice above it. All were effective, but rather at the expense of spoiling the draught, and there was not much fast running with them. Later, less stifling, arrangements were inside the smokebox.

THE FORNEY

In the United States, the "American Type" (4-4-0, with outside cylinders) long maintained its position, and was expanded by further coupled axles. The six-coupled version already was of some antiquity. Now eight-, and even ten-coupled versions appeared. On the Central Pacific Railroad—partner in the great transcontinental route of 1869 and later a constituent of the mighty Southern Pacific—A. J. Stevens' 4-8-0 locomotives climbed up and braked down both sides of the high Sierra in the early 'eighties. There was one 4-10-0, magnificently named *El Gobernador*, but a little before her time. Already, as we have seen, there were big and powerful locomotives in the mining valleys of the East, and of these we show (p. 156) the *Champion* of the Lehigh Valley Railroad in Pennsylvania, a very elegant example of the 4-8-0 type, though elegance was not what people generally expected in the Eastern coalfields of the United States, however beautiful were some parts of the country.

The 4-8-0 type was generally called "Mastodon" in the States after an extinct species of elephant whose giant fossil remains had lately turned-up in the Tertiary strata of both Europe and America. Americans loved such type-names; we shall encounter others. The "Mastodon", however, was less widely used than the "Mogul" (2-6-0) and its 2-8-0 development for heavy freight, called in America "Consolidation". Both these were used all over the world. The "Mogul" on p. 106 was built for the Baltimore and Ohio Railroad in 1875.

A very different type of American locomotive was that first schemed by, and named after, Matthias Forney. It was in essence the common four-wheel American switching engine of the mid-nineteenth century, but with the frames extended to take tank and coal-space instead of having a separate tender. It originated in the 'sixties, the first example having a bottle-shaped vertical boiler, a form usually deficient in steaming power. In the 'seventies, 'eighties and 'nineties great numbers of "Forneys" were built, sometimes for the rural—often narrow-gauge—"short lines" of New England and elsewhere, but most importantly for the city lines of which the New York elevated railways, trestled over the long-suffering streets, formed the finest examples. Though junior to the underground system in London, they made one of the earliest examples of *Rapid Transit* in cities, and were worked by hundreds of Forney locomotives until their electrification early in the twentieth century. For a "Forney" of the 'eighties, we show (p. 153) one built for the New York and Harlem Railroad. Derivation from the ordinary switching engine is particularly apparent in this, which looks more like that than a proper tank engine. Later examples were more compact, and larger, as far as weight restrictions on the trestle structures would allow. The New York and Harlem engine was rather a small suburban locomotive than an "Elevated" type, but she admirably shows the classic Forney arrangement.

These American city lines had their stations very close together, well in sight of one another down New York's long, straight Avenues. Driving an "L" train under steam was a matter of continually releasing brakes, giving steam, hooking-up the gear, shutting-off steam and braking to a stand all the way from Yonkers to down-town Manhattan, and back again. Lovett Eames' vacuum brakes were used, and this brings us to the subject of brakes.

America was the native country of powered brakes for trains, and to George Westinghouse, who first successfully applied braking by compressed air, on an experimental Pennsylvania Railroad passenger train in 1869, the whole world owes a debt not yet repaid. In its perfected form, the Westinghouse brake system depended on a powerful steam air-pump on the locomotive, constantly maintaining pressure in air reservoirs all down the train, supplying the cylinders which applied the car brake shoes, and it was *automatic in action*. That meant that in any case of failure (short of *losing the air* through arrant carelessness) all the brakes went on immediately. If a coupling broke, the connecting pipes broke with it, and the detached portion of the train came rapidly to a stand instead of colliding with the front part when that was pulled up by its anxious engineer; or, with even more frightful consequences, running backwards downhill and hitting something in rear. It may be remarked here that there was a very dreadful collision of this last kind, killing eighty persons, on the Great Northern Railway of Ireland in 1889. It moved the British Government of the time to make immediately compulsory the use of automatic power brakes on all passenger trains in the British Isles.

The culprit in this Irish case was a non-automatic vacuum brake invented by one S. Y. Smith (a compatriot of the great Westinghouse, one regrets to remark!). Air brakes would not do, however, on the New York Elevated lines; the short hops from station to station allowed no time for the engineer to work up his air pressure; hence the use of the Eames vacuum brake. Vacuum automatic brakes came to be used very widely in the British Isles and in various other countries, thanks largely to John Aspinall in England. The Tunisian Railways used a vacuum brake (Clayton's) until the early 1950s. Air was exhausted by a steam ejector, just as, in the Westinghouse and in later, kindred brakes, motive air was compressed by a pump. In the vacuum brake, application was by atmospheric pressure, always there, on the vacuum being destroyed. The appliance was thus not even dependent on a pump for its application; any mechanical failure meant that the brakes went on, or could not be released. Vacuum was less powerful than straight air, but sufficiently strong for the lighter trains east of the Atlantic, as for the very light, though often crowded trains of the American elevated and other city lines.

British horror of monopolies, comparable in the last century to American horror of socialism in the present, had absurd results, for some British railway companies used air, and some used vacuum. Through coaches and sleepers therefore needed to be dual-fitted (i.e. with two sets of brakes) to suit their various operating companies. There were two changes in braking between London and Aberdeen via the East Coast; one between Brighton and Plymouth in the South. Nor was Continental Europe faultless. The old-time Orient Express was air-braked twice and vacuum-braked twice on its long march from Paris to the Bosphorus (about 1,750 miles in sixty-five hours). Until the end of last century, its most important extra-Continental connection, a short one between London and Dover, was in the hands of two rival companies with different routes. Of

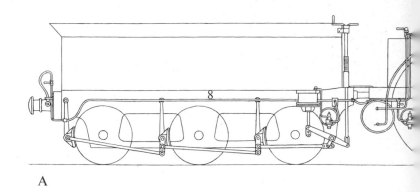

A

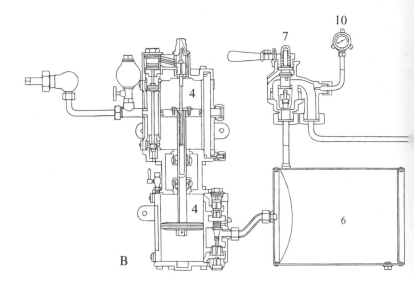

B

The Westinghouse Automatic Brake
Fig A shows the Brake complete on an Engine and Tender. Fig B is a diagram showing the operation of the Brake, from the Air Pump to the end of a vehicle. It is not to scale, and is intended simply to show the relation which each part bears to the whole.

The Engine, Tender, and every vehicle of a train is fitted with the following parts, to be found on Figs. A and B:– A Triple Valve, 1, by means of which the instantaneous automatic action is produced, in conjunction with a small Reservoir, 2, in which is stored the compressed air for applying the Brakes; a Brake Cylinder, 3, with pistons and
rods connected to the Brake Levers and Blocks. Upon the Engine is also placed:– The Steam Engine and Pump, 4, which produce the compressed air; a Main Reservoir, 6, for storing the air necessary for releasing the Brakes and recharging the small Reservoirs: a Driver's Brake Valve, 7, which regulates the flow of air from the Main Reservoir into the Brake Pipe for charging the train and releasing the Brakes, and from the Brake Pipe to the atmosphere for applying the Brakes. A single line of pipe, 8, called the Brake Pipe, extends the whole length of the train. Each van has a Guard's valve, 9, connected to the Brake Pipe, and a gauge, 10, to indicate the pressure of air.

118

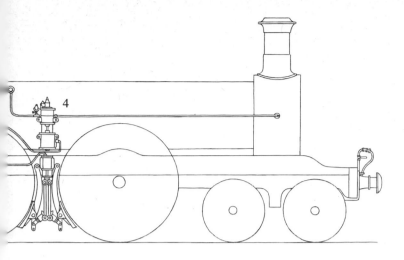

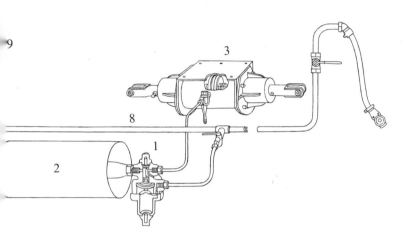

these, the South Eastern Railway used vacuum brakes and the London Chatham and Dover Railway used Westinghouse air. No wonder some visiting Frenchman shrugged off the madness of the English as he stood surveying at Dover the two London expresses whose brakes, tickets and city terminals were all different!

Back to M. Forney's locomotive: Europe used it little. There was an isolated class on the Caledonian Railway in Scotland. In England the Yorkshire Engine Company built it for South Russia of all places. It appeared on a few Swedish and Danish branch lines. All these European examples, unlike the Americans, had plate frames, though the outline remained more-or-less American.

British railway companies, however, made much use of a somewhat similar tank engine, still 0-4-4, but more compact, with inside cylinders, stemming from Stroudley's express engine which we have just noticed, and with capacious side tanks. Dugald Drummond, a fierce but gifted Scotsman who had been this Stroudley's Works Manager, was responsible for some of the most successful examples, though Samuel Johnson, who had been with both in Scotland and personally disliked them quite intensely, was first with the type on the English Great Eastern Railway.

We exemplify on p. 155 one of Drummond's earlier specimens, built for the Caledonian Railway in the eighteen-eighties, for branch passenger service. The same designer, from 1897 onwards, built a very much larger version on the London and South Western Railway, capable of taking an express passenger train at a pinch, running both fast and steadily so long as the road were decently solid. The little Scottish engines did not vanish until the nineteen-thirties, and of the sturdy London and South Western class we saw a last-survivor at Salisbury, in the South of England, as recently as April 1964.

This type was almost unknown outside Great Britain, where it was widely and most happily used in Scotland, the South, the Midlands and the North East. Long ago an American fellow-student, contemplating one and never even having seen a "Forney", complained that it was *all pfui*; to his eyes, back-to-front. It was nevertheless a most useful and remunerative type of locomotive; handsome too, in its portly way. It was many people's best investment.

The American Forney engine's effective survival was much shorter. It could not run fast, even when provided with an extra carrying axle in front, with a Bissell radial truck, as on the Illinois Central Railroad's suburban services around Chicago, making it 2-4-4. The 2-4-4 type of tank engine, however, was very successfully built in Germany by Krauss of Munich, with the Krauss-Helmholtz bogie. In this last, the leading coupled wheels shared a bogie frame with the leading carrying wheels, with suitable side-play in the coupling rods, only the driving axle being rigid to the main frames, for the remaining axles were on an Adams bogie. Helmholtz and Adams between them (they had their copyists) produced the two classic locomotive bogie trucks. The Bissell radial truck was by comparison a poor thing against these, though one regrets to record its considerable use in both America and the British Isles, sometimes with unfortunate results at high speed. The trouble with radials was that they suited only their own radii, while railway radii are variable.

THE FAIRLIE AND THE VICTOR EMANUEL

This business of flexibility in long and relatively heavy locomotives engaged many engineers, as we have seen in connection with the Semmering Trials of Austria. Robert Fairlie in England cribbed every idea he could and like many improvers got remunerative results. (In what Americans sometimes call "British English" he was, in some ways, *a nasty piece of work*.) The "Single-Fairlie" locomotive—like a "Forney" but with the motor unit also pivoted, with all the complications of flexible steam-pipes, was a wretched thing. New Zealand alone, on 3 ft. 6 in. gauge, managed to employ it with some usefulness on main-line service of a sort. (One of the engines once over-ran the pier at Lyttelton; its motor bogie dropped off into the harbour!)

Much more interesting and successful was the "Double Fairlie", with two motor bogies and a double-barrelled boiler as in Cockerill's engine at the Semmering Trials. Several were built for minor railways in Wales during the 'sixties, and very small examples may be seen to this day there on the Festiniog Railway, now run by a preservation society. From the 'seventies onwards, large numbers of these Fairlie engines were built, some of considerable size, for Russia and Sweden, and most notably for Central and South America where gradients were very steep and curves very severe. We show an early specimen built for the Ichique Railway on p. 155. The last and largest were for the Mexican Railway, well into the present century. Weak points were in the steampipes, which had to be either flexible or to have flexible joints, but these were largely overcome to produce a very powerful, very flexible, but rather slow locomotive. As the first two things were most important on steep mountain lines, and the defect scarcely mattered, the engines had quite a vogue in some places. One of the big Mexicans once ran away, from summit to foot of a most vertiginous mountain descent, reaching the bottom at far higher speed than her own steam might have managed, but undamaged with all wheels on the rails.

As suggested, the "Double Fairlie" was scarcely suitable for fast passenger trains, but that Fairlie himself optimistically planned such use is shown by a drawing signed by him and with annotations in both French and English, with metric dimensions. It undoubtedly shows a Fairlie express engine, though we have no evidence that it ever was built. The shape of the frames below the outside cylinders is that of Allan and of Buddicom in France, and whether desire outran achievement or no, one suspects that it was intended for the French Western Railway, whereon English influence was for many years very strong.

As to the other important articulated type of steam locomotive in the nineteenth century—the Mallet—that must be deferred for a few pages as its history is tied up with compound expansion. Of orthodox types, the most important to appear from European works was the *Tenwheeler*—the 4-6-0 or 2-C— which America had been building for a long time as we know, though generally subject to light axle loads. Honours for European introduction might have been shared by Italy and Scotland (we are considering standard-gauge or broad-gauge engines for main-line traffic; there had been 4-6-0 tank engines for some time already). As Italy built the type for home traffic while Scotland built it at first for overseas use, let Italy have the kudos!

Cesare Frescot was Chief Mechanical Engineer to the Upper Italian Railways, and of its successor the Mediterranean System at Turin for many years of last century and for a few of the present. His company needed something that could take heavy passenger trains, as well as freight, on steeply graded and severely curved lines of Northern and Western Italy. (Special engines, including heavy tank engines coupled back-to-back in pairs, had long been used for banking on the Giovi Pass north of Genoa, but there were many other difficult lines.) For the Upper Italian Railways, therefore, its Turin Works produced the very competent and workmanlike design on p. 130. The prototype engine, built for the new (*Succursale*) Giovi Line, was subsequently named *Vittorio-Emanuele II*, after the first King of all Italy, and later engines built for the succeeding Mediterranean company were named after eminent Italians. *Cavour,* needless to say, followed closely after the Royal Opportunist.

In style and arrangement, Frescot's earlier engines were an interesting mixture of French and German classical practice. There was little of British or American influence in them. The *Vittorio Emanuele* was, however, an entirely native Italian design. The drawing is sufficiently explanatory (there were two cylinders, with simple expansion) save that the engine was generally more massive than the American ten-wheeler of the period. The class continued to be built with slight alteration into the late 'nineties. It was not a graceful engine. The very short bogie in advance of the "works" prevented that. But it had a smart, soldierly appearance, with some of the brassy glitter soldiers were still expected to bear without being killed. From youthful days we recall sitting up and looking round, the first time we saw one. (It was in the engine's extreme eld, at Florence in 1922.)

Many "Victor Emanuels" were built, and were found very useful over many years. In the year of the first, 1884, Dübs and Company of Glasgow (Scots firm with German founder) brought out a very handsome 4-6-0 engine for general service on the broad (5 ft. 6 in.) gauge Indian State Railways, up in the mountainous North-West of what is now Pakistan, though later examples were built also for India proper; for the Bengal Nagpur Railway and the Guaranteed State Railway (lovely title!) of His Exalted Highness the Nizam of Hyderabad. Immense numbers were built. They were still usefully employed in the nineteen-thirties, right up in the barren dun-coloured mountains of Scinde. An enlarged version by David Jones (who was probably the original, anonymous designer for Dübs) appeared on the Highland Railway in Scotland, in 1894. In the same year, something outwardly like the Italian engines, though much enlarged, with four cylinders and compound expansion, came to the Gotthard Railway in Switzerland. The Swiss engines perished by electrification in the nineteen-twenties, but one of the

In order to burn low-grade coal, Belpaire built a greatly increased grate area. The old-fashioned iron grate was replaced by thin steel plates, rivetted together so as to allow air to pass easily through the centre surface. The old system of staying the firebox was abandoned and replaced with horizontal and vertical stays. His first fireboxes had round tops externally but from 1864 they had the characteristic flat crown and flat-topped casing.

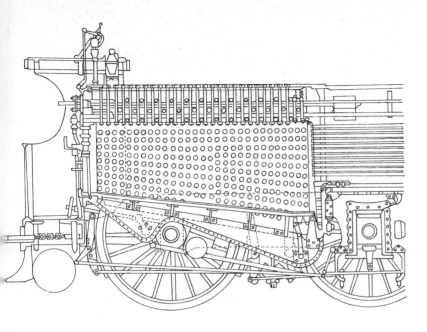

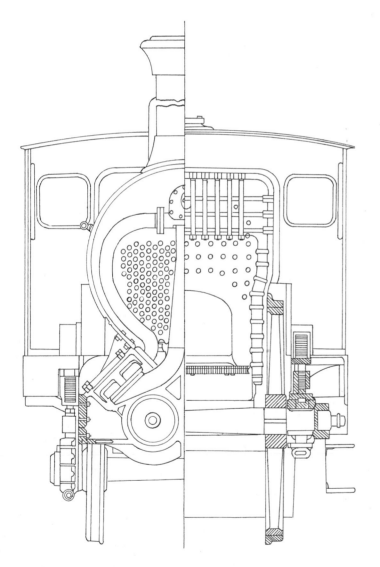

Scots, now lovingly preserved, took the last steam train out of Inverness in the late summer of 1965. These were very handsome engines with big inclined outside cylinders centred over the long-framed bogie.

A quite different type of main-line engine, which in America was but barely represented, on the Philadelphia and Reading, and on the Chicago, Burlington and Quincy Railroad, was the 2-4-2 for fast passenger traffic. It was much used on the Orleans, State, and Paris-Lyons-Mediterranean lines in France—with outside cylinders as in the rare American examples—and owed its origin to Robert Sinclair, a Scot, who designed it for the Great Central of Belgium as far back as 1860 and was copied by the Moscow-Warsaw Railway a little later. The trailing axle greatly steadied, in the French examples, what was basically the vertiginous Stephenson "long-boiler" type.

THE BELPAIRE FIREBOX

That great man Alfred Belpaire, however, produced quite a different form for the Belgian State Railways, which was built by Cockerill and others through the 'eighties into the 'nineties of last century. It had the very long, flat-topped firebox always associated with his name, capable of getting steam out of the most appalling muck the Railways Department could buy cheaply from the collieries of Charleroi. The cylinders were far forward and inside a set of very substantial double frames. It was an engine built like a battleship, of immense solidity. The driving wheels were large, but with plenty of steam behind them. The stack, very carefully calculated to promote a good even blast on the frightful fuel, was square in plan and tapered towards the top, in earlier examples, though later ones had the form of a truncated cone, likewise wider at the bottom. The design was built by Cockerill also for the Hessische Ludwigsbahn, with radial connection to the tender, but Belgium alone could stomach that square stack! A 2-6-0 version was built, with smaller wheels, for passenger traffic through the Ardennes.

Improvements in steaming efficiency, as well as mechanical and dynamic improvements, as in valve-gears and front-end passages, were becoming ever more necessary and important. Enormous freights were being handled all over the world, as well as coal and iron-ore. The feeding of great cities such as New York depended on wheat and stock trains rolling east from the Prairie States. More wheat trains in Canada, and stock trains in Argentina, fed London, thousands of miles across the Atlantic sea-routes. The Canadian Pacific Railway, backed by the legendary Hudson Bay Company, had reached the Pacific Coast in 1886; most South American railways were British-owned and equipped. In Northern Europe the great ore trains were beginning to rumble down to the Baltic from Lapland as well as from the Bergslag in Central Sweden. *Ergo,* bigger, more powerful and more efficient locomotives! People were travelling as never before; hence faster locomotives!

Coal was now the usual fuel, whether it were American anthracite, or best hard Welsh, or soft stuff from Belgium. After many experiments with water-partitioned fireboxes and combustion chambers, efficient combustion was very simply promoted by a deflector plate at the firedoor and a brick arch across the back of the firebox, though different forms of the latter suited different fuels; narrow long grates for good hard coal, wide ones for soft coal or low-grade anthracite, and so forth.

COMPOUND LOCOMOTIVES

Compound expansion—using steam first in high-pressure and then in low-pressure cylinders before exhausting, was one way to fuel economy, though complex. As far back as 1852 John Nicholson had experimented in England with what he called "continuous expansion", meeting with the frustration of many pioneers. Anatole Mallet, a Swiss, built the first entirely practical compound locomotive for the little Bayonne and Biarritz Railway, France, in 1876. Several systems of compounding appeared later in the century. Von Borries in Germany used two cylinders; a small-diameter one for high pressure steam and a large for low pressure, resulting in a curiously slow exhaust beat. A small von Borries compound passenger engine of the Hannover Lines, Prussian State Railways, is shown (p. 110). The system was once common in Central Europe, and a form of it was still to be seen in Northern Ireland in the nineteen-forties.

Alfred de Glehn was an international figure, born in England of a Baltic father and a Scots mother, and by adoption an Alsatian. His system of compounding involved four cylinders; two for high pressure and two low-pressure, beginning with an engine built for the Northern Railway of France in 1886 (preserved today). His finest work must be ascribed to his partnership with Gaston du Bousquet of the latter company. In the 'nineties, successively bigger de Glehn compound engines came out on the Northern Railway of France and were paralleled on other lines. That shown was one of a set built in the late 'nineties for the English mail and passenger trains between Paris and Calais. One reason for the success of the de Glehn-du Bousquet arrangement was their scientific study and application of his theories on free steam passages, both admissive and for exhaust. The technics of these things need a complete book to themselves and here we must stick to general arrangement.

Both the French de Glehn-du Bousquet and the German von Borries engine, it will be seen, had their high-pressure cylinders outside and driving the rear axle, a disposition of T. R. Crampton's, with, except in the initial French engine, coupling rods to the preceding axle which was driven by the inside low-pressure cylinders.

We show next a heavy compound freight locomotive designed by M. Henry of the Paris, Lyons and Mediterranean Railway and built in 1888. In this the high-pressure cylinders were inside, between the leading and second coupled axle and driving on to the third. Many larger engines of the same type were built for the P.L.M. from 1893 onwards, and were to be seen for over half a century longer.

Francis Webb, an English designer, at this time attracted much attention by his three-cylinder compound locomotives on the London and North Western Railway. He used outside high-pressure cylinders and a single very large low-pressure cylinder between the frames, with divided drive and, in the case of the passenger engines, uncoupled driving axles as in de Glehn's French engine of 1886. We show (p. 160), however, a Webb three-cylinder compound freight locomotive, 0-8-0 like the Frenchman, built for the London and North Western company in and after 1893 for heavy coal traffic on this great British line. Webb's compound engines, though ingenious, had certain undoubted defects, though hundreds were built. They *could* do excellent work, but it needed an artist to drive one. Maintenance was heavy. Austria, France, India and the Americas sampled the type—but no more!

Of American compound locomotives, those under Vauclain's patents mounted high- and low-pressure cylinders together, outside, with a single cross-head to each pair of piston rods. Many such did well, but the arrangement entailed very heavy reciprocating masses. The same defect applied to various compound locomotives in both America and Europe which had the high- and low-pressure cylinders arranged in tandem with common piston-rods.

Karl Gölsdorf in Austria produced some remarkable compound locomotives under his own patents, which hauled both passengers and freight over the Alpine passes—Arlberg, Semmering, Tauern and Brenner. They were variable engines; earlier examples steamed badly, and an old Gölsdorf was not to be compared with the de Glehn-du Bousquet engines, working very fast express trains on the great French main lines. At one time and another, the finest fast express work in the world was to be found between Paris and Calais.

SLEEPING CARS

Mention of the increasing weight and speed of trains turns us to car design (*carriages and wagons* in all British or British-influenced countries). In passenger service, we have seen how American design was improved by G. M. Pullman. By the end of the century, the native Pullman car was an enormous thing; still built chiefly of wood but spacious, of great length and formidable weight. We show (p. 124) a standard Pullman sleeper for United States service, built in 1898. The wide vestibules and closely engaging gangways with friction plate contact, one to another, were the work of Henry Sessions of Pullman's works, one of the truly historic coachbuilders. The clerestory was to remain supreme in American passenger car design for many years.

America clung faithfully, and for as long, to the old centre-aisle arrangement of curtained sleeping berths, though private compartments, reached by side corridors, could be reserved for a higher fee. European users invariably preferred these and were prepared to pay for them, even though on older cars it might entail sharing a small bedroom with three total strangers, as in the Mann-Nagelmackers arrangement.

To the best of our research, the first standard sleeping cars to provide single-berth

Alfred-George de Glehn, 1848–1936. Born in England and educated at King's College, London, he went to France after finishing there because he could not find suitable work. After working for two years in a marine engineering works he became involved in the Franco-Prussian war of 1870. Afterwards he applied for a job at the Société Alsacienne de Constructions Mécaniques in Mulhouse—unpaid. After 10 months he was put on a salary of 100 francs per month and after two years he had risen to the position of Director of Locomotive Engineering. He collaborated with Gaston du Bousquet, Chief Engineer of the Chemin de Fer du Nord, in designing the compound locomotive on the opposite page (above).

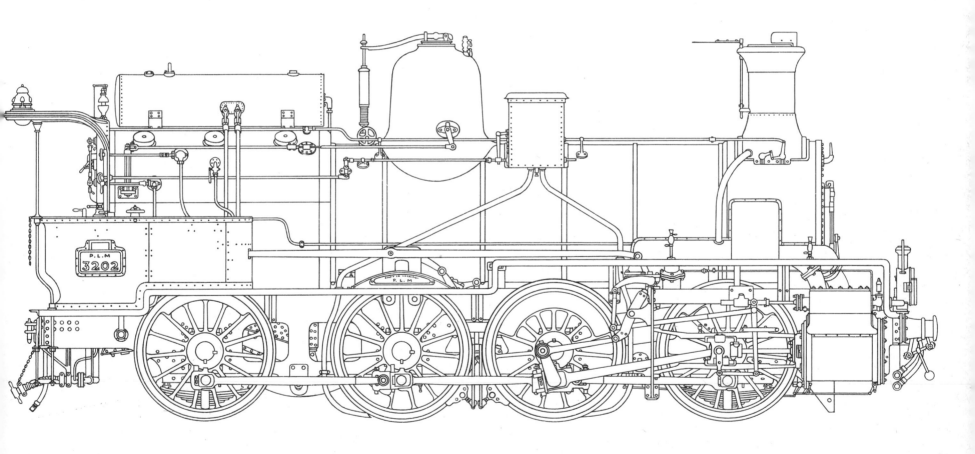

(top) The de Glehn/du Bousquet
Compound Locomotive No. 2160,
built in 1897 for the Chemin de
Fer du Nord.

(below) Henry's 0-8-0 four
cylinder Compound Freight
Locomotive, No. 3202, was built
in 1888 for the Paris, Lyons and
Mediterranean Railway.

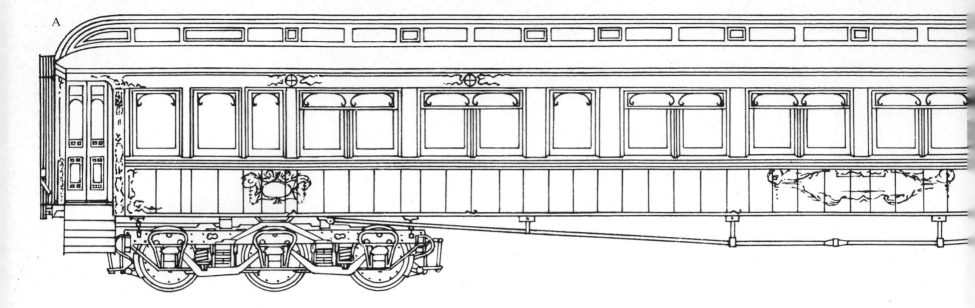

cabins for ordinary passengers appeared on the East Coast expresses between London and Edinburgh, in 1895; the work of David Bain of the North Eastern Railway in England. These cars also provided double-berth compartments for couples, and on p. 169 we show the original outline. Apart from the wide vestibules (at first without connecting gangways) that outline suggests a much older American car. But—oh blessed single bedroom! Bain's car became a prototype for all Europe, where the Wagons-Lits company took it up later for the more luxurious international expresses.

Sleeping cars were generally for first-class passengers only, though Russia, the Western United States, and Canada (which delicately called the vehicles "colonist cars") provided rather Spartan folding berths for unmoneyed migrants. As to heating, while England had a touching affection for the portable metal foot-warmer on the carriage floor, stoves of variously frightful sorts abounded. America, which could be *very* cold in winter, used the Baker heater, a stove-fired, closed-circuit, hot-pipe system using either water or a saturated saline solution which would not freeze when out of use. On the Belgian Great Central Railway (1875–76) M. E. Belleroche furnished a highly advanced hot-water circulation system throughout the train, using tender water from the engine, warmed by a special injector. In spite of the hazards of early hose connections, it answered quite well. Contact with the passengers was through copper floor-plates called chaufferettes which cooked one's boots and anything else inadvertently dropped or spilt on them. Warm water heating was general in the Netherlands.

Low-pressure steam heating of trains from a reducing valve on the locomotive ultimately superseded hot-water systems (introduced on the Eastern of France in 1874). W. S. Laycock's, with steam piped to storage heaters under the carriage seats, appeared in England in the early 'nineties, and other systems gradually followed, though in old English local trains the wretched travellers continued for some time to sit and shiver in winter.

Lighting greatly improved. England pioneered gas lighting of trains as far back as 1863. Later, compressed oil-gas superseded coal gas, as in the Pintsch system. Kerosene lamps were still much used in America, and candle-lamps in Russia. The first electrically-lit car was a solitary Pullman in England, on the London-Brighton line in 1881, but the necessary batteries were clumsy and very heavy. Until, right at the end of the nineteenth century and in the British Isles, J. C. Stone perfected self-generating and self-regulating electric lighting equipment, oil lamps and gaslight held their own in most places. A great pioneer of electric light was the Great Northern Railway of Ireland which *never* used gas. Both gas and petroleum were liable to set trains ablaze after an accident.

Passenger communication was for long very bad. *Pulling the cord,* which *might* ring a bell, was the alarm signal in many places. Passenger's emergency-access to the continuous brakes was first provided on the Grazi-Tsaritsin Railway in Russia, by its Scots engineer, Thomas Urquhart, in the 'eighties. It was the precursor of all modern systems.

A *This Pullman car was the type in common use in America, c. 1898.*
B *This delightfully named "Lavatory Bogie Composite Coach" was built at the Stratford Works in 1901 for the Great Eastern Railway, England. It is a fine example of the European compartment-type coach for ordinary trains at that period. Many English railways had gone over to a two-class system by that time—the equivalent of the American chair-car and coach—and England, being English, had chosen first and third class. The body was made of teak, heating was by low-pressure steam and lighting was by compressed oil gas. The roof had a handsome clerestory with both ventilators and decklights. It was designed by James Holden.*

1 Mirror
2 Decorative photographs
3 Lamp
4 Stuffed seats covered with blue cloth
5 Stuffed seats covered with crimson buffalo-hide
6 Woven wire seats covered with "railway-carriage" cloth (for third class)
7 Corridors with linoleum on the floor
8 Third-class lavatory
9 First-class lavatory
10 First-class smoking compartment
11 Luggage compartment

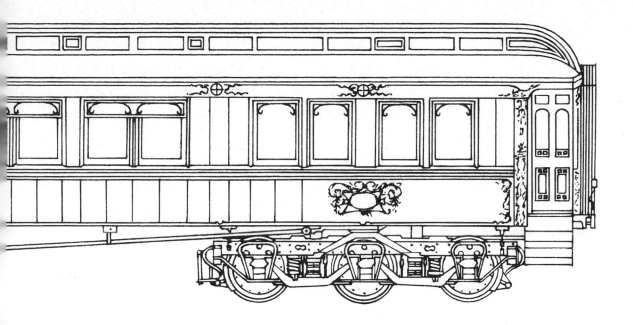

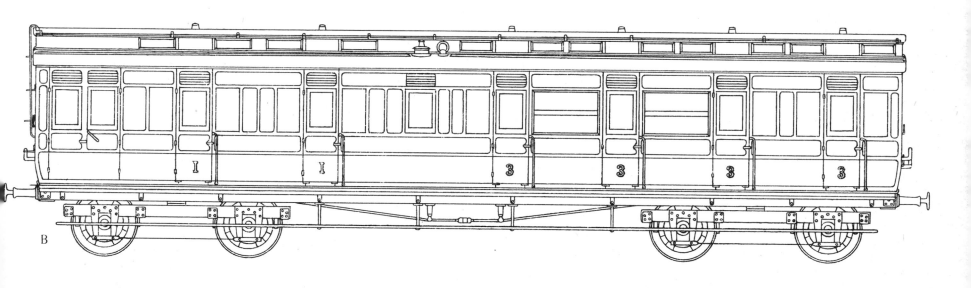

B

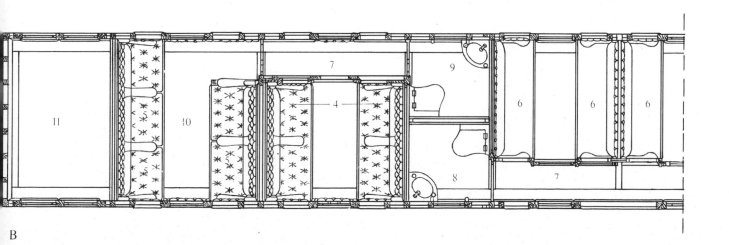

B

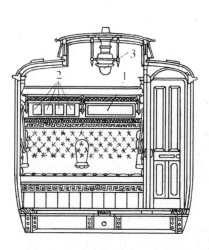

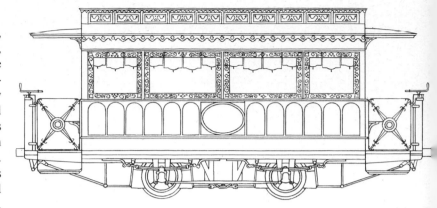

While the American ideal of aisled or gangwayed cars spread to much of the world, closed compartments remained usual for coaches in many Western European countries, and is well exemplified by this English carriage (p. 125) one of a series built for the Great Eastern Railway at the turn of the century. Though small, its third-class compartments and its water-closet access were both excellent. As long ago as 1875, the mighty Midland Railway—stretching from Bristol and London to the North of England, had cushioned the seats of *all* coaches, a most radical reform which other British companies had to copy to compete with each other. In form this Great Eastern carriage was much akin to Prussian practice of the period, though not in its provision of third-class plush.

The best Prussian carriages of the 'nineties—the famed *D-Wagen*—were prototypes of the usual Continental European passenger car of today; vestibuled and gangwayed like Pullman cars, but internally furnished with compartments and side-corridors. Ordinary French carriages of the same decade, alas, were a reproach, though the best cars could be handsome enough.

In Eastern Europe and Scandinavia, the American plan was widespread, though modified. In the Netherlands this was favoured only by J. W. Verloop on the Dutch Central Railway, of which we show (p. 174) an elegant second-class car for local traffic. (The rigid-wheelbase arrangement of six wheels, by the way, was unknown in North America. It was rough-riding, yet steady.)

Only in England (not even in Scotland!) and in North America at this time, did one find any sort of ornament about coaches for passengers paying the minimum ordinary fares. In Continental Europe, however, the *second* class was often elegant as well as comfortable, while in England, where the *third* class rapidly improved, second class became gradually moribund on the main lines. Two classes were enough, like day-coach and Pullman in the States.

Dining cars are of some antiquity. The first of which we have actual record was a convertible diner-sleeper (an "hotel car") on the Great Western Railway of Canada in 1867, about two years after Pullman's sleeper *Pioneer* in the States, though there was a diner in South Russia about the same time. A straight Pullman dining car appeared on the Chicago and Alton Railroad in 1868. The first dining car in Western Europe was a converted Pullman parlor-car called *Prince of Wales* between London and Leeds on the Great Northern Railway (England) in 1879. In all cases the term implies meals cooked in the same car *en route*.

Both Old World potentates and New World business nabobs at this time travelled in private cars—and, in the case of the monarchs, in whole special trains—of great sumptuosity. Some of the richer Americans, indeed, outdid the kings during the late 'nineties and early nineteen-hundreds. One doubts that there was ever anything on wheels more sumptuously decorated than the State coach of Maximilian II and Ludwig II of Bavaria, but their train had no bathroom. Nor had Queen Victoria's in England. But Colonel William Jackson Palmer had one on the Rio Grande Western in 1892, and so had other men like him. One reads even about marble tubs and gold-plated faucets.

Even those not quite in a position to own or permanently command such things were able to hire them in the United States. In Europe a few had them, like the Chancellor Prince Bismarck and the Duke of Sutherland. With the British aristocracy and richer bourgeoisie, the hired family saloon was a recognized institution. It was sufficient to pay so many fares and then temporarily set up house in one.

Mails had been carried by public transport in the days of the Caesars, though the service doubtless went down in the Middle Ages, when a mounted, armed courier carried them. Postal authorities quickly recognized the value of the rail. The Travelling Post Office, which meant not only the carriage but the reception and sorting of mail *en route*, originated in the English Midlands in January, 1838, at the instance of F. Karstadt, doubtless a German by descent. By May, John Ramsay of the British General Post Office had devised apparatus for picking up mailbags without stopping. Ten years later, John Dicker, also of the British G.P.O., had perfected apparatus for both pick-up and delivery of mail-pouches at full speed, still widely used on the great British main lines, and, at one time and another, in Prussia and France, though less extensively. The first French Travelling Post Offices worked between Paris and Rouen in 1844. Post Office sorting cars made their first American appearance on the Hannibal and St. Joseph Railroad during the Civil War, at the instance of W. A. Davis, an inventive postal clerk at "St. Jo." The *T.P.O.* spread.

In America it was the *R.P.O.*; the Railway Post Office. In an age of mail-bearing air-

In 1883 Ireland saw the first use of electric traction with hydro-electric power on the little Giant's Causeway line from Portrush. This is a 20-seat car built for the line by the Midland Railway-Carriage and Wagon Company, Shrewsbury, England.

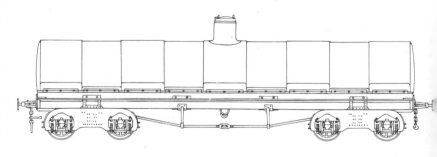

A Russian tank-car for petroleum, 1894. The increased demand for petrol which came with the popularization of the motorcar was to necessitate the shipment of millions of gallons of crude and refined oil by rail and tank-cars became bigger and bigger.

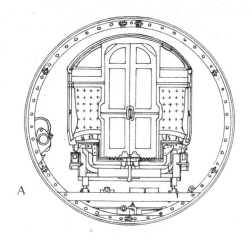

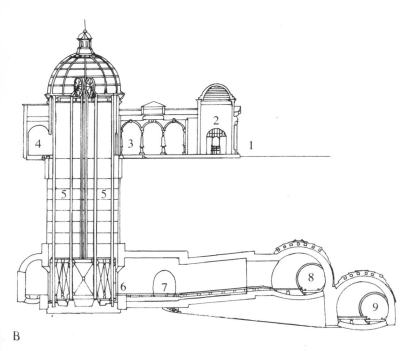

craft, the postal train holds its own on overnight inter-city service by its virtue of being an office as well as a conveyance. In pioneering England the all-postal trains to-and-from Scotland and the West run as of yore. They have no room for passengers.

Of European freight-cars in the late nineteenth century, one cannot say much, but the great distances of both Russia-Siberia and North America demanded—and got—vehicles of very substantial sort. We show here a tank car for petroleum, built in 1894 for the Russian line between Baku on the Caspian and Batoum on the Black Sea. The American freight-car of this time was a huge oblong box with a cat-walk along the top for the nameless heroes who, in the iciest weather, skipped from brake-wheel to brake-wheel as their train screamed down some vertiginous grade, were it in the Rockies or the Alleghenies. From such horrors was George Westinghouse beginning to deliver them. The diamond-frame truck was its tower of strength.

THE FIRST ELECTRIC LOCOMOTIVES

Car design brings us rather abruptly to the very first electric trains, themselves closely akin to street-cars or trams of American origin. George Stephenson himself had foreseen the ultimate triumph of electric power. Germany was the cradle of electric traction, though there had been experiments in many places. Behind its advance was the great Siemens family, of whom Wilhelm Siemens became an English knight though it was Werner von Siemens who first successfully conveyed passengers (p. 142), on a narrow-gauge line in the Berlin Trades Exhibition of 1879. Haulage was by a motor mounted over and geared to four solid iron wheels, taking current from a third rail. The motorman sat astride. On May 12, 1881, a tram-car with electric motors inaugurated the world's first public electric railway at Lichterfelde, Berlin. On August 3, 1883, Magnus Volk opened the first section of his famous narrow-gauge electric railway along the sea-front of Brighton in the South of England. It is still there; antique but well-patronized in summer, and affectionately regarded by many.

It was in Ireland that water power was first used to generate electric energy for traction. In the words of its sponsor and builder, William Acheson Traill, the Giant's Causeway, Portrush and Bush Valley Railway and Tramway Company, on the 3 ft. gauge, "was a bold venture, a Utopian scheme", for he proposed "a new traction power to supersede the long established horse or steam power for the working of tramways or railways; and, wilder still, the idea of utilising the waste forces of our rivers to generate electricity to propel tram-cars along a tramway miles away from the source of power." Traill's Consultant was Wilhelm Siemens. Turbines and dynamos were installed at a 24 ft. fall of the River Bush, though here there was some delay and spare steam-powered generators were installed at Portrush. A trial trip was made on November 21, 1882. Teething troubles were many, and two steam-tram engines were wisely acquired, but regular electric services began on November 5, 1883. Steam was used in the streets of Portrush, where the raised electric conductor rail was out of the question. Indeed for many years the little line was as much what the Hollanders called a *Stoomtram* as an electric railway. Overhead contact ultimately replaced the troublesome *hot rail*. Tramway or railway, it was the ancestress of mighty electric lines powered by falling water, stretching from Lapland to Sicily, and in many other places both European and Asiatic.

The world's first electric underground line was in England, where the first part of the City and South London Railway was opened by the Prince of Wales (later King Edward VII) on November 4, 1890, using very small electric locomotives to haul three-car trains through deep-level tunnels in the London clay. Although a rather fearsome conveyance (the citizens at once named the narrow, almost windowless cars "padded cells") it was an immediate success. Electric underground lines were ultimately to serve most of the great cities of the world.

Though America had pioneered elevated city railways, it was England that first built one with electric traction, the Liverpool Overhead Railway of 1893. Elevated city lines were less favoured than underground ones. Today they are gone from both New York and Liverpool, though they may yet return as traffic problems worsen, possibly in the form of monorails, the oldest of which, at Wuppertal in Germany, dates back to the end of last century.

But back in the last quarter of last century, the electric train was still a mechanical curiosity. In Scotland, the usually shrewd city of Glasgow so far distrusted it as to build

A *An example of the "padded cell" type car in the tunnel on the London Underground in the 1890s. The tunnel was 10 ft. 6 in. in diameter and the cars were 6 ft. 10 in. wide.*

B *A cross-section of the Oval Underground station in South London.*

1 Entrance
2 Booking office
3 Entrance to elevators
4 Exit from elevators
5 Lift shaft
6 Landing
7 Passage to down platform
8 Up line
9 Down line

an underground line with cable traction (1896) and to regret this error of mechanical judgement for the next thirty-nine years. (The line was electrified in 1935!)

William Buchanan was born in Dumbarton, Scotland, in 1830 and emigrated to the United States with his family when he was still a boy. He began as a blacksmith-machinist on the Hudson River Railroad and rose to the position of Superintendent of Motive Power for the New York Central system and its controlled lines. He designed the New York Central 999 on p. 132. It was an enlarged version of the traditional American 4-4-0 and its type was in use as late as the 1930s.

SPEED RECORDS

The sun of steam was still rising to zenith. Except for use of superheated steam, which really belongs to the present century, advances meant increase in size, above all in North America. By the end of the century, American locomotives were powerful, effective, and in some cases both speedy and very handsome. In Continental Europe there was an ugly phase. British engines were elegant but usually small.

The *American Type* (4-4-0) remained the *old faithful* for fast passenger service, almost to the end of the century, and perhaps the finest examples of this were Theodore Ely's on the Pennsylvania Railroad, and William Buchanan's on the New York Central, though other lines had many worthy designs. If an Anglo-Saxon author may criticise America, let him remark that Buchanan's achieved the greatest international fame, while Ely's were most beautiful to the eye.

New York Central No. 999 is (for she is treasured to this day) a Paul Revere among locomotives. By our records she was the first man-made machine to run at a land speed of 100 miles an hour or more, by responsible calculation. (There had been hundreds of irresponsible claims, almost since locomotion began!) She was built in 1893, and was a star turn at the Chicago World Fair of that year; furthermore, she was designed for a speed demonstration rather than for general service (later her driving wheels were reduced for that!). With the original 86 in. driving wheels, on May 10, 1893, No. 999 was timed at 112·5 miles an hour over a measured mile near Batavia, N.Y., with a four-car train. This was an official road test, though without a dynamometer car, and there is no reasonable cause to doubt its authenticity. It was to remain a world record for some years, though European opinion, jaundiced by many older and quite irresponsible American claims, was sceptical. The fastest authentic maximum speed previously had been one of 89·5 miles an hour attained by an ancient Crampton locomotive, Eastern Railway No. 604, rebuilt with a patent boiler by Flaman, on the Paris-Laroche line (June 20, 1890).

Speed-for-speed's-sake was indeed something of a fetish at this time with competitive railroad companies, as between New York and Chicago in the United States, and London and Aberdeen in Great Britain. Over the latter stretch there was a regular race, night after night, during the summer of 1895, using quite ordinary English and Scottish locomotives over rather exacting roads. Average speeds were what counted. The highest were attained by the West Coast Route (London-Carlisle-Perth-Aberdeen) on the night of August 22–23, when the 540 miles were covered in 512 minutes with three station stops of two minutes each. The fastest "hops" were at 67·5 miles an hour from Crewe to Carlisle (142 miles, London and North Western engine *Hardwicke*, Driver Robinson) and Perth to Aberdeen (89·7 miles in 80·5 minutes, or just under sixty-seven miles an hour with Driver Soutar on Caledonian Railway engine No. 17). Excellent work was done by both routes, allowing for the lightness of the trains (about four small wooden coaches or sleepers). The little engine *Hardwicke* is preserved in London. As far as any lessons were drawn from these picturesque pranks, they were, firstly, that locomotives would take bigger payloads if the proportion of boiler power to cylinder capacity were increased, and secondly—a negative one—that most passengers had little wish to be turned out into a still sleeping city with little prospect of breakfast. In the following year, the London and North Western company had a bad derailment at Preston through high speed round the curves there, and further "racing" was voted off.

But in that year, the standard Caledonian passenger locomotives acquired much bigger boilers, as in John F. McIntosh's *Dunalastair* which basically was of Dugald Drummond's old type dating back to the 'seventies. So successful was this modification that numerous "Dunalastairs" were built under licence for, of all outfits, the Belgian State Railways, which used them on the Brussels-Ostend and Brussels-Antwerp lines. The 4-4-0 engine with inside cylinders remained for years a British national type—in India and Australia too—as well as being much used in Holland and Sweden. In France it was rare, except on the Western Railway. In Central Europe it was almost unknown (exception in Baden) while in America there was no revival of the "inside-connected" engine. It made a strong and solid engine, but the machinery was somewhat inaccessible.

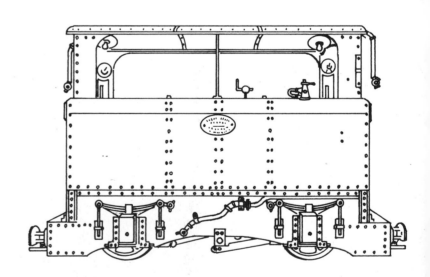

This electric locomotive was built for the City and South London Railway in 1890 by Mather and Platt in association with Beyer Peacock. It ran on the first tube railway in the world and pulled trains on such lines as that shown on the previous page.

Jules Petiet, Chief Engineer of the Chemin de Fer du Nord, 1845–1872.

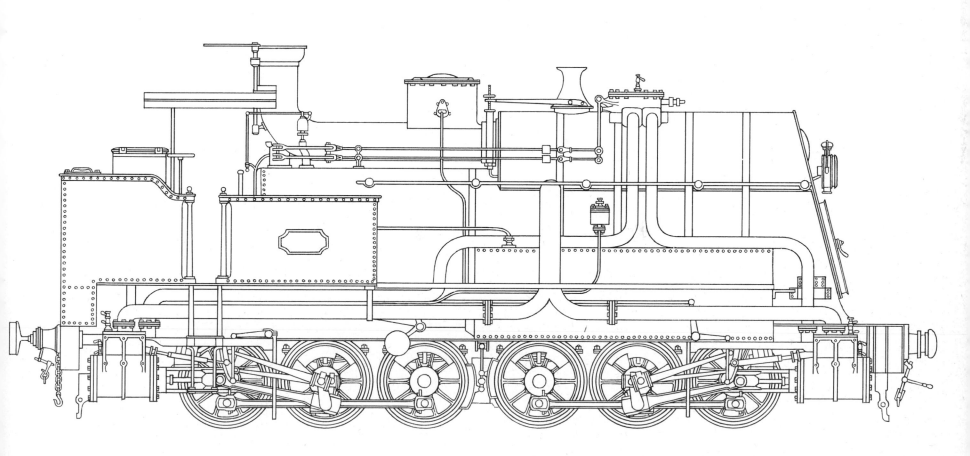

PETIET BUILT THIS TANK-ENGINE FOR THE CHEMIN DE FER DU NORD IN 1863. IT WAS USED FOR FREIGHT HAULAGE.

Vittorio-Emanuele

CESARE FRESCOT BUILT THE FIRST VITTORIO EMANUELE TYPE FOR THE UPPER ITALIAN RAILWAY. THIS BECAME A CLASSIC ITALIAN TYPE.

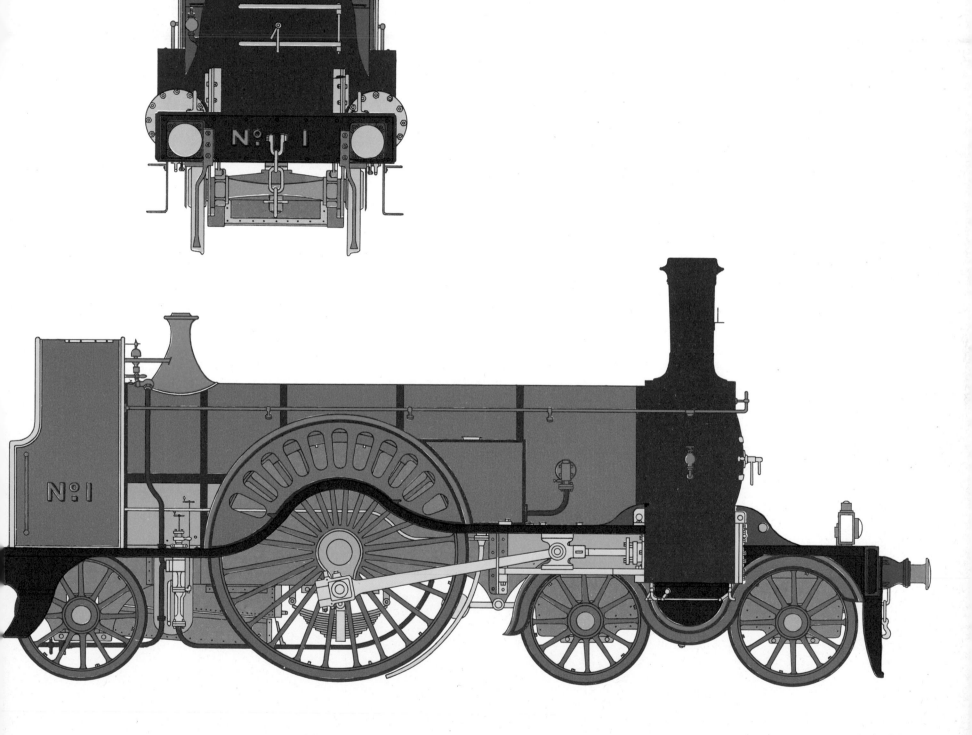

PATRICK STIRLING DESIGNED THIS LOVELY ENGINE FOR THE GREAT NORTHERN RAILWAY IN 1870. SHE HAS A 5 FT. 6 IN. FIREBOX AND 4 FT. 1 IN. TRAILING WHEELS.

New York Central no. 999

THIS IS THE FAMOUS ENGINE WHICH ESTABLISHED A WORLD SPEED RECORD OF 112.5 M.P.H. ON A RUN WITH THE EMPIRE STATE EXPRESS IN 1893. IT IS A LARGE VERSION OF WHAT WAS THE TRADITIONAL 4-4-0 TYPE. WILLIAM BUCHANAN DESIGNED IT.

THIS WAS THE FIRST PASSENGER SERVICE ENGINE OF THE MOGUL TYPE TO BE USED ON THE BALTIMORE AND OHIO RAILROAD. IT WAS DESIGNED BY JOHN C. DAVIS IN 1875.

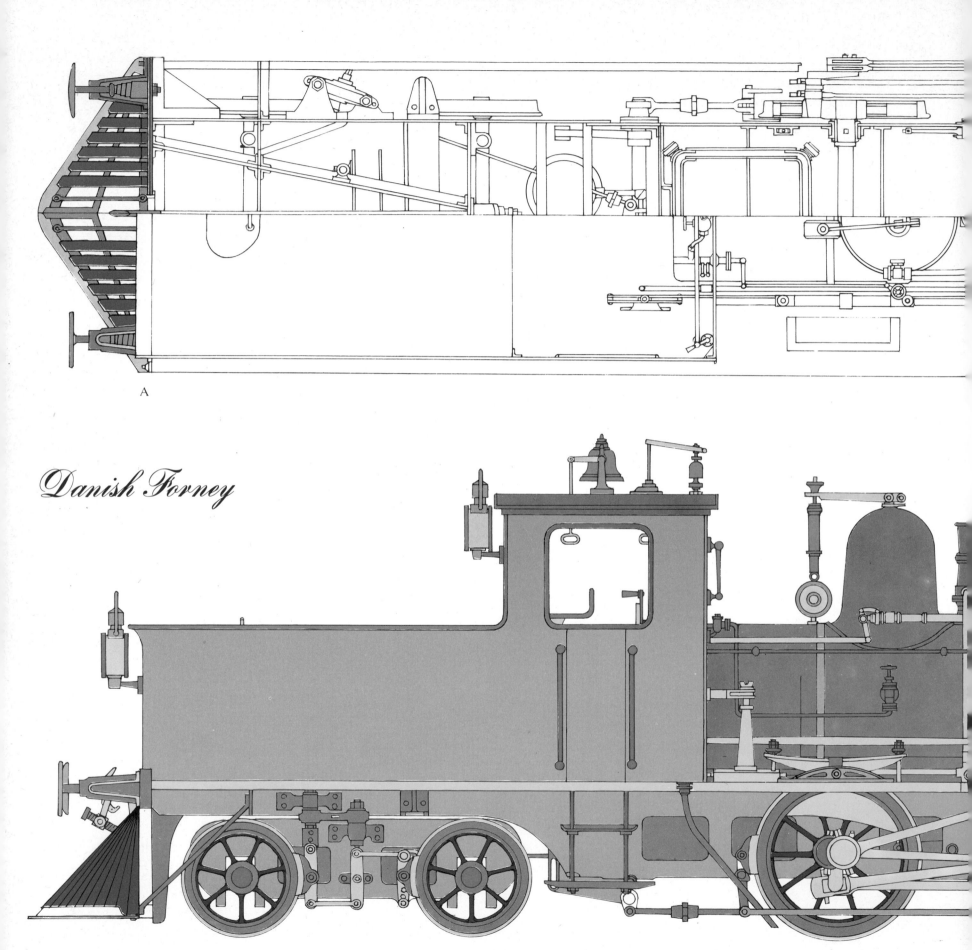

Danish Forney

THIS FORNEY LOCOMOTIVE WAS BUILT FOR THE THYLANDS RAILROAD, DENMARK. THE DESIGNER WAS OTTO BUSSE.

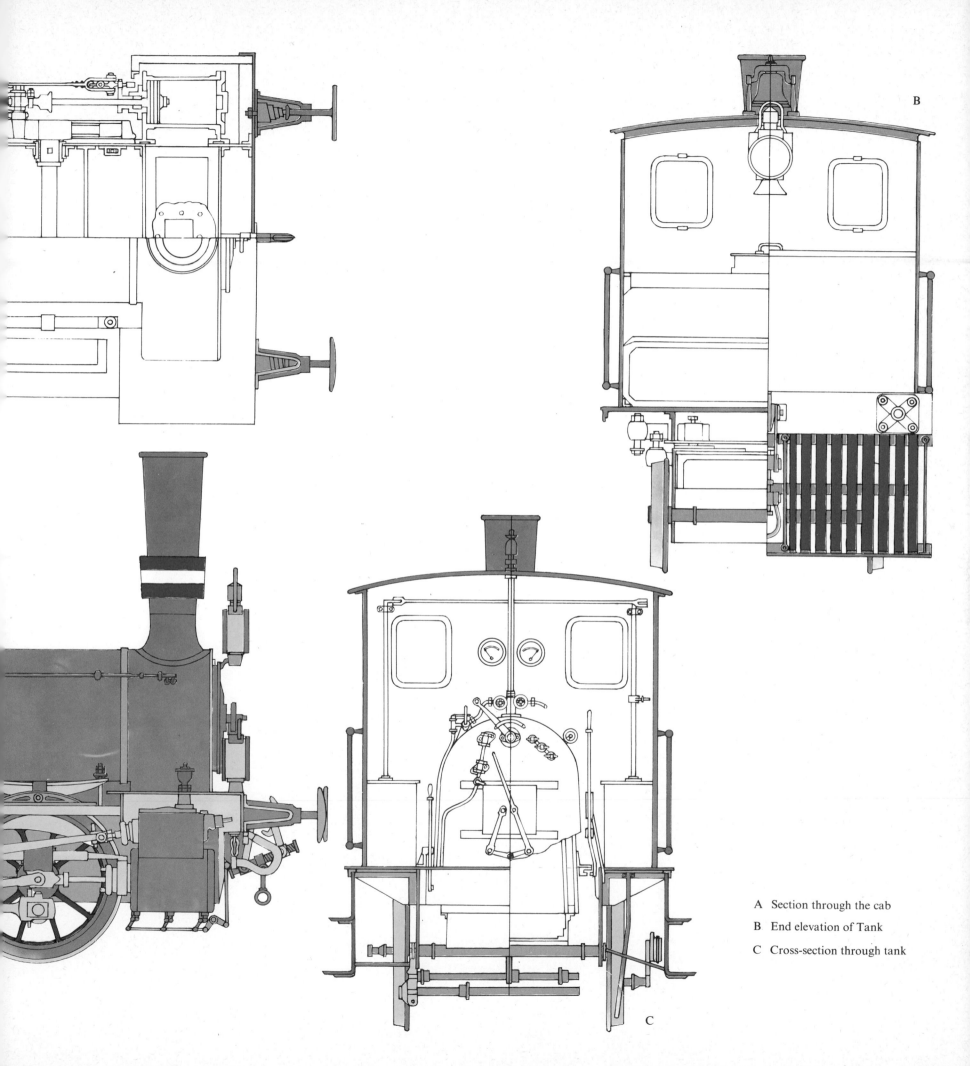

A Section through the cab

B End elevation of Tank

C Cross-section through tank

THE DOM LUIZ WAS BUILT FOR THE SOUTH EASTERN RAILWAY OF PORTUGAL BY BEYER PEACOCK OF MANCHESTER IN 1862.

Atlantic Type

THIS LOCOMOTIVE DID HEAVY DUTY ON THE CONCORD AND MONTREAL RAILROAD FOR MANY YEARS.

In France, however, we see during the 'nineties some early attempts by modified external surfaces to reduce air resistance on fast passenger locomotives. Baudry's work on the Paris, Lyons and Mediterranean Railway could not be called streamlining; "windcutting" was the vernacular word (Coupe-vent), and it involved wedge-shaped casings to smokebox, stack, and the front of the cab, and lenticular casings to the domes. F. U. Adams had tried something of the kind—and with fully streamlined cars at that— in the United States during the 'eighties, but the time was not yet ripe for these. Ricour tried the *coupe-vent* style on the French State Railway as far back as 1887, too. The odd thing was that the mighty P.L.M. was by no means "fast" by French standards. Its trains were often heavy; they rumbled rather than raced.

There was one feature of steam locomotive working peculiar to Great Britain, the French State Railways between Chartres and Bordeaux, and to certain lines in the Eastern United States, but unknown everywhere else. That was the laying of immensely long water troughs on level stretches of track, whence the engines took water at full speed (in good American "on the fly") so that very long runs could be made without need for water stops. It was an English invention, by John Ramsbottom of the London and North Western Railway, and dating back at least to 1860. Pickup was by a hinged scoop, on the tender. The arrangement lasted for as long as steam traction did; it accounts for the very small tenders of many otherwise large and important British locomotives down the years.

Invention of steam sanding gear caused, on British lines, an astonishing revival of the passenger locomotive with single driving wheels, which had never quite vanished from them. Such engines continued to be built to the end of the century, and we show (p.172) a very handsome example by Samuel Johnson, the Midland Railway's *Princess of Wales*, built in 1900. Remote descent from the Stephenson "Patentee" is discernible. The engine was shown at the Paris Exposition of 1900, causing some French astonishment but winning a gold medal. Some of these Midland "single-wheelers" lasted into the middle nineteen-twenties. They were extremely fleet engines and could move quite surprising loads.

Small single-drive tank locomotives were built for local services over many years, notably in Austria and Sweden; the last for Latvia in 1928, but outside England (which built four very large ones for China as late as 1910) express locomotives with single driving wheels were by now extremely scarce. There were the short-lived "Bicycles" on the Reading Company's Atlantic City service, also in the 'nineties, and a few (British-built) in Argentina. Those Reading "Bicycles" had a virtue purely incidental to their single driving wheels. Use of a carrying axle at the rear allowed for a much larger firebox of the sort pioneered on the same road by Millholland. American designers now went for a coupled passenger locomotive with this same advantage. Briefly the 2-4-2 type, already much liked in France, was given a trial, but the important development was the 4-4-2, known immediately as the Atlantic type from having made its first appearance on the Atlantic Coast Line in 1894, from Baldwin Locomotive Works. It had the steadiness the 2-4-2 type lacked, as well as a more adequate boiler. We show (p. 136) a similar engine, built soon after for the Concord and Montreal Railway linking New England and Canada. By 1896 American "Atlantics" were being built for the Central of New Jersey, Lehigh Valley, and other railroads, with very wide fireboxes and with the engineer's cab mounted saddle-fashion on top of the boiler. They were often called "Camelbacks", though this tended to confusion with the ancient types of Winans and Hayes on the Baltimore and Ohio. "Mother Hubbard" was at once a less confusing and more endearing nickname. The unfortunate fireman had a wet and windy perch in rear of the firebox.

In the same decade, the Atlantic type arrived in Europe. There were 4-4-2 express engines with inside cylinders on the Palatinate Railway in Germany, and on the Lancashire and Yorkshire Railway in England, but the true Atlantic had the cylinders outside, driving the second of the two coupled axles, and this was built in England by Harry Ivatt of the Great Northern Railway from 1898 onwards. The original engine, soon after named *Henry Oakley*, is preserved at York. Still boilers were inadequate; much bigger ones could go on to such a locomotive, and so they did in the early years of the following century. Ivatt's later examples in England were to give useful service through nearly half a century, including two major wars.

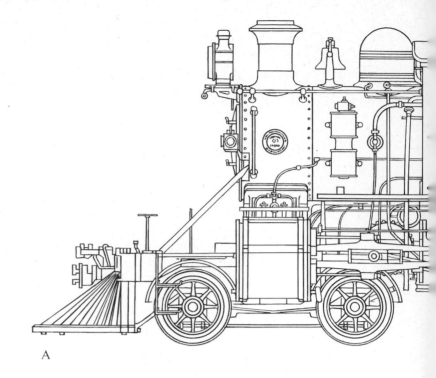

A

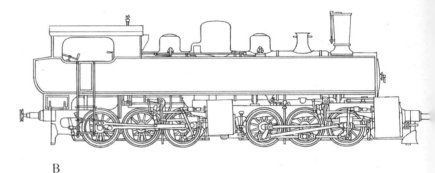

B

(previous page) Clapham Junction by Terence Cuneo. The scene is an enormous transfer station which serves two of London's main terminals. The time is the 1950s. The commuter traffic by rail in London beggars description, even by the standards of Tokyo and New York, but Cuneo has gone for the majesty of steam movement at a quieter time than rush hour. The stately Pacific engine will have brought in an express train from England's West Country; the little wing-tank engine is for shifting empty coaches.

A The Reading "Bicycle" was the brainchild of L. B. Paxson and was designed by W. P. Henszey of the Baldwin Locomotive Works. The dome was placed over the firebox and

behind the cab. Although this was unusual, it gave the driver and fireman a roomy cab and good visibility.

B J. A. Maffei's Mallet compound locomotive for the Gotthard Railway, Switzerland, 1890.

C The first electric haulage of main-line trains took place in August 1895, on the Baltimore and Ohio tunnel section of the Baltimore and Ohio Railroad in America. The locomotive was built by Westinghouse who also electrified the line. Power was collected from overhead by the pantograph, side and end views of which are shown. Note the roller bearings on the pantograph.

C

C

In America, the Pennsylvania Railroad was to produce the type to absolute maximum dimensions, and one example. No. 460, achieved a latter-day record when Colonel Charles Lindbergh made the first Atlantic solo flight in 1927 with the aeroplane *Spirit of St. Louis*. The films of Lindbergh's arrival were developed in a Pennsylvania baggage car for immediate showing on Broadway, and the engine in question covered 216 miles in 175 minutes. Be it remarked that this was, by then, with an old-type locomotive (P.R.R. Class E 6) taken straight from stock. The world's last "Atlantics" in steam were some of Denmark's beautiful Class P, still about in the nineteen-sixties.

Back to the eighteen-nineties; a funny thing happened in America. Just as certain Englishmen believed that only with a single driving axle could one get a "free-running" engine capable of really high speed, so did many Americans believe that no more than two coupled axles were permissable to the same end. Six-coupled wheels were all very well for fast freight, or for heavy passenger hauls over mountains, but——

At that time and for many years, there was intense competition for the New York-Chicago traffic by, respectively, the Water-Level Route of the New York Central and its ally the Lake Shore and Michigan Southern Railroad, and the rival route over the Alleghenies, which was a preserve of the Pennsylvania Railroad. The rival business interests, those of the Vanderbilts and the Depews, were more than just that; they were mortal enemies, but on the whole they confined their warfare to rates and rival services. (It was the rascally Jim Fisk of the Erie Railroad who got himself shot dead; and that was over a girl, though doubtless there were dry eyes in the Vanderbilt family on its being informed.)

But "Chicago in Twenty-four Hours" was the ideal of both parties in New York. By a chance of rostering, one of the Water Level Route's demonstration trains, on the Lake Shore and Michigan Southern Railroad, was headed by a little fast-freight 4-6-0 engine (No. 564) between Erie and Buffalo Creek, and covered the 86 mile stretch at a start-to-stop average speed of 72·91 miles an hour. To conventional American thought, it was as if someone had won the Kentucky Derby with a plough-horse. The "big wheel" idea died in that hour, as far as America was concerned. There were no more "Bicycles". Take a free-running engine, with good front-end arrangements, as in admission and exhaust, and a boiler making plenty of steam, and speed as well as power would look after itself! Already the Chicago, Milwaukee and St. Paul Railroad had produced a 4-6-2 type for heavy passenger service, though the extra axle had been by way of lessening axle loading and not, as in the Atlantic type, as a support for an extra-large firebox. It was not yet the Atlantic's successor, the Pacific Type locomotive. That would belong to the next century.

But the ten-wheeler—the 4-6-0 engine—which for so long had been the recognized American fast freight locomotive, came into its own for heavy passenger haulage while the 2-8-0 took more and more of the country's freight and mineral traffic. In the same decade these two arrived in Russia also, and more and more in Western Europe.

In the Alpine lands, Anatole Mallet's semi-articulated locomotives found their numerous "feet" at this time. It was in the next century that they were to take North America by noisy storm. The essential feature of the Mallet locomotive lay not only in its two sets of coupled wheels, but in the fact that only the first set was pivoted, forming a motor bogie. The after set was mounted in rigid frames; hence our term "semi-articulated", for the fully articulated engine was exemplified in double-bogie designs, as of Fairlie and Meyer.

Further, Mallet had been primarily interested in compound expansion, and his original conception had been that of a compound locomotive mounting its low-pressure cylinders on the leading bogie, thus having all axles powered while the engine as a whole was flexible to an extent impossible with the multi-coupled types of Central Europe and North America. There was less difficulty with flexible steam-pipes when these involved only low-pressure admission. Mallet's effective experiments took place in the late 'eighties, as the Englishman Fairlie's had done in the 'sixties. In 1890, under his patents, Maffei of Munich built for the Gotthard Railway in Switzerland what was then the largest locomotive in Europe and one of the largest specimens in the world, even allowing for North American prodigies. She was a tank engine, double 0-6-0, or, *auf deutsch* C-C. Her fault was that common one of the time; her boiler was not big enough. Had it been so, her axle-loading, with the track standards of the day, would have been too high.

At first, smaller examples of the Mallet type were much more successful, notably on the metre-gauge Landquart-Davos Railway in Eastern Switzerland and in a design that

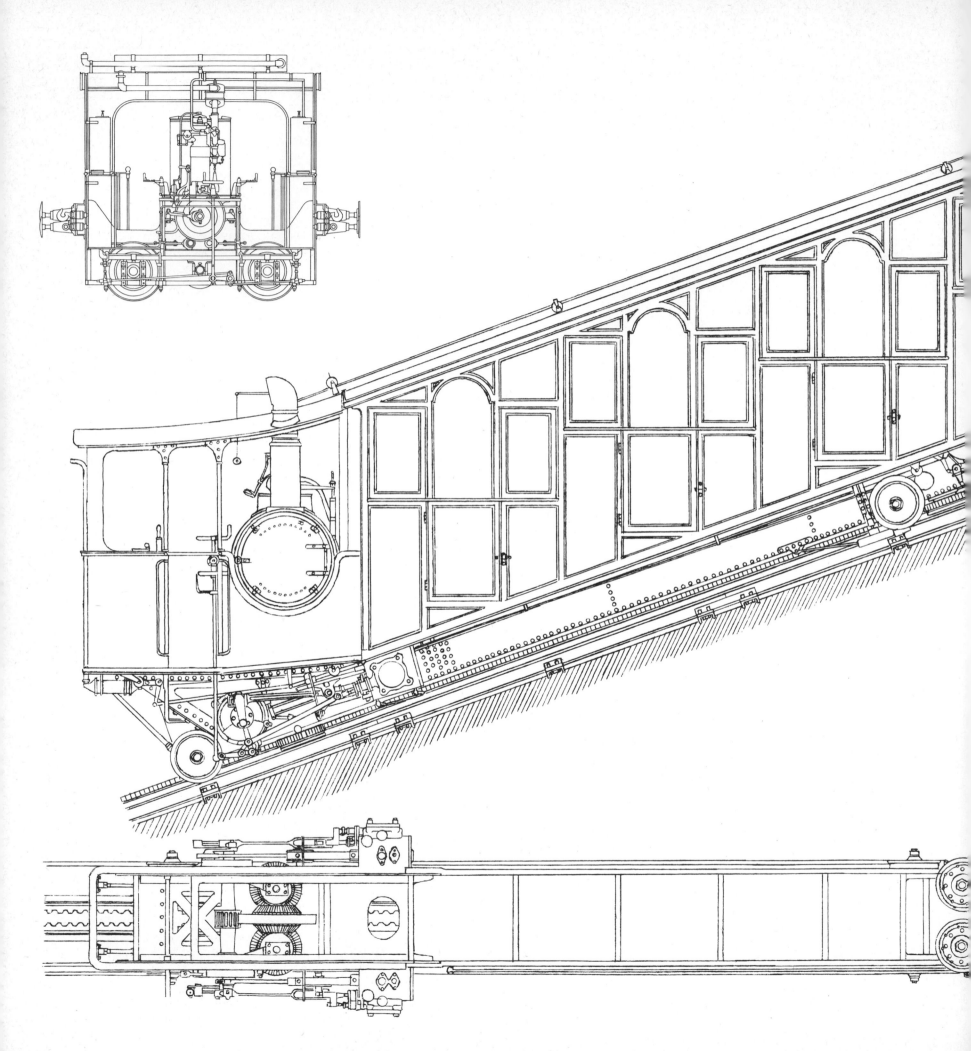

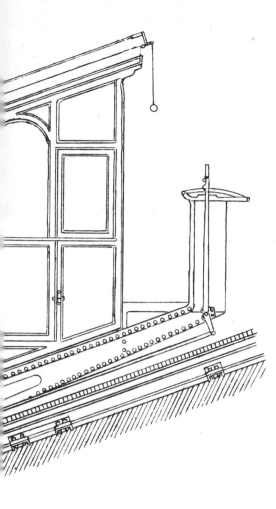

was practically identical on the Yverdon and Ste. Croix Railway in Western Switzerland and on the Provence Railway—the lovely, vanished *Ligne du Sud de la France*—both also metre-gauge. A very fine early Mallet tank engine on standard gauge, once belonging to the Swiss Central Railway, is preserved in the Verkehrshaus at Lucerne, in all her splendour of green and red.

By the end of the century, the steam railroad had conquered most of the world's great land masses, including some of the greatest mountain ranges. The locomotive was a part of people's lives as no machine had ever been before. It conveyed the emperors and the kings and nabobs; it hauled the emigrants from Ukraine and Silesia to the Channel Ports, and from Montreal or Jersey City to the Far West. It took wealthy tourists to classic lands and cheap trippers to the mountains or the seaside. It took artisans and clerks by the million in and out of the world's greater cities. As for freight, the steam train had become the overland ship. But already new challengers had appeared over the horizon.

We have noticed already the modest arrival of the electric train, at first as little more than a mechanical side-show. But when people had seen the first electric underground city railways, steam was doomed below the streets. Certainly, the steam underground lines of London—and, from the middle-eighties onwards, of Glasgow and Liverpool— were cordially detested. Their atmosphere at busy times beggared description, like something out of Dante or Milton.

It was Baltimore, in the United States, that saw the first transformation. There, between the Waverly and Camden stations, was a succession of excessively foul tunnels, and this was included in a three-mile stretch electrified by the great Westinghouse company in 1895. Haulage was by paired or articulated locomotives, each double unit on four fully-motored wheels to make what we would nowadays call a Bo + Bo machine, collecting current from an overhead *rail* (not a wire supported by catenaries, such as we know) by means of a collector shoe on a folding steel arm suggestive of a draughtsman's pantograph. These "motors" as they were at first called, took entire trains in and out of Baltimore, the steam train-engines being hauled together with their cars, with steam off and valve-gear neutral. This was the first movement of full-size trains by electric power on a standard-gauge railway. It was an undoubted "American first", to the particular credit of the Baltimore and Ohio Railroad which, years before, had taken the first train into Washington. One could see the shape of things to come through the mirk of other city railways, and also of the great mountain tunnels.

But there were other shapes of things to come, which common observers took even less seriously than they took electric traction. On the roads of both Europe and America, the motor car had emerged from the experiments of Karl Benz and Gottlieb Daimler. From 1896 onwards, even cautious England allowed it to proceed without having a red-flag man in front, while France and America received it with delight. Not yet did people imagine the motor car as a rival to the train itself. Its capacity was small; it was extraordinarily expensive; it was a sport of the rich.

Internal combustion locomotives are younger than motor cars on the road, which is odd, seeing that Karl Benz was initially a locomotive engineer. Not so odd, perhaps, considering that revolutionaries are often entirely so!

Briefly to recapitulate mechanical history: The first practical internal combustion engine was of course the gun, though it did not make anything *go* except some poor wretches' arms and legs. Huygens in the seventeenth century aimed—though no more— at the development of motive power from such a source (1673) but it was not until 1860 that Etienne Lenoir produced a workable gas engine with electric ignition. In the meantime, about 1820, something like a "modern" internal combustion engine had been schemed and even made in a laboratory form by W. Cecil, one of those remarkable English parsons of the period who applied themselves to physics while (usually) their curates read the Offices in Church. He used hydrogen mixed with air, which must have needed considerable faith in divine protection. In 1838, W. Barnett struck upon the idea of compressing the mixture before firing it, and their work was of first importance to Lenoir in the production of a commercial—and still stationary—gas engine. Improvements continued through Nikolaus Otto and Eugen Langen. Otto produced the four-stroke engine about 1876, and Sir Dugald Clerk, a Scotsman, made the first two-stroke engine in 1881. Petroleum spirit was the fuel used by the great motor-car pioneers Gottlieb Daimler (1834–1900) and Karl Benz (1844–1929). During the 'eighties, first Herbert Ackroyd-Stuart in England, and then Rudolf Diesel in Germany, devoted their energies

(inset) The little Daimler motor-locomotive built at the Esslingen Works, 1892.

The Swiss Pilatusbahn is the steepest railway ever worked by steam locomotive power. With a maximum gradient of 1 in 2, the Locher system of rack-and-pinion was employed, having a double horizontal rack between the running rails gripped on each side by the toothed driving wheels.

Instead of separate locomotives propelling cars, there were self-contained steam cars with the engines at the downhill ends. Boilers were horizontal and mounted transversely. This incredible railway opened on June 4, 1889 after some three years in construction. The steam cars worked until 1936 when the line was electrified. There remains no other railway quite like it in either hemisphere.

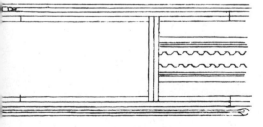

to the production of stationary engines which would consume crude oil with ignition by compression. Both produced satisfactory stationary engines, by the standards of the time, but it was long before compression-ignition oil engines were to furnish locomotion. One notes at once that Benz gave his name to refined petroleum for fuel and Diesel to the compression-ignition engine we now know so well.

The history of internal-combustion engines is a study in itself, like that of steam in the eighteenth century. Suffice it now, that in 1892, a very little industrial railway locomotive, powered by a Daimler engine, was built by the Esslingen Engine Works, Emil Kessler's old foundation which had built steam under Crampton's patents some forty years before. She is on p. 140—necessarily somewhat sectioned—with her double-buffer arrangement for moving both railway wagons and factory trams! Few could have guessed, either then or at the end of the century some eight years on, that by the nineteen-sixties internal combustion of one sort or another would be moving almost the entire overland transport of North America, and of many other parts of our long-suffering planet! As yet, straight steam had a long way to go!

At the Berlin exhibition in 1879, this little electric locomotive pulled the above "train". It was designed by Werner von Siemens and built by his firm, Siemens & Halske. The driver had to sit astride the locomotive. Few people saw the beginning of the end for the steam engine in this plaything.

In England, birthplace of the commercial steam railroad, people fixed its conventional beginning to the year 1825, whatever may have happened in 1804 or 1812. Opening of the Stockton and Darlington Railway was taken to be "Milepost Zero". In 1875 there had been quite a ceremony over the *Railway Jubilee*. Nobody bothered much about the seventy-fifth anniversary at the turn of the century. In 1925 there was a tremendous celebration of a Railway Centenary up at Darlington, with the Duke and Duchess of York (later, *malgré eux*, to be King and Queen) as Guests of Honour, the London and North Eastern Railway Company running the show, and enthusiastic support from Belgium, Italy and Ireland who sent ancient locomotives for exhibition, or, in the case of the Italians, presented a magnificent iron plaque honouring George Stephenson.

In the last quarter of this Railway Century the steam locomotive had really begun to encounter its mechanical challengers: On the rail, it was already fighting a rearguard action against electric traction, not only in city railways but in mountain countries where a great fall of water produced corresponding something-for-nothing (subject, of course, to immense capital costs and reasonable maintenance thereafter). In those years, too, the compression-ignition oil engine emerged, a difficult child at first, after equally difficult travail. Further, and not on the rail, but with a here-I-am flourish on the old roads, there had arrived the mass produced motor-car, beginning with Henry Ford's first T-Model. But in those years 1900–25, the steam railway-engine was yet a lusty old buffer, and was to stay so, in many places, for yet another half-century.

There were improvements and new inventions galore. There was the limited burning of oil instead of coal for steam raising, pioneered in Russia by that ingenious Scot Thomas Urquhart, and furthered, though to a limited degree, in Pacific-Coast America and East-Anglian England. The thing that really mattered during this time was the super-heating of steam in an otherwise entirely orthodox locomotive, and for that we must thank—for all the years over which it has benefited us—Wilhelm Schmidt. Allow some credit, also, to the old Royal Prussian State Railways—the K.P.E.V.—which believed in it, and built the apparatus, and showed it to be good!

The idea of drying live steam on its way from the boiler to the cylinders was ancient. The point had been the question of how to increase its temperature, and therefore its efficiency in those cylinders. Old English ideas embraced a drying chamber in the smoke-box, but that was not enough. In France, Jules Petiet had put it on top. Where was the real heat? In the firebox indeed, but that had business enough! Where next? In the flues!

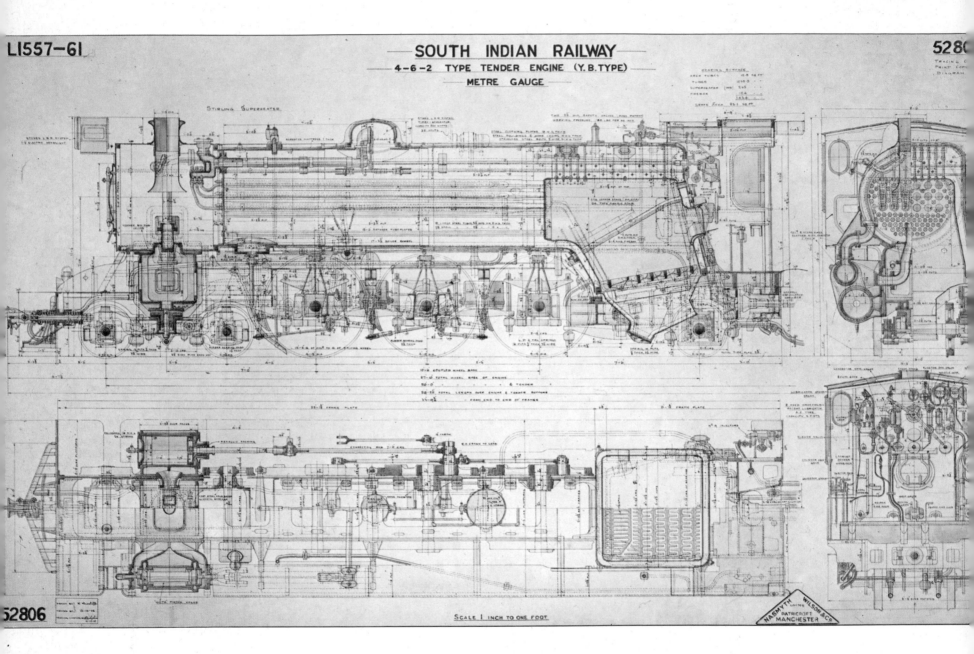

SOUTH INDIAN RAILWAY
4-6-2 TYPE TENDER ENGINE (Y.B.TYPE)
METRE GAUGE

LI557-61

SCALE I INCH TO ONE FOOT

144

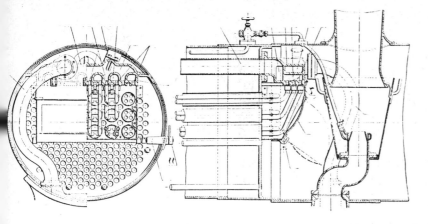

*Schmidt's superheater, 1898,
became extensively used on steam
locomotives throughout the world.*

Therefore, by Schmidt's physics, let the steam be taken through the flues! How, in the name of all that was impossible?

The answer, said Schmidt after some thought, was quite simple!

At least, so it seems in retrospect, though there was long experiment with all the toils of trial and error. The basic arrangement of the Schmidt superheater, and of the numerous other apparatus in the same family, which came later, was this. Instead of the live steam passing straight from the dome or other boiler steam space to the steamchest and thence through the valves into the cylinders, the steampipe was divided, its upper portion leading to a header whence a large number of small steam pipes or *elements* were led into, and again out from, a corresponding set of enlarged flues in the upper part of the boiler. Each element followed the line of a woman's hairpin. The live steam, passing through these, was thus subjected to the fierce heat of the firebox gases in the large flues before passing to a second header, usually combined with the first, whence main steampipes took it to the steamchests. At the first header, the steam was *saturated*. At the second it was *superheated*. The stuff was, in Richard E. Trevithick's happy phrase, *strong steam.*

In 1898, the first two locomotives to be in regular service with the Schmidt superheater appeared, as suggested, on the Prussian State system. The apparatus was applied to Prussian Class P 4[1], a 4-4-0 type with outside cylinders and Heusinger valve gear, that was a characteristic German express engine of the period. In 1900 it appeared for the first time on a tank locomotive, again a Prussian State 4-4-0 (Class T 5[2]), for the Berlin Metropolitan Railway. In this, an enlarged and much extended smokebox was used, and this came to be a usual complement to the Schmidt and kindred superheaters, which spread through Continental Europe, the British Isles and the Americas from about the middle of the succeeding decade.

For the next quarter-, indeed the next half-century, the orthodox steam reciprocating railway locomotive was to be distinguished apart from increasing size by the use of the superheater, steadily increasing pressure, generous firebox space, and the supersession of link motions by radial valve gears of the Walschaerts/Heusinger sort. As working pressures rose, and especially with the introduction of superheating, piston valves came to replace slide valves for steam distribution though even those were of some antiquity. They had appeared prematurely and disastrously in the England of the 'seventies. France in 1884 was more fortunate; on her old State Railway, Ricour produced successful piston valves with air-admission valves. By 1910, piston valves were *in*. For a locomotive of this phase we exemplify in a coloured chart a characteristic British-built locomotive for the South Indian Railway, additionally interesting in that it shows a relatively large locomotive on one of the narrower gauges (one metre).

Gauge variations we have mentioned before. Though the greatest of all rail-gauges—the generous 7 ft. of the Great Western Railway in England, had come to an end in 1892, variety continued. North America, Mexico, and Western Europe apart from Ireland, Spain and Portugal, had long settled on the classic Stephenson gauge of 4 ft. 8½ in., or 1·435 m. Doubtless out of strategic considerations, Imperial Russia adopted a gauge of 1·524 m. (five English feet) which persists in the Soviet Union from its western borders (including Finland) to the Far East. China, however, has the Europe-America gauge. The broadest gauge in general use has long been that of 1·676 m. (5 ft. 6 in.), which is that of India, Pakistan and Ceylon, Spain, Portugal, Argentina and Chile. All these lands apart from the Iberian Peninsula were long under British railroading influence. The 5 ft. 3 in. gauge (1·600 m.) is that of Ireland, Brazil and the southernmost parts of Continental Australia. The last-mentioned country, however, had (in other people's eyes and latterly in its own) about as cock-eyed a gauge policy as any country in the world; early-Victorian England, pre-Civil-War America, and Sweden included.

In last century, the several Australian States were full of jealous small-nationalism. Customs barriers were set up, and the several States had their own rail-gauges, usually chosen to be different from anything next-door. Thus Victoria and South Australia chose the Irish gauge for their main lines, New South Wales chose the European and American standard, while Queensland in the East, and Western Australia at the other end of the Continent, chose the 3 ft. 6 in. gauge (1·067 m.) which Tasmania also used, not to mention New Zealand and the great systems of South Africa, Japan and the then Dutch East Indian islands. But Australia has long rued her legacy of mixed gauges. In 1915, even, the Trans-Australian Railway was completed with largely New South Wales equipment, making two more breaks. Further, South Australia used the 3 ft. 6 in.

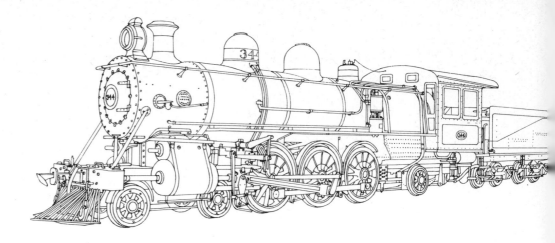

gauge for certain up-country lines, as well as the broad gauge on main and inter-city lines. As we write, there are still three gauges in Port Pirie station, South Australia, a situation we remember also in Växjö, Sweden, and on the Franco-Spanish transfer at Hendaye, whence, Gustavo Reder remarks, begins the largest metre-gauge network in Europe, even bigger than the Swiss, and serving Pullman type express services west of San Sebastian.

The 3 ft. 6 in. gauge (1·067 m.) was the third one at Växjö, as was the metre gauge at the end of France. It is a surprisingly adequate gauge for mountainous countries—Norway once ran expresses to Trondhjem on it—and today South African trains are otherwise the dimensional equals—or even superiors—of many in Europe, with great locomotives that have even impressed visiting Americans. Metre gauge has been much used for secondary lines in India, and in Malaysia and East Africa also. Many narrower gauges have been used about the world since the first public narrow-gauge railway was opened between Portmadoc and Blaenau-ffestiniog in North Wales, away back in 1836. Its gauge was one of two English feet, which latterly became the rather curious one of 1 ft. $11\frac{1}{2}$ in. The widely-used Swedish narrow gauge of 0·891 m. has stirred curiosity in other countries. Why such a gauge? Or so ask both Americans, and other Europeans, for by English measure it is 2 ft. $11\frac{25}{32}$ in! Quite simple, though! It comes to exactly three Swedish feet and that is a solution pleasing to any artist previously puzzled by figures.

In this first quarter of the twentieth century, the world's railway map became almost complete. Great estuaries had been bridged as man had not previously imagined, and train-ferry ships had spanned similar, and much greater gaps. Both these things began in Scotland on the Forth and Tay estuaries where still one may see some of the greatest bridges in the world. North America was long spanned, and several times over, by thin, steel-blue tracks. Russia and Japan both went for Manchuria, whose crossing Russia won at the cost of a subsequent, rather humiliating war. On January 1, 1903, by dint of the Trans-Siberian and the Chinese Eastern Railway (which also was Russian-owned, on the Russian gauge which was so minutely over-standard) it became possible to travel by train—or rather trains—from Calais on the Straits of Dover (la Manche to certain old and well-loved friends) to Vladivostok on the Sea of Japan in rather more than a fortnight. There was a train-ferry crossing on Lake Baikal, elimination of which was hastened by the immediately impending Russo-Japanese War. At the other end, the Channel Tunnel had been talked of since the eighteen-seventies, but as yet there were not even train-ferries, though an Englishman, that unhappy genius Sir Thomas Bouch who built the first, disastrous Tay Bridge in Scotland, had been their father. Later, too, came the very circuitous all-Russian route to Vladivostok by the Ussuri line through Khabarovsk.

Nearly complete was the railroad map of the world, but it was still almost entirely a steam realm, and that brings us back to the development of the ever-bigger steam locomotive engine.

Firstly; to the fast passenger locomotive! We have seen the arrival of the Atlantic type from America. We have seen that the 4-6-2 type had appeared in the United States quite accidentally, owing to a matter of axle-load restriction with the heavy ten-wheeler, plus the needs of experiments, in another case, under the Strong Patents. The true Pacific —the elongated Atlantic with three coupled axles—was also American in origin but not in application.

Baldwins built it in the States; but first for New Zealand, which Americans then regarded as a British colony, whatever New Zealanders might think. (It was then gene-

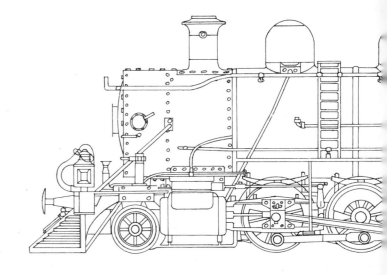

(left) New Zealand Railways Class Q, built by the Baldwin Locomotive Works, U.S.A., in 1901, is usually considered to be the first "Pacific" class in the world, although individual locomotives with the same wheel arrangement had been built earlier. This class became the most popular and versatile in the 20th century. Its wheel arrangement (4-6-2) gave good riding at speed and also room for the largest boiler and cylinders that could usefully drive six coupled wheels in general mainline work. This class survived until 1956.

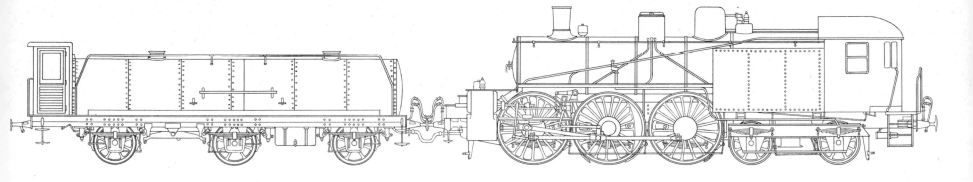

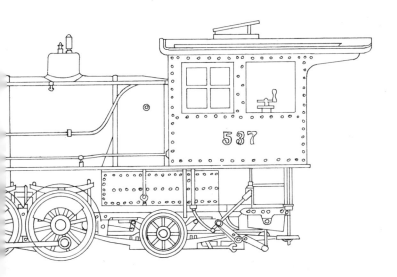

rally English down to the middle of South Island, and extremely Scottish at Dunedin and all points south.) The New Zealand Pacific type engines were in every way American; further, they anticipated on a small scale what was to be the conventional fast passenger locomotive in the States and in Canada for the next twenty-five years, with a big firebox overlapping the main frames and supported by a small pair of trailing wheels. The real object was to allow for a wide grate burning low-grade New Zealand coal.

Akin to the 4-6-2, but originally intended for fast freight haulage, was the equally American 2-8-2 engine, and here again it was first built for export before running in its native continent. Japan had the first examples, hence the American type-name Mikado. Over forty years later, the type was still being built in immense numbers for American military use, and then for post-war replacement service.

But at this time, at the beginning of the new century, there were other attempts to achieve a steam locomotive steady in running yet with plenty of space for a big firebox. None was less conventional, yet at the same time workable, than that of Giuseppe Zara, using Plancher's system of compound expansion, on the Italian Southern (Adriatic System) Railways, from 1900 onwards.

Our drawing is fairly explanatory. An old-fashioned Irishman would say that the front-end was at the back and, accepting that term, he would be entirely right. Having the boiler reversed allowed for ample firebox space over the bogie, and also placed the cab in front, with a free view of the road ahead. It was a most beneficial arrangement for long tunnel working. The engine was four-cylinder compound. Its only serious disadvantage was the need for side coal bunkers, with consequently uncomfortable firing. The long cylindrical tender was for water only. The type was sometimes called *Mucca* (not quite a compliment), and one of the first (No. 3701) was shown at the Paris Universal Exhibition of 1900, a wonderful show of contemporary locomotives, of which this was surely the most advanced by the standards of the time.

Many more of the "Mucca" type were built in the next few years. We saw them working some of the best expresses between Milan and Bologna in 1922, and over ten years later they were still serving those on the Milan-Verona-Venice run, a remarkable achievement for what was regarded as a rather eccentric design.

Later, in the United States, the Southern Pacific Railroad built enormous "back-to-front" locomotives, on the Mallet semi-articulated plan, for heavy pulling on the slopes of the Sierra, and in these the use of oil as fuel ruled out the old disadvantage of side bunkers.

Placing the cab in front was, of course, one of the great advantages of the electric locomotive which was now on its cautious way in, as of the oil-electric locomotive in later years, but there were several more attempts to do it with orthodox steam locomotives. In France there was that of Thuile, whose engine was also exhibited in Paris in 1900, of which the less remembered the better. She turned over on her trials and killed her unfortunate designer, so that was that. She was remarkable in having 7 ft. 4½ in. coupled wheels. Henschel and Son of Kassel, makers of so many memorable German locomotives down the years, built two remarkable cab-in-front locomotives in 1904. One, a 4-4-4 (2-B-2) express engine the Prussian State classified S 9 (p. 175), had coachlike casings with side windows over both engine and tender, with a pointed front, making her look like an engine with an electric "top" (apart from the protruding chimney) and a steam "bottom"; cylinders, valve-gear and all. Firing her was an abominably hot business. The other was a 4-6-4 tank engine with a cab at each end (Prussian Class T 16) with a double set of controls but, of course, with the fireman at the firebox-and-bunker end.

(above) The "cab-forward" 670 class 4-6-0 was designed for the Southern Adriatic Railway in Italy by Guiseppe Zara in 1900. The point of the design was to lessen the smoke nuisance to enginemen in tunnels. The last of this class was in service until 1942. The tender contained only water and a brakeman's shelter.

(below) 2-8-2 Mikado-type locomotive which was bought from the Baldwin Locomotive Works in the U.S.A. by Nippon Railways, the pioneer and largest private railway in Japan, in 1897. This was the first-ever engine with a 2-8-2 wheel arrangement and it soon became popular throughout the world as a freight locomotive.

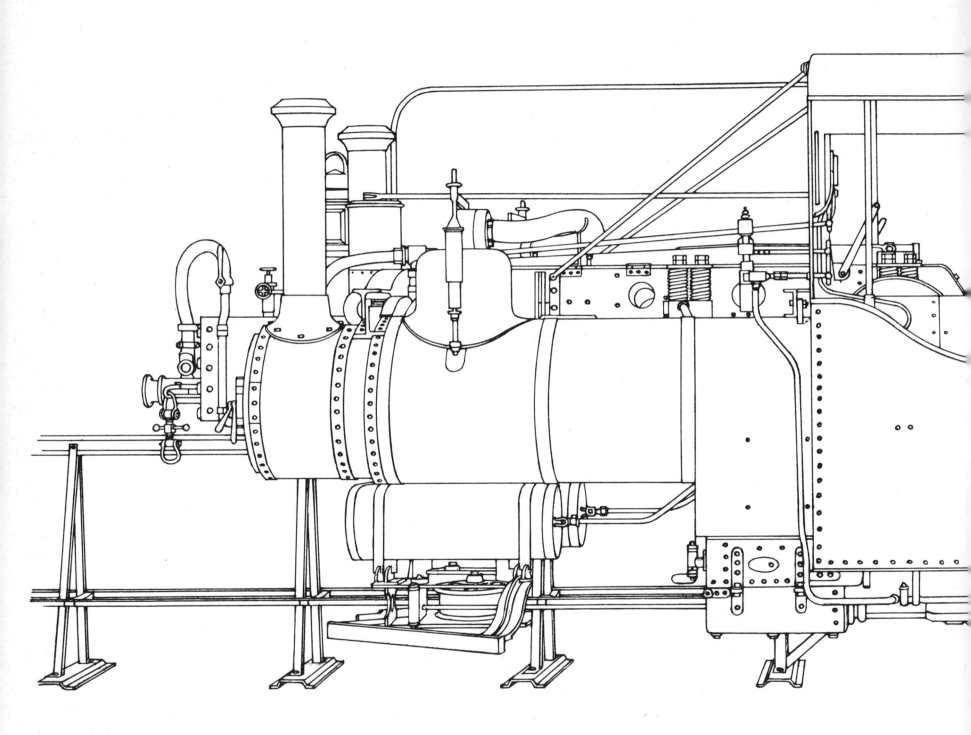

Lartigue's Monorail ran on an iron or steel trestle of triangular section with the running and traction rail on top and guide rails on each side. It was used from 1888 to 1924 for a light railway in the south west of Ireland. It was the longest running of any of the steam monorails and was an object of great wonder.

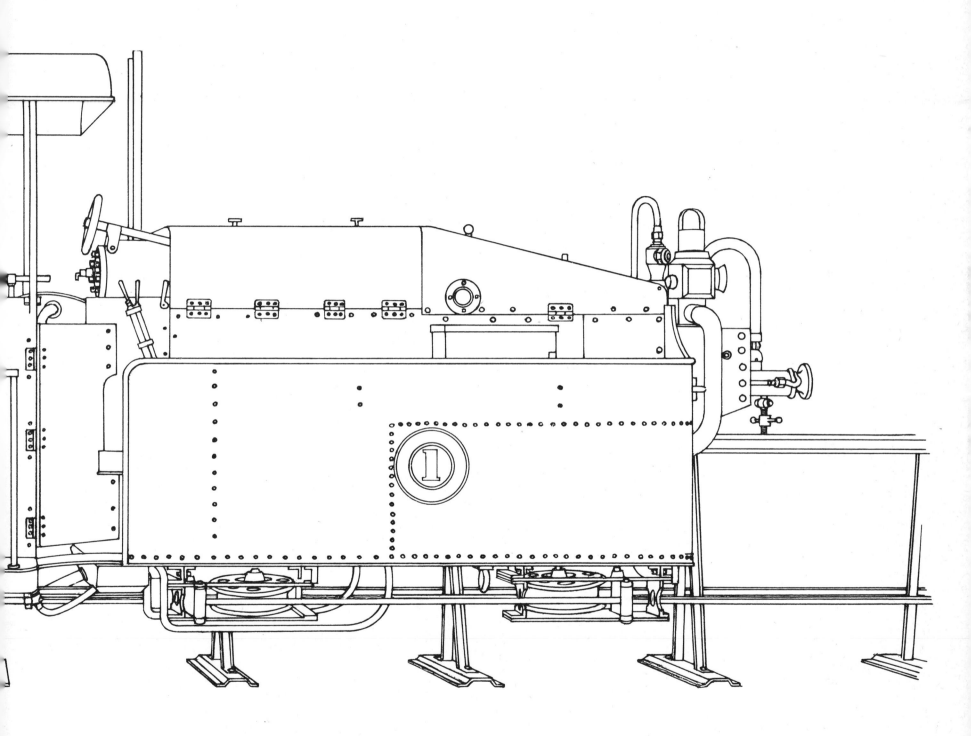

The Prussian 4-4-4 by Wittfeld is sometimes instanced as the oldest example of a stream-lined steam locomotive, though in France Baudry, with his *coup-vent* engines, was aiming at that, and the idea was older still, going back at least to a completely streamlined experimental train on the French State Railways, by Ricour in 1887, using Etat loco-motive No. 2072.

Let us now turn awhile from steam to that energetic infant the electric locomotive. We left it with steeple-cab double-unit machines under Baltimore, and self-propelling gin bottles deep down in the London clay. The turn of the century saw the emergence of the electric main-line locomotive.

As noted, it had begun in the States in 1895 and soon after the original twin units came Baltimore and Ohio electric locomotives in one piece with eight wheels coupled by side rods, steam fashion. In 1899 appeared the first main-line electric locomotives in Europe, on the Burgdorf-Thun Railway in Switzerland. There was a pair of them, equipped electrically by the Brown-Boveri company of Baden and constructed, as to their mechanical parts, by the Swiss Locomotive Works of Winterthur. They were four-wheelers, with drive from two 150 h.p. low-speed motors through gears, jackshaft and side rods, fed at 750 Volt from twin overhead contact wires (not grooved overhead rails as on the Baltimore and Ohio line). Both were in service until their quiet little railway, so useful to bygone tourists, was converted to 15,000 Volt single phase alternating current in 1933. Even the earliest electric locomotives had, like their steam precursors, long life-expectation.

THE TWENTIETH CENTURY

So we cross the century-line; for in 1902 the Oerlikon company and the Winterthur works jointly produced the first single-phase alternating-current electric locomotive in the world. It was at the Oerlikon company's own risk, and the testing ground was the little Seebach-Wettingen line in Switzerland, about 20 km., or less than 13 miles in length.

All electric trains so far had run on low-voltage direct current. But on the Seebach-Wettingen line, the voltage was 15,000 at overhead contact. The locomotive carried a rotary converter, and was powered by two 200 h.p. 700 Volt motors, one on each of its two motor bogies. The axles of each bogie were coupled with side rods to jackshafts driven by the traction motors. The machine was at once the first electric locomotive carrying its own transformer equipment and the first to be fed by high tension single-phase current. It was the archetype of the locomotive so many electric railways have known since then.

Already, in 1901, the General Electric Company (A.E.G.) in Berlin had made the Winter-Eichberg single-phase motor and had tried it out with a car on a line between Niederschönweide and Spindlersfeld. During the winter of 1903–4 the Oerlikon company was experimenting with single-phase traction motor in a locomotive, again on the See-bach-Wettingen line. Initial difficulties were overcome by using a frequency of 15—later $16\frac{2}{3}$—cycles with the line tension of 15,000 Volts. What one might term the Alpine System of electric railway traction was born.

But several other systems were to appear, and to be used from those days to this. Cautious England was to make great use of direct current at low voltages—600–660—with third rail contact, beginning with the new and the converted underground lines of London and Liverpool. Today it still serves the immense passenger traffic of the southern triangle, rooted in London and covering almost exactly 1,000 miles of route, or first track. The beginning of that was almost comic, in the anxiety of the London and North Western and the London and South Western companies in 1914–15 to have their suburban trains share lines with London underground services, dating from 1905. That is the expla-nation, not often given in print! Today, visiting Frenchmen make great merry on finding their overnight Wagons-Lits from Paris rolling behind a third-rail locomotive between Dover and London. For France knows a thing or two about early suburban electrifica-tion! Her Western lines from Paris to Versailles were equipped with 650 Volt d.c. in 1902, and the old Orleans terminal scheme, Paris Orsay-Austerlitz, dated from 1900.

City legislation in New York forced the hands of American railroad companies. The century was still new when these had an ultimatum on the use of smoking locomotives within Manhattan. The New York Central, Pennsylvania and New Haven companies had to electrify or get out, even though heavy electric traction was at best still adolescent. Conversion was carried out initially during 1906–7, with 650 Volt direct current, heavy

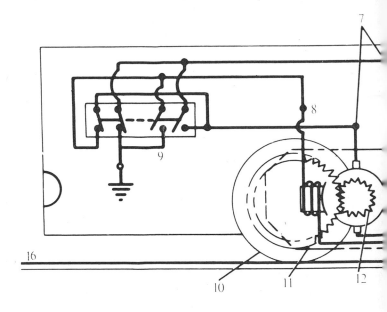

The Seebach—Wettingen locomotive for single phase current of one of 15,000 volt, 15 cycles (originally 50) was built in 1904 for the Oerlikon company.

Simplified schematic drawing showing arrangement of power and control circuits of typical electric locomotive. (Courtesy of General Electric Co.).

1 Control switch	4 Trolley wire
2 Fuse	5 Resistor
3 Trolley pole	6 Contactor
	7 Armatures
	8 Field
	9 Reverser
	10 Wheel
	11 Gear
	12 Pinion
	13 Motor
	14 Rail
	15 Controller
	16 Rail
	17 Headlight

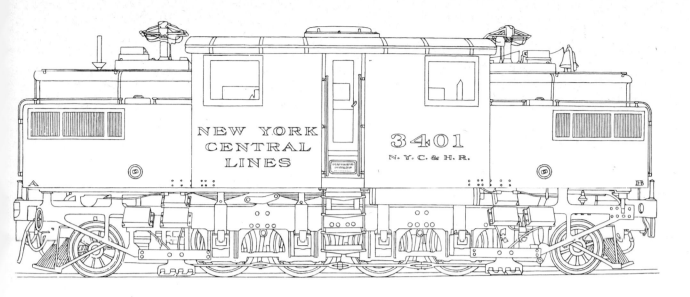

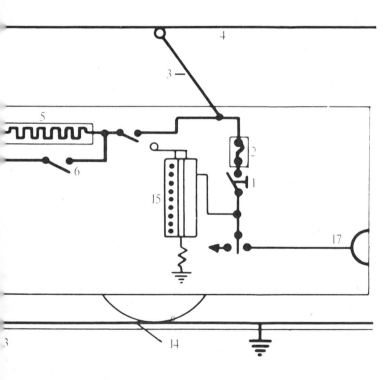

The electric locomotive built for the New York surburban service on the New York Central and Hudson River Railroad.

locomotives handling cars from outside the area. For city and suburban traffic, here and elsewhere about the world, thanks to that nearly forgotten American Sprague, multiple-unit trains were used with motor cars, or alternate motor and trailer cars, control circuits making all motor cars subject to the motorman in the leading car.

The Hungarian firm of Ganz about this time was pushing a three-phase system, with its complication of twin overhead conductors. At its own expense it equipped the Colico-Chiavenna branch of the Italian Adriatic System in 1901. That line, and its connecting Lecco-Colico-Sondrio line went over to 3,400 Volt, 15·8 cycles per second three-phase in October, 1902. This is claimed to have been the world's first high-voltage electrification. The same thing nearly happened on the older London underground lines when these were to be converted (1905) as the primeval Metropolitan company favoured it. One fancies that it would have been a nuisance under a great city.

Italy long favoured the three-phase system, on 3,700 Volts, $16\frac{2}{3}$ cycles, thus equipping the steeply-graded Giovi line in 1911 and the Brenner line as late as 1929–34. Long ere that, the Swiss Federal Railways adopted it through the new Simplon Tunnel in 1906, between Iselle and Brigue, later extending it to Sion. (In 1930 it went over to single-phase at 15,000 Volts, $16\frac{2}{3}$ cycles, thus conforming with what had by then become a vast electrified network in Alpine Europe.) The same system was adopted by Sweden, beginning with the Lapland Ore Line and its Norwegian extension to Narvik in 1915. It was in the latter year, too, that America saw her first heavy main-line electrification; that of the Chicago, Milwaukee, St. Paul and Pacific company's Mountain Division, using 3,000 Volt direct current. In all such, overhead contact was invariable.

Electric traction was still very limited, outside the great cities (which of course used it for innumerable tramways or street-car lines in both hemispheres). In a supposed railroad map of the world, the electric lines, even in 1915, would have suggested a few twigs mixed into a vast expanse of hay. In the United States they were considerably represented by the once powerful inter-urban lines, which achieved almost heroic status in the Middle West, with luxurious cars for those ready to hire them and—in our recollection—at least one slow but steady inter-urban sleeper. To the European, these were still *trams*, although (also in our recollection) there was at least one diner service, or at any rate a buffet car, in the Lower Rhine area of Germany.

At present, though, the steam locomotive was undisputed Empress of the World's Railroads as some American *siderodromophile*—or perhaps business-booster—might have put it. (That word, which we believe we invented, is quite good Greek, though not Classical Attic!) The less ornate American word of our day is *railfan*. Germans in particular regarded the electric locomotive, which their fatherland had sired, as a subject for laboratory treatment. Trials were held on a military railway—Marienfelde-Zossen—with an experimental locomotive and two equally experimental motor cars in 1901 and 1903. Three-phase traction was used. In 1901 the top speed attained, with the Siemens and Halske locomotive, was 101 miles an hour. In 1903 both cars attained 130 miles an hour, which remained a rail-speed record until 1931. Observers noted the noisy impact of pebbles against the car floor. We have known people incredulous about this, but we had an isolated experience of it, lasting a few seconds only, with steam traction on the

London and North Eastern Railway in 1935. The speed at that time was just over 112 miles an hour. The phenomenon depends on air currents and the state of the roadbed.

On the Great Western Railway in England, with a special mail train from Plymouth to London, Charles Rous-Marten recorded a maximum speed of 102 miles an hour (plus a fraction) while running downhill east of Exeter, on May 9, 1904. More importantly, on that run the initial engine, *City of Truro*, ran the fifty-two miles from Plymouth (North Road, pass) to Exeter (St. Davids, pass), over a quasi-mountainous route, in a fraction under fifty-six minutes, and averaged just over seventy miles an hour, pass to stop, from passing Exeter to stopping outside Bristol. Thence to London (Paddington) with the train lightened to a mere 120 tons of mail cars, the engine *Duke of Connaught* took just over ninety-nine minutes for the stretch of 118·5 miles. This was a run in regular public service, not a trial for show, as in the case of New York Central No. 999 a decade before. Learned attempts have been made to disprove both claims, but without convincing success. It should be added that at the time, in England, the Great Western company was in fierce competition with the London and South Western for the Plymouth traffic, and very energetic running was made by both companies then and for several years after. They culminated with an accident, as had the old races between London and the Scottish cities. The South Western company spilt its train all over the Salisbury curve in 1906, with heavy loss of life, and that was followed by a *working agreement* between the interested companies. Actual racing by rival railway companies between the same cities was a prank peculiar, to our knowledge, to the British and the Americans. What is remarkable is that the locomotives employed by the Great Western were of relatively archaic type. Both had inside cylinders and double frames, stemming from the Stephensons and their contemporaries long ago. Neither was particularly large, though *City of Truro* had a generous boiler with a Belpaire firebox. *Duke of Connaught* had very large single driving wheels; she was *almost* a giant Patentee with a leading four-wheel truck for steadiness. Both were of fine, ornate, Victorianly-brassy aspect, quite different from rugged Pacifics and suchlike!

Still as industry and liberal capitalism expanded, the mass movement of freight, fuel, ore and passengers spread with it. Vehicles grew heavier and trains larger. In the States, the mighty Pennsylvania Railroad released a photograph, doubtless with pride, of three 2-8-0 locomotives toiling hard with sixty coal cars. In passenger service, ordinary cars grew more elaborate, apart from the expensively luxurious vehicles of such companies as Pullman and Wagons-Lits. Travel in an American chair-car from Chicago to St. Louis, or in a good English third-class carriage from London to Plymouth via Bristol, fairly comparable in distance and time, could be not just tolerable but agreeable, on plush and quite elegant surroundings, and while both Englishmen and Americans were supercilious about the hard third-class of Continental Europe, Germany and Scandinavia in particular furnished a very superior second-class at quite cheap rates. Second-class was extinct in Scotland and moribund in England. In Democrat-Republican America, "class" was as dirty a word, still, as it was to be in Russia after 1917. Realist Germany under the last of the Emperors made tremendous use of fourth-class which, in our own experience, was all right for journeys of necessity or for spending a jolly Sunday among mountains. But all these things made for heavy trains, with bigger and yet bigger engines.

Queen of steam locomotives for fast passenger trains, in North America and Western Europe during this quarter century, was the Pacific—the real Pacific, 4-6-2 with long frames and ample firebox—whose prototype we saw built by America for New Zealand at the beginning of the century. Her kind was a classic. In the early nineteen-hundreds, canny American companies, which nevertheless worked their equipment to death and then bought new, took it up. Let us take our first instance from the Pennsylvania Railroad, though one seems to remember that the Chicago and Alton showed the way.

On June 11, 1905 The Pennsylvania company revived its famous Pennsylvania Special train, competing with the Vanderbilts' New York Central Lines, and scheduled it to link New York and Chicago, both ways, in eighteen hours. That meant an average speed, including stops, of 50·2 miles an hour, which by the standards of the day was extremely creditable. It entailed an average speed of 57·8 miles an hour over the first 189 miles from the old Jersey City Terminal to Harrisburg, with one intermediate stop, which was still more creditable. The engines at that stage headed the train as a couple of stately Atlantics, or even as one over the initial level section, e.g. Class E3d with piston valves.

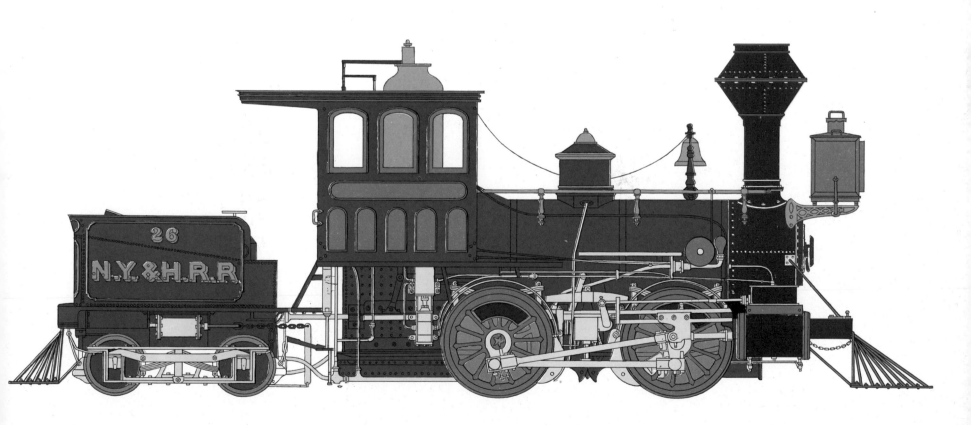

THIS FORNEY TANK ENGINE WAS BUILT BY THE SCHENECTADY LOCOMOTIVE WORKS IN 1876 FOR SUBURBAN TRAFFIC ON THE NEW YORK AND HARLEM RAILROAD.

French Fairlie

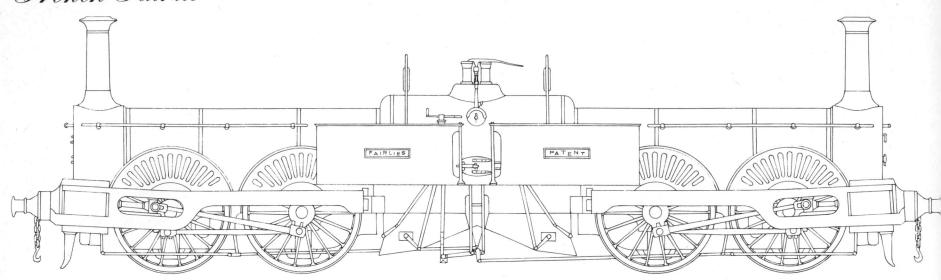

THIS ARTICULATED LOCOMOTIVE WAS INTENDED BY FAIRLIE TO BE A FAST PASSENGER ENGINE BUT THERE IS NO EVIDENCE THAT IT WAS EVER BUILT.

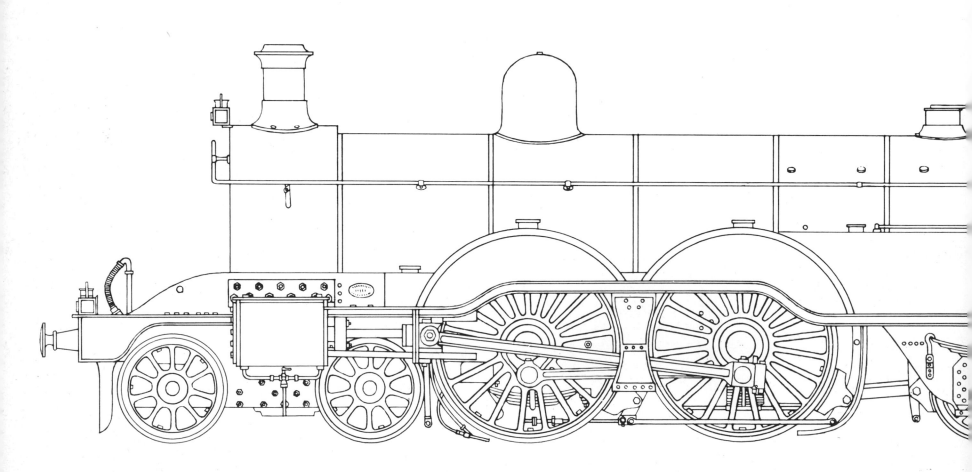

THIS 4-4-2 EXPRESS PASSENGER ENGINE WAS DESIGNED BY HARRY IVATT AND BUILT BY THE GREAT NORTHERN RAILWAY OF ENGLAND.

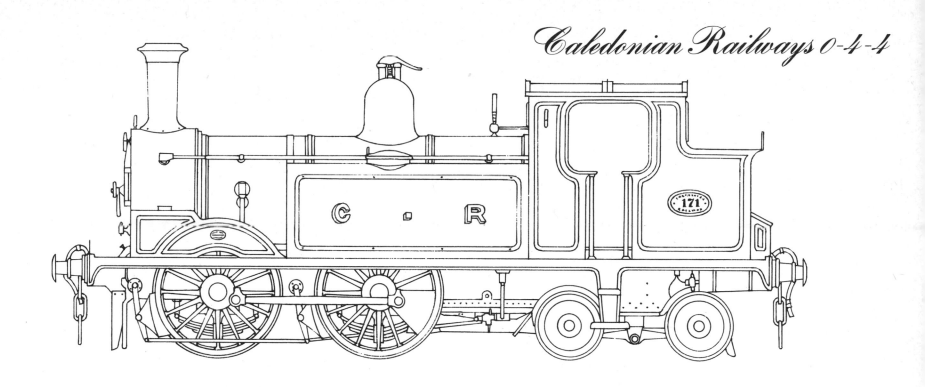

THIS LITTLE TANK ENGINE WAS DESIGNED BY DUGALD DRUMMOND IN THE 1880S AND USED FOR BRANCH PASSENGER SERVICE.

G N R no. 990

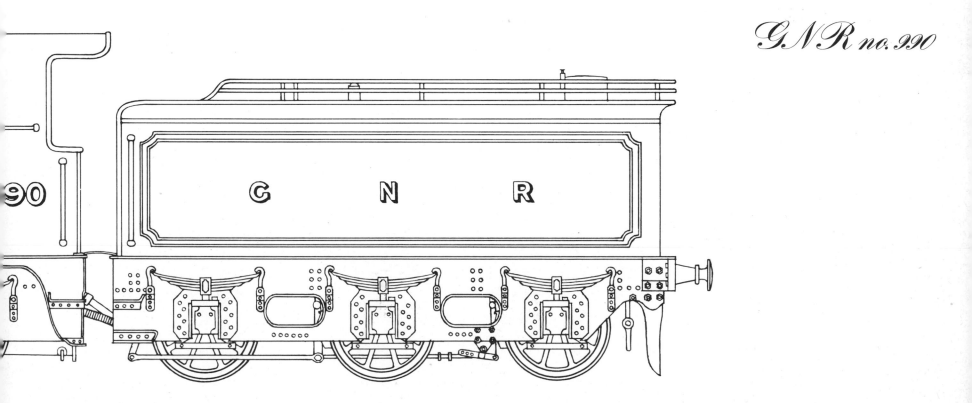

Champion

THE LEHIGH VALLEY RAILROAD BUILT THIS EIGHT-COUPLED BOGIE LOCOMOTIVE IN 1882 FOR HAULING COAL. IT WAS DESIGNED BY PHILIP HOFECKER. MASTER MECHANIC ON THE RAILROAD.

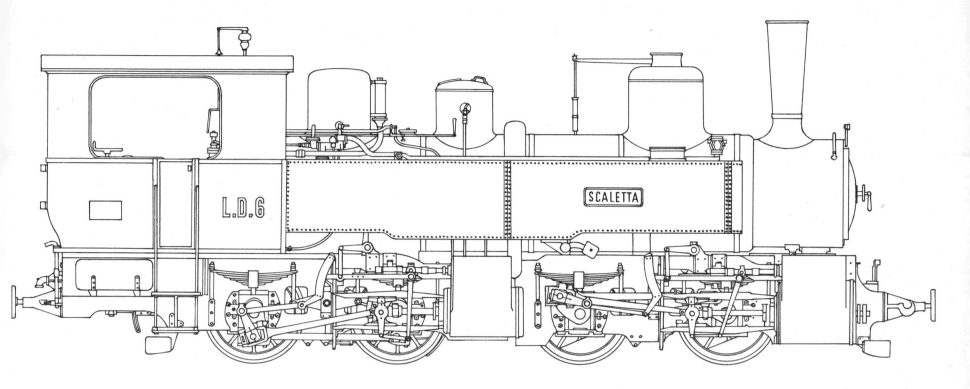

ONE OF THE EARLIEST MALLET COMPOUND SEMI-ARTICULATED LOCOMOTIVES, BUILT BY MAFFEI OF MUNICH FOR THE LANDQUART-DAVOS RAILWAY, SWITZERLAND.

Gladstone

THE FAMOUS GLADSTONE, BUILT IN 1882 FOR THE LONDON, BRIGHTON AND SOUTH COAST RAILWAY. IT WAS DESIGNED BY WILLIAM STROUDLEY.

Belpaire 2-4-2

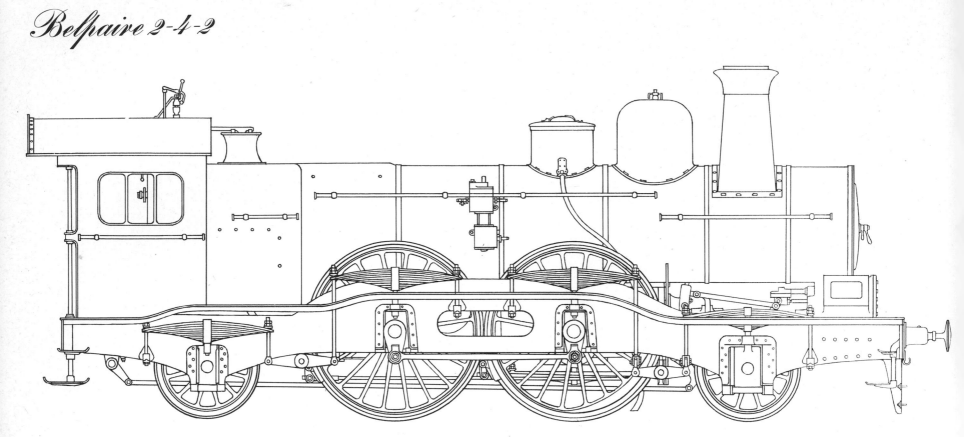

THE BELGIAN STATE RAILWAYS ORDERED THIS EXPRESS ENGINE FROM THE SOCIETÉ COCKERILL WHO BUILT IT AT THE SERAING WORKS AND EXHIBITED IT AT THE PARIS EXHIBITION.

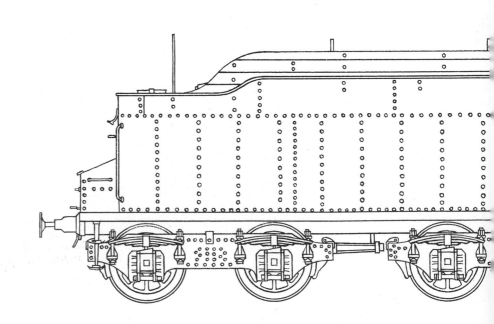

Alfred Belpaire, 1820–1893. Born at Ostend and took charge of the Belgian State Railways' Works at Malines at the age of 20 years. He rose to the highest position in the Belgian Railways Administration which he held until his death at the age of 73. He was President of the second Railway International Congress Commission. In 1860, he invented the firebox which bears his name. From 1835 to 1853 the Belgian Railways had used only coke and briquettes with very large lumps of coal. Naturally the cost of this was very high and it was in order to use the low-grade, small Belgian coal that Belpaire built his firebox. His name is also associated with the invention of a combination reversing gear with lever and screw combined and with a large number of different locomotive types which were used mainly for the Belgian State Railways.

Russian Freight Locomotive

THE 0-10-0 FREIGHT LOCOMOTIVE WAS MUCH FAVOURED IN RUSSIA. THIS EXAMPLE WAS ONE OF 66 DELIVERED BY NYDQVIST AND HOLM OF SWEDEN.

Webb's Compound Locomotive

BUILT AT THE CREWE WORKS OF THE LONDON AND NORTH WESTERN RAILWAY IN 1893, THIS THREE-CYLINDER COMPOUND COAL ENGINE WAS DESIGNED BY FRANCIS WEBB.

THE PACIFIC

In 1905 the Pennsylvania company invested in its first Pacific, an experimental engine classified K 1, from the American Locomotive Company (the "Alco" of later years). In 1910 Class K 2 was designed and built, in increasing numbers, from 1911 onwards. This had the big, broad Belpaire firebox. Modified for superheater, in 1913, the design developed into Class K 3. By that time the Pacific had generally arrived in North America.

In Europe it arrived during the two years 1907–8. France built it, initially in the very successful and handsome Paris-Orleans No. 4501, a de Glehn-du Bousquet compound by the Societé Alsacienne of Belfort. Then, under that great man Anton Hammel, the German firm of J. A. Maffei built it for the Badenese State Railways. In 1908 another giant of locomotive design, George Jackson Churchward, built a solitary example for the Great Western Railway, whereon it was something of a white elephant, being barred west of Bristol owing to insufficient clearances. (The boiler, too, was too long between tube-plates.) Churchward, indeed, had already produced a highly efficient type of four-cylinder simple 4-6-0 engine which, with successive enlargements, were to suffice his company to the end of its days in 1957. (Pacifics were not to become familiar in Great Britain until the nineteen-twenties.)

To Hammel of Maffei's works in Munich belongs the credit for producing the perhaps finest of these early European Pacific-type locomotives, and certainly one of the most beautiful. This, originally Bavarian State Railways class S 3/6, was an enlarged, superheated, big-fireboxed version of Hammel's S 3/5 Atlantic and, even more nearly, of an experimental 4-4-4 engine produced in 1906 for high-speed demonstration, and now in Nuremberg Transport Museum. The S 3/6 was four-cylinder compound, produced first in 1908 and last in 1931, with but little variation down the years, an historical circumstance with little parallel in the history of steam locomotive design. That design in itself was a remarkable marriage of European and American tradition, certainly influenced by Bavarian purchase of a pair of Baldwin Atlantic-type engines at the turn of the century.

It was not a big engine by American, or later European standards, as Pacifics went, but down many years it could handle with no apparent effort anything from a heavy international express to a Sunday excursion train between Munich and the mountains. Visually it was most beautiful, a study in visible as well as of mechanical balance. The last examples were in service until 1965. Two have been preserved; one in the German Museum, Munich, and another in Switzerland. To many Germans they were *die schönste Lokomotiven der Welt*.

Yet for all this impact of so splendid a locomotive type, Europe was shy. France, to be sure, received it with joy; all her great regional companies took it up. North Germany would have none of it until the middle nineteen-twenties. Sweden alone in Scandinavia produced it (Swedish State Class F) in 1914. Like the Bavarians, these were four-cylinder compound engines with the low-pressure cylinders outside (and in this case sharply inclined). The Swedish engines, later displaced through electrification, went to Denmark, as a result of which the class was to last over half a century. The French Pacifics, both simple and compound, did some of the finest fast passenger work in the world over many years. Largest and most powerful of the older European Pacifics were those of J. B. Flamme on the Belgian State Railways. Some of these also survived for upwards of fifty years, though others had been lost by war when still quite new.

Italy cautiously took up the Pacific, and Russia and Hungary even more cautiously. These countries were to use very extensively the 2-6-2 type of express engine, which the Middle-Western United States were already calling the Prairie type, and at moderately high speeds it served them well over many years of steam traction. Austria and Hungary, both made use of it. Hungary built 950 from 1909 onwards, plus twenty for Slovakia in 1942, all of one class (324) and 105 of other classes. One should record here that it was the success of the Italian and Austrian engines that led to the production of the very successful—and in our opinion very handsome—Russian Class Su, which continued to be built long after the Revolution.

Russia at that time—before 1914—made much use of the Mogul engine, the 2-6-0, and so did many other European states, though it was beginning to be regarded as effete and old-fashioned in North America where freight trains in particular were growing heavy beyond the worst nightmares of old-time locomotive men.

Prussia, Bavaria, Italy, all the Scandinavian countries, and to an increasing extent England were finding it an extremely useful locomotive for both the lighter freight and the slower passenger trains, and Italy in particular had produced in her State Railways' once-famous 640 class what was for a while a highly satisfactory express passenger locomotive, to be seen even in the nineteen-sixties on the level lines in the North, still under steam traction in a much-electrified land. Italy's first superheater type, it was an admirable locomotive for moderate traffic, whereon it lasted on more lightly laid lines in both the Americas (usually either English- or Scotch-built in the South American republics, most of whose railroad systems were British-owned throughout the Steam Age). For a curiosity: England's only two Moguls, over more than a decade, were two of a very English design which South America, Australia, Spain, and several other parts of the world knew well enough. They went to a rather remote English company—the Midland and South Western Junction—which had lately fallen on evil days but had recovered under brilliant management, and the first of them came to it owing to some other insolvency in South America. Countries with railways under company management sometimes saw this sort of thing; State railways rarely went bargain-hunting though now and then they sold their obsolete equipment to smaller and less opulent outfits. Even the British Government, long years after, managed to *flog* some ageing, surplus War Department locomotives to the Shanghai-Hangchow-Ningpo Railway, and the same sort of thing was to happen, from both the British and the American Governments, when the fighting stopped in 1945, still longer years after!

In Austria, at this time as at others, there was unorthodoxy, not of an idle sort. That great man Karl Gölsdorf was no longer as young as once but he was far from being *vieux jeu* in his work and perhaps only he would have produced what we call, in all humility, the *reversed Pacific*. It perpetuated the Italian Zara's "Mucca" idea of putting the great firebox over the bogie. But his engine was nevertheless front-end-forward, for she was 2-6-4; still a four-cylinder compound.

She had the big cone-barrelled boiler which Churchward was using with great success on the Great Western Railway in England, and at which other British locomotive men were looking with much distrust, for it put them in mind of the modified American wagon-top type. (Gölsdorf of Austria and Churchward of England certainly visited each other, and exchanged notes!) The new Gölsdorf express engine of 1910 was 2-6-4, but under her front-end she had not that mechanical abomination, the Bissell radial truck. She had the Krauss-Helmholtz bogie, incorporating the leading coupled wheels, with suitable flexibility in the forward coupling rods, which made her, as far as curvature went, the equivalent of a 4-4-4 engine. In Italy, G. Zara designed a very similar arrangement. Great Britain to our knowledge, and North America to our belief, would never touch these admirable trucks, which was one of the curiosities of mechanical history.

The Austrian 2-6-4 express engine was one of the classics of its day. Prussia made a close copy, though not extensively, and examples of this went to Poland, just as the native Austrian article found its way elsewhere when the Empire broke up in 1918. For mountain service, Austria produced a 2-12-0 design, dimensionally akin to the 2-6-4, but on traffic of this sort a 2-10-0 was found adequate, as in many other European countries. These later Austrian engines had an inimitable elegance of their own, unlike anybody else's. Uniquity of this kind could be claimed for several styles of this period—those of the Great Western in England, of the Pennsylvania in North America, of Maffei in Munich and of the Northern Railway of France—but not for many.

Before we turn to freight haulage, we should consider passenger conveyance. In one of its least exciting yet most important forms, this involved the transport of immense numbers of people daily in and out of the world's largest cities. Some of these, such as London, Berlin, Hamburg, Paris, and rather surprisingly Chicago, saw great use of the side-door coach, either with compartments or, as in the American cities, variations on the compartment plan with long cross benches. Chicago, be it added, had found their advantage in traffic to and from the World Fair of 1893, and for some years the Illinois Central Company standardized side-door cars for what America had come to call *commuter traffic*.

As that term has come into general use in the English speaking countries to denote twice-daily movement of office workers in city areas, whatever the form of transport, let it be at once explained. A commuter was simply a person who, by virtue of making regular journeys by public transport, had his fare *commuted* to a much reduced sum payable by periodic contract; weekly, monthly, quarterly or even annually. In the

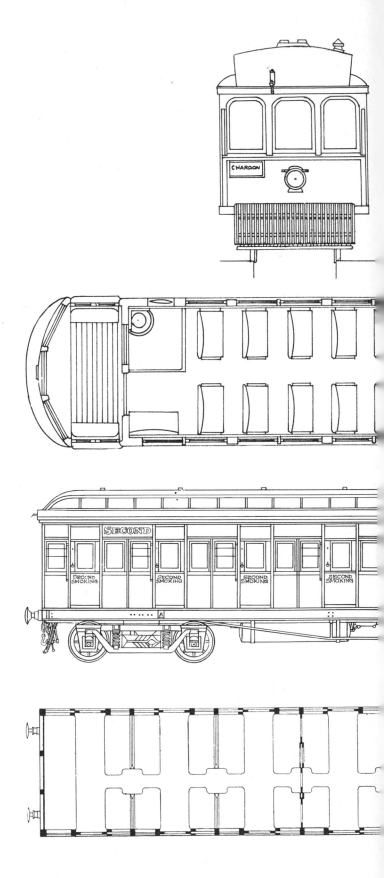

This surburban car was built by the St Louis Car company about 1900 for the Cleveland and Eastern railway.

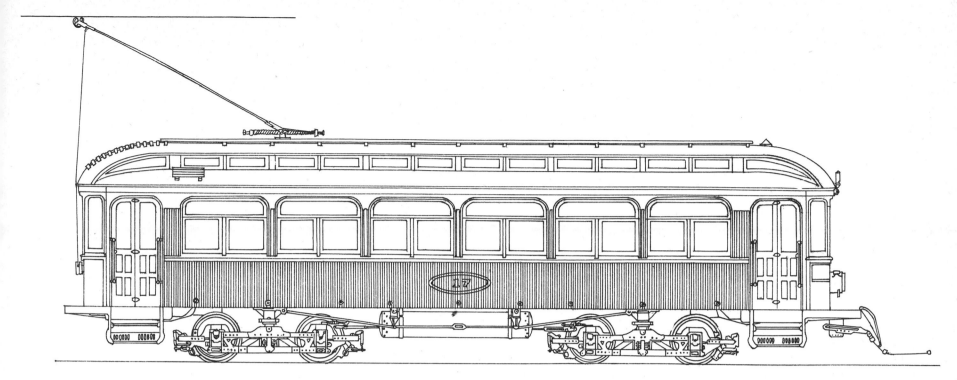

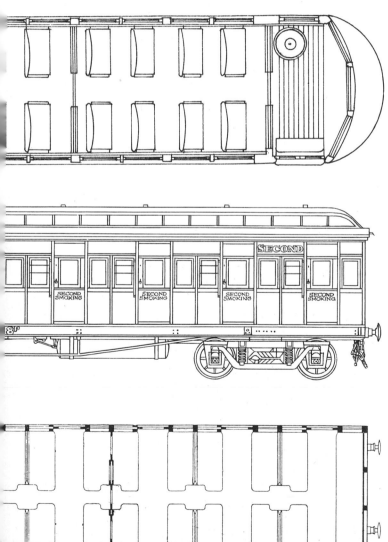

The Tait surburban second-class car was designed in 1911 for use in Melbourne, Australia. It seated 92.

phraseology of Southern England, he was a *season-ticket-holder*. In that of Northern England he was a *contract-holder*. In America he was a *commuter*. The term "commuting motorist" for a man who drives himself to and from town, which is regrettably used in many areas now, is a terminological absurdity.

The American commuters' car was generally the same as an ordinary American daycoach, extremely difficult of egress and access at terminals. In the early nineteenhundreds certain American designers added middle double sliding doors to help things out. Boston cars, thus equipped, were closely copied in England by the District Railway on its electrification in 1905. The District company was just a little too clever. With the best intentions, it tried to make the doors automatic, with opening and closing by little air engines worked off the main brake-air supply. The things speedily caught in an inexorable grip people's arms and legs, as well as old gentleman's beards, ladies' long skirts, and other appendages, with variously shocking results. This first attempt at automatic doors—now so familiar—lasted some six weeks, and then it was subjected, to your author's knowledge, to an official Act of Oblivion. For many years after, the thing was unmentionable in London Transport circles. A remotely-remembered Peter Arno cartoon ("By God, suh! I won't forget this insult!") suggests that America also had troubles of this sort, even more thoroughly wiped off the slate of history. Early London underground cars, through the influence of Charles Tyson Yerkes, were extremely American, and very good cars at that, except when the sliding doors were left open on a winter night. On hot summer nights, passengers inclined to leave them open a-purpose, except when the cars were so crammed that the passengers would inevitably spill themselves out on the tracks and get irreparably damaged.

The Illinois Central cars followed American contours, and had sliding doors, as did, a little later, the Australian commuters' cars far south in Melbourne. We show here a Tait suburban car—prototype of these—from a diagram book of 1911. The very narrow gangway was to enable rush-hour passengers to distribute themselves up-and-down the car after their first scrimmage at the doors. Cars of this type, and also of the old swinging-door sort with that peculiarly Anglo-Saxon abomination, the full-width closed compartment, were later converted for electric working in multiple-unit.

In fairness to your author's own race, let it be added that those closed compartments were common enough at the time in North Germany, France and many other European countries from the Peninsula to the Peloponnesus. They had an awful habit of turning up on the less respectable trains over longer distances, especially on cheap excursions, where their frequent lack of water-closets originated all sorts of curious stories, amusing to those who had not themselves suffered. Alas, not so long before, this defect had distinguished nearly all Western European trains! Blessings on those nameless Americans and Russians who first made suitably-adorned holes in car floors! Germany showed up well, from the eighties onwards.

163

PASSENGER CLASSES

Throughout the world, there remained two conflicting ideals of the railroad passenger car; the "open" type chiefly favoured by North America, Russia, South-west Germany, much of Eastern Europe and Scandinavia, and the compartment-form of Western Europe and of most countries under British influence including India but, rather surprisingly excluding New Zealand, which, where railroads were concerned, was decidedly American in practice. Both types had their earnest protagonists. Abroad from America, Mark Twain lamented his isolation, and possible immolation with a troublesome drunk. Abroad from England, Rudyard Kipling wrote of an Egyptian train: that she reminded him of a South African train and that consequently he loved her, adding that the familiar arrangement of compartments served by a side corridor equally annoyed his American companions (who may have included Mrs. Kipling).

So far, passenger cars had been very generally made of timber, at least as to the bogies, which made them comfortable by good insulation but liable to burn-up in a wreck when lit by gas or kerosene. One recalls awful classics of this brand of smash from Ashtabula in the States, Gretna in Scotland, Bellinzona in Switzerland and a good many other places before and within our time. To be fair to the Swiss, whose fault it was that their trains collided, it was a German gaslit coach that burst into flame and instantly affected an Italian wooden one.

In the United States, land of cut-throat competition, the more wealthy companies answered public scare over these things first by building much more substantial cars—almost invariably to what one may conveniently call the Pullman outline—and then making them entirely of steel. Less wealthy companies sometimes covered their existing wooden cars with thin steel plates, studded by ostentatiously massive rivets, to kid their patrons into believing that this was indeed an all-steel car. "The all-steel Columbian" was a publicity-department definition of the period, by the Chicago, Milwaukee and St. Paul company, whose other crack train was called the Olympian.

Some of these old American transcontinental trains were of quite astounding sumptuosity. A barber-shop was a sort of status-symbol, and so was the observation car at the rear, whereon one could either sit out in a folding chair on the back platform, watch the scenery, and put up with the dust, or sit on a handsome plush one inside with the *Wall Street Journal* and let the scenery take care of itself. The Milwaukee company, boosting its electrified Mountain Division, reminded its patrons that they could sit outside *with no smoke to annoy, or obscure the view* (cf. *The King of the Rails*, 1915). They were lovely things, those old American railroad brochures! North of the 49th Parallel, in the Canadian Rockies, the Canadian Pacific Railway was already using a form of glazed observation car which anticipated the "dome cars" of both Canada and the States in later years. Remote origins of the arrangement were in Russia, under Winans' influence, back in the eighteen-sixties.

American passenger cars at this time were almost invariably of the clerestoried shape, still favoured also by Prussia and Scandinavia, the Midland Railway in England, and (where it was to last longest) in South Africa.

Passenger accommodation was very variable indeed, according to the country and the sort of user. The most comfortable ordinary arrangement for daytime travel throughout North America was the *parlor car,* a Pullman or Pullman-type vehicle with superior overstuffed chairs on fixed pivots, set singly each side of the central aisle. It had been used on several British railways, chiefly in the South, since Pullmans were first imported in the middle-seventies, but in 1908 came the first British-built Pullmans, still with single chair seating, but with the very massive and comfortable chairs movable on legs.

America's chair car was arranged like her ordinary day-coach, but with adjustable seats and more support to the back. European coaches followed their traditional form, though more and more with vestibules and side corridors. England's remarkable third-class we have noticed already. The farther east one went, from Europe into Asia, or south into Africa, the cheaper became the third-class fares and the more austere the third-class carriages; also in some countries the dirtier they were. A colleague told us, of Europe in the 'thirties: "The bugs begin east of Budapest!" Highest standards of European cleanliness were undoubtedly in Scandinavia, where, also, the Swedish State Railways introduced third-class sleepers in 1910, with three superimposed berths to each compartment. Some years later these were copied in Germany, and later still in France. For all the excellence of her third-class day coaches, England held off third-class sleepers until

An artist's impression of the smoking lounge and library of an Orient Express in the 1880s. (Courtesy of the Radio Times Hulton Library).

1928, when they took the form of four-berth compartments, sleeping two each side as in a rather indifferent second-best-first-class arrangement which the French called *compartiments à couchettes*.

On an ascending price scale, American Pullmans contained many sorts of sleeping compartment, with side-corridor access, in addition to the traditional open section dating back to 1865. A *bedroom* resembled a European two-berth Wagons-Lits. A *drawing room* was more spacious. A *master-room* was fairly plutocratic.

With the general introduction of steel cars, design became highly standardized. A Pullman berth on the Florida East Coast, rolling out over the old viaducts to Key West, half-way to Cuba, was exactly the same as a Pullman berth on the Great Northern, headed for British Columbia; green plush and all. D. H. Lawrence found the same thing in Mexico, though with a whiff of bloody-handed brigands somewhere beyond its close-shaded windows. In Europe, you could not possibly mistake a car of the Holland Railway for one of the Prussian State, or either for one of the London and North Western, though most of them were of the primeval side-door type in the earlier part of this century. Some of the Danish State carriages were more like those of the Italian Mediterranean Railway than those of the Hessleholm-Hälsingborg just across the water, but still very different. Even the mighty and far-reaching Wagons-Lits company, the nearest approach to America's Pullman undertaking, was lusciously variable.

Eastern third-class carriages were fairly fearsome, quite apart from the fact that they were invariably crammed. In India, each long compartment had four wooden benches—the middle ones back-to-back, with access to a small Oriental-type latrine. The late Mr. Gandhi, with all India at his feet, always went third-class as a man of the people. Rich Indians, and official and Army English travelled first-class in dusty luxury. Babu-class Indians went second-class. Some Eurasians and *poor-whites* used a thing called intermediate-class, lower than second, and in Kipling's words, "very awful indeed".

Japan, and Japanese-controlled railways, had quite admirable cars, latterly very American though on a smaller scale. South Africa had many beautiful trains, with a class system similar to, though less complex than, that of India. Their third-class was necessarily Spartan for conveyance of the poor Bantu and never used by Dutch or English. *Apartheid* was thus automatic. The third-class carriages were simply marked *Kleurlingen* or *Natives,* in Afrikaans or English respectively. They were what, in the southern United States, would have been called "Jim Crow cars", and so they are still. In America, old cars were used, not specially designed ones. Of course, where the work-grimed or the frankly unwashed travelled in large numbers, something of the sort was unavoidable. Even the plushy British railways had wooden-furnished coaches for miners' and quarry-men's "paddy trains". Pit-head baths were as yet rare. Car weights in, say, 1914, were very variable on standard-gauge alone: eighty tons or more for a massive American Pullman, half that for a German D-Wagon or a large English diner, and possibly no more than eight tons for some old fossil on a French or Spanish branch line. Running was equally variable. The Pennsylvania Railroad and the London and North Western Railway both claimed, with some justice, to furnish the smoothest travel in the world. One could also find the contrary on certain lines of both England and America.

We may notice here an interesting thing shown at the German Railway Technological Exhibition at Seddin in 1924; a sleeping car with single-berth compartments for first- and second-class passengers. The latter needed to be rather acrobatic, and by no means a claustrophobe, which may be why the arrangement did not go into large-scale production. But in the first-class compartment was the prototype of the American Pullman "roomette", which was to advance with singular success in the nineteen-thirties.

Observation cars were rare in Europe. In 1914 there was a solitary, very sumptuous, British-built Pullman observation car in Scotland. As Scottish weather, blowing westerly straight off the North Atlantic, is nearly as hazardous as the Scottish West Coast is beautiful, the rear end was entirely glazed. About the same time some Canadian Pacific observation cars found their way to Austria, Tyrol, under very curious circumstances having to do with the Canadian Pacific steamships. (There was even an anti-British row about them in the German-language newspapers!) They ended their days in Italy long after World War I, again under very curious circumstances. One, perhaps the last, was at Voghera for breaking-up in 1961. Goodness knows who, if anyone, paid for them!

Apart from traditional car-classics—American, European and Eastern, there were many combinations of these. In Central America and in parts of South America one could see cars of absolute North American type, but with second-class seating very like

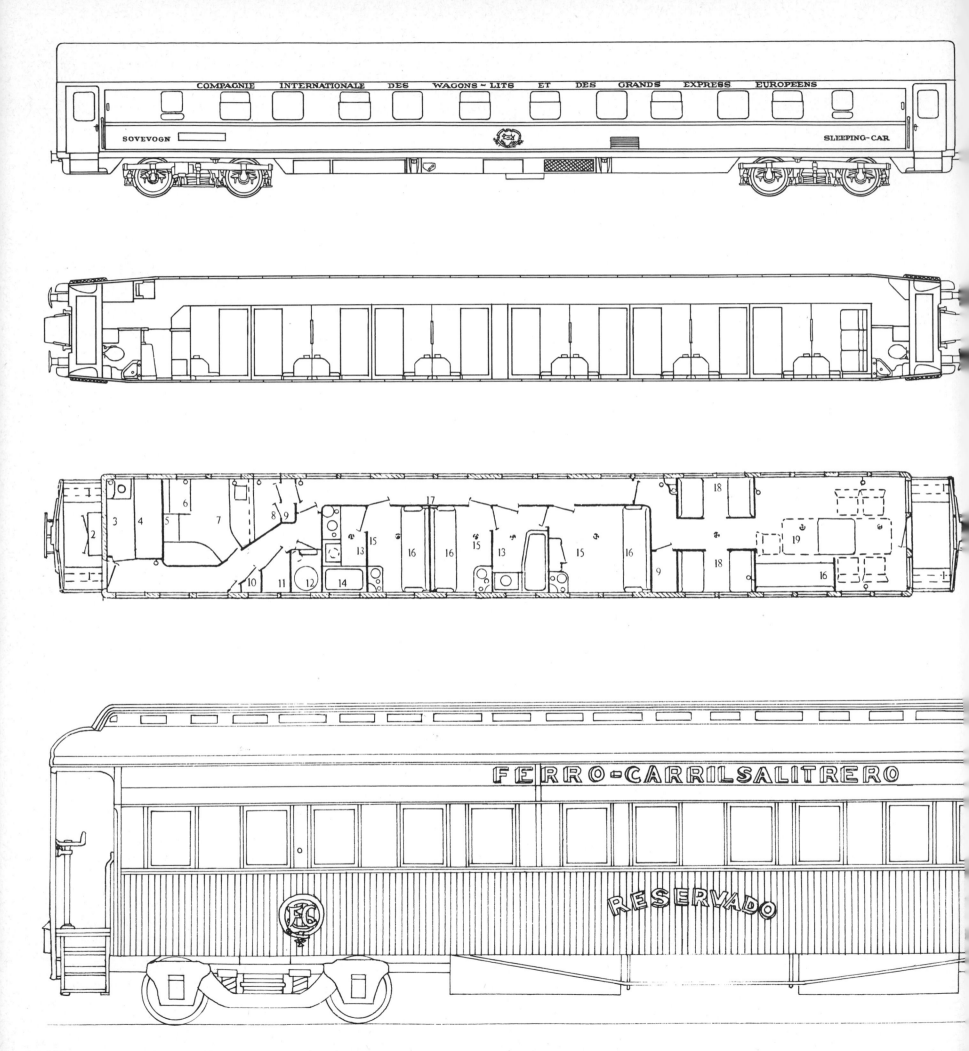

COMPAGNIE INTERNATIONALE DES WAGONS~LITS ET DES GRANDS EXPRESS EUROPEENS

SOVEVOGN   SLEEPING-CAR

FERRO-CARRILSALITRERO

RESERVADO

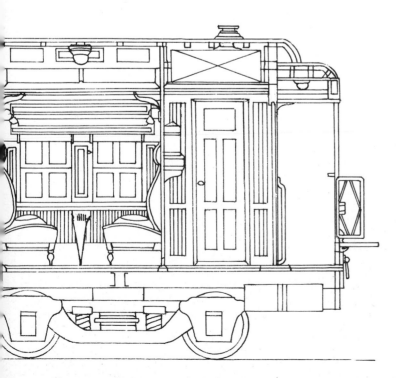

Indian third-class of that time; back-to-the-wall each side and back-to-back in the middle. South American cars, often built in England or Scotland, and beautifully done-up in Argentine ox-hide, combined features of European and American practice, though the motive power might be, and probably was, as British as the cities of Glasgow, Newcastle or Manchester. South American day-cars looked British as to coachwork, but were seated American-style in most cases. We exemplify a contrary example, in a Scottish-built first-class carriage (*reservado*) on the Chilean Nitrate Railways, entirely European within but, outside, rather Old-American. Made as late as 1927, it perpetuated the clerestoried wooden body, which was already obsolescent in Europe.

There was a handsome smoking saloon which belonged to a twelve-wheel Pullman parlor car built in the United States for the London, Brighton and South Coast Railway in 1906. It was one of the last three American cars imported by an English company. The style was classic Pullman of the period, though the provision for smokers was much more liberal than in American smoking compartments of the time, which on Pullmans were combined with the men's lavatories. (Your non-conformist either washed in front of a row of cigar-impaled grins or else smoked amid half-bare dripping bodies!) The true rock-bottom of American car construction was that chassis and body were made in one piece. The old English ideal of body-on-underframe died hard.

FREIGHT ENGINES

Now to that important, and very different, thing which is the haulage of freight! We have already noted the appearance of the Mallet semi-articulated steam locomotive in Europe from 1889 onwards. America was cautious, but in 1904 J. E. Muhlfeld, Chief of Motive Power on the great and venerable Baltimore and Ohio Railroad, took it up for heavy coal haulage, in an enormous double-0-6-0 (C-C) locomotive, of which an example was fortunately preserved. It was an immediate success. America took the Mallet to her ample bosom, where it prospered like many immigrants. Europe was ever cagey about it. The engine was sluggish, but immensely powerful, and easy on the road. How odd that the very earliest Mallet of which we have record was a tiny little double 0-4-0 tank engine which could do useful work on Decauville's portable railways, useful alike on mobile industrial work and in war! In America the Mallet became the tireless giant in heavy traffic—the sort of thing J. A. Maffei had in mind on building the grandmother-engine for the Gotthard in Switzerland—and thereafter, whenever one heard or read of *the biggest locomotive on earth* one could bet that it was a Mallet in the United States!

Muhlfeld's had been that, and there were to be many successors down to the end of steam traction in North America. A prodigy was an engine (p. 178) called *Matt H. Shay* on the Erie before World War I, which not only had two sets of four coupled axles each but a third under the tender, making the combined wheel-arrangement 2-8-8-8-2, with the type-name Triplex. There was nothing new in steam tenders; they had been made in both France (Eastern Railway) and England (Great Northern Railway) in the middle of the previous century to assist traction on starting and on heavy grades, but there was the same pitfall before them all. That meant too many cylinders for the boiler to supply, and all steam men have been ever agreed that, short of accident, there could be nothing worse than losing one's steam. Even the mighty "Shay" was not immune!

Another problem with these much-elongated locomotives was that of boiler-barrel length, and there were desperate attempts to make the boiler bend in the middle by what one can only describe as a bellows-connection, with the front half as a feedwater heater of sorts. One would think that this was asking for trouble, and unfortunately we have not met any man who had to do with such a thing—and would talk! It did not persist, but the Atchison, Topeka and Santa Fe Railroad certainly built this type, with six coupled axles in two sets, making it 2-6-6-2. Weight in working order was 308 tons, to which the twelve-wheel tender added 117 tons. Oil was the fuel.

Mallet locomotives appeared in many other parts of the world, though not on such a gigantic scale. British firms built them for South Africa, Burma and China. The type appeared on the Eastern Railway of France, and, from Maffei, on the Bavarian State Railways; all these on a much larger scale than in the early days of the Mallet in the Alpine countries. The same applied in Hungary. German works built broad-gauge Mallets for the Central Aragon and Zafra-Huelva Railways. In Scandinavia the Mallet was scarce, though an admirable narrow-gauge type by Atlas of Stockholm worked for many years on the ·891 m. Dala-Norrsundet Railway in Sweden. Two survive in reserve.

The interior of an early sleeping-car of the Pullman type.

A dining car in Germany in the 1880s.

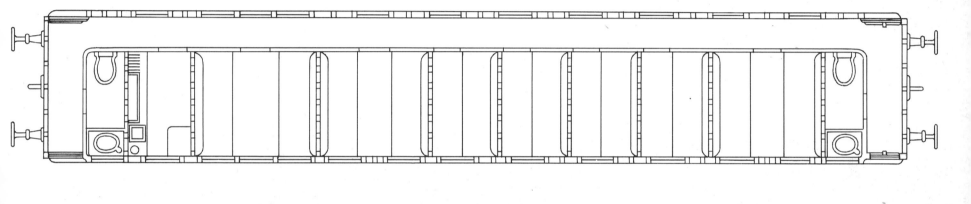

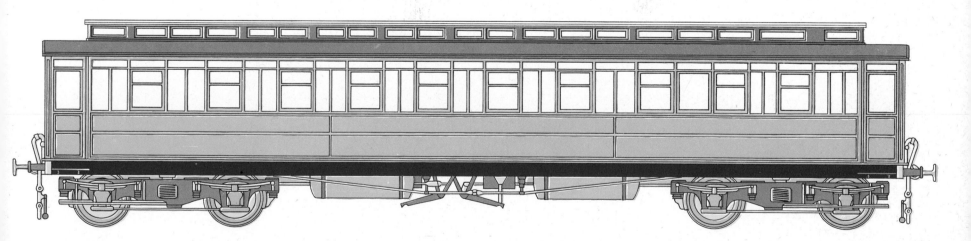

IN 1894, THE NORTH EASTERN RAILWAY BUILT THIS SLEEPER, DESIGNED BY DAVID BAIN, WHICH CONTAINED THE FIRST SINGLE-BERTH COMPARTMENTS IN GREAT BRITAIN.

French 4-4-0 Express

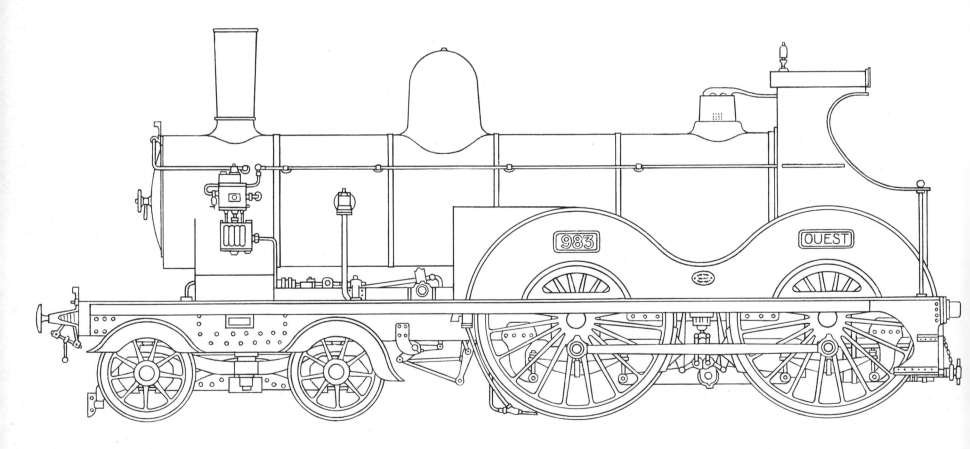

ENGLISH INFLUENCE ON THE WESTERN RAILWAYS OF FRANCE AT THE TURN OF THE CENTURY. THE COMPANY WAS STARTED WITH ENGLISH CAPITAL.

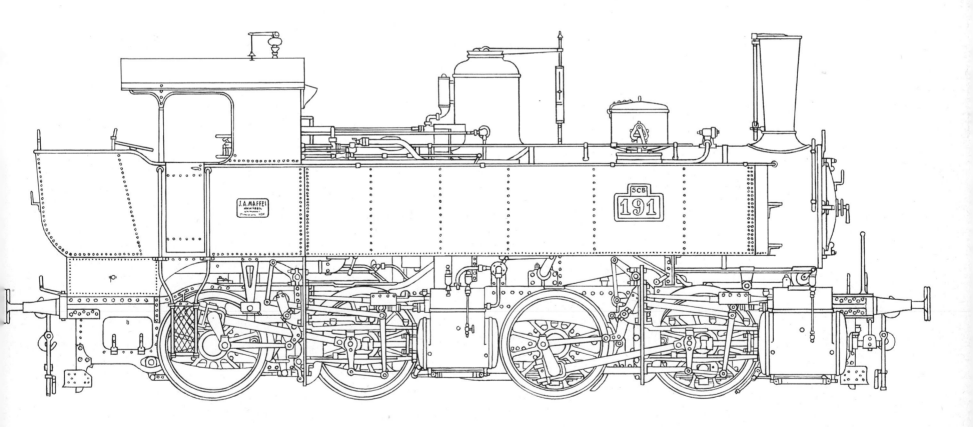

J. A. MAFFEI'S **MALLET TANK ENGINE** , CLASS C 4, NO. 191 ON THE SWISS CENTRAL RAILWAY, WAS DESIGNED IN 1890 AND BUILT IN 1894.

THE END OF THE SINGLE-DRIVER LEGEND IN ENGLAND: SAMUEL W. JOHNSON'S 4-2-2'S WERE THE MOST POWERFUL AND THE LAST SINGLE-DRIVERS.

Dutch Second-Class Carriage

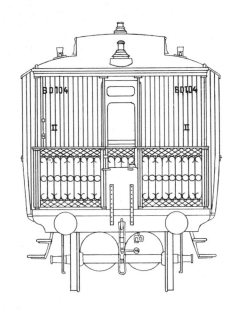

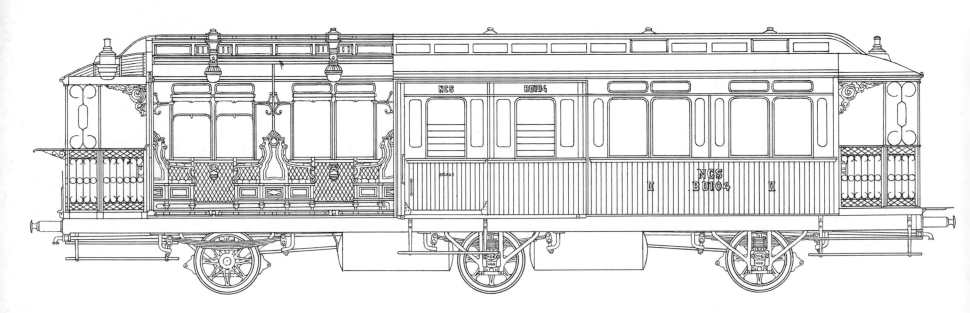

THE NETHERLANDS CENTRAL RAILWAY BUILT THIS UNUSUALLY ELEGANT DESIGN FOR USE ON ITS INTERNAL SERVICES, EARLY 1900S.

HENSCHEL AND SONS' ATTEMPT AT A STREAMLINED STEAM LOCOMOTIVE FOR THE PRUSSIAN STATE RAILWAYS (CLASS S9), 1904.

Dunalastair

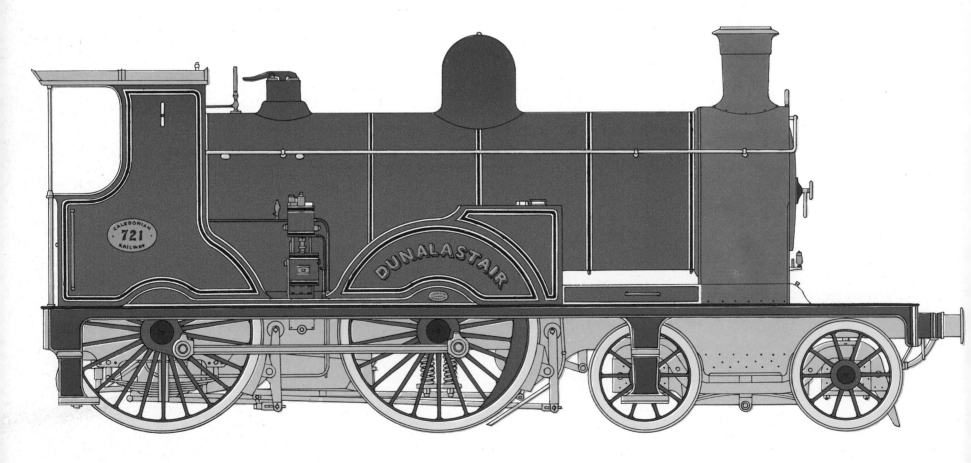

JOHN F. MCINTOSH DESIGNED THE DUNALASTAIR TO BE A STANDARD PASSENGER LOCOMOTIVE FOR THE CALEDONIAN RAILWAYS. THE TYPE WAS ALSO BUILT FOR THE BELGIAN STATE RAILWAYS.

THE BEYER-GARRATT

England produced a type of articulated locomotive which later was to be so widely and successfully used that Americans (who never bought it) sometimes called it the "British Mallet". This was the engine known down the years as the "Beyer-Garratt", for Herbert Garratt, an Englishman in Australia, invented it, and the great Manchester firm of Beyer, Peacock and Company acquired his patents.

Basically, the Beyer-Garratt consisted of two distinct locomotive units, each supporting through pivots and bearings a proportionately large boiler on a girder frame between them. Garratt's original idea had been to produce thus a powerful yet flexible large-wheeled passenger engine, with no interference by the height of the wheels in the dimensions of the boiler. He had also ideas for a locomotive gun carriage, the guns being mounted on top of the substantial tanks which were immediately over the engine units and balanced the heavy boiler between them. The express engine, with its wheels arranged 2-4-0 + 0-4-2, was indeed built for the San Paulo (Brazilian) Railway in 1915, but the very first of the type were small double-0-4-0 locomotives for very narrow gauges; for an isolated 2 ft. gauge of the Tasmanian Government Railways in 1909, and in 1911 for the vertiginous Darjeeling Himalayan Railway in India. Few would have guessed that the Beyer-Garratt of later years was to be a giant. Almost invariable features of the type were outside cylinders with radial valve gear of Walschaerts type. The little Tasmanian was exceptional in having compound expansion, like the Mallets of the period. She is preserved today (p. 179) by the Festiniog undertaking in North Wales, having gone half round the world and back again.

Various other articulated locomotive types saw much use in the first thirty years of this century. The Meyer type dated back at least to 1873 in Belgium and, by drawings and derivation (e.g. from the Semmering trials) earlier than that. Here again there were two motor bogies, as in the Fairlie, but with the leading one on a spherical pivot and the after one on transverse members, both supporting a single, reasonably large boiler. The main frames were those of the two motor units, which carried the couplers in consequence, while the boiler supported the tanks. There were separate exhausts, fore and aft. Such an engine was built for the Belgian Great Central Railway (that was the essay of 1873), but it was not until the 'nineties that the type really *arrived,* at the instance of Robert Stirling on the Anglo-Chilean Nitrate company's railway, who suggested it to Kitson and Company in England, who in turn built it (p. 179).

In this version the boiler, tanks, bunker—in fact the "top works"—were mounted on two parallel girders which rested on the bogies. These locomotives in Chile managed well on a seventeen mile line with a gradient of 1 in 25, about three-quarters of it additionally curved on a radius of 181 ft. The type achieved, in the present century, great success on other lines in the Andes, *viz.* both the Argentine and the Chilean Trans-Andine Railways, all on narrow gauge. The largest were in a set built, not for the narrow gauges of the Andes, but for the big broad gauge of Spain on the Aguilas-Lorca and Baza (Great Southern of Spain) Railway, a very considerable carrier of iron-ore. Kitsons held the Meyer patents, just as Beyer Peacock held the Garratt ones, and as the Great Southern of Spain was a British company until Spanish Communists got it, everybody was for a while happy. The engines were certainly a good investment. Other articulated steam engines of this period included not only the later Fairlies but the "modified Fairlie" and Maffei's "Garratt Union", both of which owed much to the genuine Garratt, and the Hagans type which, in two sets of coupled wheels, incorporated a derived drive to the rear set. It was built for the Prussian State Railways in 1893, and also, like the very different, pioneer Garratt, for the Tasmanian Government in Australia's Island State.

Summing up the distribution of articulated steam reciprocating locomotives, it was the Swiss-born Mallet that conquered the mountains of North America (latterly without compound expansion in most cases), the Garratt that came to possess African heavy haulage (South, East, West and more briefly Algerian), the Meyer that managed the Andes, and the old double Fairlie that held out for long in Mexico. All were slow and plodding engines except the Garratt, which could and did work express passenger trains in such widely dispersed countries as South Africa, Kenya, Angola, Algeria and even Spain on the Aragon Central Railway, where it succeeded the Mallet as it had done in South Africa. The Aragon Central company had a solitary Garratt express engine, a "double-Pacific", as well as the more usual heavy freight type. It was a wonderful engine.

Many railway authorities, however, stuck to heavy locomotives on a rigid, multi-axle wheelbase. The 0-10-0 engine was much favoured in Central Europe, by Prussia, Bavaria, Austria, Sweden, Italy, and perhaps most of all by Russia, where an admirable design, produced first before the first World War, was to be built in many thousands, notably as an all-work engine in the hard years after the Revolution, when large numbers were built by Nydqvist and Holm in Sweden and by many German Works such as Vulkan of Stettin and Humboldt of Köln-Deutz. These three firms all had the advantage, when it came to building broad-gauge locomotives, of access by waterway. From Lomonossov in Russia came staggering orders for 700 in Germany and Sweden. We show on p. 159 the Nydqvist and Holm engine, though the same drawings were used by all, and only minor modifications were made in later Russian construction under the first of J. Stalin's five-year plans in the late nineteen-twenties. In Victorian English phraseology, they were not beautiful, but they were very useful. They were also simple, straightforward engines without bothersome gadgets, suitable to a vast country emerging from industrial and social chaos.

In North America, the 0-10-0 locomotive was used only as a heavy switcher in the great freight yards, for pushing wagons over the humps of such tremendous outfits as Markham Yard, Illinois. The ordinary American freight hauler of the time was more likely to be 2-10-2, easier on the road than an entirely rigid engine. The 2-10-0 engine, of which a solitary de Glehn was built for Alsace-Lorraine Railways in 1904, was much liked in Europe, especially in Austria and the Balkans where it was to become even an express passenger type, at first on such lines as the Austrian Semmering, Tauern and Arlberg railways before their electrification, and latterly in Greece, where engines of obvious Austrian style, built by Skoda in Czecho-Slovakia after the break-up of the Empire, toiled and groaned through classic mountain places with the Athens portion of the Orient Express. One feels that they ought to have had names like *Leonidas, Alci-biades* and *Brasidas,* in a good Greek soldierly tradition, for they were most formidable and alarming-looking engines. By then, however, the naming of locomotives was mostly long out of fashion except in Great Britain, which ever loved this endearing custom.

Athens, be it added, was the last major European capital to be linked physically with the Continental network, apart from British and Scandinavian cities still dependent on train-ferries. It had long been possible to take one's choice of steam or electric trains between Athens and Piraeus, or to go loafing out on narrow gauge to Corinth and the coastal parts of the Peloponnese, but the south to north line through the great mountains, to link the Piraeus and Athens with Salonika via Larissa, was not completed until 1916, by the closing of the northern gap between Papapouli and Platy. Northern connections had been Turkish, with a good deal of French capital behind them, indeed foreign money went into most of Turkey's lines; French into the Oriental Railways, German into the Baghdadbahn, and British into the ponderously-named Ottoman Railway from Smyrna to Aidin. Their equipment reflected their origins.

This great 2-10-0 type of steam locomotive was, however, essentially a freight engine in Europe apart from these exceptions, and we show (p. 180) one of J. B. Flamme's for the Belgian State Railways' heavy coal traffic, after it had been rebuilt in the nineteen-twenties with improved front-end arrangements including double blastpipe and stack.

(above) This compound duplex locomotive was used for heavy coal trains on the Baltimore and Ohio Railroad, 1903.

(centre) Herbert Garrat's first articulated locomotive built for the Tasmanian Government Railway's 2 ft. gauge in 1909.

(below) Kitson and Company of Leeds, England, built this Meyer locomotive for the Anglo-Chilean Nitrate Company.

The Matt. H. Shay's *wheel arrangement was known as triplex, i.e. it had three sets of four coupled axles—making it a 2-8-8-8-2. It was used for freight haulage on the Erie road.*

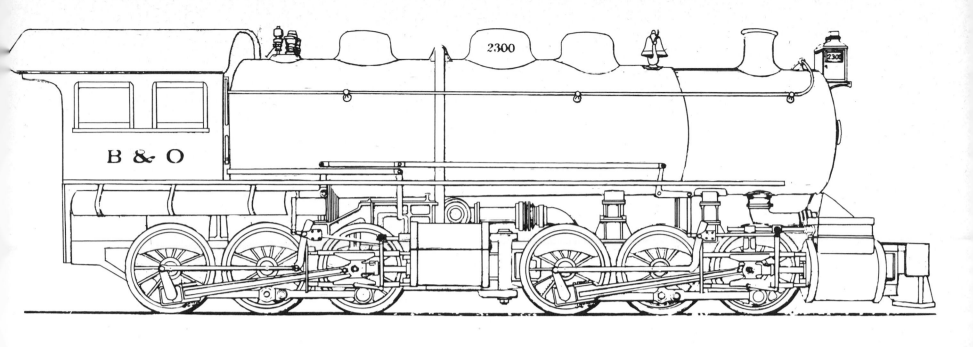

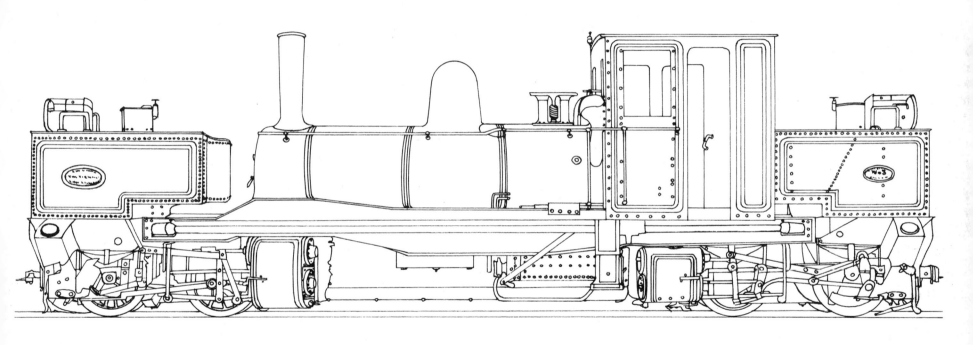

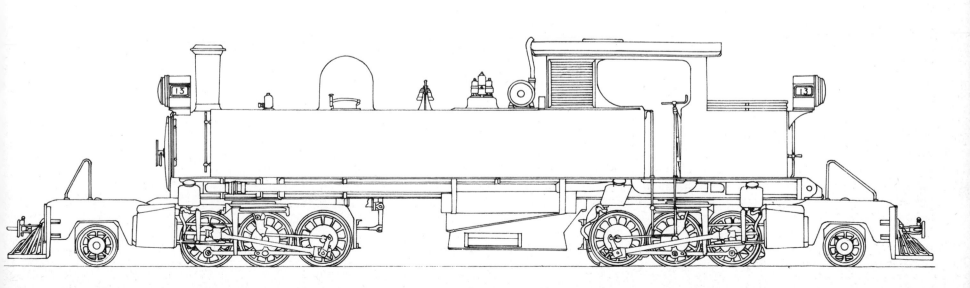

Though more constricted by loading gauge than many European engines, these were in their day the largest and most powerful on the Continent. They were closely akin to Flamme's great Pacific type express engines of the same period, and like them suffered from the hand of war.

Austria, regarded popularly and not without reason as the European home of the big steam locomotive, essayed a 2-12-0 type in Gölsdorf's later years, and so did Württemberg which bequeathed it later to the German State Railway (a post-war corporation), but the coupling of six axles was fairly rare in Europe and uncommon even in North America. A quite recent example of the 2-12-0 was the A 1 of French National Railways (1948). The old Württemburg type ended its days on the Semmering line in Austria. Articulated grouping of wheels, as in the Mallet and Garratt types, and in later electric locomotives of the period such as the famous "Crocodiles" of Switzerland and Austria, served their purpose better; indeed the very long coupled wheelbase died early. It had one last desperate puff in a monstrous 4-14-4 coal engine produced by Soviet Russia in the early nineteen-thirties, shown on p. 197 as a mechanical curiosity. It seems to have been made in opposition to a vast 4-8-2 + 2-8-4 Beyer-Garratt imported from England in 1933. They were the largest steam locomotives in Europe. Neither was repeated.

A few notes on accessory machines before we summarise general trends in steam design: Ever since the *Comet* ran over a wheelbarrow in 1830, trains had met occasional obstacles and hazards. Means for lifting derailed locomotives had advanced from primitive hand-crane to steam crane fairly early. As engine-weights grew, so side crane-lifts. It took two cranes to lift a locomotive bodily, with much preliminary work, especially if she were down on her side in the mud. In Europe, about 1910, ordinary lifting capacity might range from 20 to 60 tons; in the Americas it would be much more. Notable makers were Ransomes and Rapier in England and Bucyrus in the States. A modern American wrecking crane will have a lift of 250 tons at about 17 ft. radius with a lift of

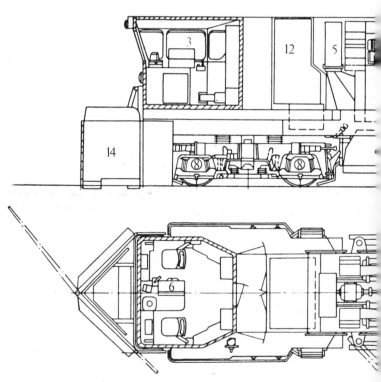

*The 1650 HP Diesel
Electric Bo-I-Bo Snowplow and
locomotive type B can be used for
shunting when not in service as a
snowplough.*

1 Diesel Engine
2 Main Generator
3 Control cabinet
4 Air compressor
5 Main generator and traction
  blower

6 Control stand
7 Engine cooling fan
8 Traction motor
9 Fuel tank
10 Battery
11 Diesel engine heater
12 Hydraulic equipment
13 Control cabinet
14 Front plow
15 Side plow
16 Draw plow
17 Turntable

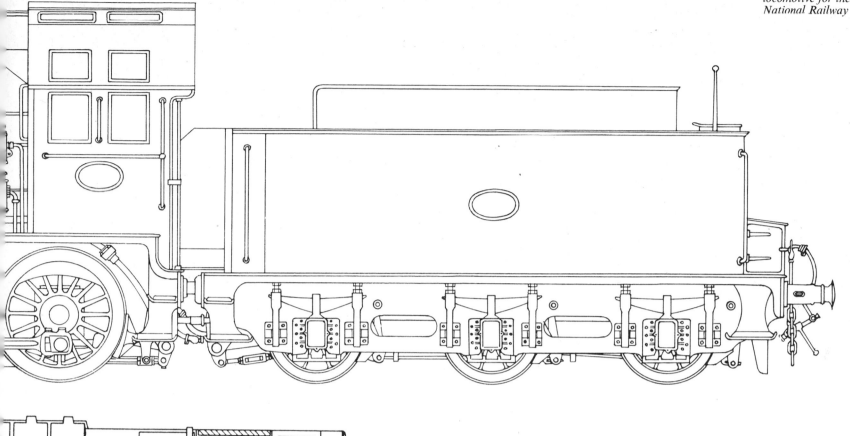

J. B. Flamme's 2-10-0 freight locomotive for the Belgian National Railway Company.

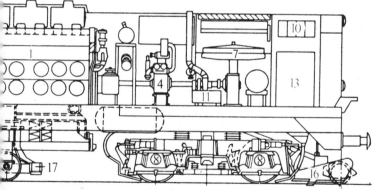

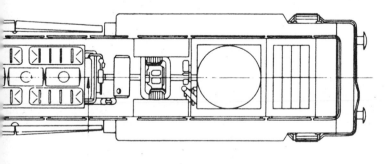

50-60 tons on the auxiliary hook at the extremity of the jib.

The primeval snow-plow, whether mounted on the front of a locomotive or running as a separate heavy vehicle, was prow-shaped, and it is a useful thing to this day on routine snow patrol, though old style snow-bucking can be a hair-raising experience of charging headlong into the drifts with three locomotives behind the plow. The Leslie power-driven rotary plow, with a vast hooded, feathering screw, appeared in the United States very early in the 'nineties, and its use rapidly spread to most of the colder parts of the world. We show on p. 180 a modern, Swedish snowplow built by ASEA. Sweden was the first country to adapt electric power to the doughty rotary plow, on the Lapland iron ore line between the Gällivare-Kiruna area and Luleå on the Gulf of Bothnia and Narvik on the Norwegian North Atlantic coast. In the steam form, a high-speed geared engine was made to drive the rotor, supplied by an ordinary locomotive-type boiler inside the all-over cab, with a small tender in the rear. For Sweden, too, Henschel in Germany built a Diesel-engined rotary plow.

Now to ordinary locomotive practice of our rather elastic period: England, motherland of the steam locomotive, ever paid the price of pioneering in restricted clearances where her great main lines, most solidly constructed, thrust through the hills instead of skirting them. Restrictions plus magnificent formations caused multi-axle locomotives to be extremely rare. There had been a solitary ten-coupled tank engine on the Great Eastern in 1902, built for purely business reasons to show Parliament that a commuters' steam train could accelerate as rapidly as an electric rival then threatening the Great Eastern company. Another 0-10-0 locomotive, having four cylinders with simple expansion, in pairs with two valves and crossed ports, was built in 1919 by the Midland Railway for banking or pushing over the very steep Lickey Hills passage south-west of Birmingham. Otherwise the type did not appear on British rails until the advent of the 2-10-0 war engines in the nineteen-forties, some of which were to end their days on

Dutch and even Swedish railways. (We have seen the famous *Longmoor* of these just twice; firstly when she went on the train-ferry at Dover, and the second time in the Netherlands Railways Museum at Utrecht.)

English conditions prevailed likewise in Scotland, whose railway system was geographically an extension of England though her old railway companies were distinctive, like the Austrian systems compared with the German though on a smaller scale.

Most of Great Britain's immense freight traffic was quite adequately shifted by six-coupled locomotives, with 0-8-0 or 2-8-0 for coal and other heavy minerals. Her equally astonishing passenger traffic (the London Brighton and South Coast, a fairly small railway, carried more passengers than the Canadian Pacific!) was dealt with over longer distances by modest 4-4-0 (the commonest), Atlantic, and 4-6-0 locomotives with axle-loads which some people would have found formidable, though the engines' aspect was modest by Continental, let alone American, standards. They were very compact, and usually most elegantly styled; further they were often painted (and kept very clean) in rich liveries of green, red or blue. As there were about 120 different British railway companies until 1923, there was plenty of variety at such great centres as York, Carlisle and Perth, which formed company frontiers. All the vastitude of America could not match those mechanical pageants of a British boyhood, though in Continental Europe there was a whiff of it at real frontier stations, and places like Antwerp and Frankfurt. One remembers with affection the fine brassy engines of the Low Countries, the majestic green ones of Bavaria, and the red-white-red collars about the necks of old Danes. As yet there were fewer national characteristics of style in electric locomotive design, save that they had pilots and central automatic couplings in North America and Mexico, and screw-coupling with side buffers on European standard and broad gauge.

The 4-6-0 steam locomotive was to be found from Western Portugal or Northern Scotland to the Urals and beyond; indeed it was one of the most widely-distributed passenger types over much of the world. There were such varieties as the Prussian P 8— one of the most numerous classes ever built—the famous four-cylinder simple engines of the Great Western in England, the Swedish State Class B, built over the decade 1909–19 (on the Stockholm-Västerås-Bergslagen in 1944!) and surviving to the last days of steam, the handsome Class A 2 of the Victorian Government Railways in Australia, and the slightly variable Indian "mail engine", British in origin, and built over a period even longer than that of the Bavarian S 3/6 Pacific, a remarkable record.

Very many Europeans, and numerous visiting Americans, have seen the Prussian P 8, from Biscay to the Baltic and the Black Sea, for under the misfortunes of war it was vastly migratory. So it is a Prussian S 10 that we show here, a handsome four-cylinder simple express engine with the inside piston-valves worked through rockers by the outside valve gear. Four-cylinder compound 4-6-0 engines were common in France and in some parts of Germany, and in countries influenced by these. As hinted, four-cylinder simple 4-6-0 engines were most successfully built in England by George Jackson Churchward of the Great Western Railway, which was still turning them out in the war-battered nineteen-forties. Contrary to the Prussian S 10, these English engines had their outside piston valves worked off the inside gear. Also, they invariably had coned boiler barrels without domes, and Belpaire fireboxes, as well as that gloriously brazen Victorian aspect which distinguished the Great Western Railway for well over a century.

In both England and Scotland the 4-4-0 fast passenger engine was far from dying, however moribund it might be in the Americas or on most lines in Continental Europe apart from the Holland Railway guided by Ir. W. Hupkes, who was to become President of the Netherlands Railways through the heartbreak years to 1946. For an example let us take a design less well-known, for there were only two of them, designed by Christopher Cumming and built in a mighty hurry for the northern section of the Highland Railway, Scotland, in 1916. This hitherto remote line had suddenly found itself providing two railheads (Invergordon and Thurso) for the British Navy. *Snaigow* and *Durn,* as the sisters were named, worked innumerable naval trains. For all our qualification, we could scarcely call these "fast" on their final northern lap. British sailors in two wars called the journey *The Thirty-nine Stops.* Unusually, low platforms and splashers were combined with Walschaerts gear; aspect was rather austerely elegant, chaste as a bottle of malt whisky.

In North America the Pacific type locomotive had truly arrived for fast and ordinary passenger work. North of the 49th Parallel, the Canadian Pacific Railway cheerfully headed it into the Rockies, though the 2-8-2, originally built for Japan, helped more

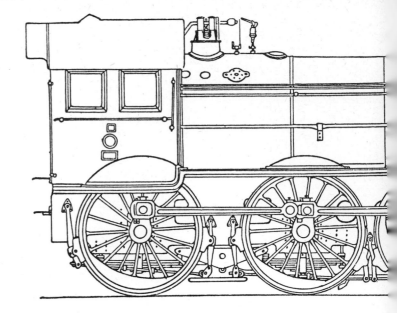

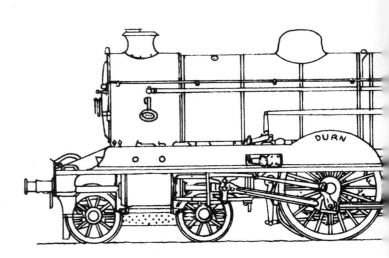

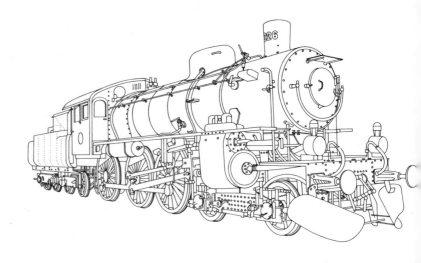

(*above*) The Prussian State Railways Class S-10.

(*centre*) The Highland Railways passenger engine Durn *was built in 1916.*

(*below*) The Swedish State Railways steam locomotive Class B *had a maximum speed of 90 km/h and was used for hauling all sorts of trains.*

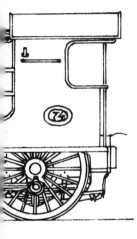

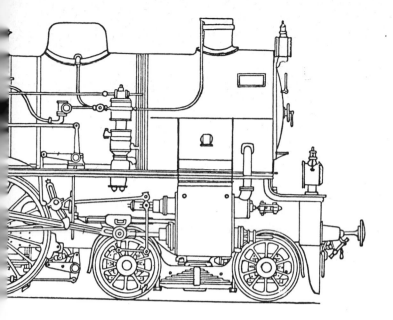

(below) The Indian "mail engine" was built by the Vulcan Foundry in England.

than somewhat. On the broad-gauge lines of South America, such as the Buenos Aires and Pacific in Argentina and the Sao Paulo in Brazil, both British-owned and using the Spanish and Irish gauges respectively, Pacific locomotives had shorter wheelbase, and narrow-grate Belpaire fireboxes instead of the wide-grate type of the true Pacific. In aspect they were English, yet with no counterparts in England; one of the curiosities of international capitalism blended with mechanical engineering tradition. On narrow-gauge lines—in South Africa, Japan and South-east Asia, the true Pacific was eminently suitable, as in New Zealand, and it flourished.

All the same, shorter engines for passenger work did not yet fade away from the United States where, said some un-American party, the companies bought their loco-motives off the hook, drove them to death, and bought new ones. Many North American lines were faithfully served by mild little Moguls—excellent things for branch lines before the automobile killed these—and the mighty Pennsylvania went on building large ten-wheelers and even portly Atlantics for country passenger traffic, including outer suburban trains on what the late Lucius Beebe called its Child of Sorrow, the Long Island Railroad.

Lest there should be European sneers at the American custom of buying, driving hard, and chucking aside, let us recall that a ten-wheeler type of the Milwaukee Road, built by Baldwin in 1900, was hauling branch sections of the Hiawatha train about 1938, albeit much rebuilt and with a streamline casing on top. To be sure, there cannot have been much of the original engine left apart from the frames and the wheel-centres; certainly the original Vauclain arrangement of compounding on four cylinders, super-imposed in pairs, had long vanished.

There was something of an English parallel. From 1946 we recall trans-Atlantic air-line specials (two Pullmans and one baggage) being worked between London and the old Hurn Airport by Drummond eight-wheelers which had also been built in 1900, for the London and South Western Railway. Thanks to a few superheater elements, later installed, they behaved in very sprightly fashion!

From the lyrical to the practical; and harsh are the words of Apollo after the songs of Orpheus! The years immediately before war came in 1914 saw the first, stumbling entry of the Diesel locomotive. There were several essays with rail-motor cars running by compression-ignition on crude oil, in Germany, but in 1912 the Prussian State Railways had commissioned a large diesel locomotive to be built jointly by Borsig of Berlin and Sulzer Brothers of Winterthur. It appeared in the following year. Outwardly it suggested electric practice, with the wheel arrangement 2-B-2 or 4-4-4, with side-rod drives. Diagonal two-stroke engines gave direct drive through a jackshaft to the two coupled axles. There was no other transmission, and compressed air had to be used to bring the engines up to at least 60 r.p.m. before ignition began. The diesel was an ailing child, and war necessities brought an end to this experiment. Most mechanical revolutionaries were looking rather to increased electric traction.

Railroad traction by oil engines, thus initially dogged by transmission problems, belongs to later years, so let it briefly stand over. Rudolf Diesel was a cosmopolitan German, born in Paris in 1858, educated partly in Munich and partly in England. He published his *Theory and Construction of a Rational Heat Motor* in 1894. In 1913 he was invited to England for a talk on engines with the British Admiralty, but he mysteriously disappeared. His supposed body was taken from the Scheldt a long time after. Sinister stories were told, from different points of view, of *whose* secret agent was supposed to have tipped him over the ship's rail, and why. But it may have been that the unfortunate genius was leaning too far over when seasick, to take an involuntary header into the dark North Sea when nobody was looking. We are unlikely ever to know.

As a less sombre conclusion to this period, let us note monorails, which in the first decade of the century were attracting a good deal of attention. There was, of course, the Wuppertal line in Germany, the *Schwebebahn* with suspended electric cars, which is still with us and has lately acquired very modern rolling-stock, but the idea was much older than that. Even in the eighteen-sixties there was an arrangement for locomotives and cars to run on a single central rail with driving and balancing wheels to the roadway or ballast each side. This was more correctly a guide-rail line than a true monorail and it was quite workably applied to the Lisbon Tramways. We show (p. 184) one of the locomotives, built by Sharp Stewart, then of Manchester, in 1872.

Lartigue's monorail (p. 148) was incorporating an iron or steel trestle of triangular section with the running and traction rail on top and guide rails each side. It was demon-strated in Brussels, saw a very brief and unfortunate public service between Feurs and

Panissières in France, and was used from 1888 to 1924 for a light railway from Listowel to Ballybunion in south-western Ireland. Never a goldmine, it was finished by damage in the Irish Civil War, repair of which was beyond the little company's means, but it was the longest-running of any steam monorails, and people travelled from distant places to see it and to ride in its rattle-drumming, pannier shaped cars. The locomotives had twin boilers, each side of the engine on the top rail. There were odd disabilities. It was impossible to convey a single cow; there had to be another to balance her on the other side of the rail. One way was to borrow two calves and then send them back one-each-side.

In Belgium, Behr's monorail was demonstrated with such apparent success that a company was formed to build the Manchester and Liverpool Express Railway, and got its Act of Parliament in August, 1901. In Behr's system, the rail was trestled on the same triangular supports as in Lartigue's, but with more guide rails and much more substantial construction. It was to be worked by very large, very fast electric cars, providing a purely inter-city service with short intervals. The London and North Western, and other companies, were much agitated, but the investing public fought shy and the line never was built.

Louis Brennan demonstrated a pure monorail whereon motor cars, balanced by large gyroscopes, ran with double-flanged wheels on one ordinary steel rail laid on the ground, or even on a steel cable. The railed version greatly excited people at an exhibition in London, in 1910. A similar car was sponsored by the newspaper king August Scherl and built in Germany at this time. Many said that the steam railway was imminently doomed. But it had yet a long and honorable way to go!

Dr. Rudolf Diesel, 1858–1913, was the German engineer who invented the diesel engine. He had studied the steam engine and had found that much of its potential energy was not being converted into useful work. He invented an engine that would burn its fuel actually inside in the cylinder, igniting it by heat produced by air compression. He took out a patent on the engine in 1892. Its chief advantage is that it gets far more work out of its fuel than does the steam engine.

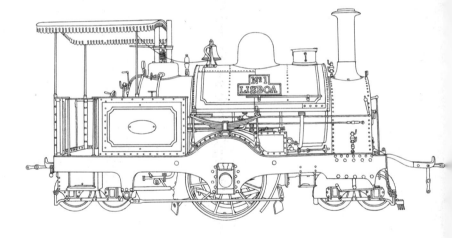

The Lisboa *was one of 15 single rail locomotives supplied by Sharp Stewart of Manchester, England to the Lisbon Tramway Company in 1872. It was a two-cylinder engine with two driving wheels on the road and two guiding wheels at each end which ran on the central rail. The wheel arrangement could thus be described as 1-1-2-1-1.*

The "Golden State" Diesel-electric engine in the Arizona Desert, passing Picacho Peak. Courtesy Standard Oil.

Chapter 7 THE TRAIN IN OUR TIME

On a steam engine the enginemen could be sure of one thing—by the end of the journey he was going to be dirty! What with the coal and the lubricating oil, his overalls were very necessary. The driver of the electric locomotive has no such problem, however. He will have as clean and comfortable a journey as the passengers, though not so relaxed. He has to keep his eye on more clock-faces and dials than did his steam-engine counterpart. He keeps in direct contact with the signal control centres by telephone. It is strange to think that developments in signalling may mean driverless locomotives in the future!

In the nineteen-twenties the railroads, as an industry, and the railway train as a machine, first really began to encounter that dire Nemesis which is the breaking of established monopoly. We have seen this already in respect of the steam locomotive, but from the nineteen-twenties onwards it was the train itself. Hitherto it had been the only important form of mechanical land transport over appreciable distance. Now the motor and the aeroplane, rapidly developed under urgent war economy, moved in. The commercial motor was something very different from the rich man's private car, just as, after a second great war, the air-liner of our time is a very different thing from the old Fokkers, Junkers and Handley-Pages of the 'twenties and early 'thirties. That the train has survived to this last, though by no means everywhere, is a token of its strong superiority for certain sorts of traffic.

Certain other sorts of traffic have simply vanished, most rapidly in wealthy or war-winning countries where there is the additional urge—psychological as much as big-businesslike—to scrap the old and get on with the new. The last of Europe's great railway companies—those which maintained a monopoly in the British Isles until 1947, and certain important undertakings in Sweden, showed wisdom when they sold out to Government, even under onerous terms imposed by Socialist Administrations. One recalls angry scenes at the last annual general meeting of the London Midland and Scottish Railway, and has heard Swedish remarks about the rape of the Bergslagernas Jarnvägar which, to the last, was *a rather good business.* But the United States of America had an armour-plated *credo,* that of free enterprise. It has resulted in our time in the persistence of company-owned railroads (or none) except in the new pioneer State of Alaska, and to achieve that business-happy object, many of the surviving railroad companies have been at great pains to shed their passenger traffic altogether. Not unreasonable, in some places! Even when we were in studenthood, an American fellow student (in Munich of all places) said then when he got home he was buying a *flivver,* which would solve all his own travel problems up to 400 miles, which to us meant the distance between London and Edinburgh. *Flivver* meant not a giant Cadillac; it meant Mr. Ford's T-Model. Germans had invented the motor car. Frenchmen made it great. Americans, already, were making it part of the American Way of Life. Later results are just beginning to be a shade ironical.

There is our background to the sober mechanical history which must now ensue!

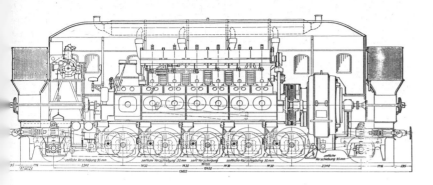

The I-E-I Diesel-electric locomotive built for the U.S.S.R. in 1924 at Esslingen, Germany.

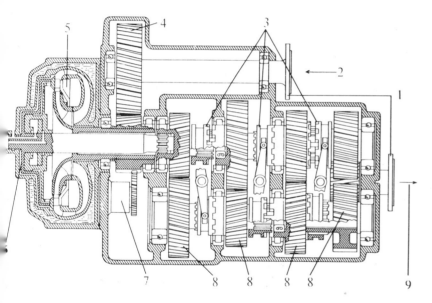

Longitudinal cutaway, of Mekydro mechanical-hydraulic torque converter, a mechanism used for transmitting Diesel engine power to wheels of locomotive.

1 Flange
2 From diesel engine power shaft
3 Clutches
4 Step-up gear
5 Hydraulic torque converter
6 Oil pressure cylinder
7 Oil pump
8 Sets of four-speed drive gears
9 To driving wheel axle

It is interesting that it was from Switzerland, home today of one of the most advanced railroad systems of the world, that we first heard—even in the nineteen-twenties—of what could only be called a sinister idea; that it would be a good thing to scrap the Swiss railway system (in the middle of Western Europe with all its international connections) and turn the old formations—yea, the great Gotthard itself—into motor roads. There were not many motors around then, but doubtless that could be remedied. The thing was that Switzerland's railroads were in a very bad way with an enormous deficit. The tourists had vanished in the war years, and of the surrounding countries, France and Italy were at war with Austria and Germany,   so there was nothing to be had from neighbours' misfortunes, as there would be in a later war when Germany and Italy were aligned. Further, it had been very difficult to get foreign fuel. Switzerland's only fuel was falling water. The only Swiss railroad using it on a grand scale was the Bern-Lötschberg-Simplon, financed largely in France.

The Federal Government of Switzerland wisely cancelled its railways' unpayable debt, having embarked on a national policy of railroad electrification. It was begun, and ultimately done. A time was to come when in all south-western Europe (after the next war) they would be the only major railway undertakings to remain (in bankers' language) viable. The idea of transport being a national service, as against a commercial undertaking, was little in countenance as yet save in newly-communist Russia and grandly-capitalist Switzerland.

There was the background. In the foreground of mechanical history of that period are the interesting facts that Switzerland, full of water-power, went for that with willing capital expenditure, while Russia, with much unrealised wealth of oil, put into service some of the very first heavy Diesel locomotives on her long-neglected and war-battered railways. The Russian essay was not to bear much fruit for a long time to come, and ironically the most important railways in the Soviet Union were ultimately to go electric. But in the Swiss company went Italy, France, Germany, Sweden and Austria, as rapidly as they could afford from the middle nineteen-twenties onwards.

The rest of the railroad world carried on, in general, with coal-fired steam, though Russia used oil-fired steam in many places, as she had been doing to a limited extent for a long time already. Finland managed uncommonly well on wood fuel for many of her trains. Fiji and some other places happily ran narrow-gauge steam on sugar-cane trash, which was not nearly so absurd a fuel as some people might imagine.

In 1925 the London and North Eastern Railway, as remarked earlier, celebrated a Railway Centenary by virtue of the Stockton and Darlington opening, and one of the events was a procession of locomotives and trains, ancient and contemporary. As we remember it, everything in that procession was steam-propelled except Stephenson's *Locomotion*, which had a petrol engine hidden in the tender and some old motor tyres acridly burning in the firebox for dramatic effect, and a petrol-electric railcar. A large North Eastern electric locomotive, built for a York-Newcastle scheme that to this day has never come off, was rather ignominiously towed past the stands by a little tank engine. It might be the afternoon of steam in those nineteen-twenties, but still it was Steam's Day!

Already, however, and quite long ago at that, Atlas of Stockholm and A.S.E.A. had produced the first Diesel-electric traction in the world, to which we will shortly come again, and by 1924, when Sweden had made twenty Diesel-electric railcars and twelve locomotives—mostly for narrow gauge—the rest of the world started to follow Sweden. The Hohenzollern Engine Works of Düsseldorf in Germany sponsored, while Esslingen actually built for Soviet Russia a most ambitious Diesel-electric locomotive to the designs of that great Russian Professor Lomonossof, already distinguished in steam, especially in the design of valves and front-end arrangement. A diagram best serves our purpose, showing the marine-type engine coupled to its generator, and the traction motors below, driving five independent axles. The electrical portion rather resembles that of the original New York Central design for working down into Manhattan after the famous "ultimatum" from the New York City Fathers, which banished steam early in the century.

In his conception of an electric locomotive carrying an oil-engine-powered generator on her back, Lomonossof was anticipating worldwide practice of much later years, and if it were for this alone, he has his place among the great mechanical pioneers, and this machine was, had people known for certain, an arch-prototype. But as yet the diesel remained for some time a rather frustrated newcomer in railroad motive power. Lomonossof himself inclined towards using mechanical transmission, exemplified in a locomotive built for Russia, again by Hohenzollern. (How odd, this association of a company associated with a scarcely liberal dynasty, doing business with a People's Commissariat of Ways and Communications! Still, history is full of such things.) The second Lomonossof-Hohenzollern Diesel locomotive for Russia was 2-E-1 with side-rod drive from a geared jackshaft driven by an eleven-hundred horsepower M.A.N. (Maschinenfabrik Augsburg-Nürnberg) Diesel engine. It was to be found—by the bitter way of trial-and-error—that mechanical transmission for railroad traction could not deal with the power-output of engines above 500 h.p.

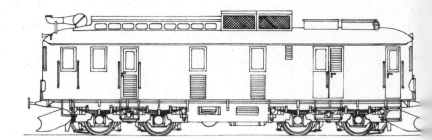

One thing was that the combination of electric locomotive with oil-engined generator was extremely expensive. People were trying to produce an oil-driven locomotive comparable to a steam locomotive—keeping separate things separate—and to this end some remarkable practical experiments were made, at immense cost. (We remember the M.A.N. company at this time earning its bread-and-butter with some admirable new tram-cars, notably for Munich.)

The Esslingen Engine Works, in collaboration with M.A.N., was working through the middle nineteen-twenties on a large oil-pneumatic locomotive which below platforms resembled a 4-6-4 or 2C2 steam locomotive with outside cylinders, piston valves and gear of the Heusinger family. Above and inside the all-over cab, a six-cylinder M.A.N. Diesel engine drove a compressor to provide "steam" (i.e. air) for these orthodox-looking "works". It was quite a courageous attempt, like an engine built in England by Kitsons of Leeds soon after, on the Still principle, in which, on starting, steam was on one side of the pistons and oil under compression-ignition on the other. The Still locomotive broke Kitsons!

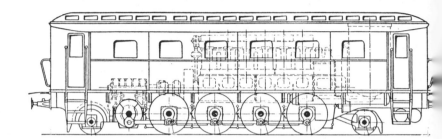

Transmission was ever the bugbear. Air under compression is a very hot motive agent. The idea of hydraulic transmission was still in a laboratory stage. But in those nineteen-twenties, people did not know that the Diesel locomotive would arrive with electrical transmission in heavy units, and mechanical in light switching and motor railcar applications. Sweden's pioneering has been noted, but we should add that Germany could claim a Diesel railcar as far back as 1914, for the Saxon State Railway. The experiment was squashed by the outbreak of World War I.

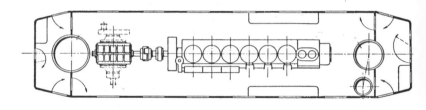

As remarked, Diesel-electric propulsion was in first cost quite damnably expensive. Who could know that in 1948, following the delays of war, there would be over 8,000 Diesel-electric locomotives in the United States, and in the summer of 1953 nearly 22,000! Back in the nineteen-twenties the work went quietly on in Central Europe, with many disappointments and little public awareness save one of frightful exhaust stinks when something was out on the road. We first encountered that *smell* in Denmark in 1929. There the great firms of Frichs at Aarhus, and Burmeister and Wain, both distinguished builders of marine engines, applied themselves most diligently to Diesel railway traction, as well they might in a country with neither native coal nor water power.

Even in Sweden, which had the latter, and had used Mather and Platt (English) electric cars on the little Djursholm line as far back as 1895, and a Swedish-built industrial electric locomotive in 1892, and was already embarking on a national policy of railway electrification on the State-owned main lines and on such company-owned enterprises as the Nordmark-Klarälven Railway, there were pioneering essays in Diesel locomotion. The example illustrated was built for Halmstad-Nässjö Railway, an entirely steam-worked cross-country line with no large cities on its route but considerable timber traffic. This company made notable experiments at private risk. Its locomotive No. 5 appeared early in 1928. Transmission was electric, as in the first Lomonossof locomotive. There was an eight-cylinder 200 h.p. engine working at 500 r.p.m. and the generator supplied two motors geared to the driving axles on a ratio of 19/77. Three of these very early Diesel-electric locomotives were built for the Halmstad-Nässjö company, which also had one small and two large railcars or motor vans. Engines were by Atlas of Stockholm and electrical equipment by A.S.E.A. It was a courageous essay for a modest undertaking in a country which, while she imported nearly all her mineral fuel, was rapidly developing her copious hydro-electric resources.

In the early nineteen-twenties the German firm of Linke-Hoffman-Lauchhammer was making practical experiments in hydraulic transmission between Diesel engine and locomotive driving axles, using the Lentz hydraulic coupling. A small switching engine on this principle worked for two-and-a-half years without trouble on the private line of the Linke-Hofmann company at Breslau. A much larger example was designed for experimental service on the German State Railway. But the day of large scale Diesel-hydraulic traction was not yet, by a long way. One should draw careful distinction

(above) This 200 HP Diesel-electric locomotive was built in 1928 for the Halmstad-Nässjö Railway in Sweden.

(below) The German State Railways Diesel-Hydraulic engine built by Linke-Hoffman.

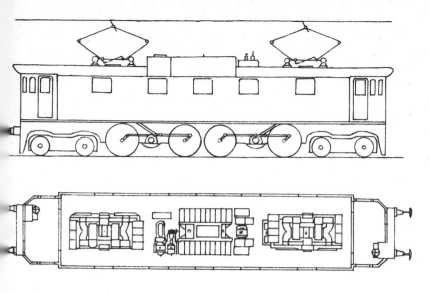

The Bavarian EP5

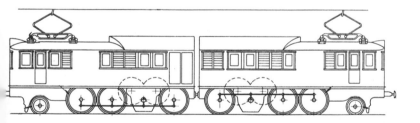

This Swedish State Railways I-CC-I was used for hauling ore-trains from Kiruna.

between hydrostatic and hydrokinetic transmissions. The former were used most notably by German makers in the nineteen-twenties. They gave trouble through the very high pressures imposed on the fluid, especially with larger engines. Voith's, in Germany in 1931, was the first practical hydrokinetic system, quickly followed by the Lysholm-Smith arrangement in Sweden. Nevertheless, in recent years both French and British makers have been using hydrostatic transmission for low-powered switching tractors, it having been revived in Italy in 1950 with the Swiss Hydro-Titan system, made possible by advances in the mechanical arts. Even the Diesel-electric locomotive was in its infancy, but we show the largest version of these early Diesel-hydraulic experiments for its historical interest. For what was then the present, Diesel traction was to be most imposing in small railcars and shunting "locomotors", not in heavy locomotive application.

Pending that, let us turn to straight electric traction, already tried and proved in countries rich in water power, and also in coal countries like metropolitan England, Saxony and the Eastern United States where heavy traffic density justified its use. Of the "water countries", Switzerland had become the classic land; in her neighbourhood, things were moving rather rapidly in South Germany, Austria and parts of France, while Italy had an expanding electric system in the North, on the 3,700 Volt three-phase system at $16\frac{2}{3}$ cycles which she had adopted rather precipitately. (One may fairly compare the price paid by the British railroad pioneers, who made their great tunnels too small!) Switzerland, Austria and Germany all standardized on 15,000 Volt single-phase at $16\frac{2}{3}$ cycles, as did the Swedish State Railways far to the North. France on the other hand, converting the Orleans and Midi main line systems from 1922 onwards, used 1,500 Volt direct current, which was to be widely extended, almost invariably with overhead contact as in the single-phase and three-phase networks of other countries, though there was some use of third-rail contact on the P.L.M. Alpine line between Culoz and Modane (1930–33). By 1939 most of the Alpine lands were served by electric railways which stretched in unbroken sequence from the Danube to the Tiber. By the way, on that interesting hike, one saw still plenty of steam though precious little Diesel. It was one of the most pleasant stages in European railroad travel, unless one were a political fugitive.

There was much electrification in Sweden, some in Northern Spain, and little in Eastern Europe apart from Hungary. In England it was immense already in the southern counties and the commuter-lands, but negligible elsewhere. In the Southern Hemisphere was a curious reflection of England, whether in South America or in Australia and New Zealand. Australia possessed in Flinders Street, Melbourne, the busiest railway terminal in the world (it was not an actual terminus) but there was not an electric long-distance train in all the continent. New Zealand had indeed what we may call an Alpine electric line, through the great Otira Tunnel, the Central Railway of Brazil had electrified, and Chile had electrified her Andean approach.

In North America, the United States certainly showed imposing mileage of route, but still proportionately small, with isolated networks in the Eastern States, of which the Pennsylvania company's was incomparably the finest, and the mountain lines of the Milwaukee and the Great Northern companies. To most Americans in the 'thirties, the term "electric railway" meant an interurban line, then still widespread, if not entirely flourishing.

As to the electric locomotives, there was marked variety, much more than in steam during the corresponding years of last century. American specimens, like the steam they had supplanted in certain areas, were often enormous. The Milwaukee company favoured very large gearless machines on its Mountain Division, and staged a priceless piece of practical publicity by making two heavy-freight steam locomotives push one, first "dead" and then with regenerative braking which brought them to a protesting stand. Power was then reversed, and the single electric engine pushed the slipping steamers back.

At first, the Pennsylvania company favoured huge low-speed motors with jackshaft drive to coupled wheels, as did the Alpine countries in Europe. An early Pennsylvania class (DD 1) was arranged 2-B-B-2, and mechanically rather anticipated a design classified EP 5 on the Bavarian network of German State Railways, built in 1925.

In other respects there was much difference. The Pennsylvania type dated back to 1910, the year of the company's Manhattan line, which included the great marmorate Pennsylvania Station, and like the rival New York Central Lines in New York City was run on direct current at 650 Volts. It was, in Scots phraseology, *no mean locomotive* of its time. The coupled wheels were 6 ft. in diameter, fully in the American fast-passenger-

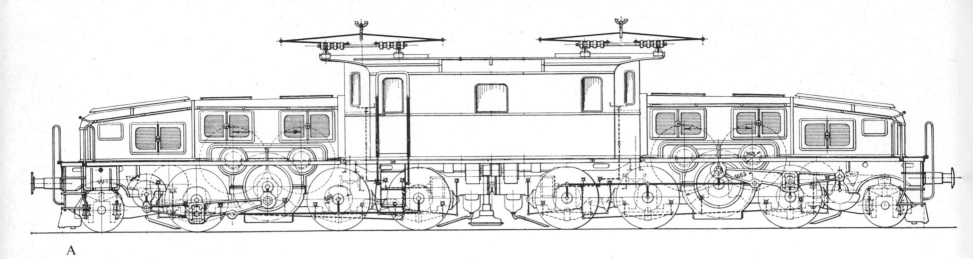

A

steam tradition, though no great speeds were attempted between Manhattan Transfer and Sunnyside, the limits of the company's New York electrified route at that time, in New Jersey and on Long Island N.Y. respectively. The two huge Westinghouse low-speed motors developed a rated maximum of 4,000 horsepower between them, giving the locomotive a tractive effort, on starting, equal to 66,000 lb.

The Bavarian EP 5, sixteen years later, was modestly rated as a *Personenzugsloko-motive,* which could and did mean haulage of ordinary hard stopping trains from Munich to Regensburg, but from 1926 we remember them with affection as well as appreciation on the night expresses and others to the North over the same route. These German lines, as remarked, ran on 15,000 Volts, $16\frac{2}{3}$ cycles.

Ere that, Switzerland and Austria, especially the former, were making tremendous use of the low-speed-motor, jackshaft-and-side-rod electric locomotive on the same system. The great firm of Brown-Boveri in Switzerland was making the electrical equipment for both, which included the famous "Crocodiles"—long articulated electric engines. 1-C+C-1, with the cab-part pivoted on the two motive units. The same wheel arrangement was used by Sweden and Norway for the great ore trains in Lapland, though these rather amounted to twin locomotives coupled tail-to-tail, like the earliest Milwaukee type. Ultimately both expanded to triple-unit form.

Much more modest-looking machines were fully capable of handling ordinary traffic, with the gear ratios varied for fast passenger or freight traffic, e.g. that Swedish State Class D, first built for the Stockholm-Gothenburg service in 1925 and still to be seen half a century later.

There were several varieties of the 2-6-2 or 1-C-1 electric locomotive, with jackshaft or yoke drive, in Europe during these years. Switzerland (on a small scale) and Italy both used it. The wheel arrangement itself was yet popular in certain countries for steam locomotives subject to the use of bogies of Helmholtz, Deichsel, or kindred types involving the leading or end coupled axles. Omission of this in favour of Bissel radial trucks had been the undoing of the American steam Prairie type which, in the earliest days of that celebrated train, the Twentieth Century Limited, had worked it into and out of Chicago on the old Lake Shore and Michigan Southern line.

Generally, large electric locomotives mounted more driving axles than three. Also in the early nineteen-twenties, the Swiss Federal Railways produced, instead of their initial side-rod types, geared electric engines, still with large driving wheels and the motors above. Buchli's great gears were on one side only, so that the outline was elegant on the other side and lumpish on this, but it answered very well for many years, first in a 2-C-1 and soon after in a 2-D-1 arrangement.

But at this time, the whole business of electric locomotive transmission was in a state of flux. Side-rod drive through jack-shaft was essentially steam-inspired; indeed it went back to early patents of T. R. Crampton in England (where incidentally it never was used with electric traction). There was, however, a new form of power transmission between

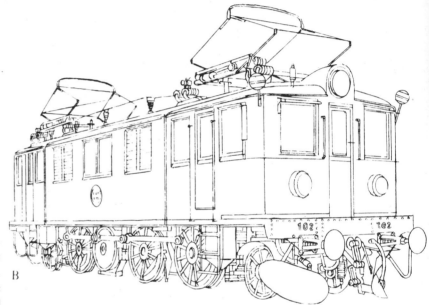

B

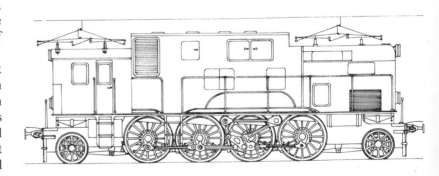

C

A   *The articulated electric locomotive belonging to the Swiss Federal Railways. It was known at the "crocodile" and had a maximum speed of 65 km/hr.*

B   *The Swedish State Railways Class D electric locomotive has* *been built in greater numbers than any other Swedish locomotive type. It has been used for both passenger and goods trains and is still in use.*

C   *The Austrian I-D-I electric locomotive.*

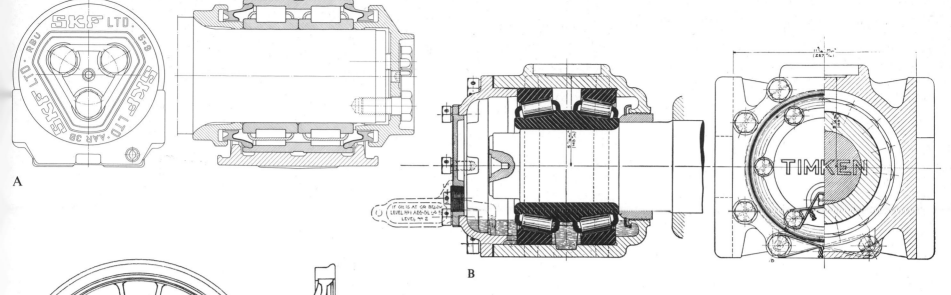

A

B

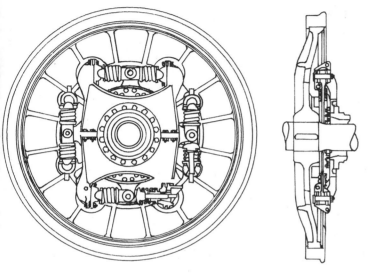

C

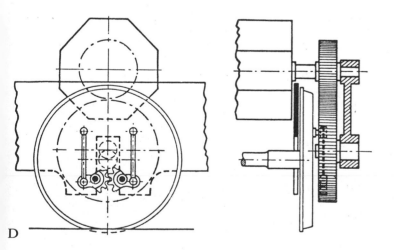

D

A   The SKF railway bearing unit,
    RBU was designed in the late
    1950s and is now used all over
    the world.

B   The Timken bearing is in much
    use in America.

C   The quill drive arrangement

D   The Buchli drive

electric motor and driving wheels, known in English as quill-drive. That is an etymological curiosity worth noticing for its own sake! The critical word is the German *Feder*, which means at once a feather, a quill or any other pen, and a spring. In primitive language, quill-drive means the bearing of sprung members on the substantial spokes of locomotive driving wheels, giving a cushion effect.

For an early example of this we show (p. 218) a design of the French Southern (Midi) Railway based on a previous one of 1923 (two engines arranged 2-Co-2) the cypher after the C for three driving axles indicating that they are uncoupled.) During 1922–23, French engineers in particular had been considering the mounting of motors with their armatures and driving shafts vertical, driving through bevel gears. These Midi locomotives were the practical outcome. In the diagram of the quill-driven wheel will be seen a roller bearing. Ball-bearings and roller bearings were an early contribution to mechanical engineering, though like all such, they had a hard way to go through both prejudice and the accidents of early application. They had indeed to wait for the advance of metallurgical methods in tail—not in advance—of mechanical ingenuity. As far back as the early eighteen-sixties, a train on roller bearings ran in fast passenger service on the Great Eastern Railway in England—for what seems to have been a very little while—for the experiment was not repeated for many years. The bold spirit behind it had been that of Robert Sinclair, another of the cosmopolitans. He was Scots; he had been works manager to Allcard and Buddicom in France: he became chief engineer to the Great Eastern company in England; he ended his days at a great age in Florence, steeped in Italian poetry; indeed a character! Ball- and roller-bearings were late in coming to railroad traction. Great names in the ultimate years of their success were those of S.K.F. (Swedish) and Timken (American). A century ago, the idea was good but the material inadequate.

Reverting to the Midi designs, these were of marked elegance, in terms of the functional line, as were much more famous and more advanced French electric locomotives of later years. They had splendid symmetry, which was more than could be said for some electric locomotives of the period. Types with a single cab at one end were the worst in these respects. The arrangement was all right for steam, to which it *fitted*, but what once was called the double-ended locomotive, were it straight electric or oil-electric, there were only two satisfactory cab arrangements. There was the central cab, with bonnets fore and aft (known in America as "steeple-cab" and in England, which used it a little in the North-East and more briefly in the north of London, as "camel-back", which meant something quite different in America). The other arrangement entailed having a cab at each end, with duplicated controls, and is today the commonest for large electric locomotives. For an example of the cab-on-end electric locomotive we show a 1-D-1 design for Austria, with somewhat ingenious rod-coupling to two large motors, from 1924. The leading and trailing carrying axles were radial, their suspension equalised with that of the adjacent coupled wheels.

East Africa, by Hamilton Ellis. Drawings cannot fully convey the aspect of a Beyer-Garratt articulated steam locomotive. This one heads a freight train from Mombasa, high up on the Kenya Plateau. The great Garrat double locomotive became the typical engine of East and South African railways over more than a quarter of a century. Courtesy of the Locomotive and Allied Manufacturers' Association, London.

BROWN-BOVERI AND COMPANY BUILT THIS ELECTRIC LOCOMOTIVE FOR THE BURGDORF–THUN RAILWAY IN SWITZERLAND IN 1899.

THE 2-8-2 MIKADO TYPE PASSENGER LOCOMOTIVE, TYPE 5, WAS BUILT FOR THE BELGIAN NATIONAL RAILWAYS AND WAS EUROPE'S MOST POWERFUL PASSENGER TYPE OF ITS TIME.

Bavarian S 3/6

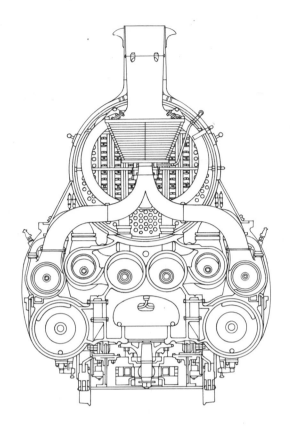

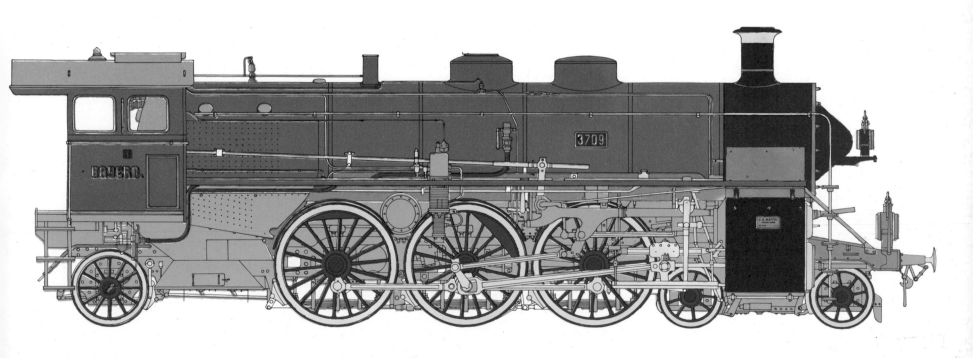

J. A. MAFFEI BUILT THIS EXPRESS 4-6-2 STEAM LOCOMOTIVE IN 1923 FOR THE BAVARIAN STATE RAILWAYS.

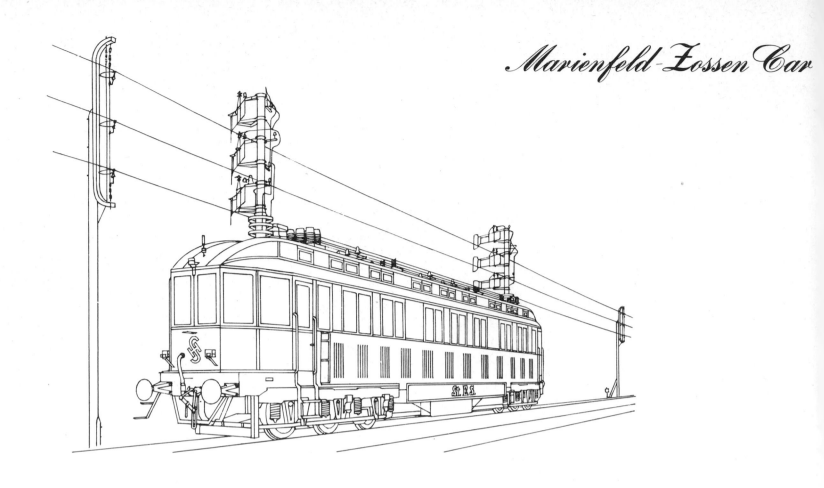

IN 1903, ON THE MARIENFELD–ZOSSEN LINE IN GERMANY, AN EXPERIMENTAL ELECTRIC MOTOR CAR SET UP A RAIL SPEED RECORD OF 130 M.P.H.

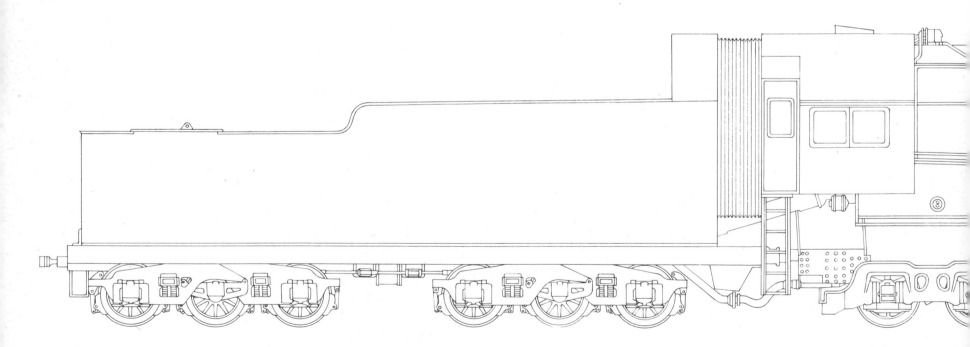

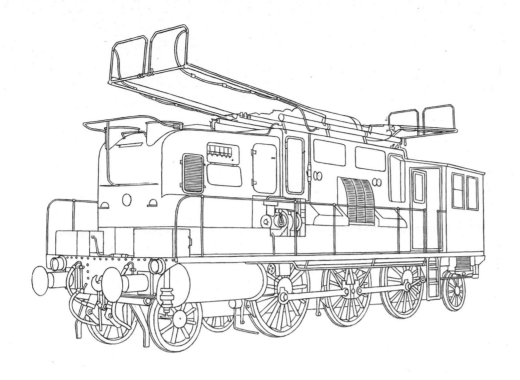

Italian State E333

THIS I-C-I ELECTRIC LOCOMOTIVE WAS BUILT IN ITALY IN 1922.

Russian Giant

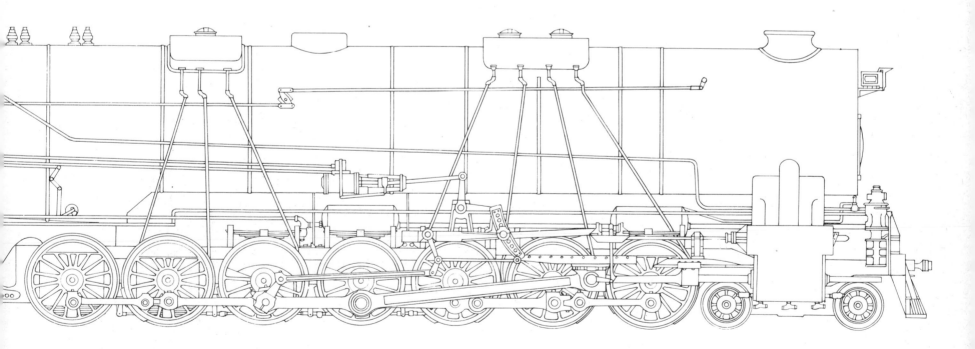

IN 1934, THE RUSSIAN RAILWAYS BUILT THIS STUPENDOUS 4-14-4 STEAM LOCOMOTIVE AT THE VOROSHILOVGRAD WORKS, FOR COAL HAULAGE ON THE DONETZ–MOSCOW LINE. IT WAS UNSUCCESSFUL.

NO. 471 WAS BUILT FOR THE LONDON AND SOUTH WESTERN RAILWAY IN 1884. WILLIAM ADAMS DESIGNED IT.

City of Truro

THE **CITY OF TRURO** WAS BUILT FOR THE GREAT WESTERN RAILWAY IN 1903. WILLIAM DEAN WAS THE DESIGNER.

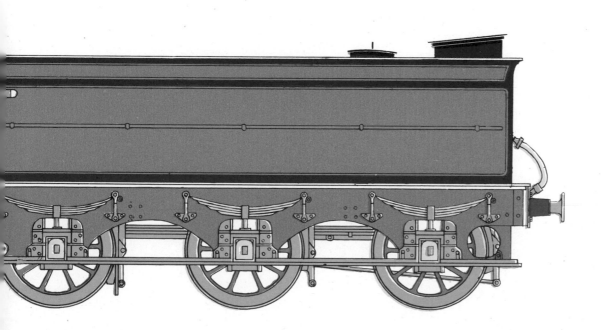

Henry's Windcutter

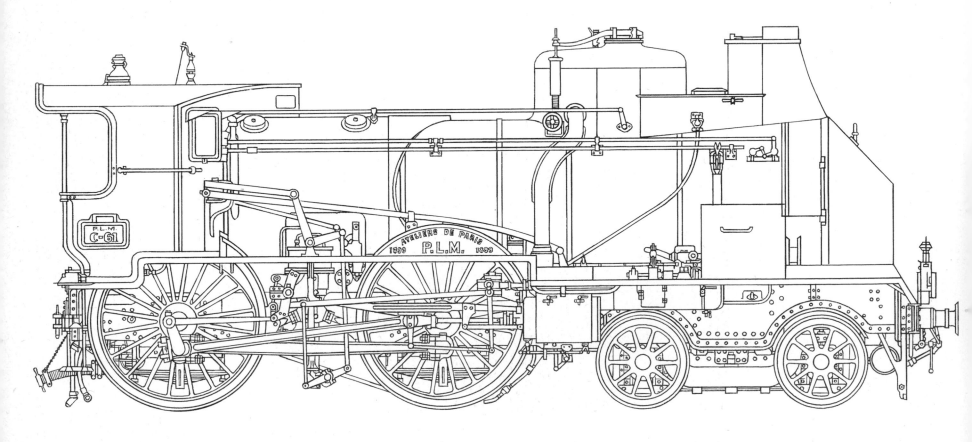

HENRY'S 4-4-0 FAST PASSENGER ENGINE WAS BUILT FOR THE PARIS, LYONS AND MEDITERRANEAN RAILWAY IN 1899.

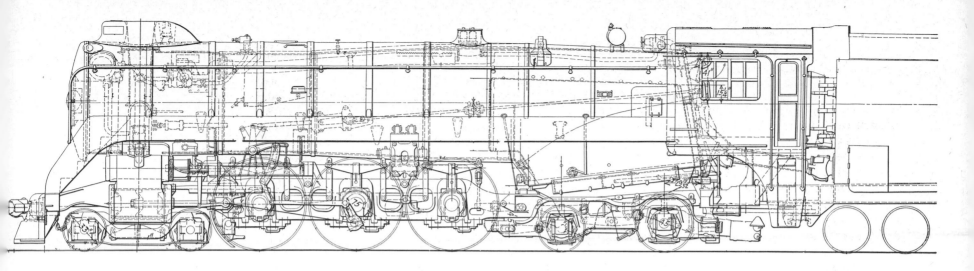

THE HUDSON AND MOUNTAIN TYPES

At this stage, direct steam traction was very far from dead; indeed, it was kicking as well as alive. On some lines in the United States, the revered Pacific was being elongated into both the Hudson (4-6-4) and Mountain (4-8-2) types. The former had originated in two experimental locomotives by Gaston du Bousquet for the Northern Railway of France, back in 1910. They were intended for the Nord Express between France and Northern Europe. Their designer consequently named the type Baltic. It differed from the later American Hudson in having bogies at both ends, for the Hudson had a radial truck at the rear. This distinction seems not to have been noted in English-speaking countries.

As for the 4-8-2 engine, it had made several appearances in North America by the nineteen-twenties. Taking the Pennsylvania Railroad for once in a while on its own evaluation—*the Standard Railroad of the World*—we may remark that it had its first Mountain type in 1923, (Class M 1) built at Altoona under J. T. Wallis, and that following practical experiments with this, a modified design was worked out and 200 were ordered, 175 from Baldwins and the rest from Lima Locomotive Works, for heavy passenger and fast freight haulage, notably over the Allegheny Mountains between Altoona and Pittsburgh. True to Pennsylvania practice, a firebox of Belpaire type was used, but with a great combustion chamber extending over eight feet into the barrel (an old arrangement, justified by the extra value of firebox-heating surface, but rarely carried out on this scale). Again true to Pennsylvania tradition, the engines had very handsome lines. Dimensionally they were scarcely bantam-weights. The working pressure was 250 lb. per sq. in.; the cylinders (two) were 27 in. diameter with a 30 in. stroke, the distribution was by 12 in. piston valves, the boiler had 6,332 sq. ft. of combined heating surface, and the engine weighed 382,400 lb. without the tender, which came to 217,900 lb., in working order. In 1930 the company built twenty-five at Altoona, with fifty more by Baldwin and twenty-five by Lima (Class M 1a). We are not giving much of dimensions in this chronicle; those must serve as a sample of the big orthodox-type steam locomotive in North America in the nineteen-twenties.

Also in 1923, Canadian National Railways produced a very comparable Mountain type engine, and likewise based later standard designs on this. Canadian locomotive design continued to follow United States practice very closely, though not utterly, and the standard Canadian National "Mountains" appeared in 1929 for the Winnipeg-Edmonton run. In 1925 the type made its appearance on European main lines, on the Eastern Railway of France, which was followed by the Paris, Lyons and Mediterranean Railway. The type name was preserved. It was *Le Mountain* (not, observe, *Montagne*!). The name, like Hudson, remained American. French railways made famous use of the type on certain lines, and so did Czecho-Slovakia and Spain, though the latter greatly favoured the 4-8-0 type, long discarded by the Americans but introduced to the Northern Railway of Spain by the Yorkshire Engine Company in England. The type was very

The Canadian National Railways 4-6-4 Hudson

successfully used by the Hungarian State Railways for more than forty years. Ex-Hungarian examples went to North Korea to replace ravaged machinery after that recent war. Their "day" in Hungary was broadly from 1924 to 1964. British railways however were to make little use of eight coupled wheels for fast passenger traffic, rather favouring, on the two big northern lines into Scotland, the modestly stately Pacific. Austria reversed the Mountain arrangement into the 2-8-4, an enlarged version of the late Gölsdorf 2-6-4 type. The thing was that passenger trains were becoming yet heavier, though not much faster.

In the depression years of 1929–32, some long-distance American trains were combined into enormous loads while others, less fortunate, were withdrawn.

Weimar-Republican Germany had, during the nineteen-twenties, the largest national railway mileage in the world after the United States and worked a great part of it with our old friends the P 8 and with eight- or ten-coupled freight engines, though for fast passenger traffic in the South there were the beautiful Pacifics of Munich and Esslingen, with larger versions being built in the North by such firms as Borsig of Berlin, and Henschel of Kassel. These also produced from 1924 2-8-2 locomotives for all sorts of trains, from the rather leisurely German *Schnellzug* of that time to fast freight, with heavy ordinary passenger service in between. Previously, the Saxon State Railways had built the first 2-8-2 express engines with really large coupled wheels, as in a Pacific. The English would have called the Reichsbahn type mixed-traffic engines, though this had nothing to do with that picturesquely awful thing the Spaniards called, in the way of trains, a *mixto*. (It generally meant a few old third-class carriages at the end of a cara-van of local freight.)

For an example of a European 2-8-2 steam locomotive we give (p. 194) a remarkable engine which we first encountered at Liége in 1930. It was a design made for the old Luxemburg line—121 miles long from Brussels to Arlon with a ruling gradient of 1 in 62 —and was for express passenger service, to succeed the Flamme Pacifics. F. C. V. Legein, Flamme's successor, was the designer, and he used the American bar frames and Alco type piston valves while retaining many traditional Belgian features. The great firebox had four arch tubes (water-tubes supporting the brick arch) and the boiler carried a work-ing pressure of 200 lb. per sq. in., which might have been made higher. Even so, the new Belgian Type 5 was the most powerful passenger type in Europe at the time. It was a simple engine with two $28\frac{3}{4}$ in. by $28\frac{3}{8}$ in. cylinders (thus exactly square in longitudinal sec-tion). Styling was classic Belgian, which meant that it stemmed from that of Belpaire, though the design did not have his flat-crown firebox, such as the Pennsylvania in America and the Great Western in England so faithfully retained.

The 2-8-2 type for fast passenger work was used in various other European countries, notably in Italy and in Scotland, but many stuck faithfully to the Pacific, while America was going on to the 4-8-4 which first appeared late in 1926 on the Northern Pacific Railway. This type had many local names. We will consider two less familiar examples from the then very prosperous British steam locomotive industry; a broad-gauge (5 ft. 6 in.) Pacific by Armstrong-Whitworth for the Central Argentine Railway and a 4-8-4 for the Chinese National Railways by the venerable Vulcan Foundry (now part of the great English Electric organisation). This fine Argentine locomotive was notable, among many down the years, for her classic British lines in American proportions and on broad gauge (5 ft. 6 in.). She had three simple-expansion cylinders $19\frac{1}{2}$ in. by 26 in., $74\frac{1}{2}$ in. driving wheels and a working pressure of 225 lb. per sq. in. The Vulcan Foundry engine for China was not, for all her myriapod aspect, an absolute giant of the American sort, but she exemplified a fine combination of adequate power with remarkably low axle-weights. Her contours, to be sure, were tremendous. In China, as in Russia and the Americas, there was plenty of room to build locomotives upwards and outwards. In England, the problem was that of getting them to the docks for shipment. They could not go by rail in such sizes as these. Terrified motorists sometimes encountered them, at strange hours, on vast, crawling motor carriers. Armstrong-Whitworth was fortunately close to the river, but Vulcan Foundry was not.

In North America, the 4-8-4 was being used more and more for freight and certain heavy passenger service. Over the Rockies, the great Canadian Pacific Railway was using the 2-10-4 to hoist the great transcontinental trains up that tremendous climb known so modestly as Field Hill. (Understatement is a Scots habit, and the Scots pioneered those parts. At home they still describe a gale as being "breezy".)

At this time there was much fast running in few places, which sounds Irish but in fact

Broad-gauge Pacific locomotive for the Central Argentine Railway

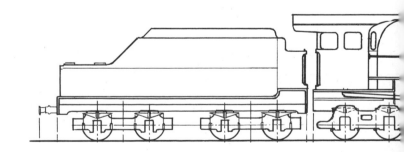

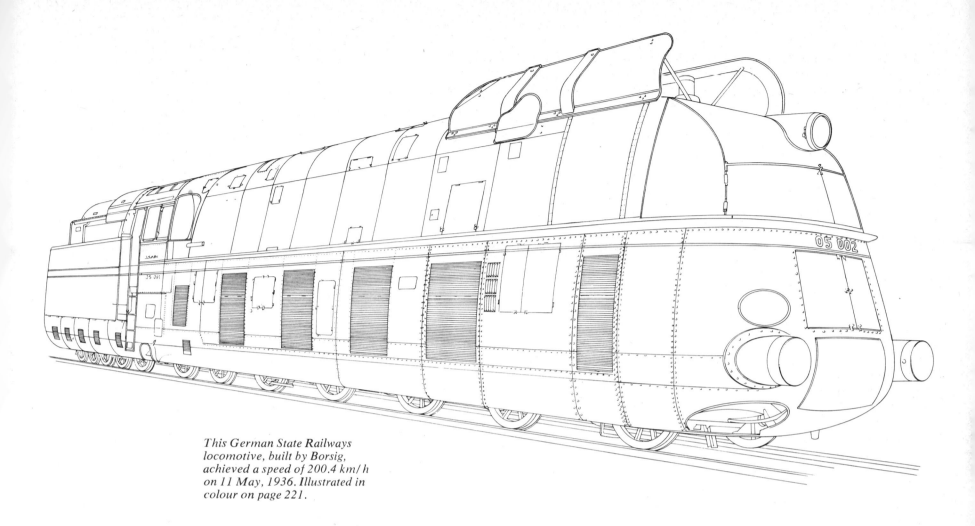

This German State Railways locomotive, built by Borsig, achieved a speed of 200.4 km/h on 11 May, 1936. Illustrated in colour on page 221.

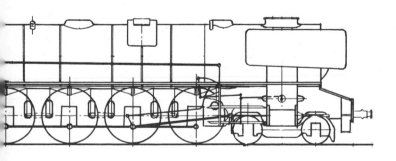

A 4-8-4 steam freight locomotive for the Spanish National Railways

means very good passenger speeds on railroads one could pinpoint on the globe, such as the Northern of France, the Great Western of England and a few railroads in the Eastern United States. The British had long had a weakness for very long runs without stops, and England for many years had had the longest non-stop run in the world, from London to Plymouth (225¾ miles in four hours). In 1928 the London and North Eastern railway announced that it would run from London to Edinburgh without any intermediate stop, and it built corridor tenders for Nigel Gresley's elegant three-cylinder Pacific engines which it had built over the past six years, so that relief enginemen could come through from a reserved compartment halfway between the two capital cities. (This would be at Alne, near York.) The distance via the East Coast route was just over 390 miles. Those were the days when railway companies still competed up and down Britannia's jimp waist, and the London Midland and Scottish Railway on the West Coast side got in first, without warning, by running from London to Edinburgh without a stop, with four men on the engine, which was a modest three-cylinder compound 4-4-0 type heading six light (but quite civilized) wooden coaches. That was on April 27, 1928, and although it were a most unbusinesslike piece of fooling, the British public briefly loved it. In certain countries there was ever a sporting element in railroad operation, though it was not often officially recognized. Two successive kings of Bulgaria loved to drive loco-motives and did so whenever they could. Then there was the Duke of Zaragoza who liked to drive the Spanish royal train, and who once bawled at the King, across a waste of dun-coloured frontier platform: "Buck up, Alfonso! We'll never be away on time!" The Duke still held his official certificate over twenty years after, and sometimes drove between San Sebastian and Hendaya when in his middle seventies. *Muy hombre!*

In those still heroic days of steam—in the nineteen-thirties—the Diesel was creeping up where electric traction hesitated. It was rapidly worming itself a long way from its first commercial railway service, which had been scarcely noticed at the time, on the little Södermanland Midland Railway, Sweden, in 1912, when Atlas of Stockholm and

A.S.E.A. produced a modest but workable oil-electric rail-car; a genuine Swedish "first". Things which happened thereafter we have already noted. It was not in Germany, or Russia, or Scandinavia that the Diesel really arrived. It was in the United States. The Americans went at first for the Swedish rail-motor-car idea, rather than the German and Russian heavy-locomotive one, and, being Americans, went for bigger and brighter Diesel-electric rail-cars, or rather sets of light-weight motor and trailer cars for limited inter-city passenger service at very high speeds. Here indeed was a complete reversal of American railroading tradition which had been to make trains as massive and heavy as possible with the idea that this safeguarded life in a wreck and consequently inspired customers' confidence. Light stainless steel and alloys where once cars had been like cruisers and locomotives like battleships! One notes the impact of motor practice.

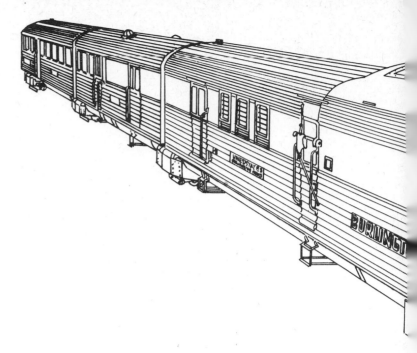

One of the famous Burlington Zephyrs

Notable pioneers were the Union Pacific Railroad, the Burlington and the Rock Island companies, all shrewd Middle-Western corporations which already had some idea of retaining passengers which the Eastern railroads were losing heavily to the automobile. The Union Pacific's pioneer train, later called *City of Salina* and ultimately broken up without regret like any other old car, appeared in 1933. It had a rated maximum speed of 110 miles an hour and could maintain an average of ninety. It had three car bodies having all-up weight comparable to that of one heavy Pullman car, the leading one containing the engine and transmission to a single motor bogie and mounting large radiator grilles below the engineer's cab. The three bodies were articulated over intermediate trucks in the style of the Gresley and Jakobs bogies of England and Germany respectively, whereof the former went back to 1907. (No slur is implied; it was a most ingenious arrangement.) Contemporary, or nearly so, were the Zephyrs of the Burlington company and a little later came the Rock Island Rockets.

On May 26, 1934, the first of the Burlington Zephyrs ran from Denver to Chicago at an average speed of 77·6 miles an hour throughout the 1,017 miles. Late in October, the Union Pacific train averaged 92·1 miles an hour over the 129 miles from North Platte to Alda, with a maximum of 120 and a pass-to-pass speed of 102·8 over sixty miles. Endurance was an even more important thing than spectacular bursts. In the same month, on a demonstration run, the 3,248 miles from Los Angeles to New York were covered, without trouble, in 56 hours 55 minutes.

In Europe as early as 1930, Germany was experimenting with Maybach 410 b.h.p. engines for fast rail propulsion, and out of these experiments emerged the two-body unit called the Flying Hamburger, between Hamburg and Berlin. The Germans had already established a world rail-speed record (maximum 143 miles an hour for 6¼ miles between Karstadt and Dergenthin) with a very light four-wheel car 95 ft. long powered by an aero-engine with a four-blade screw, but this was scarcely practical railroading.

The Flying Hamburger *was* so. Through the winter of 1932–3 it was covering the 178·1 miles between the cities, which included marked restrictions at each end and a very severe one through Wittenberge, in 138 minutes westbound and 140 minutes eastbound. It provided, of course, a supplement-charging business service, on second-class plush, which was equivalent to a chair-car in the States. In the matter of high-speed railcar pioneering, one should recall an idea put forward by our learned collaborator Gustavo Reder, then with "Eva" (Eisenbahn-Verkehrsmittel-Anstalt) for incorporating the Maybach Diesel engine then being made for Zeppelin airships. Such a railcar was built after Reder's return to Spain, and was shown at the Seddin Railway Exhibition in 1924, a most noteworthy pointer to the Flying Hamburger which was to come later.

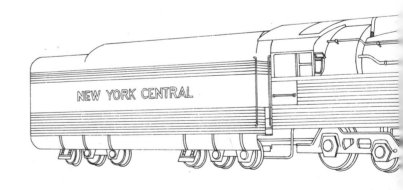

The 4-6-4 Hudson was first built in 1927 for the New York Central Railroad. This example was especially streamlined to pull the Empire State Express in 1941.

There were many experiments during the nineteen-thirties with light-weight or railcar-type trains. Bugatti of motor-racing fame made a type of railcar, on two four-axle bogies, driven from a conning tower in the middle of the roof, and demonstrated them in France from 1935 onwards, when one averaged 87·6 miles an hour over the 219 miles from Paris to Nancy. Subsequently a Bugatti car touched a maximum of 115·5 miles an hour near Le Mans. Light electric multiple units were in the running too. On July 20, 1939, an Italian State Railways three-car unit, on the 3,000 Volt d.c. system, ran from Florence to Milan, 195·8 miles via the Appenine Tunnel, at 102 miles an hour start-to-stop with a maximum of 126. (The Italian State Railways rather craftily *stepped-up the juice* that day, from 3,000 Volts to 4,000 Volts!) A month before, on June 23, a German railcar train of the improved Flying Hamburger type hit a maximum speed of 133½ miles an hour.

These speeds attracted relatively little attention outside railroading circles, for they were far outstripped in common opinion by those of racing motor-cars. The world's

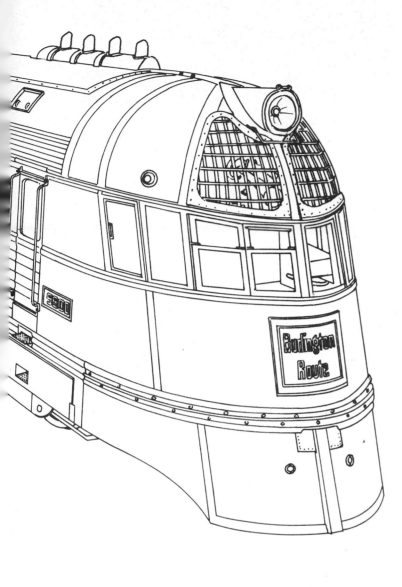

land-speed record had passed from the train to the motor as far back as 1909 when Hemery, driving a Benz, touched 125·95 at Brooklands in England. A reputed 127·1 miles an hour by Pennsylvania Atlantic type locomotive No. 7002 still lacks absolute authentication, and Mariott's 127·66 with a Stanley steam motor-car at Daytona in 1906, though vouched for by the Automobile Association of America, was not ratified in European motor-racing circles. But thereafter, land-speed records remained with the motor-car, challenged only by rocket-propelled sledges and things, which to be sure are "rail" of a sort. What is important is that in land transport, as opposed to land sport, the train has ever held its own.

For all these high jinks with railcars, the orthodox, relatively heavy train was not to be left behind. About 1933–34, Nigel Gresley, Chief Mechanical Engineer of the London and North Eastern Railway, contemplated something on the Flying Hamburger model for the London-Newcastle business service. But Gresley was a conservative man whose aristocracy was venerable. (A Normandy Gresley had truly fought the English at Hastings in 1066, and so the Gresleys had become Englishmen!) This Gresley consulted with one of his younger colleagues, Oliver Bulleid, a New Zealander, who except in his politics was distinctly un-conservative. It was decided that steam could do the job, with a train adequate but of strictly limited weight, carrying first- and third-class passengers in remarkable comfort. Dimensions of the already standard three cylinder Gresley Pacific engine were modified to this end: (Less on the cylinders put the pressure up to 250 lb. per sq. in. The drivers were 80 in.) Oscar Tietgens in America and Dendy Marshall in England had for some time tried to give academic demonstration of the aerodynamics of heavy railroad equipment at high speed. Racing motor designers had long since taken up these things. Germany was already carrying out the stream-lining of steam locomotives, but Gresley did not look to Germany. Bulleid is believed to have suggested the use of an aerofoil shape in the design of steam locomotives outside casing: anyway, Gresley carried it out. With the engine went a light train, weighing just under 220 tons behind the tender but seating seventy-eight first-class and 128 third-class passengers, with a kitchen unit in the middle. The object was to run a four-hour schedule over 268·3 miles. It was kept with ease, but we recall a more rip-roaring journey than this stately progress at 67 miles an hour start-to-stop, with maxima about 90, and that was the Press run on September 27, when we were above the hundred mark for twenty-five miles, averaging 107·5 pass-to-pass with a maximum of 112·5. It had been a straight trial to see what the engine would do, with a view to its availability in general service. For seventy miles the average had been 91·8, compared with 89·9 with the Milwaukee company's 4-6-4 engine No. 6402 (Class F 6) for 68·7 miles between Mayfair and Lake, on a run from Chicago to Milwaukee, eighty-five miles, in 67 min. 35 sec. The English run had been rather longer, rather more than 105 miles, and more undulating. Power-to-weight proportions had been fairly comparable. The American engine weighed 292 tons with her tender and hauled 380 tons behind that. The English engine and tender weighed only 165·5 tons and the cars 230 (with passengers).

For in America too, steam was fighting a doughty action agains the upstart oil engine, even though, as some party said at the time, the American rail-roads were selling out to General Motors. *Certes*, G.M. established what it called its Electro-Motive Division, making very large Diesel-electric locomotives! The Chicago, Milwaukee, St. Paul and Pacific Railroad certainly aimed at fast passenger haulage by steam; at first with a very advanced Atlantic type of locomotive covered with an air-smoothed rather than a truly streamlined casing, and then with the magnificent Hudsons (Class F 7, streamlined, built in 1938). The train was called *Hiawatha*, after that noble, mythical, honorable red man immortalized in English verse by that most nice Yankee Henry Wadsworth Longfellow. *Hiawatha's* cars also looked very nice in the bright yellow and red which the Milwaukee company laudably perpetuated for many years in a generally drab world.

Those old Eastern stalwarts, the New York Central and the Pennsylvania companies, likewise stuck to steam most bravely for as long as they could in a country becoming dominated by its oil and motor kings, and so, north of New Haven, did their modest companion the New York, New Haven and Hartford Railroad, serving the New York—Boston fast trains with singularly handsome, as well as effective, streamlined Hudson type steam locomotives. There was much of what we must call phoney-streamlining about at this time, based on ever-vulgar fashion and not on wind-tunnel tests, but the motor-car suffered most. The theory of streamlines was best expressed by a seventeenth-century

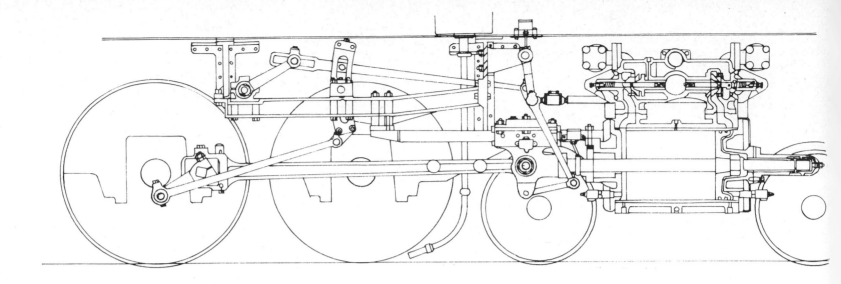

shipbuilder who said that his craft, below the waterline, should have the head of a cod-fish and the tail of a mackerel.

In the steam locomotive, as in other engines then, since and henceforward, quite a lot of the streamlining was internal, as in steam and exhaust passages and, for that matter, in our own internal organs. The high spots of speed with entirely orthodox, streamlined, steam locomotives were achieved by two engines, English and German respectively. One of Gresley's, the *Mallard*, which had been modified as to the front end with the French Kylchap exhaust arrangements, having a double chimney, attained 125 miles an hour during brake tests on July 3, 1938, with a very brief burst at 126 on the dynamometer-car's chart. In May, 1936, one of three experimental Hudson-type German locomotives (Reichsbahn Series 05) had shown 124·5 on the dynamometer chart. These fireworks were the high rockets of the steam reciprocating locomotive. The British *Mallard* and the German 05·001 are preserved at Clapham and Nuremberg respectively for those who knew and loved the prime of steam and for those who will have never known it. The German "O-Fives" lasted in service until 1958; the British engines, forming a larger class, worked into the middle-nineteen-sixties on Scottish services.

The Kylchap blast-pipe, noted previously, combined features of the Chapelon arrangement in France and of Finland's Kylälä blast-pipe, hence its name. It incorporated four nozzles or jets, usually paired below a double chimney, making eight nozzles in all. It was one of the many improvements in exhaust and front-end arrangements that were being made about this time, perhaps most notably by André Chapelon. There were indeed many experiments at this time in steam locomotive development. The noble old engine was fighting for its life against the electric motor and the internal-combustion engine. One offensive—not a very happy one—was with the use of very high pressures, as with the Schwartzkopff-Löffler and Schmidt types from Germany, certain quite academic designs by the Delaware and Hudson Company in the United States, and a remarkable 4-6-4 express engine in England wherein Gresley of the London and North Eastern made an immensely expensive adaptation of the Yarrow marine watertube boiler. With the Schmidt type, which included a closed-circuit system of tubes—steam to heat steam—there were some blow-ups with tragic results. It was tried in Germany, England, France and Canada.

Piston valves having largely superseded slide valves, there was a vogue for poppet valves, following motor practice and sometimes worked by rotary-cam instead of radial valve gear. Lentz (in Austria) and Caprotti (Italian) poppet valves were about the most successful and were widely used, though the piston valve scarcely retreated.

An interesting arrangement of the early 'thirties was the Cossart valve gear, now shown in a rebuilt Northern of France Pacific. The engine had been one of Breville's improved de Glehn-du Bousquet type of 1924 and was thus modified by his successor Lancrenon, as a four-cylinder simple engine. Outside arrangement of the gear is obvious from the drawing, but there were four valves for each cylinder, in pairs at each end, and of the piston-type set vertically, rising and falling through levers and springs, with a rotary camshaft. This particular transformation seems to have been unhappy, but later use of the Cossart system of distribution was justified by many years' service, not finished as we write.

The Lentz poppet valve

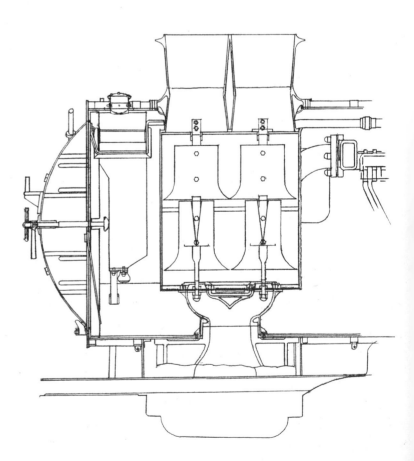

The Kylchap blast-pipe

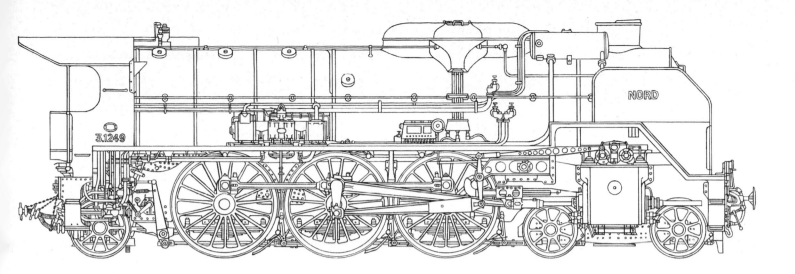

Otherwise, this Bréville-Lancrenon locomotive is noteworthy, like early engines on the Northern Railway of France, for the use of a long, narrow firebox, such as the Great Western Railway invariably favoured in England. Both companies achieved very fine performances with what Americans considered small engines. The Great Western boasted awhile, in the early nineteen-thirties, *the fastest train in the world*. The claim was quite authentic for regular service: Swindon to London (Paddington), 77·3 miles in 65 minutes. On June 6, 1932, it was done in 56 min. 47 sec. (engine *Tregenna Castle*). This was a publicity boost. Rather slower services with much heavier trains between London and Plymouth were really much more interesting, with a mountainous road in the West Country. The Great Western engines, like the French ones, were among the best for their modest size in the world.

Many appliances were going to improve the basic steam locomotive still. The principle of thermic syphons in firebox was ancient (cf. J. H. Beattie in the 'sixties). The modern Nicholson form was applied on certain American locomotives and in England (Gresley and Bulleid on the London and North Eastern Railway) at the beginning of the nineteen-forties. Absolutely essential, of course, was the big boiler supplying plenty of steam on a high pressure. Past were the days when partly through the need for keeping down axle loads, what had otherwise been very good engines were spoilt by boiler inadequacy, as in the eighteen-nineties.

In the late nineteen-thirties, such firms as the American Locomotive Company, and, as noted, General Motors Electro-Motive Division, were building larger and more powerful Diesel electric locomotives for both fast passenger and heavy freight service in the United States. Certain American railroads stuck faithfully to steam for a very long time. The New York Central's legendary Twentieth Century Limited continued to roar along the water-level route behind its magnificent Hudson. The Norfolk and Western Railway, a very heavy coal carrier, showed quite fanatical loyalty to steam, even scrapping electric traction which it had installed before 1920. It is interesting to recall that as late as 1957, when the Diesel conquest of America was far advanced, the Norfolk and Western had 408 steam locomotives (including one terrific turbine-electric unit) called *Jawn Henry* and but sixty-two Diesel-electric. At that time there was no more steam on the New Haven, the Missouri Pacific, and many other Class I railroads. The New York Central had 122 steam and ninety-three electric locomotives out of a total of 2,168. Making European comparisons, in 1955 British Railways, under State ownership for the past decade, had still 17,955 standard-gauge steam locomotives against 532 of all other sorts, including 407 Diesel-electric and but seventy-one straight electric. The disappearance of classic British steam, little over a decade later, seemed unthinkable! West Germany, in 1956, had 9,533 steam, 525 electric, and 223 Diesels of all sorts. America undoubtedly was the first great country to be possessed by the Diesel.

Her steam locomotives had been vast things over many years. In North America, and in other countries of mighty steam engines, it had long got beyond the power of any long-suffering fireman to shift coal into those cavernous fireboxes, and the steam-driven mechanical stoker came to his aid, or rather to *their* aid where two firemen were needed to maintain steam. Its principle was that of one of the senior mechanical appliances, the *Archimedean screw* (Third Century B.C.). As so many American examples

A 4-6-2 two-cylinder express locomotive, no. 3.1249, Chemin de Fer du Nord, 1934.

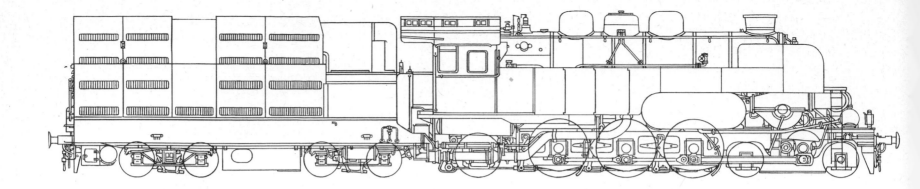

have been illustrated in past books, we show a diagram from the Polish State Railways. But yet it was in America that the appliance became universal on all big engines, and widespread in parts of Africa and the East. British home railways never took it up. Their engines were necessarily small from first to last, and even some Beyer-Garratts on the Midlands-London coal trains went only as far as self-trimming bunkers which brought the fuel within easy reach of the strong man with the shovel.

Pulverised fuel, as an alternative to low-grade stuff, was tried at the expense of elaborate machinery for firing. Old Archimedes again was an essential contributory inventor. One should remark great progress in the use of pulverised fuel on the East German State Railway after World War II.

As the orthodox steam locomotive was being prepared for its last mortal battles, more and more accessories had been brought into common use. Boosters—small auxiliary engines on back axles to assist on starting and on heavy grades, were most used in North America, though very early examples (mounted forward) were experimentally applied by Krauss of Munich, at the end of last century, and auxiliary steamtenders to the same end were an ancient French invention; (e.g. Verpilleux' *La Jumelle*, 1843). Unsuccessful through lack of boiler capacity, they reappeared, and again disappeared, in England in the eighteen-sixties. The giant Erie specimen we have noticed. It was the old business of trying to make two and two add up to six. But the small booster, in its day, was a great success within its limits.

Boiler accessories, such as water purifiers (called top-feed in England) went back to Wagner in pre-Imperial Prussia. Feedwater heaters were increasingly used, though these again had quite ancient antecedents. Notably successful were those of Knorr (the German air-brake firm) and A.C.F.I. in France.

Experience of even torque, as with electric motors and turbine steamships, stimulated awhile the turbine locomotive. At a remote time there had been a plucky but fruitless attempt in the United States to make a steam locomotive go by an enclosed reaction turbine driving through belts. Ramsay's turbine locomotive experiments in Scotland and then in England bear mention. But there was brave work in Central and Northern Europe in the early nineteen-twenties. The Swiss Engine Works of Winterthur, and Krupps of Essen, both built notable turbine locomotives under Zoelly patents, using condensers as in marine practice. Rather oddly, it was the non-condensing turbine locomotive, with the usual open exhaust, that was to be a practical proposition in public service, while the huge, tender-mounted condensers were found useful for ordinary reciprocating locomotives in South Africa, and by both the Russians and the Germans, especially when they were both fighting and moving traffic in waterless country.

Previously, Ljungström in Sweden had produced a remarkable condensing turbine locomotive, a larger version of which later appeared in England and certainly hauled some Midland expresses. The boilers of these were on the tenders, with turbine and condenser on the engine proper, a transposition which has foxed many innocent scribes. But most successful of the Ljungström sort were three non-condensing turbine locomotives built by Nydqvist and Holm in and after 1929 to the order of Harry O. Johnson of the Grängesberg-Oxelösund Company, a heavy iron-ore mining and carrying undertaking in Sweden. They were the most successful turbine steam locomotives ever built for they worked the great ore trains down to the Baltic Coast until the line was electrified (1947–56, in stages) and then were kept in reserve and not immediately scrapped or sold. Their short, high tenders were necessitated by small turntables. These famous three (1929 and 1936) had a long-legged sister in England, a Pacific type express passenger engine built in 1935, structurally the same as the orthodox Princess class of the London

The turbine locomotive built under the Zoelly patents

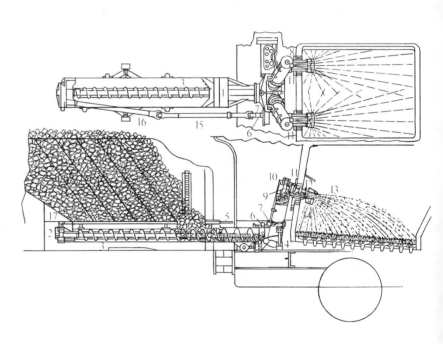

A mechanical stoker, made in America, which was used by the Polish State Railways on two of their largest class of goods locomotives.

1 Coal crusher	6 Regulating shutter
2 Spur gear driving feed screw	7 Base of vertical elevators
3 Feed screw	8 Orifices for distributors in firebox wall
4 Flexible mounting for feed gear	9 Elevator screw
5 Tender footplate	10 Fuel outlets
	11 Distributor hoppers
	12 Steam jets
	13, 14 Mouths of distributors
	15, 16 Driving shafts
	17 Pushers

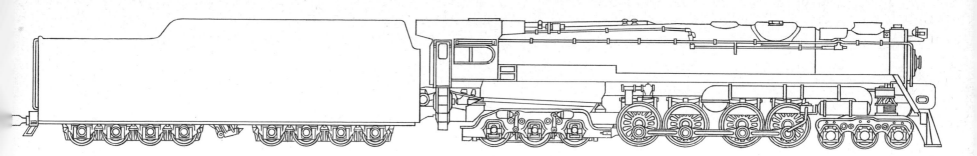

Midland and Scottish Railway, and happily familiar over many years of peace and war on the Merseyside Express between London and Liverpool (how beautiful to us was that brief rising hum when she was given steam at the start!). At last, when her turbines were worn out, the State-owned British Railways. turned her into an ordinary Princess (*Princess Anne*) and as such she came rather soon to a shocking end in England's worst-yet railway accident at Harrow in 1952. She was a good engine, deserving better memories.

Most magnificent of the *turbomotives* were some Americans. We have mentioned *Jawn Henry* on the Norfolk and Western (whose old age also was marred by collision, though less gorily than *Princess Anne's*). Three turbine-electrics were ordered by the Chesapeake and Ohio—the Norfolk and Western Railway's old neighbour and rival, with perhaps a love-hate relationship—and the first of these appeared (Baldwin and Westinghouse Electric) in the summer of 1947, for fast passenger trains between Washington and Cincinnati. There was a conventional boiler (310 lb./sq. in.) and the locomotive was arranged from the front in this order: coal-bunker, mechanical stoker, boiler with firebox forward, main turbine, reduction gearing, and exciters, with water-tender in rear. There were fourteen axles (excluding tender) eight of which were motor-driven. Maximum tractive effort at start, and maximum speed, both limited by traction motors, were 98,000 lb. and 100 miles an hour respectively. Such a mechanical prodigy was more like a self-propelling, massively-hauling power-station than anything in transport outside the world of ships. This magnificent box-of-tricks weighed 367·4 tons, with a tender weighing 166 tons. We have rolled on the unkind Atlantic in a ship of less than half that tonnage! To be sure, she was a venerably old ship!

The Pennsylvania Railroad's straight turbine locomotive of the nineteen-forties followed on a grand scale those which had successfully worked in Sweden and England in the 'thirties, and were still going well. She was arranged 6-8-6. A Pennsylvania reciprocating locomotive of 1940 had been 6-4-4-6. As in the European engines, there was a main turbine for forward running (maximum speed 100 m.p.h.) and one for reverse running (25 m.p.h.) on the right and left sides respectively. Drive was through double reduction gears and quills to the two inner coupled axles, with roller bearings throughout, including the side rods. Pressure was 310 lb. per sq. in. (285 lb. at turbine inlet).

There is little doubt that had not the oil industry come to dominate world commerce and politics, far-advanced methods of using steam on the locomotive itself would have become commonplace wherever it was uneconomic to use it in central power-stations for electric traction and where water-power was weak. The Germans in particular made most interesting practical experiments with what we might call the steam-motor locomotive—i.e. one with geared high-speed engines.

As it was, the steam locomotive fought her last actions in what might have been called conventional armour, that of the reciprocating engine with direct drive and with such boiler and front-end improvements as mechanical science had already produced. On very heavy haulage the giant American Mallets—ever more gigantic, pursued their dogged way, and, in what we still tend to call the Old World, especially in the African countries, there was the Garratt. The classic American Mallet—though she was not without her rivals even in size, was the great design carried out by Alco for the historic Union Pacific Railroad in and after 1941. A locomotive of orthodox type, having a working pressure of 300 lb./sq. in., an evaporative heating surface of 5,755 sq. ft. plus a super-heating surface of 2,043 sq. ft., a grate area of 150·3 sq. ft.; a locomotive with four cylinders 23¾ in. by 32 in. (12 in. piston valves with 7 in. maximum travel) driving sixteen 5 ft. 8 in. coupled wheels with a four-wheel truck fore-and-aft; a locomotive weighing 772,000 lb. excluding her 348,000 lb. tender (two-thirds loaded) on five fixed

The Pennsylvania interpretation of the non-condensing turbine locomotive. Conception was on the Grängesberg-Oxelösund Railway in Sweden at the end of the 1920s, and gestation on the London Midland and Scottish Railway.

209

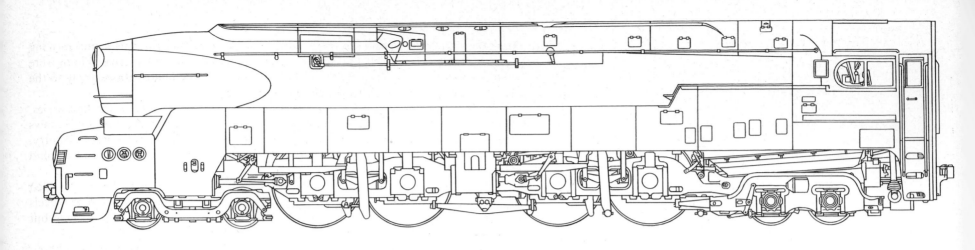

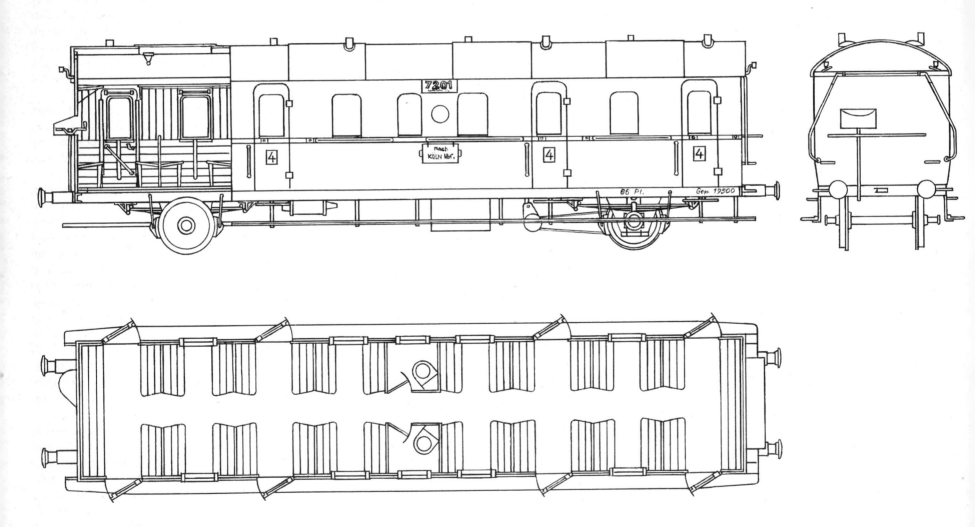

(above) The Pennsylvania
Railroad's *4-4-4-4 Class TI*. Its
total wheel base was 51 ft. 11 in.,
it had a modified Belpaire-type
firebox and a total heating surface
of 5898 sq. ft.

(below) Plan, elevation and
rear-view of the spartan though
civilized fourth-class carriage of
the German State Railways.

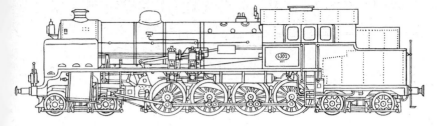

axles and a leading two axle truck, was not the sort of steam engine one found moving up and down most people's Mountain Divisions, even in North America. There were two lots; road-numbers 4000–4019 and 4020–4024. The basic figures above apply to the last five. These were the celebrated *Big Boys*.

They remained in service for as long as steam did. No. 4012, one of the first series, has most fortunately gone to Steamtown, that wondrous working museum by Bellows Falls in one of the loveliest parts of the New Hampshire—Vermont border country, where people may enjoy them—and a steam ride on the Monadnock Northern Railroad —for their own sakes.

Both before and after World War II there was experiment with what has been called the duplex locomotive, meaning that which has two sets of cylinders and coupled wheels but is not articulated like the Garratt or semi-articulated like the Mallet. It made but slight impact in Europe.

France produced some handsome locomotives of apparent duplex type but with an ingenious arrangement of inside coupling rods between the first and second sets of wheels. In the United States there were several designs for fast passenger engines arranged 4-4-4-4 which, adapting the old type-name, might have been called "Double-American". There was the remarkable *George H. Emerson*—which incidentally had very handsome lines. The Pennsylvania Railroad's Class T 1, which first appeared in 1942 and ultimately numbered fifty-two engines, sang one of the more majestic swan-songs of railway steam. (Statement made with due respect to the Norfolk and Western, and several other undertakings!) The engines were designed for a normal maximum speed of 100 miles an hour at 20 per cent cut-off and 295 lb. boiler pressure. Maximum horsepower was 6,552 (indicated) and 6,110 (drawbar). Tenders were by now enormous. That of Class T 1 ran on two eight-wheel trucks, with the waterscoop between. Engine weight was 502,200 lb.; and of tender, 442,500 lb.

North America was the land of the giant passenger and freight engine; the steam tank locomotive was relatively little known there (or, for that matter, in the Soviet Union). There *were* indeed some large steam tank engines—4-6-4 or 4-6-6—on certain commuting passenger services which had not been electrified, as on the Boston and Albany Railroad, and about Montreal on both Canadian National and Canadian Pacific services.

In many parts of Western Europe, however, there were tank engines galore; ancient, modern, diminutive, or even big to American eyes. Maffei in Munich built some tremendous Mallet tank engines as helpers on heavy grades in Thuringia. In the nineteen-twenties certain of the old British companies had built very fast-running and indeed elegant 4-6-4 tank engines for non-stop business passenger runs of fifty miles or so between London, Glasgow and Manchester, and their neighbouring coast towns. Then much larger 4-8-4 tank engines were built for Spain, France and most notably for the Netherlands Railways which used them for heavy coal haulage in and about Limburg.

One of these we show now. They were the largest and most powerful of their type in the world. A product of 1930, they were simple, reliable and very competent. One is now preserved at the Netherlands Railways Museum, Utrecht. There were four cylinders, all in line with drive to the leading coupled axle. Noteworthy was the combination of bar frames with an almost English outline. The stack had a bright copper cap, a Victorian feature favoured by the Netherlands, as well as the Great Western Railway in England, and endearing to the eye of an artist, as to an old-time locomotive man.

While in North America, the steam locomotive retreated in the way of mechanical evolution spurred by oil-business interests, in much of Europe, during the nineteen-forties, there was a massacre of another sort. In their thousands, steam engines fell to the waste of war, whether by aerial bombing or by sabotage. To take but one example, seventy per cent of effective steam locomotives in Austria were—officially at any rate— either severely damaged or quite destroyed, and (mark this!) a steam engine was the most resilient and least fragile of all locomotives. She could limp home after mischief that would have crippled anything else. One should add that no country could beat Austria at the useful business of having locomotives in reserve, sometimes with long grass about their wheels, but sound when needed!

It was in Austria that one of the last great contributions was made to steam locomotive engineering. Giesl-Gieslingen's improvements in front-end design and, particularly, in exhaust arrangements, were what earlier had been called a "break-through". But apart from the improvement of many existing engines and the better equipment of a few new ones, they came too late.

This Netherlands Railways 4-8-4 tank locomotive was Europe's heaviest. It was used for hauling Limburg coal, 1930.

Many splendid locomotives were built in those fateful 'fifties which saw the twilight of European steam. In Italy, land of so much electric traction, the Franco-Crosti boiler revived in modern form something like Petiet's arrangement from long ago, even to rearward smokestacks, and tried early on a veteran "back-to-front" 4-6-0 of Plancher's type. Germany and England both gave it fair trial. In Ireland that unconventional-conservative New Zealander Oliver Bulleid—once of the English Great Northern and later of the English Southern—made a brave attempt to produce an advanced steam locomotive running on turf. He, like ingenious Germans before him, had great ideas about steam-motor locomotives, multiple-cylindered and incorporating sleeve-valves as well as much else that old shellback engineers considered unconstitutional and thus anathema.

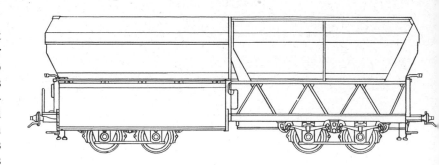

Let our last bouquet go to France, country of Marc Séguin, Jules Petiet, Baudry, du Bousquet, and André Chapelon; adoptive country of Tom Crampton and Alfred de Glehn; nation of fascinating steam! We show now French National Railways Class U, one of the last of the great French compound express engines, built in 1949 by Corpet, Louvet and Company. The chief designer was de Caso, heir to the work of such great Frenchmen as Chapelon on the Orleans and Brévillé on the Northern. In her design there were the best in tradition and also the best in novelties. Drive was divided, with high-pressure cylinders in a single casting driving the first coupled axle, and the two low-pressure cylinders outside, driving the middle one. Piston valves and Walschaerts' gear were revived. S.K.F. roller bearings were used, and lubrication was by automatic pumps. There was a mechanical stoker. This was not a big engine by North American standards, but with 300 lb. per sq. in. boiler pressure, making 270 lb. in the high-pressure steam-chest and 75 lb. in the low-pressure, the initial engine on her trials between Paris and Lille easily equalled the speed performance of the Diesel *autorails* while taking loads up to 500 metric tons at 87 m.p.h. maximum speed. High average speeds were much regarded in France, without high maxima.

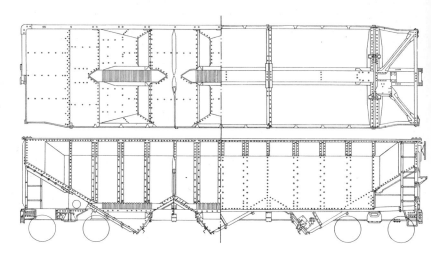

There had been many attempts, since American Civil War days, to make practical steam rail-motor-cars, and in themselves these were quite successful, though inelastic. One recalls excellent examples in America, in England, and in Germany where Henschel and Son took up the American Doble patents in the nineteen-thirties, notably on the Lübeck-Büchen Railway. Ere that, a very neat design had appeared on the Dalsland Railway in Sweden. But in the days of railway monopoly, the steam car could not, when required, be expanded into a train. In later days, *anything that went by steam* seemed to be anathema to the too-powerful oil companies. We may yet see them, in one form or another, in millions.

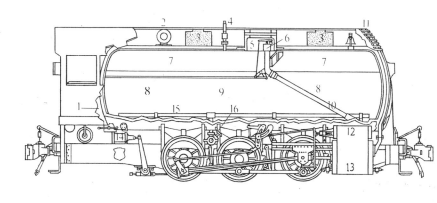

There may have been many other factors in the decline of steam traction. Discounting donnish arguments about *thermal efficiency*, there is the more potent one of availability, and on that the Stephensonian locomotive fell down. Its servicing times were terribly long compared with those of either the electric or the oil-electric engine. Further, a new generation of young men was being required to give ill-paid, devoted, *dirty* service to what it regarded as an obsolete machine, under the eyes of what it considered tyrannical old men dedicated to that same machine. Where once the enginemen were the *élite* of mechanics, now the labour exchange sent the fool of the family down to the steam shed when he wished to become an astronaut (*cf.* a juvenile delinquent in a British police court). In Germany and France, much use was made latterly of oil firing (a novice in the cab had a rather nervous impression of riding above a gigantic blowlamp, but it was quite safe, as a Scotsman had demonstrated to Russians nearly a century earlier).

Specialised steam locomotives remained few in type. The rack-and-pinion mountain engine, pioneered by Marsh in America and Riggenbach in Europe, is still with us, in a few places like Mount Washington in New Hampshire and the Rothorn in the Alps, though rackrail Diesels now growl up to the tops of Pike's Peak and Monte Generoso.

For work over rough roads, especially lumber lines in North America, the Shay loco-motive was widely used over many years. It was probably the ugliest Caliban of steam, with its boiler off the centre-line to balance a vertical engine driving a universally jointed propeller-shaft to two or three motor-trucks, but it was an ingenious machine, and extra-ordinarily useful at that within its limited sphere. Rivals were the Climax and Heisler geared locomotives, but the Shay remained the old favourite. Fireless steam loco-motives, with heavily-lagged steam reservoirs charged at strict intervals from a central supply, originated for steam street-car lines in New Orleans, back in the 'seventies, and many years later they were found useful about mills and oil-refineries where open exhaust

(above) This self-discharging coke car was used by the German State Railways in the mid-1920s.

(centre) A Bessemer and Lake Erie Railroad 90-ton triple hopper coal car.

(below) An advanced fireless steam locomotive used in the U.S.A. in the 1930s. The drawing is semi-diagrammatic. Note the succession of sandboxes with dome, safety valve and lighting generator.

1 Heavy insulation
2 Lighting generator
3 Sand
4 Safety valve
5 Dome
6 Throttle
7 Steam
8 Water
9 Reservoir
10 Dry steam to cylinders
11 Exhaust steam
12 Piston valve
13 Cylinder
14 Brake cylinder
15 Charging pipe
16 Charging connection

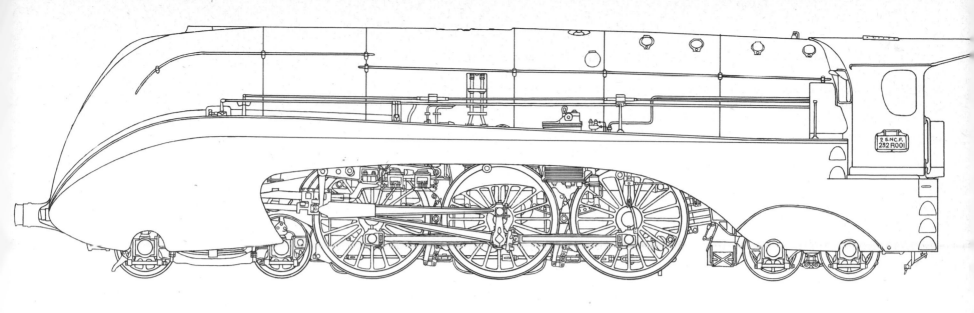

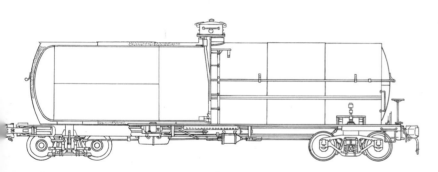

(above) French National Railways 4-6-4 Class U locomotive, built in 1949, was used in the Northern Region. A mechanical stoker was fitted and piston valves and Walschaerts gear were used.

(below) This oil tanker was built by the American Car and Foundry Company in the 1950s

might cause disaster on a grand scale. Germany in particular produced many excellent examples in the present century.

With these humble housemaids of steam locomotion, we must leave what long bygone Englishmen called the *Steam Travelling Engine*. In its day, lasting about a century-and-a-half, it has been not only one of the most important of transient machines, but one truly best-loved, both by those who had to do with its honest reliability and by those to whom it simply appealed to the senses, as the great sailing ship, the windmill, the beautiful bridge, and a few other purely functional things have appealed.

Let car history give us breathing space. We are old enough to have found the German fourth-class carriage very useful for a thrifty student on his Sunday outings, and on p. 210 is one of the early nineteen-twenties. It was neither elegant nor luxurious, but it was spartanly adequate and extraordinarily cheap to ride in. Furthermore, though grotesque to North American eyes, the two-axle car with good springing and suspension has much to commend it. It is the obvious arrangement for the light motor rail-car, much used in Europe where otherwise there were no passenger trains. Most of Europe's massive railroad freight is carried by highly developed "four-wheelers" including an adaptable type to internationally-agreed standards which can be run anywhere in Western Europe and the Balkans—from Northern Scotland to Turkey—and even in the broad-gauge Peninsula through the provision of transposable axles. The same applies between Scandinavia, Central Europe and Russia. European sleeping cars, likewise, can change gauge at frontier by bogie substitution.

Car design needs a book to itself—and has had two or three—so we must stick to a few examples. First, oil being a most important commodity of the Americas, we show a standard tanker of the American Car and Foundry Company in the nineteen-fifties, with a welded steel underframe. It is interesting to compare this with the much earlier oil-tank car of the Russian State Railways in Tsarist days (page 126). Next to coal and coal products: Eastern and South-eastern United States, Don Basin, the vast English, Welsh and Scottish coalfields, Silesia, Northern France, the Newcastle district of New South Wales, and the Indian collieries poured their black money into the great trains which took it to the ends of the earth—where the ships took over. In the middle of the nineteen-twenties, the 109 ton coal cars of the Virginian Railroad were claimed as the biggest on earth, and if it were not so, the rightful claimant was probably something else American, possibly on the Norfolk and Western.

We show now a diagram of a Bessemer and Lake Erie 90 ton car with three-hopper discharge between the trucks, and a drawing of a side-discharging coke wagon of the German State Railway during the inter-war years by way of comparison (not odious in either direction!). Refrigerated carriage of foodstuffs and other perishables goes back a good many years. By no other means could sea fish be eaten fresh far inland, whether in Vienna, Chicago or Winnipeg. On the next page is an American design of 1944 favoured by the United Fresh Fruit and Vegetable Association, with stage icing and forced air circulation. Refrigerator cars of many sorts dated back to the previous century, like most other specialised freight cars such as the warmed banana vans which were known to late Victorian England.

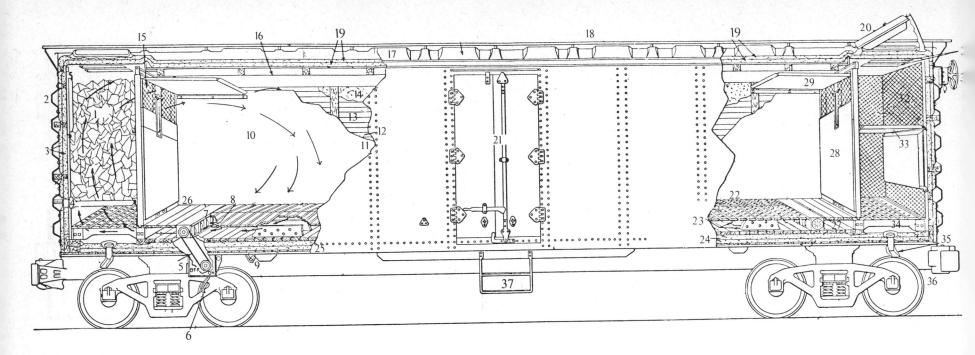

For many years, too, enormous vehicles have been built for carrying heavy power-house and marine equipment, with means—especially necessary in Europe—for slewing the load at points where it exceeds the loading-gauge. We have persistent memories of certain long, slow journeys, as of the transport of complete machinery for a glass factory from Belgium to Northern England, and of a giant stator from Newcastle-upon-Tyne to a power-station near Birmingham. It was surprising what could be got through the confined right of way.

Transport of automobiles is a thing of our own time, whether from works to market or by passenger train with the owners tucked away in the sleepers, (the latter a characteristic feature of Western European travel, beginning between London and Perth, though unknown in many other regions). It saves a long, tedious drive through the night, and gives a rail-head usually in pleasant country whence driving can be a delight. British autocarrying vehicles are completely enclosed. The later ones take their vehicles in two tiers, with power-driven lifts and fibreglass sides.

Straight passenger-car design has generally improved in detail rather than in general features, in spite of repeated efforts in both America and Europe to achieve a faultless form of pendulum suspension, and such things as the Talgo articulated train, which Spain essayed, but which a detractor—certainly he had made a journey in one—described as a string of open-ended wheelbarrows towed by a Diesel. For the record; each car has a single axle-line and is articulated to its predecessor, wide diaphragms making a continuous corridor of the very short car bodies. When it was new, its fans loved it. Novelty? Or real virtue? Certainly, in the third Spanish Talgo train, the earlier disabilities and faults in running seem to have been conquered.

One of the pleasantest sorts of car for specialised passenger service, as in imposing mountain country, has been what America called the "vista-dome" or, latterly, simply the "dome car". The idea is ancient, but Pullman and Budd in the United States have built magnificent modern examples. A Pullman is exemplified. A necessity of the dome type of observation car is smokeless traction and air-conditioning, which is possibly why it was so long a time a-coming. Tight loading gauges also rule it out, and that applies to many European countries. The Germans, indeed, made small motor or electric rail-cars, with a form of dome construction, back in the nineteen-thirties, for purely sightseeing trips, and the German Federal Railways, thirty years later, thus provided their revived and quite newly-designed Rheingold Express.

Air-conditioning again was a very old notion indeed. As far back as 1854 George F. Foote in the United States invented, and sold to the Michigan Southern and the Northern Indiana companies, a system of ventilation based partly on the miners' safety lamp (George Stephenson's original invention, incidentally, though Sir Humphry Davy got the credit) and partly on a system of air-cooling by water jets. Its troubles were with the belt-driven water-pump. R. D. Sanders made for the Great Indian Peninsula Railway a

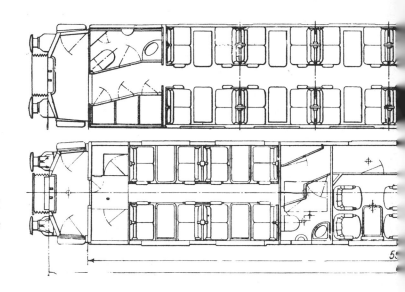

Refrigerator car for the United Fresh Fruit and Vegetable Association, in America, 1944.

1 Ice
2 Steel end
3 End insulation
4 Ice grates (full stage position)
5 Drive belt
6 Fan lever at "on" position
7 Fan housing
8 Fan intake
9 Precool motor bracket
10 Forced air circulation
11 Car wall
12 Air flue
13 Car wall sub-lining
14 Wall insulation
15 Top bulkhead opening (screens)
16 Ceiling
17 Steel roof

18 Steel non-skid running board
19 Roof insulation
20 Integral hatch cover and plug
21 Self-locking door
22 Floor racks
23 Floor stringers
24 Floor insulation
25 Sub-floor
26 Car floor
27 Air channel
28 Adjustable bulkhead
29 Hatch shield
30 Hatch openings
31 Power hand brake
32 Bunker screens
33 Ice grates (half stage position)
34 Well trap
35 Drain spout
36 Improved softer action draft gear
37 Step

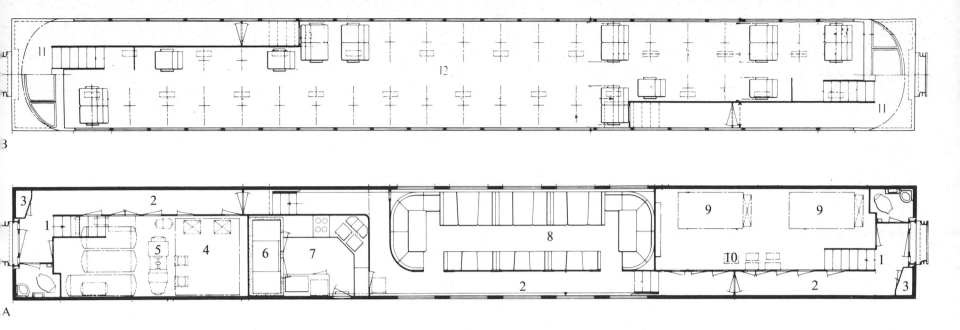

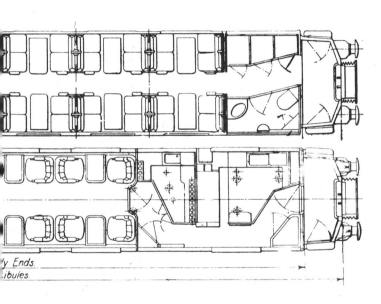

large number of first-class carriages ventilated through water-drenched cloth by means of air-scoops, the cloth being kept wet by a tumbler-flush from an overhead tank which had to be kept constantly replenished. Labour was cheap and travel slow in the India of the eighteen-seventies.

Air-conditioning today is a complex branch of mechanical engineering, whether in vehicles or buildings, and having one of its higher forms in the pressurised aircraft. Mechanical systems of air-conditioning became really workable following experiments by the Baltimore and Ohio Railroad, successfully culminating in a very handsome diner called *Martha Washington* and first being applied to a complete train in 1931; indeed, to two trains on the New York—Washington service. Thereafter, new cars were equipped, and thousands of older cars fitted, in advanced countries where climate went to extremes. We should mention, among European applications, those of the Trans-Europ-Express trains, and some in Spain, notably on the Talgos. Elsewhere, forced ventilation systems were found entirely adequate. South Africa put the air-ducts in the clerestory deck. America, in re-equipped cars, put them in the external angle of the clerestory, which was a makeshift. Car structure indeed was undergoing radical changes in some quarters, though the British peoples (excluding Canada) were hard to part from the old English idea of making body and frame separately. France was one of the pioneers of tubular construction of passenger cars. We show (p. 216) an example of the nineteen-thirties.

France, too, had been a pioneer of double-deck coaches for commuting passengers, though the early ones were extremely rough. In the United States, two levels rather than two decks gave good service and improved seating capacity. More recently, the Chicago and North Western company has made admirable commuting trains with two level accommodation. Possibly England has been responsible both for the highest combination of seating capacity and rapid access and egress, and the most elaborate high-grade cars for commuting city passengers. The first category was the work of Oliver Bulleid and Lionel Lynes jointly. Every other compartment has side doors and short-stair access to an upper one dovetailed with the lower like the Long Island sections. Those uppers were conducive to claustrophobia; after a helpless old woman had been beaten-up and robbed in one by ruffianly youths, the arrangement became most unpopular, and was not made standard. We show next two plans, third-class and composite respectively, of Pullman cars on the London-Brighton fast commuter and holiday trains when these were electrified in 1933. Though small at 66 ft., they were of admirable design. The British Pullman tradition was that one could be brought anything from a drink to a rather adequate meal without having to move. The supplement was small. London-Brighton journey time is sixty minutes, and has been so for many years. In long-distance European service, the classic *Wagons-Lits* car prevailed.

In the nineteen-fifties, over much of the world and still spreading, it became Diesel's Day. Oil engines were working more and more of the trains, where these survived (and on lesser and remoter lines the train had begun to die). They were working the heavy motors and they were driving many ships. In heavy railway traction, two transmissions had outpaced other ingenious forms; namely, electric and hydraulic. While the Diesel-electric locomotive or motor-coach is indeed an electric vehicle carrying its own power-plant, one should note the difference of the mobile power-house. This is a machine with electric motors sufficient only for its own movement, but with a Diesel generator capable of supplying also the motors of a multiple-unit electric train. Notable examples are in Argentina and in parts of Italy. In Ireland in the late 'thirties—and after—one could see steam trains hauling Diesel cars "dead" like this between city and country junction.

America first, and then parts of Europe, saw the building of many very large Diesel locomotives as steam gradually declined. American examples were often describable as "multiple-unit", in the sense that three or four could be managed by one engineer and his assistant (still called, by tradition, the fireman). Indeed, they were built thus, dia-phragmed together like coaches, and with the cab above the nose of the leading one, which we exemplify (p.223) by an Alco leading unit, of 2,250 horsepower, as built for American Class I railroads in the 'fifties. Co-designers and builders were General Electric, European and many other railroads favoured rather the single very large unit than what might be called a locomotive conglomeration, owing to the use of turntables (American radiators) rather than the widely-used American reversing Y, which takes up much space, not easily to be had in old countries. This resulted in extraordinarily powerful Diesel-electric single units. Using four units to one road locomotive, the Kansas City Southern Railroad produced one of 8,000 h.p., with a cab at each end. (The "h.p." quoted indicates brake-horsepower, by the way.) A record single-unit locomotive was the Deltic type, so named from its use of an existing marine engine thus called, made by English Electric and the Vulcan Foundry in 1955. The engine, arranged Co-Co like the Alco unit just shown, developed 3,300 b.h.p., by which it then qualified as the most powerful single-unit Diesel locomotive in the world. It was very exhaustively tried on the heaviest British service, and was adopted for the East Coast service of British Railways in 1961, where it still hauls the fastest and heaviest trains. The prototype, by the way, is now in the London Science Museum; perhaps the swiftest locomotive apotheosis ever known. The makers presented their infant prodigy to the nation, so now she (we had better give her gender) has for company such ancients as *Puffing Billy* and the original *Rocket*, and the beautiful Great Western engine *Caerphilly Castle* of 1923. A special new gallery has been built for them; they stand as in the nave of a great church.

For an example of an American general worker of this order, we show a Northern Pacific engine by General Electric, of 2,500 b.h.p. This is a most useful locomotive; one can see its kind far across North America, and in many other places too. There is little variety save in size and indicated horsepower. Even the candy-stripe finish favoured by some companies as fleet liveries is modified to something more Americanly puritan. The cab is a box (very well arranged, to be sure) at one end of a relatively narrow hood containing engine and generator. Let not Americans be angry with us for suggesting that the railed gallery each side suggests old Russian steam practice. So it does, and an excellent arrangement at that! Such are the engines by which so much American freight is shipped about and across a continent.

The English Electric Company's *Deltic* remained the world's most powerful single-unit Diesel until the advent of the Krauss-Maffei 4,000 b.h.p. Diesel locomotive of 1961, and that had hydraulic transmission. Three were delivered in that year to both the Denver and Rio Grande Western and the Southern Pacific companies, and in the following year the latter bought fifteen more, the first Diesel locomotives ever imported by the United States. The name *Deltic*, by the way; it came from the inverted *delta* section of the engine, more comparable to the Eastern *nabla*.

The summer of 1967 saw the completion and trials in England of the prototype Diesel-electric locomotive *Kestrel* by Brush of Loughborough with a Sulzer sixteen-cylinder engine developing 4,000 h.p. at 1,100 r.p.m. That made it the most powerful single-engine Diesel locomotive in the world at this time, though it was built to the necessarily modest British proportions and arranged Co-Co with a maximum axle-load of twenty-one tons. The rated maximum speed is quoted, with characteristic British guardedness, as "above 160 km./h.". Naming the locomotive after one of the smaller birds of prey is typically English, and she is appropriately painted in a rather fierce combination of chocolate and yellow. The Sulzer V engine with an alternator/rectifier unit powers six parallel connected traction motors, one to each axle.

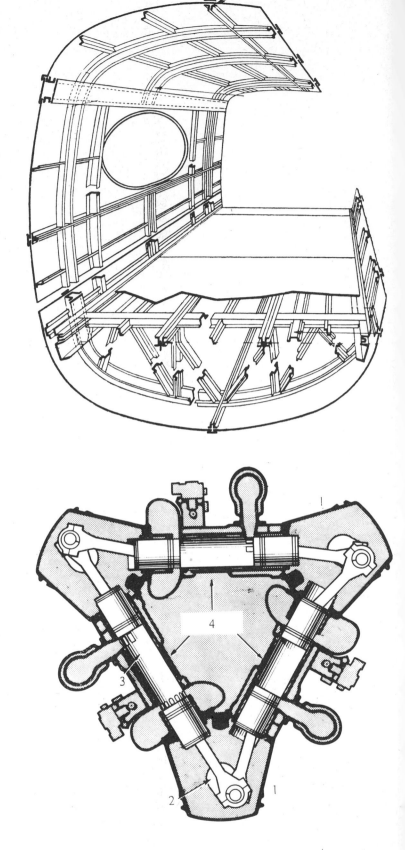

(above) Section of a coach of the French State Railways, 1939, showing the interior bracing of the shell and the substructure.

A sectional view of the Napier Deltic engine showing the general arrangement of the cylinders. They form in the end view an inverted equilateral triangle, thereby giving rise to the name "Deltic". *This triangular design results in an almost complete balance of the reciprocating forces and masses within the engine frame.*

1 Crankcase
2 Crankshaft
3 Cylinder liner
4 Cylinder blocks

GRESLEY'S STREAMLINED A/4 SIR RALPH WEDGWOOD WAS TOPPING 100 M.P.H. ON THE LONDON AND NORTH EASTERN IN THE 1930S.

Hiawatha

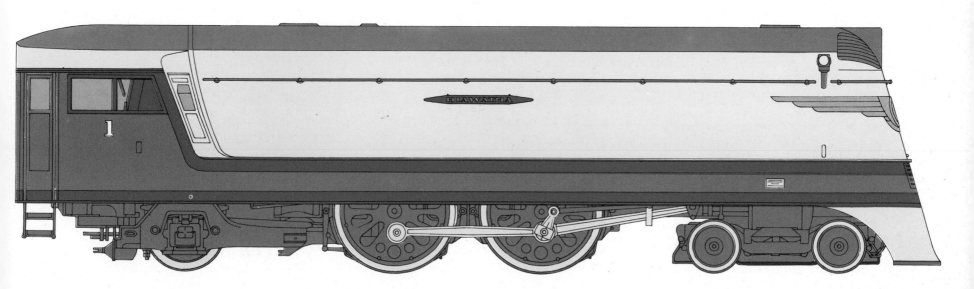

AT THE SAME TIME IN AMERICA, THE 4-4-2 HIAWATHA, ALSO STREAMLINED, WAS ALSO DOING OVER 100 M.P.H. FOR THE MILWAUKEE ROAD.

Midi Electric

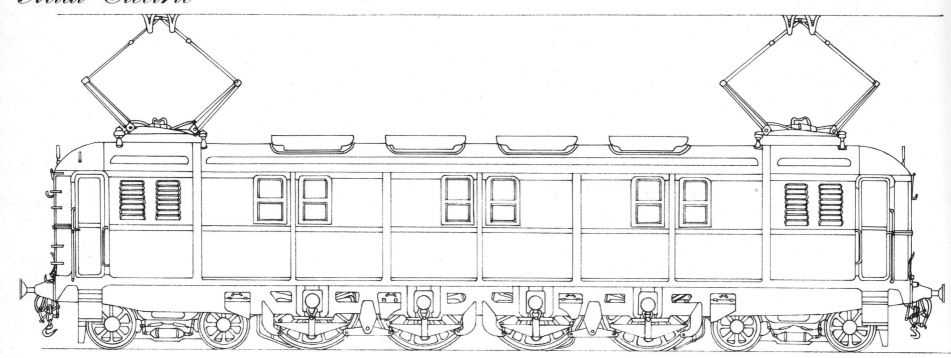

A 4-8-4 ELECTRIC LOCOMOTIVE BUILT IN 1923 FOR THE BORDEAUX–IRUN LINE OF THE CHEMIN DE FER DU MIDI.

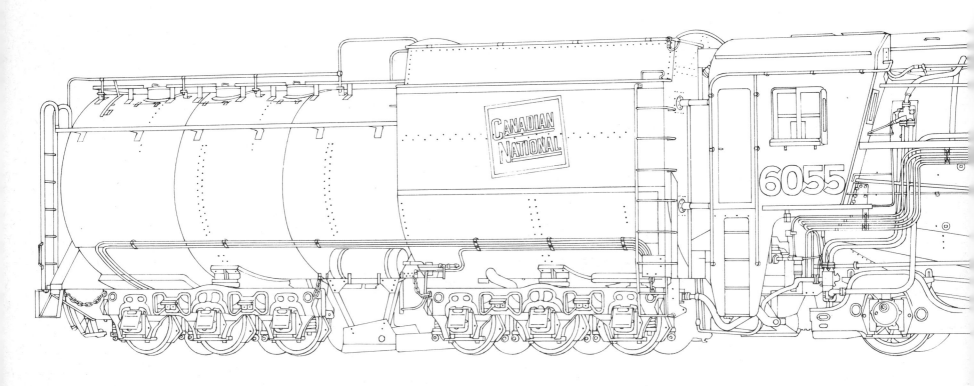

Canadian Mountain Type

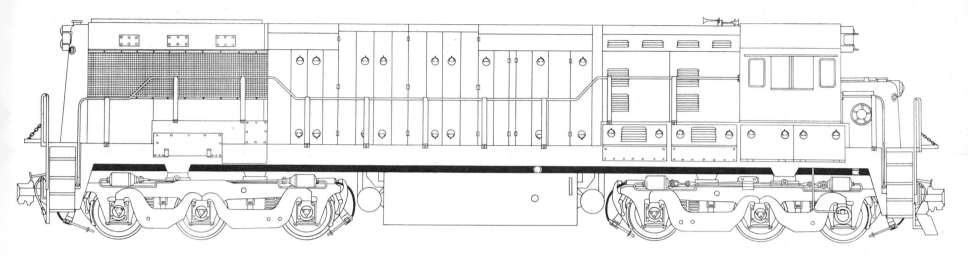

GENERAL ELECTRIC BUILT THIS DIESEL-ELECTRIC LOCOMOTIVE FOR HIGH-SPEED AND HEAVY DUTY FREIGHT SERVICE IN 1963. IT HAD A 16-CYLINDER DIESEL ENGINE, 2,500 H.P.

THE CANADIAN NATIONAL RAILWAYS 4-8-2 CLASS U-1 WAS BUILT IN 1930.

CC 21000

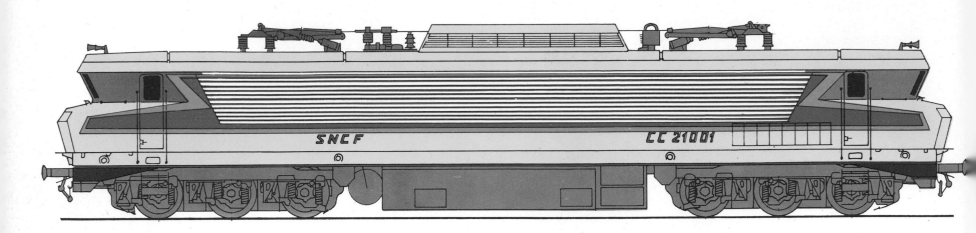

S.N.C.F.'S CC-21000 IS ONE OF FRANCE'S MOST MODERN ELECTRIC LOCOMOTIVES, BUILT BY ALSTHOM, ITS MAXIMUM SPEED IS 220 KM/H.

Big Boy

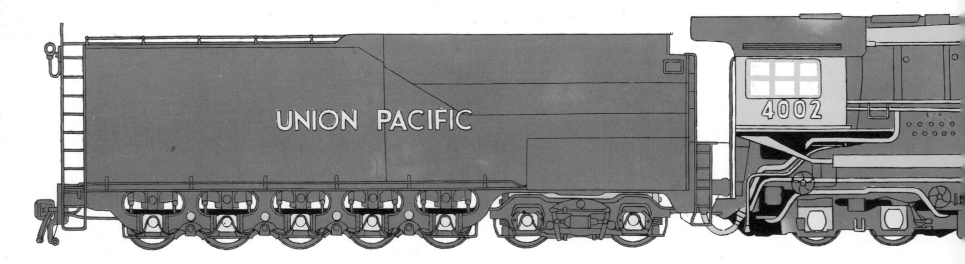

UNION PACIFIC

4002

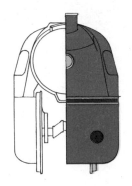

German State 4-6-4

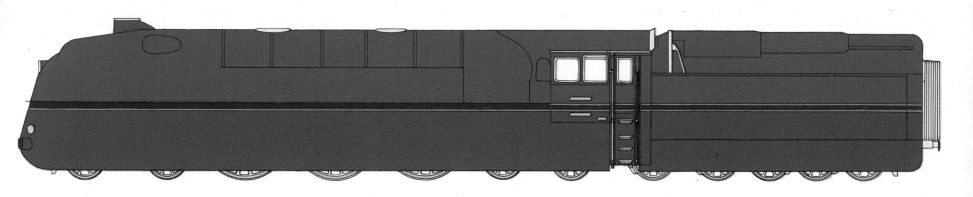

BUILT IN 1935, BY BORSIG, FOR THE GERMAN STATE RAILWAYS, THIS STREAMLINED STEAM LOCOMOTIVE MADE A RECORDED RUN OF 200.4KM/H IN 1936.

UNION PACIFIC'S 4000 CLASS 4-8-8-4'S WERE THE BIGGEST STEAM LOCOMOTIVES EVER. WEIGHT WAS 340 TONS AND THEY HAD MECHANICAL STOKERS FOR THE 150 SQ. FT. GRATE.

221

CC 7100 Class

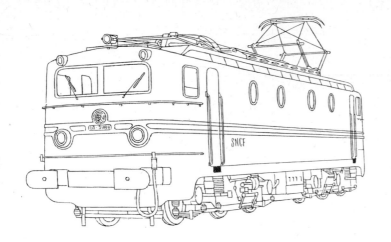

S.N.C.F.'S ELECTRIC LOCOMOTIVE CLASS   WAS THE MAINSTAY OF THE EXPRESS SERVICES FROM PARIS TO MARSEILLE. IT WAS BUILT IN 1953.

V 200 Class

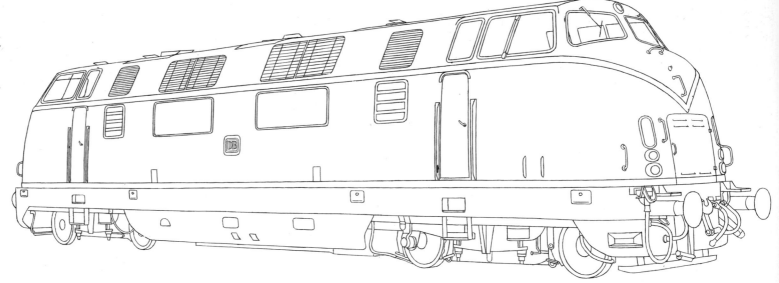

2,000 HP. DIESEL-HYDRAULIC LOCOMOTIVE BUILT IN 1954 FOR THE GERMAN FEDERAL RAILWAY.

RENFE Electric Locomotive

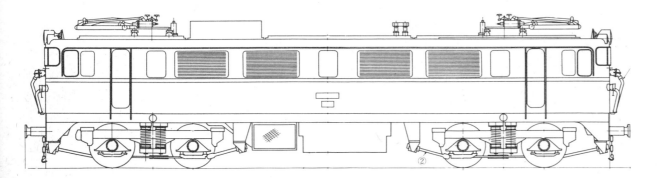

INTRODUCED ON THE SPANISH NATIONAL RAILWAYS IN 1969, THIS ELECTRIC LOCOMOTIVE IS THE FIRST JAPANESE-BUILT ENGINE TO BE USED IN EUROPE.

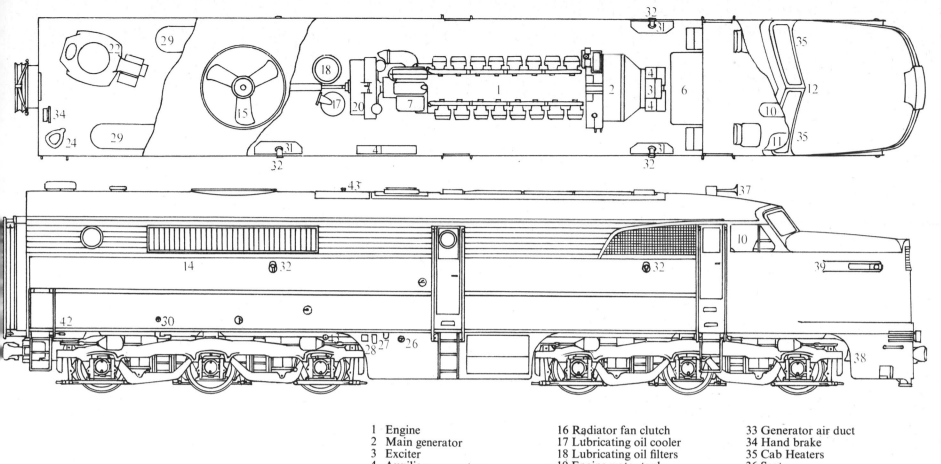

1 Engine	16 Radiator fan clutch	33 Generator air duct
2 Main generator	17 Lubricating oil cooler	34 Hand brake
3 Exciter	18 Lubricating oil filters	35 Cab Heaters
4 Auxiliary generators	19 Engine water tank	36 Seat
5 Traction motors	20 Air compressor	37 Horn
6 Contactor compartment	21 Main air reservoirs	38 Bell
7 Turbo supercharger	22 Steam generator	39 Number box
8 Turbo supercharger filters and silencers	23 Batteries	40 Tool box
	24 Sanitary fixture	41 Engine control panel
9 Dynamic brake grids and blowers	25 Fuel tank	42 Water filling connection for sanitary fixture
	26 Fuel tank filling connection	
10 Control stand	27 Fuel tank gauge	43 Engine cooling water filling connections
11 Brake valves	28 Emergency fuel cut off	
12 Traction motor blowers	29 Water tanks	
13 Radiators	30 Water tank filling connections	
14 Radiator shutters	31 Sand boxes	
15 Radiator fan	32 Sand box filling holes	

Alco G E Diesel Electric

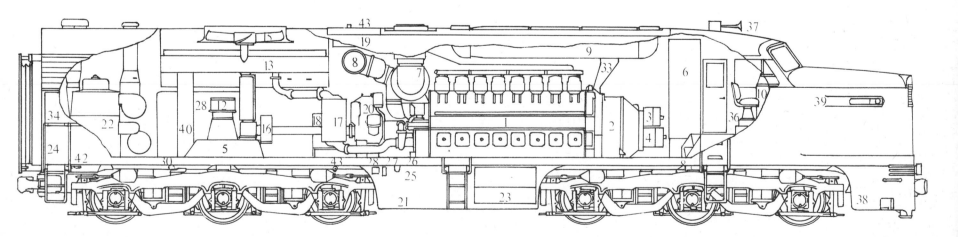

THIS LEADING UNIT OF THE ELECTRIC LOCOMOTIVE ALCO-G.E. 2,250 HP DIESEL IS A TYPICAL EXAMPLE OF THE POWERFUL ENGINES BEING RUN IN THE UNITED STATES TODAY.

Tokaido Express

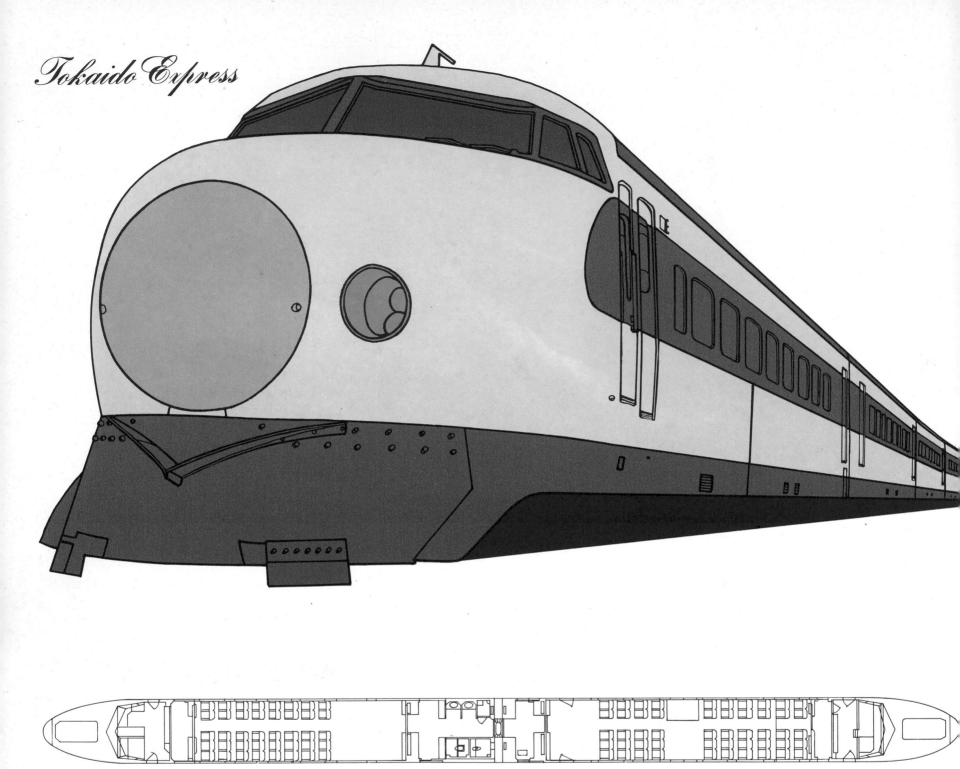

JAPANESE NATIONAL RAILWAYS' EXPRESS LOCOMOTIVE FOR THE NEW TOKAIDO LINE HAS A MAXIMUM SPEED OF 250 KM/H. IT IS EQUIPPED WITH AN AUTOMATIC SIGNALLING SYSTEM.

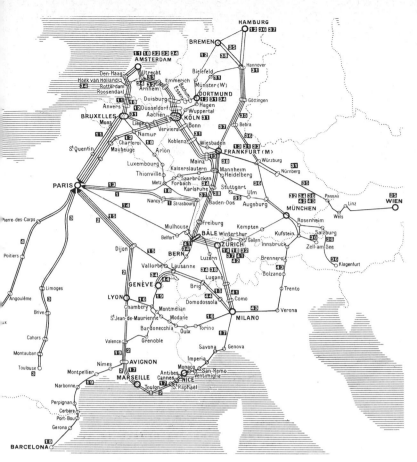

Map showing the Trans-Europ-Express routes.

DIESEL-HYDRAULIC PROPULSION

While Diesel-electric traction is almost universal in North America (a notable exception has been the use of gas-turbines by the Union Pacific) Diesel-hydraulic propulsion has been a bird of more limited flight, with a chiefly European habitat and even there, as naturalists say of birds and beasts, local in distribution. The Diesel-hydraulic locomotive has the virtue of primary motive power. The engine is the thing, not motors supplied by engine and generator. In 1962, Henschel of Kassel made and delivered to Russia a 4,000 h.p. Diesel-hydraulic locomotive with two Maybach MD 870 engines. The rated power-output was at 1,525 r.p.m. It was, like so many in recent years, a mixed-traffic engine, i.e. for either freight or passenger haulage, with a maximum speed of 100 miles an hour. The motor-bogies had drive to all axles, giving the arrangement C-C, each pair of axles being coupled by Cardanshaft.

Diesel-hydraulic locomotives have had some success in England. Although British Railways form a single State-owned network, and have done so since 1948, their Western Region showed off its partial autonomy by building Diesel-hydraulic while the Railways Board's official line was one of standardising on Diesel-electric or straight electric traction. Whiffs of Western nonconformity were doubtless a legacy of that old, highly individual English company, the Great Western Railway. All the same, its then works-commander came from the old London and North Eastern!

Use of gas turbines has just been mentioned respecting the Union Pacific company, whose courageous use of them may be compared to the Grängesberg-Oxelösund Railways' long use of steam turbines, admitting the latter's much shorter system but recognizing its heavy haulage of iron ore. The gas turbine is possibly an increasingly important thing still in its infancy apart from great application to aircraft. Both motor and railway mechanical engineers have been dallying with it for some time. A noteworthy French experiment was made by Renault. The first practical gas-turbine locomotive was, to the best of our knowledge, Swedish. In 1935, the Uddevalla-Vänersborg-Herrljunga Railway received, jointly from Nydqvist and Holm, Ljungström, and Götaverken a 1-B-1 locomotive with a marine type of gas-turbine. It had been built the year before. A Diesel motor delivered the gas to the turbine. Then in 1941, a G-T. locomotive was built in Switzerland by the great old firm of Brown-Boveri and Company, when the United States first went in grandly for Diesel-electric freight haulage and most of the other locomotive-building countries were rather preoccupied with more destructive machines. Eleven years later came the first British-built gas-turbine locomotive, from Metropolitan Vickers, though England had already seen a Brown-Boveri design from Switzerland, in which that non-conformist Western Region was interested. The future of the gas turbine on rails is to be watched. British Railways have announced its possible return. Doubtless it will have its commercial enemies; but even as we write, there are more interesting developments in North America, as in an order by Canadian National Railways for gas-turbined high-speed trains between Montreal and Toronto, and trains in the United States for United Air Corporation's Northeast Corridor service between New York and Boston.

THE TRANS-EUROP-EXPRESS

Diesel-electric multiple-unit trains have made new progress in Western Europe of late, as in the very admirable Trans-Europ-Express services (which also use straight electric propulsion, adaptable from one system to another as between the Low Countries and Italy) and in those agreeable business express trains known as Blue Pullmans in England; air-conditioned, running to schedules sufficiently fast to compete successfully with internal air-lines on inter-city routes. The Trans-Europ-Express idea came from Dr. F. Q. den Hollander, auspiciously-named President of the Netherlands Railways, in 1953. The first trains were in service on June, 1957, and we show (p. 226) a unit jointly produced by Werkspoor of Amsterdam, with Brown-Boveri electrical equipment. A T.E.E. train uses up to 2,500 b.h.p. for a single set, and the complete make-up may run to eight cars. At the other end of the scale, light four-wheel rail-buses have kept alive the passenger service on many small but otherwise sadly-missed European branch lines, notably in Germany and Scandinavia. American conditions do not favour even these, though in North America the relatively large Budd rail-cars have done a similar service for some country towns. Thinking Europeanly, one cannot imagine very small vehicles of any sort suiting the American Way of Life.

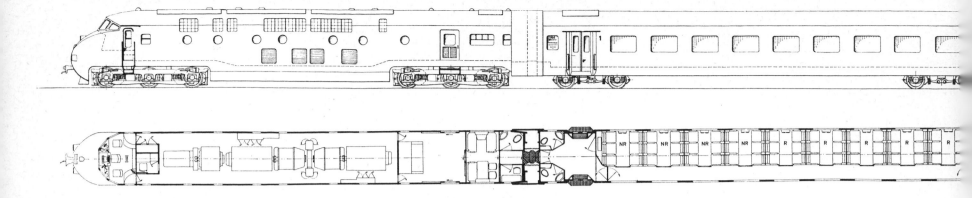

In between these extremes, we have seen the considerable success of trailer-hauling Diesel cars on various European and Eastern railways. In France and Denmark these may be of 1,000 b.h.p. and thus rateable as modestly powerful locomotives in their own right. In Scotland, the ancient and very useful Edinburgh-Glasgow line is served by Diesel multiple-unit trains, furnished to long-distance standards and with buffet-bars, outwardly so like the electric trains in the South of England that visitors often can recognize them only by the smell. (Glasgow, by the way, has very handsome electric commuters' trains, but Edinburgh, as yet, has not; a sorry thing for so lovable a capital city!)

A-propos of such services, and before we turn for the last time to electric main-line traction, we should notice the enormous expansion of what America calls Rapid Transit, including Subways; what Paris, Moscow and some other cities call the Metro; and what London, since the eighteen-sixties, has called the Underground. London, the pioneer city, indeed regarded her Underground with contempt in the years before 1905, when both she and New York electrified lines in their inner areas. (London, be it remembered, had had deep-level electric lines since 1890, and Paris since 1900 below street level.) Today such lines serve cities over much of the world. Everywhere light steel or steel-and-alloy cars are used in multiple-unit, entry and egress being by low-powered automatic doors (ref. London, 1923; a more fortunate innovation than the first attempt in 1905). Guide-rail systems with pneumatic tyres running on concrete are used on several of the Paris Metro lines, where they first appeared; indeed the use of such wheels for railway transport originated in France with the Michelin motor rail-car back in the thirties, and was applied as a practical experiment in certain main line cars of French National Railways' Eastern Region. In the latter case the treads were on orthodox rails, with guidance by steel flanges. New trains were built in 1949.

As yet, however, the old principle of steel-wheel-on-steel-rail has generally held its own, even on such recent underground railway systems as those of Stockholm and Toronto. That of Moscow, originating in the nineteen-thirties, remains notable rather for its fabulous station architecture and decorations—the full exuberance of *Art-nouveau Stalinois*—than for its trains, which though adequate to the point of excellence, are Spartan things. Several subway lines in the Old World have provided two classes of car at one time and another, even in supposedly egalitarian Paris, though only in Liverpool have we ever seen first-class subway cars *with carpet on the floors*.

City transit is rather an industry within an industry. In some places the subway may even come while the old railway goes; for instance the city of Caracas, which having long ago scrapped its mountain railway to La Guaira in favour of a motorway, has lately found itself in urgent need of rapid transit. So has Los Angeles, which for a good many years now has exemplified what we might call an autopolis, where it was difficult even to hop on a bus. Monorails may come in for something, and several systems have been successfully demonstrated in recent years, most notably in exhibitions as at Turin, Seattle and Montreal. The virtue of the modern monorail, as of the now venerable one at Wuppertal, is that it can be carried high over street or river without interference, but otherwise its advantages over an orthodox railway of either heavy or light construction—even for airport access—are less apparent than its enthusiasts would have us believe. It is relatively inelastic, and its switching and junction problems remain as considerable, almost, as they were when Lartigue and Behr were at work on their grotesque trestles.

The ten-wheeled bogie built by Michelin in France, 1949.

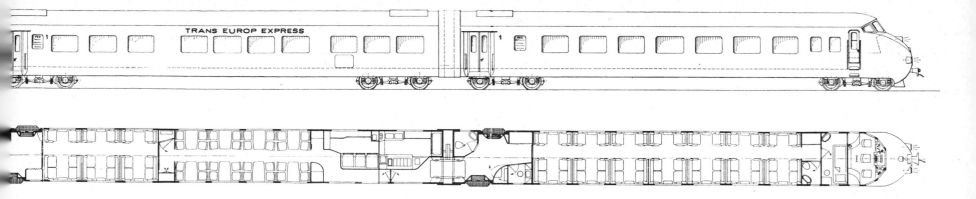

But rails, whether mono- or duo-, are becoming more than ever desirable for city-airport traffic as commercial aviation expands and advances. That admittedly delightful machine, the helicopter, furnishes but a very limited, very noisy answer to such a demand, and the motorway already shows signs of terminal thrombosis.

Meanwhile, it is the electric train that advances over large expanses of the planet where once steam was the conqueror and where the rail holds a lot of its own against both aircraft and the motorised highway.

Technically—without regard to commercial economics—the most perfect form of mass surface transport in our time is the electric train. It is clean, efficient, unlikely to break down, and capable of handling enormous loads while being also the fastest public conveyance on land. A nation with plenty of water power can use it all over the place, but countries with less of this can use it economically only in places of very high traffic density; e.g. in parts of England, the Low Countries, and the Eastern United States. The two circumstances between them account for the vast electric networks of Europe and Soviet Siberia compared with the rest of the world outside Japan. The effective life of an electric locomotive, as of a steam engine, is long. That of an internal-combustion engine is relatively short.

Nor is the electric rail unlovely. With its great, tireless-seeming trains; with its delicate overhead equipment, it gives strength to the landscape whether it be among Alpine immensities or on the great fenlands about the North Sea. But it has been somewhat bedevilled by differences in system, and further changes based on later experience. Both England and France had settled for 1,500 Volt d.c. when experiments with 25 kV. 50-cycle traction were carried out on the line from Aix-les-Bains to Annecy and La Roche-sur-Foron during 1950–51, though there had been earlier 50-cycle experiments in Germany (20 kV., Hollentalbahn, 1936) and Hungary (25 cycles per second, changed to 50 c/s in the late nineteen-fifties). The 50-cycle/sec. system allowed for very marked economies in sub-station provision and equipment, and it was shortly to see great development in both France and Great Britain. Still, the 1,500 Volt d.c. system went ahead in both countries, most spectacularly in the former, where already it extended from Seine to Biscay. In June, 1952, it reached Lyons (one of our treasures is a commemorative medallion made from the fire-box copper of a P.L.M. Pacific steam locomotive just retired).

At that same time there appeared the splendid—and indeed most elegant—Co-Co locomotives by Alsthom for this line; an English visitor called them the *Sea-green Incorruptibles,* though comparison with Robespierre may be thought rather unfair on this splendid design. It related to the colour-scheme. Of this class, French National Railways No. 7121 reached a maximum of 150·9 miles an hour between Dijon and Beaune on February 21, 1953. No. 7107 reached 205·6 between Facture and Morcenx, on the old Midi line between Bordeaux and Dax on March 28, 1955, a speed equalled by No. 9004 (a Bo-Bo) on the following day over the same line. It is unlikely that higher speeds will be attempted with conventional trains, so those who like speed-for-speed's-sake may add these things to the eternal Glory of France.

But when it came to railway electrification in Northern and Eastern France, experience with 50-cycle operation in the Alps led to its unhesitating adoption. In England, 1,500 Volt d.c. had been adopted for the Manchester-Sheffield-Wath line, with its heavy

The Diesel-electric Trans-Europ-Express belonging to the Swiss Federal Railways.

coal traffic through the great new tunnel piercing the Pennines, and to a lesser extent on the eastern side of London. Yet the latter lines were converted to 25 kV. 50 c., which system was then used for further extensions in that part of England, and for the splendid conversion of those historic lines which once had been the backbone of the London and North Western Railway, from London to the Midland cities and to both Manchester and Liverpool. Completion of this in 1966, and its attendant frequency of service with eighty-miles-an-hour average speeds including stops, including maxima of 100, as on the mighty Pennsylvania Railroad in the Eastern United States, paid off to a startling degree. Many inter-city flights were taken off. A world-flying pilot we know said that he was delighted to see the English airspace becoming less crowded for serious long-distance air traffic. *Verba sapientia!* Japan watched the French, and the British. The same thing would happen soon after on an even grander scale; that of a new railway altogether.

Meanwhile the diversity of systems still spread. Italy expanded on 3,000 Volt d.c. while her old three-phase lines retreated in the north. Belgium too adopted the former, while the neighbouring Netherlands stuck to 1,500 Volt d.c. This had interesting results when two arrangements marched at the frontier. In 1952 this had come to a head at Roosendaal, on the main Brussels-Antwerp-Rotterdam-Amsterdam line. There must be through working with no awkward stops at Roosendaal as there were at Modane between France and Italy and at the Italian borders of Switzerland and Italy, where systems clashed. So came the dual-voltage motor current-supply systems, in locomotive or multiple-unit train. Problems were simplified where the voltages were on a ratio of two-to-one, as between the Belgian and Dutch d.c. systems.

British Railways too were much interested in this. The Essex lines, as noted, were being electrified now on 25 kV., and so were the Clyde coast lines in Scotland, centred on Glasgow. Both had their terminals in great cities; in Glasgow indeed, the central section was a true underground railway, like the newly completed Midi-Nord line in Brussels and the city lines on Manhattan Island in the States. Glasgow and North-East London therefore used 6·25 kV. in their inner areas, with some teething troubles at first but lasting success; so much so that the linking of the Scottish and English 25 kV. networks became, in Scotland, a political issue. As we write there is a long Diesel-worked gap of 243·6 miles, much of it through empty, indeed mountainous country where once good steam performance was a sporting as well as a serious business. We believe that this would be good 25 kV. country, whatever it might have been on 1,500 Volts d.c.

While the great Central/Northern Europe *bloc* sticks faithfully to its 15,000 Volt single-phase international network, Russia has worked through from 1,500 Volt d.c. (1929) and 3,000 Volt d.c. (1932) to 25 kV. since 1955. On American (U.S.) railroads there remains diversity, but the Pennsylvania company continues to work one of the best inter-city services in the world—again with eighty-mile-an-hour passenger averages, on 11,000 Volt single-phase at 25 cycles.

As to locomotives, there has been diversity as wide. The 25 kV. system allows for light equipment, with quite small, compact locomotives for very heavy and fast haulage. Strangers find them deceptive, whether in France or on the old, transformed North Western line from London; whether they be in French sea-green or in British powder blue with intentionally startling yellow noses. Conversely, visiting Europeans are awed by the enormous Pennsylvania locomotives with their streamlined hooded ends. Though steam be gone, the electric locomotive can have majesty, and often does.

Of giants, there have been various examples all down the years, ever since those of 1915 on the Milwaukee Road, which became more gigantic when a third unit was inserted between the original pair. Europe's electric giants have been three locomotives of the Swiss Federal Railways, working in double-unit, particularly on international freight over the Gotthardbahn. The first of these appeared back in the 'thirties. Double-units of 12,000 h.p., one was shown in the Zürich Exhibition of 1939. Ever more impressive, to the eye and mind of an artist, is the big single unit, and perhaps our favourites in the Alps are the gently puissant 6,000 h.p. Co-Co class Ae 6/6, each named for one of the Swiss Cantons, which since the late 'fifties have worked all sorts of international traffic through those giant mountains, whether by Gotthard or Simplon. Very impressive and very recent are the Swiss Class Re 4/4 II of Bo-Bo type—6,400 h.p. on four axles only.

Detailed analysis of electric locomotive design would fill all our pages. Enough that by the nineteen-thirties, drive by yoke, jackshaft and side-rods was generally confined to smaller machines for shunting and shifting; note a parallel in the English Diesel switcher whose double frames, outside cranks and coupling rods go back to Stephensonian days!

A *Electric freight locomotive built by Krupp for the Soviet Union, 1961.*

B *Diesel electric switcher by Brush, England, 1950s.*

C *Swiss Federal Railways class Ae 6/6*

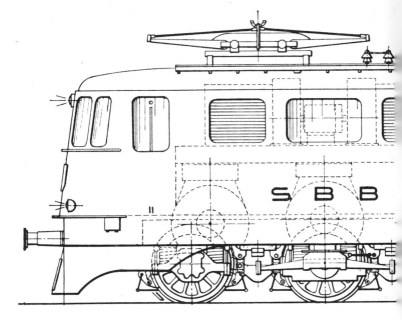

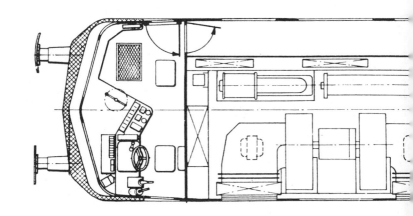

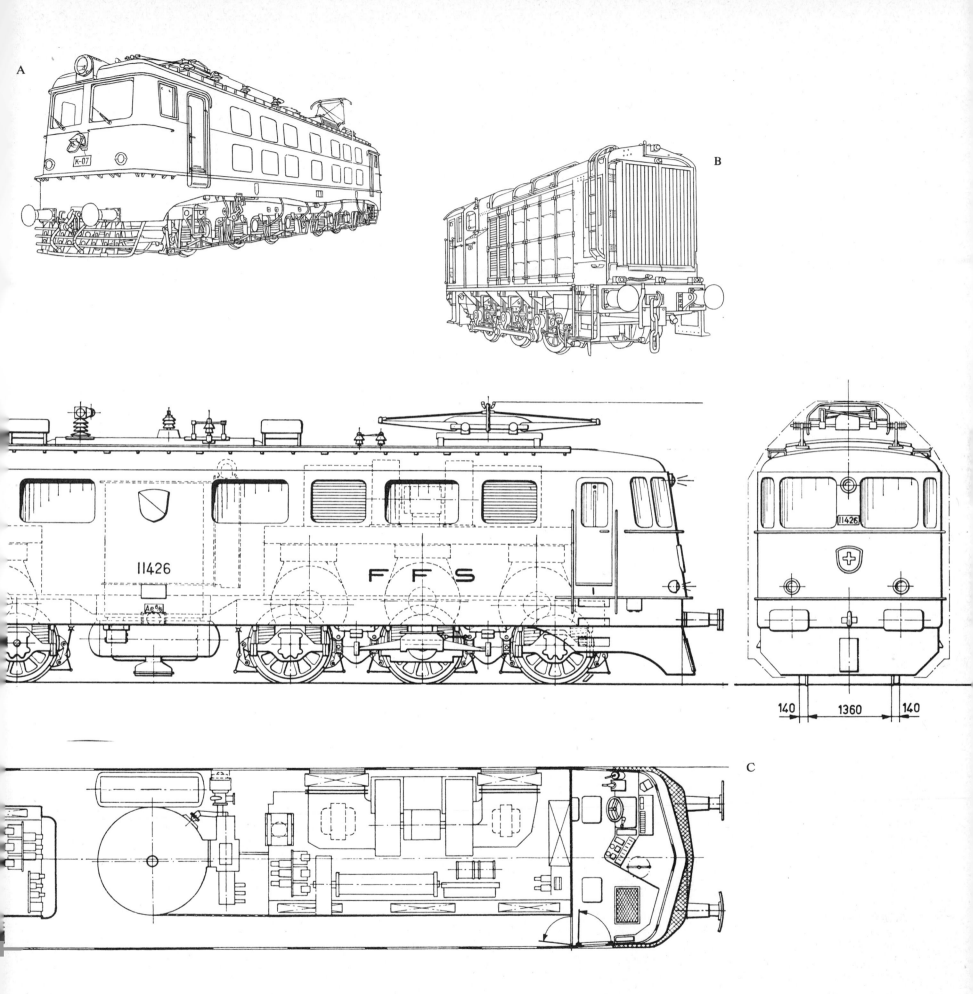

A

B

11426

F F S

11426

140   1360   140

C

By now, such things as the old and magnificent 1-E-1 of the Berne-Lötschberg-Simplon Railway were *vieux jeu,* though their kind was to be very useful for a long time yet to come. Nose-suspended motors were commonly used, these being carried on the axle through suspension bearings and held on the other side by a bolted transom on the bogie, again with springing of some sort. Though widely used, it is by many held inferior to the motor which is suspended from the bogie frame and drives the axle through a flexible coupling, being thus entirely borne by springs. It is easy on the road, always a recommendation, particularly a virtue where rail sections are relatively light. In that last case, jackshaft and side-rods, however old-fashioned and steam-style they may be, are preferable to nose-suspended motors. For all its heavy four-beats-to-the-bar (sometimes six or eight in three- or four-cylinder engines) the great steam locomotive was a gentle giant.

All the same, the later 100 locomotives for the English North Western line were given nose-suspended motors, backed by the old argument of first cost and maintenance. These locomotives have solid-state rectifiers, first applied (in the world) on a "guinea-pig" electric coach, on the now abandoned Lancaster-Morecambe line, England, in 1955. Of more recent developments one should remark the "monomoteur bogies", with axles coupled by Cardanshaft, already noted in connection with Henschel's diesel-hydraulic locomotive of 1962.

Current collection from overhead contact lines also has had its variations. At an early stage the diamond-outline sprung collector (the "pantograph") superseded the old trailing bow (as noted, its principle had been applied for the first time in connection with overhead conductor rails on the Baltimore and Ohio Railroad in the 'nineties) and in much of the world it holds its own, even in a refined form on the new Tokaido Line of Japan. The Faiveley collector, elbow-shaped, appeared in France with the use of 25 kV. in the nineteen-fifties, and since then on the Eastern and Midland lines of British Railways. While running with the "elbow" in rear, it looks most unmechanical, but French and British trains run at very high speeds with it, and without accident that could be ascribed to design faults.

From the United States, vast land of the Diesels, we note nevertheless some of the most magnificent single-unit electric locomotives in the world, the Pennsylvania class GG 1, arranged 2-Co-Co-2 which, using 11,000 Volt a.c., maintain those eighty-mile-an-hour city-to-city averages which more than adequately compete with shorter-distance airlines. And of double-unit electric locomotives, commend us the sixteen-powered-axle articulated machines of the Virginian Railway, arranged Bo-Bo-Bo-Bo twice over, and also running on 11,000 Volt a.c. In their scarcely distant day, they ranked as the most powerful locomotives in the world, as their great steam predecessors had done at one time and another. In the United States, Oil is King, though the Pennsylvania Railroad has long run a good Resistance Movement.

This great corporation apart, we who both like and believe in the electric train find hope and inspiration in Europe, in the Soviet Union, and in Japan.

Before we briefly visit the latter, we should note the returning importance of the multiple-unit, or motor-and-trailer electric train, which through many years in some countries was regarded purely as a factor in city and suburban transit. For over thirty years it has given reasonably fast inter-city service in the Netherlands and in the South of England, and Europe has since seen it blossom in the Trans-Europ-Express services about the time when the last American "interurbans" (which were generally of much older sort) were dying. In London today, at that bleak transfer station called Clapham Junction, such trains during peak periods move passengers through at the rate of one thousand every twenty seconds, inter-city trains such as those to Southampton dovetailed with the capital's commuter traffic.

Such trains, of advanced design, work the passenger traffic of Japan's new Tokaido Line, the most refined example of an inter-city railroad in five continents.

The old Tokaido Line already had been Japan's classic railway over many years, running south-west from Tokyo, first along the Pacific Coast, then inland to the ancient city of Kyoto and to the great industrial centre of Osaka, whereafter the Sanyo line proceeded to the farther South-west, by the western shore of the Inland Sea. Under steam traction it gave very creditable service on the 3 ft. 6 in. gauge with trains which a visiting Englishman of the nineteen-twenties described, not inaccurately, as German-American to South African proportions. Electric traction followed steam, but the capacity of this very busy line had reached its limits by the time of the Second World War.

In that war, Japan's railways did not suffer the tremendous destruction known by

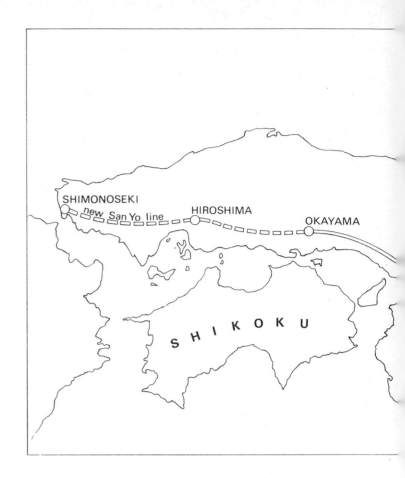

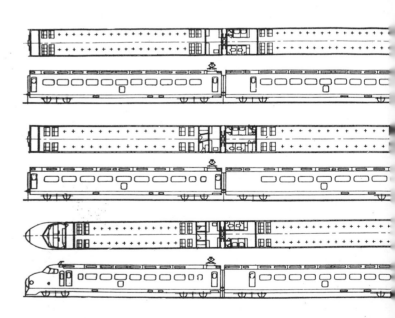

The map of the Tokaido line which was completed in 1964. The old line was not capable of taking the growing passenger volume (about 40% of Japan's population *lives along the line) and so the new line was constructed almost exactly parallel to the old. Double tracked, it is standard gauge (1.435 metres).*

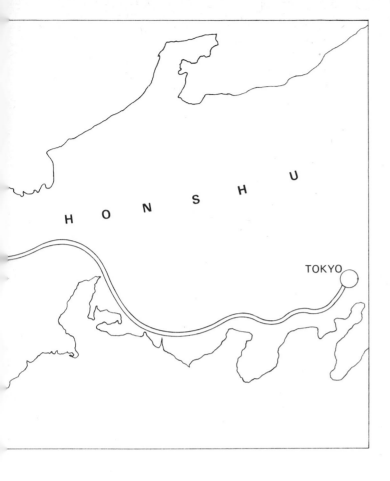

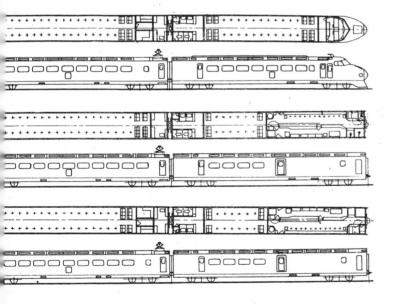

(below) Plan and elevation of a standard 12-coach train with the Tokyo end on the bottom right and the Osaka end top left. Each coach is equipped with pneumatic springs and double-glazing is used to cut down the noise. The brakes are automatically controlled, the signals being duplicated on a panel in the driver's cab. If he should fail to react to a signal the automatic safety device will apply the brakes.

those of Central and Western Europe, in spite of that appalling day when a guarded announcement told that no trains were arriving from Hiroshima on the Sanyo line, and that communication lines were dead. There's enough of that! Post-war reconstruction found a railroad system admirable of its time and sort, yet inadequate, especially as to that once proud Tokaido Line which had been the country's aorta in the days of railroad monopoly, and still was so, though now subject to thrombosis.

Was the Tokaido Line to be rebuilt? Was there to be instead, or as a supplement, a giant national highway or motorway? Would airlines relieve the pressure? The decision, as we know, was to make an entirely new railroad, on the standard 1·435 m. gauge of America and Western Europe, electrically worked, with grading and curves of a sort seldom seen, though they recalled the early work of Brunel in England, whereon speeds much in excess of 100 miles an hour, even up to 150 m.p.h., would be a commonplace of schedules. The old Tokaido Line would survive, for local traffic.

So it was! The initial scheme, covering the country from Tokyo to Osaka, was begun in 1959 and completed in 1964. The next stage was the extension—the new Sanyo Line—thence to Okayama. The New Tokaido Line has 515 km. (320 miles) of route, with ten intermediate stations between Tokyo and Shin-Osaka. Sharpest curves are of 2,500 metres standard minimum radius. The road is of long-welded rails 53·3 kg./m. laid on prestressed concrete sleepers in crushed rock ballast. The system of electrification, as with the advanced lines of France, Great Britain and the Soviet Union, is 25 kV. single-phase, but at a frequency of 60 cycles, with centralised substation control. All movements are of course subject to automatic train control (or, as it is nowadays called in England, one of the pioneer countries, automatic warning control) and centralised traffic control.

This is a brief chronicle of trains, not of railways as a whole, but these things must be noted when it comes to a railroad where the regular express trains (*Kodama*) cover the distance between Tokyo and Shin-Osaka in four hours and the "super-express" trains (*Hikari*) in 3 hours 10 minutes, with ten and two intermediate stops respectively. What might be called a feeler service was begun on October 1, 1964. Two years later came the full service, with sixty trains daily each way from six o'clock in the morning to midnight. Service is not quite twice round the clock, there being at such speeds no need for all-night sleeper trains. Night freight-train speed averages in the eighty mile-an-hour region, with loads of thirty cars or less as required have been proposed.

The passenger trains are both efficient and stylish, with all cars motored, thus evenly distributing the load and allowing for light car-bodies and light draw-gear through the lack of inter-car stresses. Collection is by small reinforced pantographs. Brakes are likewise evenly applied and can be electronically controlled from Tokyo Central if speed is excessive, as with a too-long-sustained speed, though the present maximum is as high as 150·3 (250 k.p.h.). The engineer is in continuous telephonic communication both with Control and with the rest of the train. Accommodation is after American chair-car fashion; two-by-two in the first class and two-by-three in the second, and generally resembles that of a rather comfortable aircraft. It is of course fully air-conditioned, and there is a peculiar refinement in the trains' sanitary arrangements. At very high speeds, the discharge of sewage by chute to the ground is most undesirable (one recalls an interesting, and horrifying, practical experiment made with whitewash on the London and North Eastern Railway, which never reached the technical journals!). These Japanese trains have closed cess-tanks below the water-closets, to be syphoned-off during terminal service. The practice is not new; it was adopted for main-line trains which went adventuring on the underground District line in London as far back as 1911, and lasted until 1939 when the service ceased (Ealing-London-Southend); but only on the New Tokaido line has it been adopted for regular long-distance trains. We have said that the trains are stylish. There is indeed something of the aircraft in the nose, while externally the roof contour rather suggests the ancient clerestory. Commend us the full-speed passage of one below the white cone of Fujiyama!

It is only fair to add, clownlike after the triumph, that the old Tokaido Line is useful for excess commuter, vacational rushes, variable traffic flows of all sorts and suchlike inevitable nuisances.

We have called this *The Lore of the Train*. In lore, there is no place for prophesies, unless they are old ones on record, like George Stephenson's on electric power. We can only watch tendencies, which ultimately are governed by technical advance but are also swayed by business fluctuations, whether capitalistic or collective, by politics of all sorts,

and most absurdly by fashion. There are ever old loves and old hates, for everything
that is loved by some is hated by others. The old British ruling class in the first half of the
nineteenth century—especially the English— hated the rail because it invaded the privi-
leges of property and imposed a sort of policing on those who travelled. The old British
proletarians had their horizons widened, but found themselves being brusquely pushed
around. The British bourgeoisie of the same time were most content, and many of them
became much richer than they had been. All classes in America (which was nominally
classless) welcomed the train as the bringer of progress, yet were the first to turn against it
in their sturdy individualism when the motor car gave them mechanical independence
in travel. Prussia found in the rail a strategic asset, and used it with energy to this end.
Having sojourned in Germany in the nineteen-twenties, we never encountered that latent
hostility to the railway industry which in England had never died out.

To be sure in the years of railway monopoly there had often been outrageous arrogance on the part of both railway companies and State undertakings towards their
patrons, and in the Americas there had been plenty of sharp practice too. As always,
stupidity was the jackal of arrogance. Then came the challengers; on the old roads, on
new roads, and in the air. With a less mechanically efficient transport machine than the
railroad, those challengers would have achieved a *Blitzkrieg*. Even in the nineteen-
twenties, their more ardent enthusiasts were heralding the imminent disappearance of
the train from the human scene. But it was a wishful prophesy by business rivals and,
like so many, phoney. Which was just as well for some people twenty years later!

In our time, the local country railway has withered away in many places. The train
has vanished from such small and isolated countries as Cyprus, Mauritius, Barbados
and Jersey; all islands. The position in Venezuela is odd; the once spectacular La Guaira
and Caracas Railway has been gone some time; higher up the country, great ore trains
are running where no trains were seen a few years ago. More great ore trains are now
rolling down Labrador where no trains ran before.

For the carriage of solid minerals by land, the train is as yet the only thing, just as for
the movement of city millions it is the only thing. For close inter-city traffic it remains
the best thing. For airport access it is a very good thing, whose virtues might have been
appeciated earlier. In such traffic, the train will prevail, and serve, through foreseeable
time. Just what form that train may take is a subject for lively discussion. Monorails, as
yet, are footling things. The best is still the ancient one in Wuppertal. Completely
automatic railways have been with us, though unobtrusively, for some time. The application of electronics advances. Traction by linear induction is under study and practical
experiment though British experiments so far have shown it to be uneconomic at speeds
under 200 miles (or 320 km.) per hour. These things are not yet Lore.

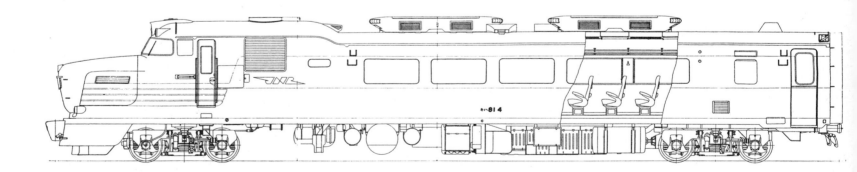

*A second-class coach with
motorman's cab from the
Hatsukari multiple-unit diesel
railcar train which operates daily
between Ueno in Tokyo and
Aomori at the northern end of
Honshu—a distance of 751
kilometres.*

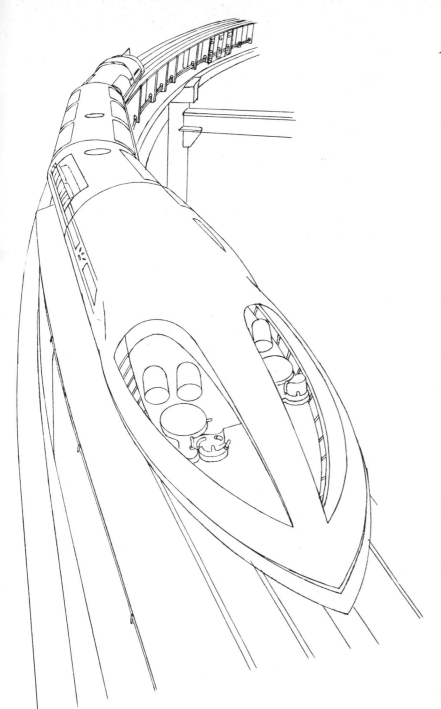

Appendix THE FUTURE OF THE TRAIN

Trains will be with us for a long time yet, that much seems certain. An enormous amount of work is going on devoted to their improvement, but here it is proposed only to examine the future of the high-speed passenger train. It is in this field that the reader is most likely to notice changes and it is for passengers that some of the more revolutionary and extraordinary trains are proposed.

AUTOMATIC RAILWAYS

Next to the provision of suitable motive power high speed depends on signalling. Often enough in the past speed has been held down by inadequate signalling (together with inadequate track and inadequate brakes, but those are different stories for which there is no room here). The basis of modern signalling is the track circuit, in which the presence of a train joins the two rails electrically and a current flows. This current can be employed in a number of ways.

The track circuit current was used originally to ensure that the signal behind the train showed danger. Then it was employed to operate an illuminated track diagram in the signalling installation—the diagram being a plan of the railways controlled on which the train showed its position track circuit by track circuit. Electric signalling installations provide for the points and signals to be interlocked electrically so that the signalman cannot make a false and dangerous move. This is done by a series of electric relays and the track circuits were integrated with this interlocking.

As the speed of the train rises the driver has less and less time to observe and act upon lineside signals. It is now generally agreed that it is unsafe to rely on the driver's unaided eyesight at high speed, probably at speeds above 100 mile/h. and certainly at speeds above 125 mile/h.

Bringing the signal light inside the cab in front of the driver improves conditions and railways have been employing intermittent cab signalling for a good many years. As a train passes a signal a similar signal lights up inside the cab for reference until the next signal is passed. For high speeds the railways are now installing improved continuous cab signalling making use of track circuits.

For some time track circuit currents have been variously pulse coded to ensure that false messages are not passed back to the signalling installation. The codes differ according to the state of the railway ahead and as the track circuit current flows it is picked up inductively by the train and used to work the cab signal. The system is continuous because the cab signal changes as the track circuit code changes, whether or not a lineside signal has been passed.

Having got a signalling electric current aboard the train it can be used for safety devices as well as for the cab signal. Thus it is almost universal that the emergency brakes are automatically applied should the driver make no alteration to the driving controls within a few seconds of a slow down warning appearing on the cab signal. This is the start of the automatic railway and already some railways are fitting braking programmers to handle routine brakings from high speeds automatically.

A decade ago a New York "subway" coach shuttling between two stations was perhaps the first orthodox automatic railway based on the above methods and more recently a whole railway has been equipped, the Victoria Line of the London "tube". In London track circuit codes start and regulate the speed of the train while the brakes are applied by high frequency "spots" in the rails, which are also picked up inductively. Unfortunately rails are not very well insulated (consider the conditions in rain or snow) nor do they conduct the alternating currents used in signalling very well. This last disadvantage is put to use in the case of the high frequency "spots" mentioned above, the frequency is so high that the current can only spread a foot or so along the rail. So to

An exhibition working model of the Japanese magnetic levitation train.

ensure safety only five track circuit pulse codes can be used at the most, which limits the information that can be passed to the train.

Automatic railways will require a great deal of information to be passed to and from the train and new systems of communication are being studied in Germany, Great Britain, France and Belgium. These depend on electric cables laid along the centre of the track, the signals in which are picked up inductively by the passing train. Electronics have made much more sophisticated equipment possible, both in the train and in the signalling installation.

In Germany a continuous series of messages are exchanged between the train and the signalling installation via the inductive link. The track cables are crossed from side to side over each other every one hundred metres which allows the train to determine its position on the railway. It reports its position and speed to the signalling installation, while the signalling installation, knowing the position on the line ahead and where the timetable stops are, advises the train to speed up, slow down or stop as required.

The British system also has two cables laid between the rails but these are used for train speed regulation only and other instructions are passed by "telegram" from special induction "spots" between the rails. Over 125 different "telegram" signals can be passed to the train. French and Belgian systems are variants on the above two, the French system being closer to the British.

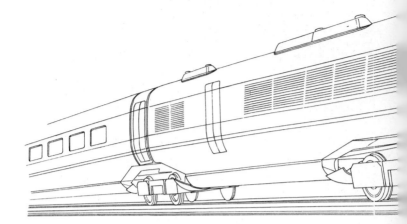

As this is being written one of the big high-speed German Federal Railways 103 class electric locomotives is running up and down between Hanover and Uelzen controlled from the signalling installation, although as it is an experiment it should be recorded that there is a man aboard just in case anything should go wrong. British Rail is so interested in the results that they have obtained that they have made a study of how an automatic railway should be organised, reaching the conclusion that each coach and wagon should be motored and run up and down the railway individually.

Each wagon and coach would be electronically labelled for its destination. Loading completed, it would run to the destination all by itself, the signalling installations making up the best timetable for it and all the other vehicles as it ran along and dealing with all points and control instructions. Perhaps the idea is too heavily based on the British conviction that they live on an island. Already plenty of foreign wagons are reaching Great Britain by train ferry and when the proposed Channel Tunnel is built there will be many more.

The above British scheme presupposes that the signalling installations will be automatic as well. For the moment signalmen are still employed in pressing installation buttons to set up routes so that trains can run according to the timetable. Automation has just appeared in the latest installations; these have electronic memories (similar to those in a computer) which aid the signalman in deciding the precedence of trains over complicated junction layouts for the best results.

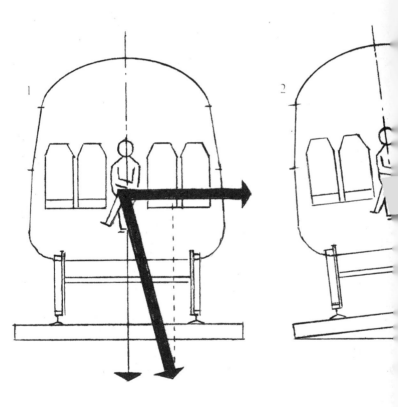

The Bay Area Rapid Transit system at San Francisco which is to open to traffic shortly will have a really large memory in its signalling installation, in fact three to take care of failure and maintenance. The memory will be programmed with a complete day's timetable, which it will signal for automatically untouched by hand. Furthermore the programmes will include instructions on what to do in case of delays or accidents. The signalman will occupy himself in drawing up fresh programmes and in watching for incidents outside the programmes being worked.

Automatic railways will probably be safer because the accident statistics of many countries show that human failures of drivers and signalmen cause many accidents while automatic devices cause few. Already modern signalling installations have removed safety responsibility from signalmen, the responsibility now falling on the signal engineer and his men. They can work at comparative leisure and above all their work can be independently checked before being put to use. Similarly the signal engineer will take over from the engine driver on automatic railways and another source of danger will be removed.

Will automatic railways be expensive? Perhaps not, for railway operating costs are substantially made up of wage costs. In Europe wage costs make up about two-thirds of the total in Germany ranging down to about half the total in Spain. Recently British Rail opened three signalling installations that reduced the number of signalmen employed in the area concerned by 550, out of a total of some 750. Labour saving on this scale will produce large sums of money to service automation capital expenditure and hopefully leave something over to allow reduction of fares and charges.

(above) British Rails Advanced Passenger Train (APT) will have a tilted body.

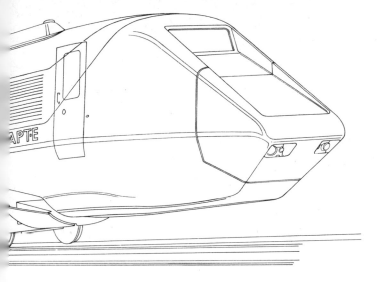

HIGH SPEED ON STEEL RAILS

Some degree of automation, if not a complete automatic railway, is necessary for high speeds. There are other impediments, such as the curves and gradients of existing railways. New straighter and flatter railways are being built, the first of them, the Tokaido line in Japan, is mentioned earlier in this book. The Tokaido line is now being extended for 350 miles and this San Yo line will be suitable for 155 mile/h. speed. The Italians are actively building a 155 mile/h. line between Rome and Florence and before this appears in print it is probable that a 185 mile/h. line will have been authorised between Paris and Lyons.

It has long been apparent that trains can safely round curves at speeds much higher than those possible for their passengers, centrifugal force throwing the latter violently about. The answer is well-known to any motor cyclist, lean inwards when going round a curve. On the railway the whole coach body must be tilted to gain a similar effect, such tilting body vehicles having the added attraction that they are a much cheaper way of accelerating trains than building an entire new railway.

Experiments were made with tilting body coaches in the United States and France in the 1950s and in the middle 1960s "Turbotrains" were built for the New York–Boston run in the United States and the Montreal–Toronto line in Canada. In all these cases the coaches were effectively suspended near their roofs so that forces acted on them as pendulums when rounding curves. They are not entirely satisfactory as the response time is too slow and the passengers still suffer sudden although reduced shocks.

British Rail started designing a tilting body train with a powered tilt in 1967, the movement of a pendulum being amplified by an electro-hydraulic mechanism to give fast positive response times. The Germans built the first powered tilting train in 1968, followed by the Swedes and the Japanese in 1969. The Germans, Japanese, British and Italians have improved trains on order. The Swedish train was the first to be electrically driven and the first to provide for the current collecting pantograph on the roof to remain parallel with the rails and not to tilt with the coach body to ensure uninterrupted power supply.

Not only complete trains are built, individual coaches are equipped with tilting apparatus. French Railways are now taking delivery of ninety *grand confort* coaches which will eventually be equipped for tilting and the Swiss and Japanese have tilting coaches on order. French Railways are seriously investigating tilting and are to try out four different powered systems for their coaches and also for gas turbine-electric trains they are having built for a top speed of 185 mile/h.

The powered steel wheel has an inherent maximum speed of about 210 mile/h. when running on a steel rail. This is because the train moves as the wheel pushes at the rail and as the wheel pushes the rail slips away behind it. Eventually the rail is slipping away so fast that the wheel can push no more and spins uselessly without adhesion. The speed limitation can be overcome by applying other sources of motive power such as the linear electric motor.

British Rail have done more than anyone else to investigate the linear electric motor when applied to a railway. They have reach the conclusion that the linear electric motor is so inefficient at low speeds that it is cheaper to stick to orthodox traction methods—low speeds in this context meaning less than 200 mile/h. An ordinary railway is so expensive to construct for speeds above 200 mile/h. that it will probably never be done.

UNORTHODOX RAILWAYS

Currently there is renewed interest in unorthodox railways, more particularly because of their speed possibilities which are needed to meet competition. Three unorthodox railways are discussed below, two tracked hovercraft systems and magnetic levitation. All three still employ a form of track, although very different from that of the orthodox railway. "Duorail" is a useful term coined to describe the latter recently, which will now be employed.

An unorthodox railway system mentioned earlier in this volume is the monorail. As pointed out, it has never been widely used because of its lack of flexibility, more particularly the slow acting and expensive points that have to be provided to move vehicles from track to track. It should be borne in mind that the three unorthodox railways now to be described are also in effect monorails and share the latter's lack of flexibility. Their

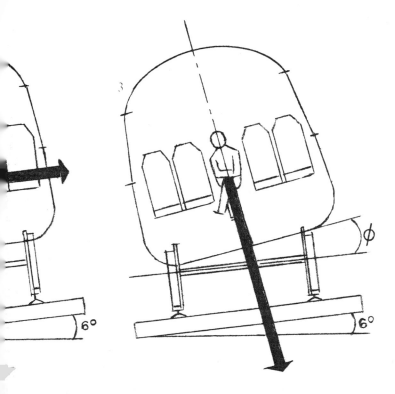

(below) This diagram shows the forces acting on a passenger in a train rounding a curve:
1 *when the rails are not super-elevated,*
2 *when the outer rail is super-elevated. The outer rail can be* super-elevated up to 6° from the horizontal at the very maximum, but no more in case the train stops on the curve,
3 *when the rails are super-elevated and the body is tilting.*

recommendation is speed and below 200 mile/h. duorail and the orthodox monorail are likely to offer them effective competition.

The French are perhaps the most advanced with a tracked hovercraft system and an eleven-mile test track has been built near Orleans for their "Aerotrain". The track consists of 65 ft. reinforced concrete beams 12 ft. 9 in. wide on top, supported on pillars, the centre of the top platform being occupied by a reinforced concrete guide rail 3 ft. high. The coach is supported on top of the platform by air cushions, additional air cushions on either side of the guide rail giving lateral stability.

The Aerotrain is driven by aircraft propellers or reactive gas turbine units, the thrust of the latter being the more effective as the jet is directed at an angle down to the platform. Speeds of up to 185 mile/h. have been attained on the test track and higher speeds are possible. At the end of each run the Aerotrain runs off its track on to a concrete field in which it manoeuvres on wheels to turn for the return journey. It is one way of overcoming the shunting and points problem, but perhaps it can be said *c'est magnifique mais ce n'est pas la guerre*.

An Aerotrain line between Paris and Orleans is proposed, and a local line in Paris. Noise pollution is a difficulty, people are not likely to approve of what is virtually an aeroplane at ground level shooting past their houses at intervals. Electric propulsion is being looked into, especially for the local line, but picking up current at high speeds is a problem. The Japanese are proposing to enclose their lines from end to end in a light plastic tunnel because of the danger from rain and falling snow at high speed. Perhaps such a tunnel would be an answer to the French noise problem.

The British have a three-mile tracked hovercraft test line near Ely. The coach sits astride a smaller concrete beam than that of the French, supported on an air cushion with other air cushions against the sides of the beam. A linear electric motor is used for propulsion and cruising speeds of about 250 mile/h. are envisaged.

In a conventional rotating electric motor the less the gap between the rotor and the stator the greater the efficiency, the gap being a few millimetres. On the British test track the comparable gap for the linear electric motor varied between 12 mm. and 125 mm. to start with and research is going on to reduce the heavy loss of efficiency that this represents.

The Japanese are working on magnetic levitation trains. Opposing magnets tend to fly apart and by arranging long lines of electro-magnets as a track and equipping the coach with opposing electro-magnets the coach can be made to rise from the ground. By varying the power of the magnets at the front of the coach it can be made to move down the track and by this means speeds of 280 mile/h. to 310 mile/h are proposed. A model has been demonstrated and now a full-sized train is being built. It is this railway that the Japanese propose to protect from the weather by enclosing it in a continuous tunnel of light plastic.

There is the snag that the powerful electro-magnets required on board the train are so heavy that there is no capacity for passengers. This has been overcome by making use of the phenomenon of super-conductivity—metals and more particularly some alloys of metals offer no resistance to the flow of an electric current when cooled to a temperature at or near absolute zero (minus 273° centigrade). Electro-magnets at this temperature can be made very much smaller and lighter while still offering the same power.

Unfortunately the electric power required to reach temperatures in the region of minus 273° centigrade is considerable for the large number of electro-magnets required. Japanese physicists have found a gallium/vanadium alloy which goes super-conductive at only minus 250° centigrade and this increase of 20° in temperature will result in a substantial drop in power requirements; so much difference is made that the whole idea of a magnetic levitation train becomes a commercial possibility.

The tracked hovercraft and the magnetic levitation train will have to be fitted in among other modes of transport in such a manner that they will pay their way. A recent British report examined the prospects of the linear-motored tracked hovercraft and came to the conclusion that it would find a use for journeys of over 100 miles and less than 400 miles. Under 100 miles there would be effective competition from duorail, about 400 miles the ordinary aeroplane would be a faster transport mode.

The report mentioned that this conclusion would be affected by the development of short take-off and landing aircraft as well as by vertical take-off and landing aircraft. Perhaps it can be said that the maximum distance to be served competitively would be reduced to 300 miles by these developments, while the report made no mention of

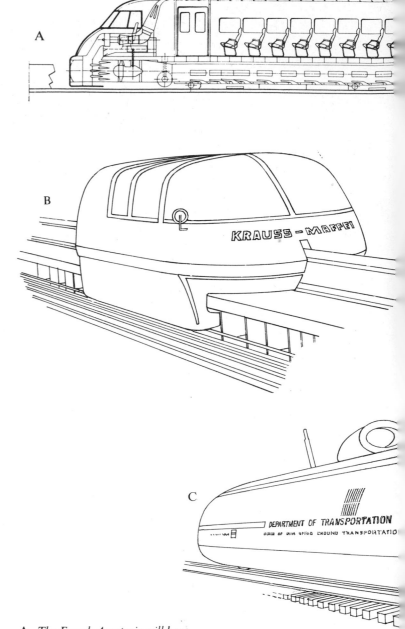

A *The French Aerotrain will have seating for 80 passengers. It is being tested at present on the test track at Orleans.*

B *The Krauss-Maffei experimental locomotive with magnetic suspension and linear motor. It is being track-tested in Germany at the moment.*

C *The American Department of Transportation has established a huge research centre in Pueblo, Colorado where the above linear motor locomotive, a Garret-Air research project, is being tested. The revival of the railroad as a means of transportation is becoming an important part of the U.S. Government's Transport and environment policies.*

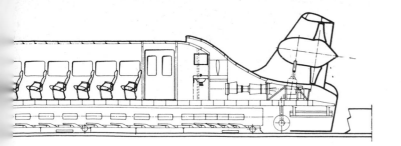

monorails or automatic railways which might put the lower limit up to 150 miles.

The report goes on to state that a minimum of 1¼ million passengers per annum will be required to allow the tracked hovercraft to pay its way. Ideally two cities are required about 225 miles apart between which an average of nearly 3,500 travellers can be expected each day in the year. Similar calculations and estimates are being made in France and Japan, as well as in the United States where the hardware for unorthodox railways is not in such an advanced state.

Present research is concentrated on effective motive power for high speed unorthodox railways. When that problem is overcome there is the problem of signalling and control. When both these problems are satisfactorily solved it appears likely that some unorthodox railways will be built somewhere in the world. When at last they are in traffic they will come up against the really difficult transport problems common everywhere, all the way from how to handle peak business and holiday traffic to how to keep lavatories clean and tidy.

Duorail, automatic duorail, tracked hovercraft and magnetic levitation railways will continue guided transport into the future with recognisable trains, reduced to single coaches and wagons perhaps at times, but still trains, and for a long time yet there will be more fascinating detail to add to The Lore of the Train.

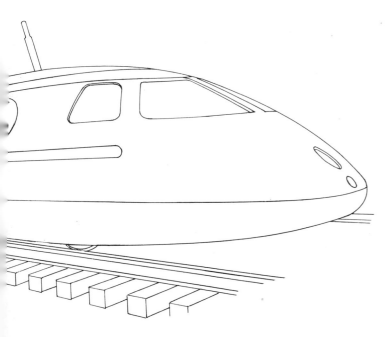

BIBLIOGRAPHY

Albers, L. J. P. and de Jongh, J. C. *Van Stoom naar nieuwe stijhl*, Amsterdam
Alexander, E. P. *Iron Horses*, Bonanza Books, New York
Allen, Cecil J. *The History of the Great Eastern Railway*, Ian Allan, Shepperton *Switzerland's Amazing Railways*, Ian Allan, Shepperton
Asselberghs, Marie-Anne. *Versierd verslag van de lotgevallen van de Stoomlocomotief*, Amsterdam, *Van d'Een Honderd Roe naar Lombardijen*, Den Haag *Met de groeten van Trijn*, Blaricum
Baxter, Eric. *The Study Book of Railways*, Bodley Head, London
Barman, Christian. *Early British Railways*, London
Bagnall, G. Philip. *The Railway Clearing Houses*, George Allen & Unwin, London
Barker, T. C. and Robbins, Michael. *A History of London Transport Volume 1 1863–1900*, George Allen & Unwin, London
Behrend, George. *Grand European Expresses*, George Allen & Unwin, London
Berghaus, Erwin. *Auf den Schienen der Erde*, Süddeutscher Verlag München
Brandt, Walther. *Schlaf- und Speisewagen der Eisenbahn*, Franskh'sche Verlagshandlung, Stuttgart
Bruce, J. G. *Tube Trains under London*, L. T. B., London
Casserley, H. C. *Preserved Locomotives*, Ian Allen, Shepperton
Cooley, Thomas M. (ed.) *The American Railway*, Scribners, New York. *History of the Baldwin Locomotive Works*, Philadelphia
Cooper, B. K. *Electric Trains and Locomotives*, Leonard Hill, London
Davis, Randall. *The Railway Centenary 1925*, London
Day-Lewis, Seán. *Bulleid: Last Giant of Steam*, George Allen & Unwin, London
Draney, John. *Diesel Locomotive*, Chicago
Ellis, C. Hamilton. *Engines that Passed*, George Allen & Unwin, London *The Trains We Loved*, George Allen & Unwin, London *The Splendour of Steam*, George Allen & Unwin, London *Railway Carriages in the British Isles*, George Allen & Unwin, London *The Flying Scotsman 1862–1962*, George Allen & Unwin, London *British Railway History Vols 1 and 2*, George Allen & Unwin, London *The Midland Railway*, Ian Allan, Shepperton *Railway History*, Dutton Vista, New York and London
Grinling, Charles H. *The History of the Great Northern Railway*, George Allen & Unwin, London
Glover, Graham and Court, John. *British Locomotive Design*, George Allen & Unwin, London
Hamilton, J. A. B. *British Railways in World War I*, George Allen & Unwin, London
Haut, F. J. G. *The History of the Electric Locomotive*, George Allen & Unwin, London
Hinde, D. W. and M. *Electric and Diesel-electric Locomotives*, MacMillan, London
Hupkes, Drs. G. *Treinen*, Amsterdam
Kalla-Bishop, P. M. *Italian Railways*, London *Tandem Compound Locomotives*, London
Kubinszky, Mihály. *Bahnhöfe Europas*, Franckh'sche Verlagshandlung, Stuttgart
Leech, K. H. and Body, K. G. *Stirling Singles of the GNR*, David & Charles, Devon
Maedel, Karl-Ernst. *Die deutschen Dampflokomotiven gestern und heute*, VEB Verlag Technik, Berlin *Die Dampflokzeit*, Franckh'sche Verlagshandlung, Stuttgart

Marshall, C. F. Dendy. *Centenary History of the Liverpool and Manchester Railway*, Locomotive Publishing Company, London
Marshall, L. G. *Steam on the RENFE*, MacMillan, London
Motojima, Saburo. *The Railways of Switzerland*, Tetsudo, Japan
Murphy, J. S. *Railways*, Oxford University Press, London
Nock, O. S. *Britain's New Railway*, Ian Allan, Shepperton *British Steam Locomotives at Work*, George Allen & Unwin, London *British Steam Railway Locomotives, 1925–1965* Ian Allan, Shepperton *Father of Railways*, Thomas Nelson, London *Historical Steam Locomotives*, A. & G. Black, London *The Great Northern Railway*, Ian Allan, Shepperton *The Railway Engineers*, B. T. Batsford, London *Railway Signal Engineers*, London
Obermayer, Horst J. *Taschenbuch Deutsche Dampflokomotiven*, Franckh'sche Verlagshandlung, Stuttgart
Ottley, G. A. *Bibliography of British Railway History*, George Allen & Unwin, London
Peynet, Henri. *Histoire des Chemins de fers en France et dans le monde*, Paris
Reder, Gustavo. *Los Ferrocarriles de Espana*, Madrid
Robbins, Michael. *Points and Signals*, George Allen & Unwin, London
Rogers, H. C. B. *The Last Steam Locomotive Engineer*, George Allen & Unwin, London
Sinclair, Angus. *Development of the Locomotive Engine*, New York
Snell, J. B. *Classics of Transportation: Trains*, MacDonald, London *Trains Seventy*, Ian Allan, Shepperton
Taylor, Boswell. *Railways*, Brockhampton Press, London
Tuplin, W. A. *Great Central Steam*, George Allen & Unwin, London *Great Western Steam*, George Allen & Unwin, London *North Eastern Steam*, George Allen & Unwin, London, *North Western Steam*, George Allen & Unwin, London
Way, B. W. *The Story of British Locomotives*, Methuen, London
Wenger, W. *Les Chemins de Fer dans le monde*, Mondo, Switzerland
Wilson, B. G. and Day, J. R. *Unusual Railways*, Muller, London

ACKNOWLEDGMENTS

These illustrations have been reproduced from books published by the following publishers who are duly acknowledged.

The illustrations on page 18 (above) and page 168 came from *Auf der Schienen der Erde*, Süddeutscher Verlag München;
those on pages 50 and 66 (c) came from *Iron Horses*, Bonanza Books, New York;
those on page 54 came from Bonnier's Lexicon, Bonniers, Stockholm;
those on pages 74–75 (below) and on page 151 came from *Railways*, Paul Hamlyn, London;
that on page 225 came from *Jane's World Railways, 1967*, Jane's Year Books, London;
that on page 55 came from *Look at Railways*, Panther, London;
those on pages 150–151 and 188 (below) came from *The American People's Encyclopedia*, (c) 1971, by special permission of the publisher, Grolier Inc. New York.

INDEX